Handbook of Spanish
Popular Culture

The ancient and the modern in Spain. A shepherd (with staff, center-right) and his flock exercise their right of passing through Madrid along one of the traditional *cañadas* or drovers' roads as Mel Gibson (*Braveheart*) looks on. Puerta del Sol, Madrid, September 1995. Copyright © Fernando Toribio Pintos Rivilla.

Handbook of Spanish Popular Culture

Edward F. Stanton

Greenwood Press
Westport, Connecticut • London

Library of Congress Cataloging-in-Publication Data

Stanton, Edward F., date.
    Handbook of Spanish popular culture / Edward F. Stanton.
      p. cm.
    Includes bibliographical references and index.
    ISBN 0-313-29885-8 (alk. paper)
    1. Popular culture—Spain—History—20th century.   2. Spain—
Social life and customs—1951-   I. Title.
    DP48.S68   1999
    306.4'0946—dc21   99-17847

British Library Cataloguing in Publication Data is available.

Library of Congress Catalog Card Number: 99-17847
ISBN: 0-313-29885-8

First published in 1999

Greenwood Press, 88 Post Road West, Westport, CT 06881
An imprint of Greenwood Publishing Group, Inc.
www.greenwood.com

Printed in the United States of America

The paper used in this book complies with the
Permanent Paper Standard issued by the National
Information Standards Organization (Z39.48-1984).

P

In order to keep this title in print and available to the academic community, this edition
was produced using digital reprint technology in a relatively short print run. This would
not have been attainable using traditional methods. Although the cover has been changed
from its original appearance, the text remains the same and all materials and methods
used still conform to the highest book-making standards.

To Melissa Ann

Contents

Illustrations

Acknowledgments

I would like to thank: the Program for Cultural Cooperation between Spain's Ministry of Culture and United States Universities, for a grant that enabled me to travel to Spain for primary research; Dr. David S. Watt, Vice-Chancellor for Research and Graduate Studies at the University of Kentucky, for matching funds; Dr. Richard C. Edwards, former Dean of the College of Arts and Sciences at the University of Kentucky, for a research grant; Ms. Irene Chico, my research assistant in the Department of Spanish and Italian; *mi maestro*, Prof. Rubén Benítez; Sr. J. A. Bardem, Spanish film director; Mitchell Codding, Director, the Hispanic Society of America; Sra. Dolores Devesa, former Director of the Library and Graphic Archive, Filmoteca Española, Madrid; Aldo D'Ambrosio Gomariz, Barcelona; Manuel Durán and Toribio Pintos, Graphic Archive, Espasa-Calpe, Madrid; Guadalupe González-Hontoria y Allendesalazar, Director of the Museo de Artes y Tradiciones Populares, Universidad Autónoma, Madrid; Gabriel Jaraba of Televisió Catalana, Barcelona; Prof. José Labrador Herraiz, *amigo del alma* and editor nonpareil; Emilio López González, Restaurante Botín, Madrid; Manuel Martín Ramos, Director of the Photographic Archive, Televisión Española, Madrid, and his assistant, Pilar López; Javier Ochoa of Bodegas Ochoa, Olite (Navarra).

Finally I would like to thank the following friends and colleagues who in one way or another helped me with the book: Patxi Alemán, manager of the Hotel Maisonnave, Pamplona; Prof. Aníbal Biglieri; Claudio Boquet; Prof. Juan Cano Ballesta; Prof. Rosario Cambria; Dr. Fernando Claramunt; Prof. José F. Colmeiro; Ernesto Delgado; Prof. Joseph R. Jones; Prof. Israel J. Katz; Prof. Douglas La Prade; Kevin F. McEuen; Profs. Leticia and Michael McGrath; Melchor Miralles, former director of *El Mundo del País Vasco*; Prof. Timothy Mitchell; Prof. Inmaculada Pertusa-Seva; Angeles Rodríguez Cadena; José Luis Romero; Prof. Juana Sabadell-Nieto; Michael Shearer; Michael Shotwell; Daniel E. Stanton; Edward F. Stanton Jr.; Prof. Shelby Thacker; Prof. Veronica Dean-Thacker; Germán Yanke of *El Mundo*, former director of the Basque Institute of Arts and Letters.

Introduction

Flocks of sheep have been crisscrossing central Spain for nearly a thousand years. They move up to high ground to escape the heat in summer and down to the plains in winter. The animals and their shepherds follow ancient drovers' roads called *cañadas*, protected by law since the Middle Ages. It is possible to be standing in the Puerta del Sol, kilometer zero for all of Spain and the thriving heart of Madrid, and see shepherds drive their flocks through the streets. (See Frontispiece.) This kind of contrast would be hard to find in other European countries. In Spain, past and present, popular culture and high technology live side by side.

"Spain is different." So ran the famous slogan created by the Franco government to attract foreign tourists in the 1960s. Since then it has been mocked and parodied by Spaniards who reject the image of a picturesque, exotic nation. When a delegation of Spanish students visited other European countries recently, they used as their motto "We are different but the same."

In fact Spain has always been different. Far from the centers of European power, it lies on the western reaches of the continent. The French like to say that Africa begins on the Spanish side of the Pyrenees. For centuries the Iberian Peninsula has been a crossroads between Europe and Africa. More than 150 years ago the great British traveler Richard Ford called Spain "the most romantic, racy, and peculiar country of Europe."[1]

One of the most peculiar things about Spain is the vitality of its popular culture. What other nation has been identified so often with the expressions of its common people? The philosopher Hegel said that traditional Spanish ballads formed one of the great treasure troves of European poetry. The bullfight, flamenco, Carmen and Don Juan are some of the most obvious examples of popular archetypes that have been forever invoked to describe the country. In this handbook I will keep a weather eye on the alert for these and other clichés, always trying to separate the facts from myths.

For centuries Spaniards and foreigners have been decrying the advances of modern life that threaten the country's traditional culture. As Spain becomes more integrated in the European Union, the dangers of conformity are greater than ever. The capitalist market seems to turn everything into a standardized product for consumption. The "culture industry" has never been more lucrative. Yet Spain has always shown resilience to change. I believe it can continue to do so. This book admits the threat of uniformity and its deadening weight while recognizing new possibilities for cultural freedom and creativeness in the twenty-first century.

On a map Spain looks small and compact, not much larger than the state of Montana. Yet many and various peoples live there. Ford, who knew the country as well as any foreigner, called it "a bundle of small bodies tied together by a rope of sand."[2] In the last quarter-century the rope has become even harder to grasp. Ever since the death of Generalissimo Francisco Franco in 1975 and the end of forty years of autocratic rule, power has been flowing from Madrid to the provinces. Under the 1978 constitution, the country has been divided into seventeen autonomous communities (see Figure 1). Andalusians, Aragonese, Basques, Castilians, Catalans, Extremadurans, Galicians, Leonese, Murcians, Navarrese and Valencians, who once belonged to separate kingdoms, may speak different languages and hold tenaciously to their unique ways of life. *A cada terra el seu ús* says a Catalan proverb: "To each land its own custom." Within the necessary boundaries of an introductory handbook, I will try to give the reader an idea of the exuberant variety of cultures in the Peninsula. If it were not so awkward in English, I would be tempted to use the plural "Spains," as some Spanish writers do. When I employ the term in the singular, I do so in the same sense as Julio Caro Baroja in his pioneer studies of popular culture: as a convenient geographic term, without ideological import.[3]

I am also convinced that we must speak of culture beyond the regional level. The rain in Spain is mostly European nowadays. As the sociologist Julian Pitt-Rivers says, the style of many customs in Spain belongs to specific regions but the content usually derives from a larger European tradition.[4] It would be shortsighted to succumb to the current political trend that always favors the local over national and global cultures. *En todas partes cuecen habas* says a Castilian proverb: "They cook beans everywhere." I will try to show the reader those places where popular culture in the Peninsula can indeed be called Spanish, Catholic or even Mediterranean. I avoid the latest fashion of flaunting place names in Basque, Catalan and Galician spellings that would be unfamiliar and confusing to most English speakers. Yet I know that languages are in flux in some regions of the Peninsula and that the reaction against Castilian dominance is a natural response to the long night of Francoist rule.

This *Handbook* will deal with various kinds of popular culture. In Spanish the term translates mostly as folklore, which is still alive in some places, especially rural Spain. In English the term often applies to an urban phenomenon linked to technology and mass culture that is thriving in most cities throughout the world. I will treat both kinds of popular culture in this book—what has been called "the folklore–popular culture continuum."[5] Some chapters like "Fiestas" (Chapter 3) will naturally focus on tradition and folklore; others, like "Radio and Television" (Chapter 8) will stress the electronic media. Yet we must remember that the tradi-

Figure 1
Autonomous Communities of Spain After 1978

Source: From *Bulls, Bullfighting, and Spanish Identities* by Carrie B. Douglass. Copyright © 1997 by The Arizona Board of Regents. Reprinted by permission of the University of Arizona Press.

tional and the modern are rarely separate in Spain and that many Spaniards live in both worlds at once, as in the Puerta del Sol when the shepherds drive their flocks through the city. In fact the speed and complexity of the country's accelerated development over the last thirty years have led some critics to speak of a schizophrenic Spanish culture.[6]

This handbook deals above all with the present. Yet in most chapters I will take a historical look at the subject in order to help readers grasp how it arrived at its current conditions. In the case of religion, for example (Chapter 2), the modern battles between the Catholic Church and its enemies could not be understood without recalling the struggles between Christians, Muslims and Jews in the Middle Ages. Modernity does not always exclude old memories and traditions in Spain but has often arisen through them, transforming them along the way.

A few words on style. Spanish expressions that are uncommon in English will appear in italics. This does not apply to political parties and organizations. Castilian words now common in English have roman characters only—barrio, flamenco, machismo. All translations are my own unless indicated otherwise. A glossary at the end of the book defines key terms, which appear in the text preceded by an asterisk the first time they are used in each chapter (*Black Legend, for example).

I have written this work with the general reader in mind. For this reason I have avoided specialized terminology and scholarly cant: it would be laughable to write a book on popular culture in a pretentious style. For the same reason I have tried to avoid excessive numbers, although they are a constant temptation in a book like this one. The reader should keep in mind Mark Twain's famous words about three kinds of falsification—"lies, damned lies, and statistics."

NOTES

1. *Gatherings from Spain* (1846; reprint, London: Dent, 1970), 50.

2. *Gatherings from Spain*, 13.

3. See *Ensayos sobre cultura popular española* (Madrid: Editorial Dosbe, 1979), 7.

4. "L'identité locale vue à travers la 'fiesta,'" in *Culturas populares. Diferencias, divergencias, conflictos*, eds. Yves-René Fonquerne and Alfonso Esteban (Madrid: Casa de Velázquez, Universidad Complutense, 1986), 18.

5. Peter Narváez and Martin Laba, eds., *Media Sense: The Folklore–Popular Culture Continuum* (Bowling Green, OH: Bowling Green State University Popular Press, 1986). There are useful discussions of the term "popular culture" in two works by John Storey, *An Introductory Guide to Cultural Theory and Popular Culture* (Athens: University of Georgia Press, 1993) and *Cultural Studies and the Study of Popular Culture: Theories and Methods* (Athens: University of Georgia Press, 1996).

6. See Helen Graham and Antonio Sánchez, "The Politics of 1992," in *Spanish Cultural Studies: An Introduction. The Struggle for Modernity*, ed. Helen Graham and Jo Labanyi (Oxford: Oxford University Press, 1995), 406–418.

—————— *Chapter 1* ——————

Languages

I speak French to men, Italian to women, Spanish to God and German to my
horse.

—Attributed to Emperor Charles V

Spain has one of the last oral cultures in the Western world. It is dying there and in
most other places. Yet it is so ancient and rooted in the Peninsula that it will be
around for a long time. For the last twenty-five years it has been changing faster than
ever before. Language is such a basic part of Spanish popular culture that it must be
the starting point for this book.

If you go into a bar or café around 8 o'clock in the evening, when the night is still
tender in Spain, you might be surprised by the noise. The locale may be full of people standing at the bar, talking, drinking and eating *tapas*, or appetizers, before sup-
per. Even if there are not many people, there will probably be a clamor. Spaniards
love to talk and talk loudly. They love to get right up next to you and talk in your face,
so close that many foreigners feel uncomfortable. To Anglo-Saxons, who often think
that raising the voice is a sign of rudeness, Spaniards seem to be angry. More likely
they are simply talking to friends in the stentorian tone they use at home, at work and
in the street. The sociologist Amando de Miguel says:

A normal conversation between Spaniards resembles a situation in which somebody needs to
convince someone who does not want to be convinced easily and is not even listening. This is
the reason for the loud voice, the emphatic tone . . . the exaggerated gestures, the tendency to
move so close that the speakers touch or exchange each other's breath. These are all maneuvers to hold the attention of an interlocutor who does everything in his power not to listen.

As Julio Caro Baroja told me in an interview, "In Spain there are many mouths
and few ears." It is a pity that so many Spaniards do not listen to each other; often
they have a lot to say and they take pride in saying it well. Some, in all social classes,

still speak with a flavor for the apt word or phrase that has almost disappeared in America. I have conversed with peasants and farmers who spoke with the dignity of great *señores*. They said things that only poets would dare to express in the Anglo-Saxon world. I remember a thousand-wrinkled old man who said, sounding like an oracle as we watched the sun sinking in the starched Castilian sky: "*La tarde aún tiene cara*" (The afternoon still has a face), meaning that there would be a few more hours of daylight.

Ernest Hemingway, who butchered Spanish when he spoke it but had a good ear for understanding it, believed that the language had not been divested of its poetic qualities as much as English, French, German, Italian and the other major Western languages. This lyric quality is seen in toponyms and street names, for example. Starting from the Puerta del Sol (Door of the Sun) at the very heart of Madrid, kilometer zero for measuring distances to any point in the country, and moving north, for instance, to nearby towns like Colmenar Viejo (Old Beehive), Miraflores de la Sierra (Looking at the Flowers of the Mountains) and San Ildefonso de la Granja (St. Alphonso of the Country House), I could go on forever across the whole Peninsula with its shape of a stretched-out bull's hide drying in the sun. It is the same with street names. Instead of your Main Street, your Elm and Maple, without leaving the capital you have Calle Lavapiés (Feet-Washing Street), Cuchilleros (Knifesmiths), Ribera de Curtidores (Tanners' Quarter), Reyes Magos (Three Kings), Pez Volador (Flying Fish) . . .

Hemingway—perhaps the American writer who knew Spain best—also believed that Spanish retains more primitive elements than other modern tongues, more double and "secret meanings from the talk of thieves, pick-pockets, pimps, whores, etc." The picaresque novel of the sixteenth and seventeenth centuries, one of Spain's greatest contributions to world literature, was in fact a repository of the argot spoken by beggars and thieves—what Peter Burke calls the "most distinctive of all popular sub-cultures." Many writers, native and foreign, have noticed the Spaniards' penchant for jargon and slang. In addition to beggars, thieves, pimps and whores, other groups have developed their own argots, sometimes unintelligible to outsiders: gypsies, bullfighters, flamenco singers, teenagers and the inhabitants of certain old neighborhoods in large cities like Madrid.

Hemingway also believed that Spanish is "the roughest language that there is." One of his favorite writers, the English Hispanophile Richard Ford, had said the same thing a hundred years earlier: "Few nations can surpass the Spaniards in the language of vituperation; it is limited only by the extent of their anatomical, geographical, astronomical, and religious knowledge." To the blasphemy of Catholic nations, they add the family and ancestor insults of the Middle East and the allusions to sex and body functions of the Protestant countries. The result is not for delicate ears. Only a people with an intimate sense of religion, like the Spaniards, could blaspheme so much and so well.

Cursing is not taboo in Spain, even for children. I remember a soccer match in Madrid where twin brothers, not more than nine or ten years old, chanted the whole afternoon at the visiting team from the Canary Islands: "*¡Tenerife es una mierda! ¡Tenerife es una mierda!*" (Tenerife is a bunch of shits! Tenerife is a bunch of shits!) The same pair alternated their favorite cheer with a theme and variations directed at the visitors: "*¡Hijos de puta! ¡Hijos de la Gran Puta! ¡Hijos de la Gran Puta que los parió!*" (Sons of whores! Sons of the Great Whore! Sons of the Great Whore who bore them!) These were interspersed with exhortations for the enlightenment of the home team such as "*¡Dales en el culo!*" (Kick them in the ass!) and "*¡Reviéntales los cojones!*" (Bust their balls!).

Spanish *tacos* or swearwords reached even greater notoriety on 23 February 1981 (popularly known as "*el 23-F*"). Lieutenant Colonel Antonio Tejero of the Guardia Civil (Civil Guard), in connivance with the army and the political right, briefly took over the Congress in an aborted coup d'état that was recorded by television cameras and radio microphones. Wielding a submachine gun, he cried out "*¡Siéntense, coño!*" (loosely translatable as Sit down, fuck!) to the assembled leaders of the nation—words that were televised and broadcast all over the country and the world.

Foreigners are often surprised when Spaniards use curses as the highest form of praise. If a soccer match, a bullfight or a concert is described as "*de puta madre*" (like a whoremother), you know it was superlative. Amando de Miguel calls this common phrase "an incredible expression that cannot be translated into any cultured language." Even Spanish Americans, who speak the same tongue, are sometimes shocked by the Spaniards' indecency.

By far the most common *taco* is the verb *joder* (to fuck) and its many variants, which occupy many pages in dictionaries of swearwords. This should not surprise us since the same verb has nearly as much versatility in some sectors of American society. Four of the most common expressions, with their amazingly similar equivalents in English, are *joderla* (to fuck up), *jodedor* (fucker), *jodido* (fucked-up) and *jodienda* (fuck-up). One difference between the two languages is that Spanish has a whole series of words that can serve as softeners or euphemisms for the real thing, allowing a series of gradations that are impossible in English, unless we include the insipid "f-word": *¡Jo!, ¡Jobar!, ¡Jolín!, ¡Jolines!, ¡Joroba!*

Another common *taco* is the word for testicles, *cojones* (singular *cojón*). It has so many uses that it fills ten pages in Jaime Martín's dictionary of cursing. A few examples follow; they could be multiplied at will. The word varies in meaning according to number: one testicle indicates value ("*Vale un cojón,*" It's worth a fortune); two, valor ("*Tiene dos cojones,*" He has a big pair of balls); three, contempt ("*Me importa tres cojones,*" It doesn't mean shit to me); a large even number, difficulty ("*Lograrlo me costó mil pares de cojones,*" It cost me an arm and a leg to do it). With the color purple the word means cold ("*Se me quedaron los cojones morados,*" I froze my balls off); with a square shape it signifies tiredness ("*Tenía los cojones cuadrados,*" He was beat). Many prepositional phrases employ the term: "*de cojones*" can mean "wonderfully" or "terribly"; "*por cojones,*" obstinacy; "*hasta los cojones,*" "up to my neck." It can be used as an interjection of surprise in a masculine genital variation of "*¡Coño!* (literally cunt): "*¡Cojones!*" There are also adjectival derivatives of this potent word in Spanish: *acojonado* = terrified, *descojonado* = fatigued, *cojonudo* = perfect, superb. The last term can even be applied to a woman, as "ballsy" can refer to a female in contemporary English, although in a different sense: "*una mujer cojonunda,*" a smashing woman.

Cursing is a well-developed art form in Spain. One dictionary of swearwords has two full pages dedicated to oaths using the word *hostia*, the consecrated wafer or host that is supposed to become the body of Christ in the rite of Communion. It is common for Spaniards to say that they "shit on" a holy person or object, such as Christ or Christ's blood, the nails of the Holy Cross, the Virgin, the dead, the host, the monstrance, the sanctuary and so on. The greatest oath I ever heard came from the mouth of an incensed bus driver who offered this posy to his admiring passengers one morning: "*¡Me cago en los sangrientos calzones de la Virgen y en la puta que la parió!*" (I shit in the bloody drawers of the Virgin and on the whore who bore her!), a sentence with more complexity than many books of theology and one with fatal consequences for the doctrine of the Immaculate Conception.

Spanish may have more dictionaries of dirty words than any other language. Camilo José Cela, winner of the Nobel Prize for Literature in 1989, has published a two-volume *Diccionario secreto* (Secret Dictionary) and a four-volume *Enciclopedia del erotismo* (Encyclopedia of Eroticism). His ingenious *Rol de cornudos* (Catalogue of Cuckolds) is a collection of quotes by Spanish writers from the Middle Ages to the modern period, along with many of his own inventions, to describe no less than 364 different kinds of men whose wives deceive them. One of my favorites is the "Sunday afternoon type whose wife cheats on him while he gets hoarse from screaming *cabrón* [he-goat or cuckold] at the referee in the soccer match for not calling obvious penalties." Some of Cela's own novels and short stories are brilliant tours de force of popular language, comparable only to Francisco de Quevedo's work in the seventeenth century. It would be hard to find similar works in classical or modern British and American literature.

While swearing used to be reserved for certain spheres of Spanish life and art, it has now become almost ubiquitous. A friend of mine who teaches at a university in Madrid says he is not popular with his students because he refuses to swear in class like his colleagues. Amando de Miguel—no prude in these matters—says that swearwords in Spanish are now so common that they have lost their old cathartic and social function: "Absolute permissiveness takes away the purpose of bad words. I do not oppose swearing from the point of view of a priggish watchdog of good manners, but rather from an almost opposite perspective. In order for cusswords to go on being healthy, they should remain forbidden, confined to certain well-defined situations."

Another characteristic of the Spanish language is its vast repertoire of proverbs (*refranes*), known collectively as the *refranero*. Along with riddles, jokes, street cries, ballads and folktales, they make up a part of Spain's rich oral tradition (see Chapter 6, "Music," and Chapter 10, "Popular Literature"). Four hundred years ago Cervantes had his unforgettable character Sancho Panza spout one proverb after another until he almost drove his master Don Quixote madder than he already was. I have heard Spanish peasants string popular sayings together as well as Sancho. They can come up with an appropriate popular saw for almost any situation. If you want to know about the weather, for example, ask someone who works the land. One scholar has estimated that every Spanish farmer knows at least 100 proverbs devoted to the subject.

The total number of refranes in use approaches 100,000. Each region has its own repertory, with original sayings or variants. There are nearly 500 anthologies. These include specialized collections on animals, medicine, the weather, agriculture and other fields.

Some scholars have attempted to show that proverbs embody a kind of *vox populi*, or popular wisdom. José María Iribarren spoke of "those phrases that express philosophy and experience, the people's wit and humor." Indeed many sayings seem to reflect a seasoned, pragmatic view of life, fit for the common people who have always borne the brunt of poverty, famines, persecutions and natural disasters. Here are a few examples out of thousands that could be chosen: "*En cada sendero hay un atolladero*" (Every road has its puddle), "*Allá van leyes do quieren reyes*" (Kings make and break the laws), "*A grandes males, grandes remedios*" (For great ills, great pills), "*Habéis sudado, y nada al cabo*" (You have fought, all for naught), "*El camarón que se duerme, se lo lleva la corriente*" (The current sweeps away the sleeping shrimp), "*La mujer, si es hermosa, te la pegará; si fea, te cansará; si pobre, te arruinará, y si rica, te gobernará* (A beautiful wife will cuckold you, an ugly one will bore you, a poor one will ruin you, a rich one will rule you). As the last example shows, many adages have a masculine point of view and do not portray women in a favorable light. There is a smaller repertoire of anti-male proverbs and traditions in Spanish folklore.

Julio Caro Baroja was very skeptical about seeing proverbs as a depository of popular wisdom. He pointed out that in addition to the kind of sayings quoted above, one can also find other points of view—epicurean, Christian, "pagan" and so on. One can also find prejudice, superstition and outright falsehood.

Proverbs, like so many other expressions of popular language in Spain, are being used less by the younger generations. I remember a talk I had with a boy in the Guadarrama Mountains, north of Madrid: when I asked him about proverbs, he said, "Ask my father—I don't know any of those old sayings." As in so many aspects of Spanish life, there is a kind of schizophrenia in the use of language by different generations.

Another form that is disappearing from Spanish speech is the *piropo*, the amorous compliment or flirtatious remark made by a man when he passes a woman on the street. The Catalan writer Eugenio d'Ors called it "an urgent madrigal." "*¿Quién te va a querer a ti, rica?*" (Who is going to love you, beautiful?), "*¡Viva tu madre, cachito de gloria!*" (Long live your mother, little piece of heaven!") and "*¡Así se pisa!*" (That's how to walk!) are examples that are neither too poetic nor too coarse. Many others could be cited in late nineteenth- and early twentieth-century theater, in the *zarzuela* or light opera, and in religious celebrations in which the Virgin Mary becomes the object of flattery by both male and female devotees. Spaniards took the *piropo* to the New World, where it also became a custom. Some believe its origins lie in the subconscious fantasy that words can impregnate a woman through her ear. The psychiatrist Fernando Claramunt speculates that the mystery of the Annunciation may derive from this psychic substrate.

Like other expressions of Don Juanism, the *piropo* often has the intention of showing a man's virility as much as a woman's beauty. The writer Fernando Díaz-Plaja says:

The declaration is made to an unknown woman who, in most cases, does not have the slightest interest in the man, an indifference that does not necessarily cause him grief; he has launched his exclamation—ardent, apparently passionate—like someone who is carrying out a necessary mission with two purposes. First, to sublimate the desire that overwhelms him at the sight of the female. Second, to show the other men around him that he is *muy hombre*, a man who can't help but react when a woman goes by. Once he has done this, he can go back to talking about the latest soccer match.

Like most male writers, Díaz-Plaja does not consider the female point of view, the humiliation suffered by women under verbal assault.

Changing reactions to the *piropo* could serve as a measure of the country's modern development. For years young ladies pretended not to hear the compliments or at most they might have blushed. With the liberation of Spanish women in the last twenty-five years, their attitude has sometimes become defiant: I remember one saucy teenager who challenged her verbal aggressor on the streets of Sevilla by asking "*¿Y qué?*" (And what are you going to do about it?). Now a woman can turn the tables and pay a compliment to a man. Imagine a lady who sees an unattractive gentleman in a luxury car, stopped at a traffic light; she says "*Me gusta el estuche pero no la joya*" (I like the box but not the jewel." Like this one, most *piropos* contain a dose of cruelty. Others can be so timely and graceful that the only possible response is a smile—from the person receiving the compliment or from passersby. In these cases the *piropo* is a true art form of popular culture. Let us hope that it survives and does not disappear in a world that is socially and politically correct, but a deadly bore to live in.

Our discussion of three bastions of popular Spanish usage—cursing, proverbs and *piropos*—shows how fast the language has been changing. In fact it has been in ferment ever since the death of Generalissimo Francisco Franco and the collapse of his dictatorship in 1975. Censorship was soon abolished and linguistic freedom became a symbol of political liberation. The minority languages—Catalan, Basque and Galician—repressed during forty years of fascist rule, returned to the schools, the streets and the media. I will discuss them later but will concentrate for the time being on Castilian, the majority language spoken by some three-quarters of the population and understood by all. Of course it is also spoken in most parts of Latin America.

Many of the changes in contemporary Spanish reflect the worldwide shift from print to electronic culture. As in other countries, lovers of the written word have raised their voices in a chorus of denunciation and lament. This is especially true in Spain, where the Castilian language is so closely tied to the people's identity. At the forefront of the counterattack against slipping standards is the Real Academia Española (Royal Spanish Academy), founded in 1714 on the model of the French Académie, with the mission of "cleansing, fixing, and adding splendor" to the official tongue. The Real Academia is supported by the state and has always been used to encourage linguistic and political unity. Its importance is hard to comprehend for most English speakers because institutional control of language is so foreign to us.

The Spanish Academy has always been known for its slow response to linguistic change. As the *New York Times* said recently, "it can take decades, even centuries for a common usage from the Latin American outback to pass the academicians' linguistic gantlet and be accepted as bona fide Spanish." But the Academy has finally begun to move faster. The latest edition (1992) of its most important publication, the prestigious *Diccionario de la lengua española* (Dictionary of the Spanish Language), was prepared by computer; it took less time to produce—eight years—than any previous edition. For the first time the dictionary was also made available in paperback. The governing regulations of the Academy have become more democratic: reforms now may be approved by a majority rather than unanimous decision. Major policies can only be implemented at the periodic meetings of the Association of Academies, whose members include many Spanish-American countries in addition to Spain. As the academician Gregorio Salvador said, "the Spanish language is not the inheritance of Spaniards; we Spaniards are merely a part of a vast dominion that is the Spanish language, for which reason we cannot make unilateral decisions that ignore the other beneficiaries of this common heritage." In effect, Spaniards now make up no more than 10 percent of the 400 million people who speak Spanish throughout the world.

In spite of these changes, the Academy's dictionary still lags years behind the speech of most Spaniards. The latest edition does not have an entry for *privacidad* (privacy), for example, a word that has already been accepted by most Spanish-American dictionaries. On the other hand terms like *sexismo* (sexism) and *chauvinismo* (chauvinism in the sexual sense) have recently been accepted by the Academia; *aventurismo* (adventurism) and *yuppismo* (yuppyism) are still awaiting their turns.

The Academy has had to deal with many different kinds of change. The European Union pressured it to make the unique Castilian alphabet compatible with other continental languages. The Spanish *ll*, for instance, is not merely a double *l* but the symbol of a separate sound in the phonetic system. Since this letter confounded European Union bureaucrats who spend their careers making alphabetical lists, they urged Spaniards to do away with it. The same held for *ch*, also listed separately in modern Spanish dictionaries. Some academicians and others considered this foreign meddling to be an affront to national integrity. Why should the Castilian alphabet be the same as every other, they asked. Yet the Academia, showing a remarkable new resilience, has voted to consider these letters respectively as *l+l* and *c+h*, and has restored them to their former places in the Spanish alphabet—following the Latin—under the letters *c* and *l*. Defending these changes against a chorus of laments, scholars reminded Spaniards that in the millennial history of the Castilian language, it has only been in the last two hundred years that these double letters have been treated as single. The change in alphabetical listings in no way alters the fact that both *ll* and *ch* represent distinct sounds of the Spanish language. In contrast to this controversial decision, the Academy has held tenaciously to the rebellious little ñ, which continues to represent a separate sound and letter, listed after the entries for n and before those for o. This is consistent with other exceptions allowed by the United Nations Educational, Social, and Cultural Organization (UNESCO), such as the German *w* and the ç of several Romance tongues. The ñ is so dear to Spaniards that it caps the logo of the Instituto Cervantes, created by the Socialist government in 1991 to be the national version of the French Alliance Française and the German

Goethe Institute. With a head office in Madrid, the new organization has some forty cultural centers in Europe, Asia, Africa and America.

Many of the current trends in Spanish spring from the growing influence of popular speech. We have already seen how cursing has spread to nearly all areas of usage. Politicians and the media often affect a plebeian tone. Young people have created their own idiom to differentiate themselves from their elders. On the other hand, people on the street, barraged by radio, television and the press, may misuse the latest jargon. Let us look at some of these trends in more detail.

While young Spaniards did not have the freedom to invent their own language during the Franco years, for the last quarter-century they have been creating a generational slang that has crossed over into other sectors of society. As in so many other aspects of Spanish life, Madrid has taken the lead with its *cheli* argot. Its principal characteristics are its own verbal system (*enrollarse*, to get in a mess or hook up with a man or woman), the deformation of standard words (*drogata*, drug addict, from *droga*, drug), new spellings (*rrollo* for *rollo*, a mess), the reliance on linguistic crutches (*tío*, literally "uncle" but meaning "guy" or "dude"), a preference for imprecise expressions (*y tal* and so on) and the adoption of Anglicisms (*beibi* = baby). Old gypsy terms have been revitalized: *pelma* (a bore), *camelo* (a trick, a cock-and-bull story). Words from the drug culture have also become part of general slang: *colocado* ("high"), *esnifar* (to snort). The increased economic power and mobility of young Spaniards have helped to disseminate their argot throughout the Peninsula. Since it was born in the late 1970s and early 1980s during the period of political *desencanto* or disenchantment, this jargon has been associated with the *pasotas* (loosely, hippies), *ácratas* (loosely, dropouts) and young leftists (*"progres"*—see below) who belonged to the first post-Francoist generation of Spanish youth. (See Glossary, *pasotismo*.)

The linguist Fernando Lázaro Carreter, president of the Royal Academy, has said:

The evidence cannot be denied that the speech of young people, in certain kinds of communication, contrasts vividly with their elders'. They laugh at the love letters their parents wrote. The greetings, the goodbyes, the style of address, certain judgmental adjectives tend to differentiate age groups clearly. . . . It would be hard to imagine a young man of today calling his girlfriend *tesoro* (my treasure), *bien mío* (my darling) or *corazón* (my heart). . . . Language is the foundation upon which youth affirms its condition as such.

Although this may always have occurred to a certain degree, never in modern Spanish history have children and teenagers developed such a distinct idiom, and never has the linguistic gap between the generations been as great as it is today.

Not all of young people's speech can be considered *cheli* or slang. Many children and adolescents overuse the adjectives *guay* ("cool") and its virtual opposite, *cutre* (grungy), for example. Another offender is *divino* (divine) in the sense of "pretty," "cute," "stupendous." The prefix *super* is even more abundant. A pop star can be *superdivino* and a landscape, a piece of clothing or a gift are often *divinos*, *superbonitos* (super-pretty) or *superelegantes* (super-elegant). Advertising companies attempt to sound up-to-date by making *superofertas* (super-offers) and *superrebajas* (super-sales) while banks create *supercuentas* (super-accounts). This popular prefix can now be used as an adverb (*superbién*, super-well), a noun (*superprofesor*, super-professor) or even stand by itself as an adjective (*una chica súper*, a super-chick). The fact that it already implies the nth degree does not prevent it from being prefixed redundantly to words that are already superlative: *superdificilísimo* (extra-super-difficult), *superextrafinísimo* (extra-super-fine).

This kind of language seems to have lost any pretense to logic. The same can be said of much speech and writing by adults. Reading the Spanish press I have been surprised to find the same kind of sloppiness that we see in the American media. Recently I read a description of an automobile that was "suffering constant improvements" and a soccer team that was "achieving bad results." More than poor language, phrases like these show an absence of common sense. As Lázaro Carreter said in a recent editorial, "Since nearly all humanism has been abolished from the school curricula, it is not impossible for a young citizen to believe that these logical absurdities are normal."

Scientific and technical inventions have given birth to new words in Spanish, often adapted from English or French. Everyday examples are *videoclub* (video club or store), *teletaxi* (a "teletaxi" or cab called by phone). Such neologisms demonstrate the larger trend of employing foreign words, even when there is a perfectly good Castilian term available for use. Sometimes they are borrowed straight from another language without being adapted to the Spanish phonetic and orthographic systems, as in sporting words like *golf, match, dribbling, deuce*. Other times the forms are Hispanized: sprint becomes *esprint* and boxing becomes *boxeo*; outside the world of sports, stress becomes *estrés* and whisky is *güisqui*. "*Puenting*," a new word for the sport of bungee jumping, is a creative use of "Spanglish": the Castilian root for "bridge" (*puente*) combined with the English suffix *-ing*. Some Spaniards love to affect foreign terms: we might hear an announcer on radio or TV tell his audience that he has a super *show* coming up, ask a guest to make a long *speech*, say that an actress has a new *look* and that a singer belongs to the *jet set*. However frivolous this sounds, it is less insidious than false cognates, or the use of Castilian words in an English rather than a Spanish sense: *regular* (for the correct *habitual*), *ancestro* (for *antepasado*), *presumir* (for *suponer*) and so on.

Another trend in modern Spanish is the use of shortened words. While this has always occurred to a certain extent (*auto* for *automóvil*, automobile, *cine* for *cinematógrafo*, cinema), it has become a modern plague. Now one is a *progre* (progressive), *retro* (reactionary), or *ultra* (ultra-rightist); one can feel *depre* (= *deprimido*, depressed) or *tranqui* (= *tranquilo*, tranquil); young men and women go to their *facu* (= *facultad*, college) or *insti* (= *instituto*, institute), while kids attend their *cole* (= *colegio*, school) where they write with a *boli* (= *bolígrafo*, ballpoint pen) and talk to the *profe* (= *profesor*, professor), the *seño* (= *señora*, the lady teacher) or the *dire* (= *director*, principal); one watches the *tele* (= *televisión*, TV) or goes to a *peli porno* (= *película pornográfica*, porno flick) or to the *pelu* (= *peluquería*, hair salon).

A related habit is to rely on abbreviations and acronyms, a plague that infects the languages of most countries in the world. The late poet and critic Dámaso Alonso, former director of the Royal Academy, has called our age "*el siglo de las siglas*" (the century of abbreviations). Classic cases are RENFE (Red Nacional de Ferrocarriles Españoles, the nationalized train system) and OTAN (Organización del Tratado del Atlántico Norte, NATO). More recent acronyms, far more common, are the inescapable IVA (Impuesto de Valor Añadido or sales tax), ONCE (Organización Nacional de Ciegos Españoles, the national organization of blind lottery-ticket vendors), and the many political parties—PSOE (pronounced "so-ay," Partido Socialista Obrero Español, the socialists), PP (Partido Popular or conservative party), PNV (Partido Nacionalista Vasco (the Basque Nationalist Party) and so forth. Leonardo Gómez Torrego says of these forms: "We are witnessing in recent years a veritable invasion that is turning Castilian into an almost cryptic language." The use of shortened words and abbreviations may be convenient at times, but it can also be a manifestation of what Ramón Carnicer calls linguistic laziness.

Other trends in contemporary Spanish reflect new social conditions. Forms of address are the most notable case. *Tuteo*, the use of the familiar second-person pronoun *tú* (similar to the archaic English "thou") has spread like a forest fire to all levels of society at the expense of the more formal *usted* ("you"). (The same has naturally occurred with their plural equivalents *vosotros* and *ustedes*.) Everyone seems to be using the *tú* form nowadays, especially children and teenagers, who rarely address people in any other way. This trend is a result of relaxed social distinctions and the general democratization of Spanish life. Like many of my friends in Spain, I prefer the greater range of nuances in the double-pronoun system that prevailed until recent times. Some Spaniards, in order to protest the rampant use of tuteo, insist on using the more distant and respectful *usted* if they are not on a first-name basis with their interlocutors. When addressed by a stranger in the *tú* form, they may react by asking something like "*¿Desde cuándo hemos comido juntos en la misma mesa?*" (Since when have we eaten at the same table?).

Another controversial trend is the creation of words for women in new professional roles. Since English is almost a gender-free language, it never had this problem. Thus when women became doctors and lawyers in the Anglo-Saxon world, these words could refer to them as well as their male counterparts. Spanish, on the other hand, classifies all nouns as either masculine or feminine. When women started entering the liberal professions in the 1970s, speakers first began to prefix a feminine article to the masculine noun ("*la médico*," the woman doctor, "*la abogado*," the woman lawyer). As more and more ladies worked in these fields and the old linguistic walls began to crumble, the next step was to make the whole word feminine ("*la médica*," "*la abogada*"), words that of course have not been accepted by the Royal Academy nor by many speakers. It takes Spanish ears some time to get used to these new forms. Resistance has come not only from stodgy academicians but also from certain women who believe the traditional masculine words command more respect. Thus they prefer to be called "*boticario*" rather than "*boticaria*" (female pharmacist), "*juez*" and not *jueza* (female judge), "*notario*" instead of "*notaria*" (female notary public). They have taken this stance in part because the feminine forms sometimes used to be employed in a derogatory way to mean "the pharmacist's wife," "the judge's wife," "the notary's wife." We must wait to see how much this trend will evolve, but the doors have been opened to further linguistic change to keep up with new social conditions.

A final trend has been called "pseudoculture," the attempt to sound educated by using elegant words, often incorrect or in bad taste. In Spain, a country that was virtually a part of the underdeveloped world a mere forty years ago, there have been great leaps in prosperity and literacy; many people have not assimilated the changes and strive to imitate the speakers they consider to be sophisticated. Unfortunately, the greatest perpetrators of pseudoculture are those with the largest audience—radio and TV announcers. They and their imitators usually prefer a long word to a short one, even when the shorter term is more effective ("*problemática*," "problematics," rather than *problema*, problem). Instead of the simple verb *acabar* (to end, finish), they prefer the fancier *finalizar* (finalize) or "*dar por finalizado*" (to declare finalized). Instead of *celebrar* (to celebrate), they say *solemnizar* (to solemnize). The extra syllables, according to Amando de Miguel, "have the purpose of breathing into these words an air of mystery and innovation." The worst part of these fashionable terms is that they displace perfectly good, simple Castilian words and destroy the spontaneity of everyday language.

A spate of -isms (*ismos*) is another sign of the same trend. As we have seen earlier, some of these new words have been adopted by the Royal Academy. Others that have been blessed with official approval in recent years are *paternalismo* (paternalism), *apoliticismo* ("apoliticalism"), *perfeccionismo* (perfectionism).

Many Spanish linguists take the middle road on this matter, recognizing the barbarity of pseudointellectual language while admitting that most linguistic change comes about through violation of the existing rules. For his part, Manuel Seco believes that this trend has its source in written language:

In effect, what movies, radio and television really give us is not *spoken language*, but *an oral version of the written language*: the reading or memorized recitation of written texts. The only exceptions, on radio and television, are certain responses by people who are interviewed; and even in many of these cases we have to take into consideration an element of *affectation* of naturalness, next to the formalizing posture that most people adopt in front of the microphone, that makes them instinctively search for an expression closest to the model of the written language.

Another form of pseudointellectual jargon is what Amando de Miguel called "*doble-lenguaje*" ("double language"), a translation of George Orwell's well-known double-talk or doublespeak. It is defined by Webster's as "inflated, involved, and often deliberately ambiguous language." In Spain and elsewhere it is the special domain of politicians. Some recent examples are former Prime Minister Felipe González's unintelligible "*hipotizar el futurible*" (to hypothesize the "futurable"), and current Prime Minister José María Aznar's redundant "*el máximo y el mayor responsable*" (the maximum and major person in charge). A member of parliament, Rafael Martínez Campillo, made a classic statement of doublespeak when he said "*Hay cosas que, aun siendo verdad, no son ciertas*" (There are things that, although true, are not certain).

Circumlocution is another aspect of doublespeak that has always had a fertile field in Spanish, "the language of bureaucracy par excellence" (Pablo Neruda). The government has recently abandoned the word *cartero* (mailman) in favor of the roundabout "*auxiliar técnico postal de clasificación y reparto*" (postal auxiliary for sorting and delivery). When my son's school in Madrid decided to celebrate one of its many religious holidays, it sent the following circular to the parents (I have translated the message into English):

The School traditionally, because of the fact that it is located on the periphery of the city, has unified the holidays of St. Joseph of Calasanz and St. Thomas Aquinas, celebrating both uniformly on the date of the latter. The reasons that moved us to do so have been, on the one hand, that of facilitating a series of services, such as dining halls and scholarly transport, and on the other, that of achieving an equality of circumstances for those teachers who exercise their activity in different parts of the city. For this series of motives and because of the perturbations that any modification would imply, we believe that during this school year the School should maintain what has already become its custom and therefore, celebrate this coming Monday 28 January as a holiday.

All of this to say that there would be no classes on Monday.

Although Spanish is undergoing the most rapid development in its history, the situation of the so-called minority or regional languages in the Peninsula has changed even faster. Spain has been experiencing a new era of local and regional power after forty years of monolithic rule under Franco. The change is of course a common one in many parts of the world in the late twentieth century.

Repression of minority languages was an important policy of the fascist government. Generalissimo Franco postulated "national . . . absolute unity, with a single language, Castilian, and a single personality, Spanish." Regional tongues like Catalan and Galician were classified as "dialects" rather than separate languages with centuries-old literary and cultural traditions. A pamphlet of the post–Civil War period gives an idea of the times: "SPEAK WELL. BE PATRIOTIC. DON'T BE A BARBARIAN. A true gentleman speaks our official language, that is to say, Castilian. . . . Long live Spain and the discipline of our Cervantine tongue. ¡¡ARRIBA ESPAÑA!! (Hooray for Spain!)."

When Franco died and a democratic government was elected, the situation began to change quickly. Article 3 of the 1978 Constitution was criticized by some but heralded by many as a radical new recognition of cultural pluralism and linguistic rights. The first clause states: "Castilian is the official language of the state." The sensibilities of the regional politicians had been so heightened by decades of linguistic oppression that this sentence caused fervent debate. The consensus of both Spaniards and the international community, and the practice of most Latin American countries were not enough to prevail upon the Congress to use the word "Spanish" in this clause. The Royal Academy–Spanish, not Castilian–attempted to intervene but was quickly silenced. What Lázaro Carreter calls the "schizophrenic foolishness" of excluding the word "Spanish" is now enshrined in the new constitution. Camilo José Cela said, "In the world there are twenty sovereign states that speak Spanish and the only one whose Magna Carta does not call its official language Spanish is Spain." Many of the regional politicians will go to any lengths to avoid using the name of the language and "Spain" in their discourse. Jordi Pujol, president of the Catalan Generalitat or autonomous government, for instance, uses classic doublespeak when he refers to the country as "the confederal Hispanic framework in the heart of a united Europe." Spaniards (or should I say "residents of the Iberian Peninsula") were practicing political correctness before the term was ever coined in English.

The second clause of Article 3 declares that "The other Spanish languages will also be official in the respective autonomous communities in accordance with their statutes." The phrase "other Spanish languages" was another sore point that pleased no one: it would be hard to describe Catalan in this way, since it constitutes a separate Romance language every bit as much as Castilian, French or Italian. Some argue the same for Galician. It is even more problematic to call Basque a "Spanish language" since it existed centuries before any of the other tongues spoken in the Peninsula and is so unique that it constitutes its own linguistic family. Moreover, some speakers of the minority languages wondered what kind of official status they would enjoy if they lived or traveled outside their own territory.

The third clause of Article 3 in the new constitution is probably the most important: "The richness of Spain's different linguistic varieties is a cultural heritage that will be the object of special respect and protection." When combined with Article 148, it has given each autonomous community the authority to foment its respective "culture . . . , and where appropriate, the teaching of its language." This applies not only to the minority tongues—Basque, Catalan and Galician—but also to the regional varieties of Spanish. These clauses have inspired work on lexical and phonological features in Andalusia and the Canary Islands, for instance, where the regional dialects are especially divergent from the Spanish of Old and New Castile. These policies have enormous consequences in determining acceptable standards of literacy and usage in schools and the media; the situation might be loosely compared to the controversy surrounding Ebonics in the United States.

Despite the ambiguities of these articles, Spain's advances in linguistic freedom over the last quarter-century are impressive. The constitution, combined with the relevant Autonomy Statutes and the Linguistic Normalization Laws, have established a legal framework similar to that in other European countries. Yet the politics of language in Spain are still contentious. While the central government considers Castilian to be "*primum inter pares*," this is exactly how the speakers of the major regional languages see their own tongues within their autonomous communities: first among peers, with the same rights and responsibilities but preferable to Spanish, all other things being equal. Let us look now at the situation of the minority languages—Catalan, Basque and Galician.

Catalan is the second most widely used language in Spain, with some five to six million speakers (depending on the source). It is a Romance tongue distinct from Castilian Spanish. It belongs to the Gallo-Romance branch of languages and is somewhat similar to Provençal, the language of southern France in the Middle Ages. Catalan has more speakers than the official tongues of several European states: Danish

(4,500,000), Finnish (4,000,000) and Norwegian (3,500,000). It is spoken in the four provinces of Catalonia proper (Barcelona, Gerona, Lérida and Tarragona), a small strip of Aragón to the west, the tiny Pyrenean principality of Andorra and the French region of Roussillon to the north, the three provinces of the País Valenciano (Valencian region) to the south (Alicante, Castellón de la Plana and Valencia), the Balearic Islands (Mallorca, Minorca and Ibiza) to the east, and even in the city of Alghero in Sardinia—a relic of Catalan expansionism in the fourteenth century. The literature in this language, some seven hundred years old, may be the most important in the world in a tongue that does not enjoy majority status. Catalans like to recall that the very first book published in Spain was in their language (1490).

In order to understand the situation today, we cannot forget that all the minority languages were banned from public use and education after the fascist victory in the Civil War (1939). In Catalonia, signs urged the people to use Castilian: "Catalans: Don't Bark! Speak the Language of the Empire!" Unlike Galician and Basque, the Catalan tongue had a cultural infrastructure dating from the early nineteenth century. This allowed it to go underground in the postwar period and to receive support from certain sectors of the intelligentsia, the Church and the bourgeoisie. When I first traveled to Catalonia in 1965, I remember seeing graffiti on walls saying "*Català a l'escola*" (Catalan in schools). The people had become virtually illiterate in their own tongue, which was reduced to the private realm of the home. Waves of immigrants from poorer regions of Spain were moving to the area in search of employment, further diluting the Catalan-speaking population. It was not until 1946 that books could be published in the language; no translations were allowed until the early 1960s. All publications were severely censored. The repression of Catalan culture during the dictatorship is revealed by the fact that the quantity of books published in the language did not reach prewar levels until 1976, the year after Franco's death. Radio and television in the vernacular were limited to a few hours per week.

With the advent of democracy, the Generalitat or new autonomous government of Catalonia created the Council of Culture to oversee efforts of "linguistic normalization." The Philological Section of the Institute of Catalan Studies in Barcelona was founded to carry out a mission similar to the Royal Spanish Academy's, with a lot less ceremony. Catalan is now the first language in government offices, in all public and many private schools throughout Catalonia. It is heard on the streets much more than Spanish. At the 1992 Olympic Games in Barcelona, it was one of the three official languages, along with Spanish and English. In the universities between 40 percent and 70 percent of courses are taught in the language. The number of books published in Catalan has soared to over 5,000 per year. Translations are numerous: one can now read Proust, Marx and most major writers of the world in good local versions.

Efforts in the audiovisual field have also been rewarding. As we will see in later chapters, there are now Catalan radio stations and television channels, independent movie producers and a lively popular music industry, all of them working in their first language as well as Spanish. This is all in addition to newspapers and magazines published in the local tongue. Foreign movies, plays and programs are translated into Catalan, and commercials are also in the vernacular.

We should note that the Valencian autonomous community, which speaks its own variety of Catalan (*valenciano*), has pursued some of the same cultural policies as its larger neighbor, with similar results. The Generalitat Valenciana has an office of "Linguistic Politics" in its Council of Culture, Education and Science. The region also has its own television channel and radio stations. In general the Valencians do not favor as much cultural independence as the Catalonians, nor do they have the Basque sense of ethnic separatism.

In just two decades Catalonia has achieved a success story that is unique in the world. People of all social classes have recovered their language, their culture and their pride. Joan Guitart, Culture Minister of the Generalitat has claimed, "in cultural matters Catalonia should be equivalent to a state"—and it practically is.

The same cannot be said of the other two minority languages, Galician and Basque. Unlike Catalan they have always been rural rather than urban languages, spoken by the poorest and most uneducated part of the population. They do not have a centuries-old tradition of printing and publishing. Each carries an onus—we could compare it to the stigma attached to hillbilly language in the United States—that the Catalan tongue has never suffered. While the language of Barcelona can serve as a symbol of social mobility, Galician and Basque have long been considered the lingo of peasants and farmers. We will look at each of these languages in turn.

The writer Gonzalo Torrente Ballester has a famous novel entitled *La saga/fuga de J.B.* (J.B.'s Saga/Flight, 1972) in which a mythical Galician city named Castroforte de Baralla levitates and disappears into the clouds as a result of the collective anxiety of its inhabitants. One critic has seen this metaphor as a symbol of Galicia's frustrated search for identity and its virtual obliteration from the cultural map of Spain. While most Catalonians are in favor of increased political and cultural independence, the inhabitants of the country's green northwest corner cannot seem to reach a consensus on the region's future. Some, the isolationists, favor a program similar to the Catalonians', but they do not have the numbers, the power nor the infrastructure that have enabled that region to achieve so many advances. Others, the reintegrationists or *lusistas* (from Luso = Portuguese), dream of returning Galicia to the fold of Mother Portugal, which has undeniable historic, linguistic and cultural ties to the area. So far neither group has been able to counter the dominance of Castilian.

In contrast to Catalonia and the Basque Country, Galicia has not been inundated with immigrants who dilute the language. For this reason a very high percentage of the population—90 percent—speak Galician, compared to 60 percent who claim to speak the vernacular in Catalonia and less than 25 percent in the Basque provinces. This means that the language has just under three million speakers in the four northwestern provinces of La Coruña, Lugo, Orense and Pontevedra. However, only a tiny minority of middle-class intellectuals write Galician and use it in anything but everyday conversation. Another key difference is that the Galicians have been an emigrant people for centuries—by land, sea and now by air to all corners of the world. This has produced what Clare Mar-Molinero has called a "conservative holding mentality," particularly among womenfolk who always seem to be waiting for the return of their husbands and sons. In this kind of atmosphere, regional identity and personal confidence are not very strong. Galicia is still perceived by many Spaniards as a cultural back-water, and its inhabitants are the butt of ethnic jokes in some parts of the Peninsula.

The Xunta or semiautonomous regional government, parallel to the Catalan Generalitat, is attempting to combat these attitudes. It has taken a clear stand against the reintegrationists in favor of Galician or *galego* as a language with a venerable literary tradition of its own, not a mere appendage of Portuguese letters. In fact poetry was written in the tongue as early as the twelfth century. Galician-Portuguese was the most prestigious language for lyric poetry in many parts of the Peninsula for at least a hundred years. Even Castilian kings, like the famous Alfonso the Wise, preferred it to their own language. Santiago de Compostela, the presumed burial site of the apostle St. James the Elder, attracted tens of thousands of pilgrims every year and became the cultural capital of the northern Peninsula. After this early period, Galician entered a long decline and was not reborn as a literary tongue until the nineteenth century. This modern revival lasted until the long night of Francoist oppression. (Ironically, Franco himself was a *gallego*, like so many Spanish politicians then and now.)

With the removal of censorship in the late 1970s, the Galicians, like the Catalonians and Basques, felt a euphoria that did not last very long. Young writers, filmmakers, pop singers, cartoonists and graphic designers from the region enjoyed a brief popularity in an ephemeral movement that was known as the *movida galega* (see Glossary, **movida*). While only 78 books had been published in Galician in 1972, the number grew to 303 by 1980, the year after the new Autonomy Statutes were introduced, and to 637 by 1989. Publishers like Edicións Xerais launched collections of popular literature, including detective novels and new journalism. Young poets like Ramiro Fonte revitalized Galicia's ancient lyric tradition. Radio stations and a television channel began local programming in Galician. The language became the official medium in the regional government, in many schools and at the University of Santiago de Compostela. The Real Academia Galega (Royal Academy of the Galician Language) was founded. In spite of all these policies, the number of people who use Galician as their mother tongue continues to fall. The language faces a long uphill climb.

With a population of less than 2.5 million, the Basque Country is the smallest of the three autonomous communities where a minority tongue is spoken. It is used by some 515,000 people in the three provinces of the País Vasco or Euzkadi (Alava, Guipúzcoa and Vizcaya), as well as in northern Navarre and the three French Pays Basque provinces of Labourd, Basse Navarre and Soule. *Euskara* (sometimes written *euskera*) may be one of the most ancient and is certainly one of the most distinct languages in the world. It is a non-Indo-European tongue and is therefore unrelated to Catalan, Galician and Spanish, not to mention every other known language. This has been one of the major obstacles to its "normalization": Basque is much harder to learn, even for the *vascos*. While thousands of Catalonians and Galicians have been able to "recover" their vernacular tongue, the process has been much more arduous in Euzkadi.

More than the other minority languages, Basque has been closely associated with the struggle for ethnic separation. The nationalist movement **ETA has used it as a symbol of identity and independence. Even before Franco's death, elementary schools known as *ikastolas* were run clandestinely. With the new constitution and the Autonomy Statutes of 1979, they became private organizations or nonprofit parental cooperatives. Now many are supported by the regional government. Since Euskara does not enjoy the long literary tradition of Catalan or Galician, the language needed to develop from an oral to a written medium, passing in a few decades through a process that requires centuries in most tongues. The Academy of the Basque Language (Euskaltzaindia), led by the linguist Koldo Mitxelena, codified the rich variety of local dialects into *euskara batua* (standard Basque). The hard-line defenders of the ancient forms have criticized this effort but have not been able to prevent the adoption of the standardized form by the media and most writers. Jesús María Lasagabaster has pointed out that "Languages are not made by academies. The success of the Basque Academy's initiative depends ultimately on those who speak the language, and here writers and cultural workers can play a vital role."

Like the Catalonians, the *vascos* have had to deal with the problem of immigration by Spaniards from the poorest regions of the country. But it is much harder for an Andalusian or Murcian, for example, who has probably gone to Euzkadi to find a job, to understand or speak Basque than it would be for him to learn Catalan, which at least belongs to the same language family as Castilian. Euskara has the additional stigma of being associated with rural people and old-fashioned attitudes; unlike Catalan, it is not the language of prosperity and success.

Another disadvantage suffered by the *vascos* vis-à-vis the Catalonians is the nature of their economy. The main actors in Catalan society have usually been small entrepreneurs, the protagonists of the region's cultural separatism. Basque capitalism has been powered by heavy industry and banking, centered around Euzkadi's only metropolis, Bilbao. This kind of economic structure requires a wider base and a "national" or international rather than a local or regional organization. For this reason the most potent members of Basque society, the great industrialists and financiers of Bilbao, along with a small group of intellectuals have nearly always preferred to use Spanish rather than Euskara.

In spite of all these obstacles, Basque has made some strides forward in the last quarter-century. For the first time in the region's long history, some good writers are using the language in their works. The most sensational example is the novelist Bernardo Atxaga, who won the National Prize for Literature for his book of stories—published in both Euskara and Castilian—titled *Obabakoak* (1989). Basque government entities and banks offer literary prizes endowed with handsome stipends. While a mere 95 books were published in Euskara in 1976, the figure had risen to 968 by 1995. Most of the earlier works were creative, whereas the more recent books cover the whole gamut of the standard UNESCO subject areas from literature to education and science. Euskara is also spoken in feature films, the performing arts and on several autonomous radio stations and TV channels. Departments of Basque Studies have been organized at some universities in Spain and abroad, including the western United States.

Euskara and Galician have a long way to go before they achieve the success of Catalan. All the minority languages are hit by a double whammy: they must compete not only with Spain's majority tongue, Castilian, but with the world's majority language too—English. Clare Mar-Molinero says:

Satellite television, international travel, computer technology, multinational business creating the so-called global village inevitably weaken the role of lesser-used languages and strengthen the position of world languages, above all English. Castilian is, of course, a widely spoken world language, and to compete with it or aspire to equal bilingualism (as stated in the declaration of aims of the respective communities' language laws) is arguably an impossible goal.

Even more impossible is the goal of saving regional dialects like Asturian (*bable*), Aragonese (*aragonés*) and Aranese (*aranés*). They survive only in remote mountain areas. In the ancient kingdom of Asturias, with a total population of 1,112,000 in 1984, only 26 percent spoke the region's dialect of Bable while a mere 9 percent could write it. Because of its richness in dialectical forms and its influence on early Castilian, it has been studied much more than other dialects in the Peninsula.

Aragonese has lingered in several forms of local speech (*fablas*) in the Pyrenean valleys of this old kingdom. It has practically become a dialect of Castilian. A survey in 1989 showed that only 30,000 people considered themselves capable of speaking or understanding Aragonese.

Aranese, spoken by some 59 percent of the inhabitants of the Pyrenean Valle de Arán in the Catalonian province of Lérida, is a dialect of Gascon, spoken in the French region of Gascony. Gascon in turn is closely related to Provençal. Although the population is very small—some 5,000 people—its isolation has helped its speech survive. Being a part of Catalonia has also favored the Valley: the Generalitat, so sensitive to the problems of minority tongues, has given this dialect the same legal protection enjoyed by Catalan itself.

A final variety of Spanish that has great historical importance is *sefardí* or Sephardic, the language of the Jews expelled from Spain by the Catholic Kings in the late fifteenth century. For centuries after this new diaspora, their descendants continued singing their folksongs and speaking the language of the land where they had lived for a thousand years. Frozen in time, Sephardic Spanish remains a curious relic that is now being studied in several universities in Spain and Israel. The Spanish foreign radio service broadcasts in this unique dialect, which is also known as *djudezmo* or *djudeoespanyol* (Judeo-Spanish).

For most inhabitants of Spain, language is an important part of their identity. For this reason the politics of language will continue to be fraught with tension and misunderstanding. At the same time, further integration of the country in the European Union will probably make linguistic uniformity less important than it was in the old nation-state. Meanwhile some 350 million people speak Spanish outside the Peninsula. The future of the language lies there more than in Spain itself, with its population of a mere 40 million. After English, Spanish is the most widely spoken Western language in the world. It is also one of the most studied: by 1995, it was chosen by more than half of foreign-language students in American colleges and universities. Spanish is now one of the world's five megalanguages, along with Chinese, English, Hindi and Arabic.

A recent statement by Emilio Alarcos Llorach, a member of the Royal Academy, might serve as a fitting conclusion to many of the themes discussed in this chapter:

In spite of so many snares that are often cited (the avalanche of technical barbarisms, the more or less impetuous flood of the vernacular languages, the negligent or ignorant lack of interest from the authorities, the idiomatic uncouthness of the media and the general public, etc.), I don't see any grave dangers for the healthy survival of Spanish.

RESOURCES

There are many sources on Spanish, Catalan, Galician and Basque on the World Wide Web. They can be accessed through various search engines, including "Olé," which specializes in Spanish topics. Some interesting sites are listed below.

The Instituto Cervantes, created by the Socialist government with the purpose of fomenting Spanish language and culture throughout the world (similar to France's Alliance Française), can be reached by mail at 122 East 42nd Street, Suite 807, New York, NY 10168; telephone (212) 689-4232; telefax (212) 545-8837; e-mail <cervanny@class.org>.

The Instituto Cervantes also has several websites: in New York, <http://www.users.interport.net/~cervante/> and in Spain, <http://www.cervantes.es/>.

The Academia Norteamericana de la Lengua Española (North American Academy of the Spanish Language), initiated by the eminent linguist Tomás Navarro Tomás, a member of the Spanish Royal Academy exiled in New York during the Francoist period, is one of twenty-one similar associations throughout the world. All cooperate with the Spanish Royal Academy and are officially recognized by this institution. The North American Academy publishes two journals, *Boletín* (Bulletin) and *Glosas* (Glosses). It can be reached at G.P.O. Box 349, New York, NY 10116; fax (202) 941-5793 and (718) 761-0556; e-mail c/o Dr. Estelle Irizarry, <hispania@guvax.georgetown.edu/>.

The North American Academy of the Spanish Language has a website at <http://www.georgetown.edu/academia/>.

The Real Academia Española can be reached by mail at Calle Felipe IV 4, 28014 Madrid, Spain; telephone 011-34-91-420-1614; fax 011-34-91-420-1478. Not surprisingly, the Royal Academy at this writing was not accessible on the Web. It can be reached through e-mail by addressing the employee's name followed by <@crea.rae.es>; but of course you may not know an employee's name! In addition to its famous *Dictionary of the Spanish Language*, the Academia publishes other dictionaries, books and the irregular *Boletín de la Real Academia Española* (Bulletin).

The Biblioteca Nacional (National Library) of Spain can be reached on-line at <http://www.bne.es/>.

Agencia Efe, the largest press agency in the Spanish-speaking world, has some very helpful and up-to-date services available on-line. You can make language inquiries on their website at <http://www.efe.es/lenguaes.htm/>. In 1992 Agencia Efe published its *Vademécum de español urgente* (Vademecum of Urgent Spanish), which is now on the Web. It is used by the agency's reporters and correspondents and can be very helpful to anyone interested in current usage.

Many Spanish dictionaries are now available electronically. The Royal Spanish Academy has not rushed to place its Dictionary on-line, but it is now available on CD-Rom.

The on-line magazine *Melibea*, with its section called "Lengua viva" (Live Language), includes a "Consultorio Lingüístico" (Language Consultation): <http://www.abaforum.es/is/melibea/numero0/mlb0009.htm/>.

The academies of the minority languages in the Iberian Peninsula can be reached by mail. For Basque: Academia de la Lengua Vasca (Euskaltzaindia), Plaza Barria 15, 48005 Bilbao, Spain. For Catalan: Secció Filológica, Institut d'Estudis Catalans, Calle del Carme, 08002 Barcelona, Spain. For Galician: Real Academia Galega, Seminario de Sociolingüística, Calle Alfredo Brasas 10, 15701 Santiago de Compostela (La Coruña), Spain.

The beautiful monthly magazine *Catalònia*, published bimonthly in English-Catalan, French-Catalan and Spanish-Catalan, is available from Centre UNESCO de Catalunya, CATALONIA Culture, Mallorca 285, 08037 Barcelona, Spain.

BIBLIOGRAPHY

Alarcos Llorach, Emilio. "No hay temor a que el español sea desarraigado en algunas autonomías." *ABCe* (*ABC electrónico*, on-line) [18 November 1997]. A report on a speech given by Emilio Alarcos Llorach of the Spanish Royal Academy.

Alvar, Manuel, ed. *Manual de dialectología hispánica: el español de España.* Barcelona: Ariel, 1996.

Baez San José, Valerio. *Bibliografía de lingüística general y española (1964–1990).* 3 vols. Madrid: Universidad de Alcalá de Henares, 1996.

Burke, Peter. *Popular Culture in Early Modern Europe.* New York: New York University Press, 1978.

Carbonell Basset, Delfín. *Diccionario de refranes castellano e inglés. A Dictionary of Proverbs, Sayings, Saws, Adages. English and Spanish.* Barcelona: Ediciones del Serbal, 1996.

———. *Diccionario malsonante inglés-español.* Madrid: Istmo, 1992.

Carnicer, Ramón. *Desidia y otras lacras en el lenguaje de hoy.* Barcelona: Planeta, 1983.

Caro Baroja, Julio. Interview with author. Madrid, Spain, 16 March 1980.

Caudet Yarza, F., ed. *Los mejores refranes españoles.* Madrid: M. E. Editores, 1996.

Cela, Camilo José. *A bote pronto.* Barcelona: Seix Barral, 1994.

———. *Diccionario secreto.* 2 vols. Madrid-Barcelona: Alfaguara, 1968.

———. *Enciclopedia del erotismo.* 4 vols. Barcelona: Destino, 1982–1986.

———. *Rol de cornudos.* Barcelona: Noguer, 1976.

Claramunt, Fernando. *Modas y epidemias psíquicas en España.* Madrid: Temas de Hoy, 1991.

Correas, Gonzalo. *Vocabulario de refranes y frases proverbiales y otras fórmulas comunes de la lengua castellana.* 1627. Reprint. Madrid: Edición Mir, 1924.

Díaz-Plaja, Fernando. *El español y los siete pecados capitales.* Madrid: Alianza, 1966.

Fernández, Josep-Anton. "Becoming Normal: Cultural Production and Cultural Policy in Catalonia." In *Spanish Cultural Studies. An Introduction. The Struggle for Modernity*, edited by Helen Graham and Jo Labanyi, 342–346. Oxford: Oxford University Press, 1995.

Ford, Richard. *Gatherings from Spain*. 1846. Reprint. London: J. M. Dent & Sons, 1970.

Gómez-Tabernera, J. M. "El refranero español." In *El folklore español*, edited by J. M. Gómez-Tabernera, 389-431. Madrid: Instituto Español de Antropología Aplicada, 1968.

Gómez Torrego, Leonardo. "La lengua española de hoy." In *España hoy*, edited by Antonio Ramos Gascón, 2: 9-47. 2 vols. Madrid: Cátedra, 1991.

Hemingway, Ernest. *Selected Letters, 1917-1961*. Edited by Carlos Baker. New York: Scribner's, 1981.

Hemingway, Mary. *How It Was*. New York: Ballantine Books, 1977.

Iribarren, José María, and Ricardo Ollaquindia. *Refranero navarro*. Burlada (Pamplona): Fondo de Estudios y Publicaciones, 1983.

Lapesa, Rafael. *El español moderno y contemporáneo: estudios lingüísticos*. Barcelona: Crítica, 1996.

Lasagabaster, Jesús María. "The Promotion of Cultural Production in Basque." In *Spanish Cultural Studies. An Introduction. The Struggle for Modernity*, edited by Helen Graham and Jo Labanyi, 351-55. Oxford: Oxford University Press, 1995.

Lázaro Carreter, Fernando. *El dardo de la palabra*. Barcelona: Galaxia de Gutenberg, Círculo de Lectores, 1997.

———. *Estudios de lingüística*. Barcelona: Crítica, 1980.

Lechuga Quijada, Sergio. *Castellanopatías (enfermedades del castellano de fin de siglo). Con un diccionario de lo que no hay que decir*. Navarra: EUNSA, 1996.

León, Víctor de. *Diccionario del argot español*. 6th ed. Madrid: Alianza, 1988.

Lorenzo, Emilio. *Anglicismos hispánicos*. Madrid: Gredos, 1996.

———. *El español de hoy, lengua en ebullición*. 3d ed. Madrid: Gredos, 1980.

Mar-Molinero, Clare. "The Politics of Language: Spain's Minority Languages." In *Spanish Cultural Studies. An Introduction. The Struggle for Modernity*, edited by Helen Graham and Jo Labanyi, 336-341. Oxford: Oxford University Press, 1995.

Martín, Jaime. *Diccionario de expresiones malsonantes en español*. Madrid: Ediciones Istmo, 1979.

Martínez Márquez, José Ramón (Ramoncín). *El nuevo tocho cheli. Diccionario de jergas*. Madrid: Temas de Hoy, 1996.

Miguel, Amando de. *La perversión del lenguaje*. Madrid: Espasa Calpe, 1985.

———. "La perversión de la lengua a través de los medios de comunicación." In *La sociedad española, 1993-1994*, edited by Amando de Miguel, 726-736. Madrid: Alianza, 1994.

Moliner, María. *Diccionario de uso del español*. 2 vols. Madrid: Gredos, 1983.

Muñoz, José Javier. *Argot del periodismo actual*. Salamanca: Cervantes, 1996.

Neruda, Pablo. *Memoirs*. Translated by Hardie St. Martin. New York: Penguin, 1978.

Ninyoles, Rafael. *Cuatro idiomas para un estado (El castellano y los conflictos lingüísticos en la España periférica)*. Madrid: Cambio 16, 1977.

Preston, Julia. "Latin Americans Declare Linguistic Independence." *New York Times*, 16 April 1997.

Real Academia Española, *Diccionario de la lengua española*. 21st ed. Madrid: Espasa-Calpe, 1992.

Rees, Earl L. "Spain's Linguistic Normalization Laws: The Catalan Controversy." *Hispania* 79 (May 1996): 313-321.

Regueiro, Marisa. "Las 'novedades' de la Real Academia Española." *Razón y Fe* 230 (1994): 41-52.

Romero, José Luis. "Antología del folklore de Villavieja de Yeltes y provincia de Salamanca." Unpublished. Madrid: 1994.

Seco, Manuel. "El léxico de hoy." In *Comunicación y lenguaje*, edited by Rafael Lapesa, 189–200. Madrid: Karpos, 1977.
Siguan, Miquel. *España plurilingüe*. Madrid: Alianza, 1992.
Stanton, Edward F. *Hemingway and Spain: A Pursuit*. Seattle & London: University of Washington Press, 1989.
Toro Santos, Xelís de. "Negotiating Galician Cultural Identity." In *Spanish Cultural Studies. An Introduction. The Struggle for Modernity*, edited by Helen Graham and Jo Labanyi, 346–351. Oxford: Oxford University Press, 1995.

————— *Chapter 2* —————

Religion

You can even find God among the pots and pans.

—St. Teresa of Avila

I'll bet Spain is the country with more faith than any other. . . . Spaniards are also the people who blaspheme the most, who build the most sumptuous cathedrals and then burn them.

—Salvador Dalí, cited in Manuel Delgado, *La ira sagrada*

There is a story about two Basque peasants who were bumping along a steep, twisting road in an old wagon pulled by a horse, when the animal slipped and sent the men hurtling into the canyon below. If their fall had not been broken by a large tree, they would have perished. They climbed back up to the road where one of the peasants dropped to his knees, clasped his hands in prayer and cried "Thanks be to God!" Standing up on his feet, the other yelled "No! Thanks to the tree. As for God, we know what he wanted!"

The story is a humorous example of the religious extremes in Spanish life. Spain has been the country of the Church triumphant, "more Catholic than the Pope," the homeland of St. Teresa of Avila and St. John of the Cross, the birthplace of the Dominican Order and the Society of Jesus. It has also been a hotbed of anticlericalism and the most violent religious persecution of modern times. All sides have tended to be passionate in their beliefs. Some Spanish atheists, for example, follow their convictions with a zeal that we normally associate with the faithful. As the great filmmaker Luis Buñuel boasted, "I am an atheist by the grace of God."

In order to understand popular religion in Spain, we must also consider the country's tradition of iconoclasm. Both were forged in the same crucible. For centuries people who lived in the Iberian Peninsula identified themselves not by the place they lived but by their religion—Christian, Muslim, Jew. Eight centuries of conflict and coexistence between the three faiths created in Catholics a crusading mentality that did not die when the infidels were forced to convert or be expelled from the land in the late fifteenth century. The modern Spanish nation was created by the "Catholic Kings," Isabel and Ferdinand, who utilized the Holy Office of the Inquisition against supposed misbelievers, heretics and witches. Spaniards then carried their missionary spirit to the New World, where the indigenous population replaced the Semites as the new infidels. The national patron saint, Santiago Matamoros (St. James the Moorkiller), who had cut down thousands of Arabs and Moors on his white steed in the Peninsula, now appeared miraculously on American battlefields to slay Aztecs and Incas. After the Protestant Reformation, Spain was the great defender of the Church and the "hammer of heretics," in the words of the conservative scholar Marcelino Menéndez y Pelayo. Militant Catholicism resurfaced in the nineteenth-century Carlist movement, a mostly rural crusade against the dominant trends of the modern age. When anticlerical movements rose during the same period, they simply followed the example of the Carlistas and the Spanish Church. If their descendants burned temples, monasteries and convents, murdered priests, monks and nuns in the Civil War of 1936–1939, they were continuing an unbroken national tradition of violence toward ideological enemies.

Julio Caro Baroja happened to be writing a study of Baroque religion at the beginning of the war, and he soon realized that powerful, ancient forces were at work. In this work he would show how the same persecution that was once carried out in the name of religion was repeated much later in the name of progress. Both believers and nonbelievers operated by demonizing their enemies. Caro Baroja had discovered the key to his country's ideological conflicts. Manuel Delgado says:

The evidence shows that mass violence against sacred objects, in Spain . . . never implied a rupture, but rather an authentic tradition. . . . The models of persecution, harassment, judgment, burning, lynching and massacre of those who were considered to incarnate social evil—identical to religious evil—had been generously tested for centuries, and historical Spaniards had been well trained in using them against Muslims, Jews, witches, heretics.

The anti-religious fury of the Spanish Civil War has been called the greatest clerical bloodletting in the history of Christianity. During a few weeks in the summer of 1936, some 8,000 priests, monks, nuns and novices were killed. To these must be added the lives of thousands of relatives and sympathizers. Nuns were violated then shot. Some priests were forced to dig their own graves before being executed. Many were found with their skulls crushed. Others were doused with gasoline and burned alive. In one town, rosary beads were forced into monks' ears until their tympanums was perforated. A priest had his eyes gouged out with the crucifix of his rosary. Another crucifix was rammed down the mouth of a mother of two Jesuits. An elderly priest was stripped and castrated; his assassins stuffed his genitals into their victim's mouth before shooting him. Don Antonio Díaz del Moral of Ciempozuelos (Madrid) was thrown into a corral filled with fighting bulls, where he was gored to unconsciousness; later one of his ears was cut off to imitate the amputation of a bull's ear in honor of a matador. These events recall eerily images from Francisco de Goya's famous series of etchings, the *Desastres de la guerra* (Disasters of War), in which

Napoleon's soldiers perpetrate horrendous crimes against Spanish soldiers and citizens, including priests, monks and women.

With the same circular violence that we have seen throughout Spanish history, the Nationalists reacted against their anticlerical enemies in the Civil War. Communists, anarchists and socialists were tortured and executed with no less pity than the priests. When his side won the war, Generalissimo Franco undid all the reforms legislated by the Republic, from the separation of Church and state and the establishment of secular education—symbolized by the removal of crucifixes from schools—to civil marriage and divorce. So many priests and monks found employment in the Ministry of Education that it became popularly known as the "Monastery of Education." Lay people, admitted one cardinal, were treated "like children in the church choir." It was literally impossible for a Spaniard to live without God. Tens of thousands of priests, monks, friars, nuns and hangers-on made their livelihood from the Church. Although nonbelievers were not dealt a physical death as in the Middle Ages, they were given a civil death by being deprived of basic rights. (They could not obtain a passport or a driver's license, for instance.) Citizens had to receive a name, contract matrimony and be buried in the name of God and the Church.

The fusion of state and Church in the Franco period has been aptly called National Catholicism (with obvious echoes of Hitler's National Socialism). According to plans by the Generalissimo himself, he was the Father, the heir apparent to the throne was the Son, and Spain was the Holy Spirit. In this trinitarian system, state, nation and Church were inseparable. Franco had a direct role in the appointment of bishops. A frequent symbol of National Catholicism, seen over and over in photographs and newsreels during the forty years of Francoist rule, was the dictator's habit of appearing in public beneath the canopy of a pallium, used for religious processions and in particular for the bearing of the Eucharist.

In spite of the efforts of the regime to enforce Catholicism, religious practice was probably much less widespread than most people suspected. In a 1972 poll, three years before Franco's demise, 84 percent of Spaniards declared themselves to be believers; yet only half the population practiced their religion on a regular basis in Old Castile, Aragón and the Basque Country, three of the most devout regions in the country. The percentage of practicing Catholics plummeted to one-third and even one-sixth in the south-central regions of the country, where anticlericalism has been vigorous in modern times. Almost two-thirds of Spaniards admitted that they did not follow Church doctrine in sexual matters.

The honeymoon between the Spanish state and Church lasted for a quarter-century. By the 1960s new voices were already beginning to be heard. The Second Vatican Council (1962–1965) created the most radical revolution in the history of the modern Catholic Church. Rite and belief, which had been considered eternal, became susceptible to change. The Council plotted a more liberal and tolerant course for the future. As the historian Stanley Payne observed, "In no Catholic society did the dramatic new doctrines of Vatican II have such a marked effect as in Spain." Although many people, especially in rural areas, objected to liberalization, most Spaniards recognized that reform was overdue. The Spanish Church underwent what has been called a "reconversion." I would suggest that it could also be described as a kind of Catholic "reformation," because it executed a series of radical measures that uncannily evoked the spirit of Martin Luther: emphasis on faith over icons and rituals, suspicion of local cults and practices. Another trend that recalled Protestantism, without the approval of the new Church, was the marriage of priests, monks and nuns.

Just as surely as we speak of the transition to democracy after Franco's death, we can speak of a religious transition that began a decade earlier; in fact it prepared the way and was part and parcel of the political change. The Church publicly distanced itself from the regime, as if it wanted to clear a guilty conscience of the abuses committed during the previous twenty-five years. "Worker priests" helped organize laborers in order to demand higher wages and the right to call a strike. Some clerics, especially from the Basque and Catalan regions, took part in political protests. There was a "massive desertion" of the Church by clerics and monks who chose to marry or live with a partner. I remember going with a Spanish friend to a priest's house in a remote village of the province of Salamanca in 1970 and seeing a poster of Che Guevara on the wall. It was the spirit of the times. The connection was not by chance: the theology of liberation, which was then thriving in Latin America, was also espoused by some Catholics in Spain.

The decline of the Franco regime, which the Church was instrumental in bringing about, paradoxically marked the end of Catholic dominance in Spanish society. As Frances Lannon says,

The two had proved strangely interdependent at the end, as at the beginning. As democracy was established and a new agenda emerged in Spain, dominated by Europeanization, capitalist growth, cultural experimentation, and the transformation of women's roles and family structure, Catholicism found itself just one influence among many in the new pluralism.

Let us look at one Spanish town before and after Vatican II in order to see how the reconversion of the Spanish Church affected people's lives. For several decades the anthropologist Ruth Behar has studied the village of Santa María del Monte (León) in the heart of Spain's Bible Belt—if that term could be used for a country and a religion in which the Scriptures have always been less important than the clergy and tradition. Don Efigenio was parish priest in the town for twenty-five years, mostly during the Francoist regime. Like the Generalissimo, he had an authoritarian personality and brooked no opposition. He lived in the village and kept his ear to the ground regarding local affairs and gossip. He demanded attendance at Mass and valued other rituals like rosaries, novenas, litanies, processions and festivals for local saints. Haranguing his parishioners with two-hour sermons, he insulted them and even called them "*burros*." His confrontational style led to open struggles in which he almost came to blows with some of the local men. These conflicts eventually caused his removal to another parish. Surprisingly, many older parishioners were sorry to see Don Efigenio leave because he embodied the style of religion in which they had been raised. This reaction resembled their attitude toward the Franco period in general. Older Spaniards still speak nostalgically of "the way things were" and regret that certain aspects of the former regime have been lost for good. Yet they know that the old politics, like the old religion, was as backward as harvesting wheat with a sickle, and they would never wish for a return to the former status quo.

Efigenio's successor in Santa María del Monte, Don Laurentino, shows the spirit of Vatican II and the reformed Spanish Church. He lives in another town and therefore does not meddle in village affairs. He downplays attendance at Mass and other rituals, believing that outward signs of devotion are less important than a deep inner faith. He keeps his sermons short and does not use a bully pulpit to enforce religious unity. Although Don Laurentino is popular in the village, some people—especially the older generation—criticize him for being away too often and for ignoring customs like the rosary, which he has not led even once since his arrival in the parish. The greatest scandal caused by the new priest occurred when he decided to take an old wooden image of St. Tirso to the local cemetery and burn it without consulting the villagers. He claimed that it was "so ugly" and such "a degradation" that it did not even deserve to be preserved in a local museum. Ruth Behar says: "The death of the image in the cemetery, in the company of the souls of the village dead, can be taken as a metaphor for the mission of the Vatican II church to put popular rural religion to rest, tactfully and with dignity if possible, or otherwise enshrined in a museum case, but to rest nevertheless." The rapidity of change has left many Spaniards, above all the elderly, with a kind of schizophrenic feeling of dislocation.

The Catholic Church may have attempted to put popular religion to rest, but in large part it has failed. In fact, it could be argued that it has put the influence of the ecclesiastical hierarchy to rest while traditional forms of religiosity have undergone a new awakening. We will see evidence of this below.

Like all other Western countries, Spain has largely become a secularized nation. The new constitution, approved three years after Franco's death, in 1978, calls for a nonconfessional state with no official religion, although it does provide for relations "between the Catholic Church and many confessions." Measures promulgated by the Republic and abolished by Franco have been restored: the right to secular education, civil marriage and divorce. In this sense the four decades of National Catholicism seem to be a mere parenthesis in modern Spanish history. Yet certain persecutory rituals have survived. As if centuries of religious paranoia were not enough, every year Spaniards symbolically repeat macabre old rituals by killing effigies of Jews or beheading Judas figures in Holy Week celebrations and by again conquering and expelling Muslims in the festivals of *moros y cristianos* (Moors and Christians), celebrated in hundreds of places all over the Peninsula and even in Latin America. The government has tried to make up for this political incorrectness, not to mention centuries of persecution, by cultivating relations with Arab countries and more recently with Israel. Yet the Spanish state's pursuit of *ETA, the clandestine organization of Basque separatists, could be seen as the latest expression of a national disease, like the terrorists' mock trials and executions of their hostages. We are dealing with a tradition that cuts across most historical, social, religious and political lines.

Other worrisome vestiges of the old Spain have survived Vatican II and the reconverted Church; they seem to carry a heavy symbolism. When a Spanish warship is launched, for example, it is done in the presence of a member of the royal family and the ritual is blessed by a Catholic priest. In the annual ceremony in honor of the apostle St. James, held every year on 25 July at the cathedral of Santiago de Compostela, the king or his son the prince of Asturias is always present to make an "offering of consecration of Spain to the Apostle." The invocation begins with the words that Franco initiated decades ago: "*Señor Santiago* . . ." (Lord St. James . . .). Remnants like these have led some critics to express concern and to call Spain a "crypto-confessional" state. The writer Eduardo Haro Tecglen says, "When I see the chief of state, or the king in front of the statue of St. James, speaking with that stone idol, I feel a considerable fear that we could return at any moment to the triumphant Catholicism of the Civil War."

One can understand the author's fear—he spent his adolescence in the war—but one must also admit that a return to National Catholicism would be inconceivable in modern Spain. The battle that the anticlericals failed to win through centuries of tireless militancy has been won quietly and bloodlessly by a gradual process of secularization. Rafael Díaz-Salazar and Salvador Giner say,

Without burning temples or assaulting convents, a religious indifference took root that was a thousand times more potent than the defeated anticlericalism of the Civil War. . . . The final result has been the most important change in the religious history of Spain since the Counter-Reformation: the appearance of a country that is modern in religion, relatively secularized and open to the emergence on its soil of a new pluralism.

The authors go on to say that the secularization of modern Spain is a relative fact. The country has a deep religious substrate. Blue laws do not need to be promulgated, for example, because for most Spaniards, believers or not, it is simply wrong to go on with business as usual on a Sunday or holiday. Today nobody ascribes to the naive ideology that once predicted the gradual disappearance of religion as the inevitable result of progress. Anticlericalism in the communist world has shown that religious persecution usually creates a boomerang effect, as Spaniards themselves should remember from the Civil War.

If it was impossible to live without the sanction of the Catholic Church in Francoist Spain, millions of Spaniards now live outside religious institutions. Attendance at Mass and confession—two of Martin Luther's main targets for criticism—have dropped sharply. The reaction against the Church is part of the general tendency throughout Spain and the Western world to withdraw from all institutions. Some critics speak of a private, interior spirituality or "invisible religion." It is certainly true that there has been a much steeper fall in religious practice than in belief. Gustavo Bueno says,

In democratic Spain one can live without God, but in fact, the majority continue living with him, even if it is in the form of a distant, residual ether that tranquilizes them and frees them from any philosophic unrest, giving them plenty of time to devote to their bank accounts, their sports, their discotheques and even, in the case of the most educated minorities . . . to the novels that hold the top places in the best-seller lists.

Religious belief and practice in Spain, the country that once prided itself on being "more papist than the Pope," are now similar to those in other modern, secularized countries. Between 1970 and 1989, a period including the end of Francoism, the democratic transition and Socialist rule, one-fifth of Spaniards "emigrated" from religious belief to atheism or indifference. During the same period, acceptance of the infallibility of the Pope fell from 76 percent (among housewives only) to 27 percent (among men and women), and belief in hell dropped from 80 percent (housewives) to 32 percent (men and women). These statistics also indicate that Spanish women have customarily been more devout than men, a fact that holds true in other Catholic countries.

The sociologist Amando de Miguel, with his typical talent for seeing through numbers to perceive larger patterns, finds a symmetrical distribution of religious belief in data from 1992: about one-fifth of adult Spaniards are practicing Catholics; another fifth have no religious life and consider themselves to be indifferent, agnostic or atheist. The remainder are Catholics mostly in name, those who are baptized, contract matrimony and will be buried by the Church; about half of these attend Mass occasionally and the other half not at all. Of course we should take polls on religion with even more grains of salt than other statistics—the salt of wisdom—since they deal with a person's most private, intimate beliefs.

Some comparisons with the United States will show to what extent Spain has been transformed into a secularized nation. We should remember that postwar America once represented the epitome of profane society for many Spaniards. As we reach the turn of the century, the United States now seems to be the most religious country in the West. In a 1987 poll, a full 96 percent of Americans believed in God, while only 52 percent of Spaniards believed "firmly" and 27 percent "more or less." At the same time 92 percent of Americans believed in the human soul, while a mere 49 percent of Spaniards believed firmly and 40 percent had doubts or did not know what to believe. (The remaining 11 percent must have lacked conviction too.) Although religion in American society is very different from Spain—often related to social acceptance as much as religious faith—the radical differences in these figures are revealing.

Other figures suggest that Spain is mostly a country of fair-weather Catholics. The sacraments that interest a majority of Spaniards today are those that are more public than private; they may have as much to do with social custom and prestige as religious faith or commitment. While less than a third of the people took Communion and only 6 percent went to confession with any regularity in 1989, an incredible 84 percent considered baptism and 75 percent a Church marriage and extreme unction to be important. (The latter, now known by the horrible euphemism of "farewell rites," is admittedly more of a private than a public ritual.) And the most amazing figure of all: in spite of the many secularizing trends we have observed, 99 out of every 100 Spaniards desired a Catholic burial. These statistics suggest that majority religion in Spain is largely a result of habit and socialization. For others, usually men, it has traditionally been a matter of convenience. As the writer Juan Eslava says, many Spanish males are religious "from the waist up." By this I do not mean to denigrate the hundreds of thousands of Spaniards who live by their deep faith.

Converts to other Christian churches in Spain tend to be more assiduous in their beliefs and practices than most Catholics. They show that the vaunted new pluralism in Spanish society is more than just a fashionable term. They no longer have a siege mentality as under the Francoist regime, when they were often banned. Yet they still attest to some discrimination by the state, the Catholic Church, the media and people on the street. For many Spaniards, especially in rural areas, to be Christian has always been synonymous with being Catholic. In fact it could be said that to be fully human also meant being Catholic. Against this kind of mentality, other Christian faiths have made an uphill climb. They did not win complete rights to worship until 1980, and they were not granted full legal footing until 1992. The result has been that Protestants in Spain have grown from approximately 30,000 at Franco's death to some 250,000 today. Of these, 90 percent are evangelical. Pentecostals now own 250 churches, while Baptists have 240. Most are concentrated in urban areas.

The overall secularizing of Spanish life has been accompanied by an extraordinary revitalization of popular religion. Something similar happened during other crucial periods in the country's past: the mid-eighteenth century in reaction to the Enlightenment, the early 1800s in revolt against the Napoleonic invasion, and the early twentieth century in resistance to the pervasive influences of modernity. This seems to be a natural rhythm in Spanish history, a series of Toynbeean challenges and responses in which European influences are countered by a strengthening of native traditions.

In the late twentieth century, the enormous richness of Spanish popular culture seems to be asserting itself once more against the forces of postmodern life. José Vericat believes the flip side of the current secularization is a "religious nostalgia" that reveals itself in the revival of communal fairs and patronal feasts, in processions, pilgrimages and other forms of popular devotion. I will introduce some of these trends in Chapter 3 ("Fiestas"), especially those, like Carnival, that show a decidedly secular character. I will discuss others here, above all those that are more closely associated with the Church calendar and ritual.

By popular religion we mean the unofficial beliefs and practices of the people. In Spain these often involve a close relationship with nature, the body and the imagination and with the oral tradition that has preserved the great myths of life, death and rebirth. William Christian calls it "religion as practiced" in contrast to "religion as prescribed." At its best, popular devotion in Spain has a wonderful richness of color, imagery and symbolism and a remarkable sense of the sacred in everyday life. At its worst, as we have learned above, it manifests ancient persecutory beliefs as well as superstition, witchcraft, sects and cults.

When we discuss religion in Spain, it is not easy to distinguish between popular and official practices. "Low" culture permeates "high" more than in most other countries, as we have seen in the previous chapter and will see throughout this book. In the special case of religion, one of the reasons for the millennial survival of the Catholic Church has been its genius for absorbing local customs, in the Christianization of ancient rites celebrated at the equinoxes and solstices, for example. (See the discussion of St. John's or Midsummer Eve in Chapter 3.)

Some important elements of popular religion in Spain include the worship of the Virgin Mary and the saints, often associated with miracles; a long-suffering Jesus in contrast to the risen Christ (see Photograph 1, Ignacio Zuloaga's *El Cristo de la Sangre*); the cult of the dead in various forms; penitence; monasticism and mysticism; processions; pilgrimages and *romerías* to local, regional and national shrines; fairs and fiestas (see Chapter 3); *cofradías* and *hermandades* or religious brotherhoods and confraternities; *compadrazgo* or "godparenthood," the linking of families through children's sponsors at baptism; superstition and witchcraft; blasphemy (see Chapter 1, "Languages"); anticlericalism and iconoclasm. Many of these elements were of course carried by Spaniards to the New World where they often blended with pre-Columbian influences and still constitute important aspects of popular devotion. We only have to remember that the Virgin of Guadalupe, the patroness of Mexico and other Latin American countries, has her origins in a small Extremaduran town of the same name in the province of Cáceres.

A map of popular religiosity in Spain would include many local and regional customs, beliefs and practices. In Galicia, the most Celtic area of Spain, we would have to emphasize witchcraft and the worship of nature, the home, ancestors and the dead—*ánimas en pena*, or the wandering souls from purgatory. Towards the ancient kingdom of Asturias, the "cradle" of Christian Spain and the reconquest, also with a Celtic past, the cult of the dead survives along with a strong anticlerical tradition among its mining population. In the Basque country and Catalonia to the east, popular religion has been associated with the modern struggle for autonomy. In Navarre, Aragón, Castile and León, the heartland of the Peninsula, there is the highest incidence of belief and practice, in contrast to the prosperous coastal areas of the Levant and Catalonia, with the lowest. Towards Andalusia in the south, spectacular displays of devotion coexist with anticlericalism, anarchism and iconoclasm rooted in poverty, unemployment and class tensions.

Marianism is perhaps the most pervasive characteristic of popular religiosity in the Iberian Peninsula; it has existed at least since the thirteenth century. In the long battles against the Moors that are collectively known as the reconquest, between the eighth and fifteenth centuries, Christians at first lacked a militant saint who could confront a crusading prophet like Mohammed, so different from the unwarlike Jesus. The myth of St. James the Moorkiller emerged to fill this vacuum and the apostle became the national patron saint. The cult of the Virgin, which developed a little later and sometimes competed with the veneration of Santiago, satisfied a need for a mediating feminine figure to counterbalance the stern, masculine God of Hosts. It was in this context that local versions of Mary sprang from the ancient Mediterranean goddesses of life worshiped in many places throughout the Peninsula.

To foreigners, especially those from northern Europe or the United States, the bewildering variety of local Virgins in Spain is confusing to say the least. These people find it hard to understand that the hundreds of Marian icons, all idolized under different appellations, in fact represent the same Mother of God. Many of her names reveal a connection to nature and the earth: Our Lady of the Sierra, the Mount, the Hill, the Valley, the Pass, the Olive Grove, the Chestnut Trees, the Elms, the Oaks, the Ever-

1. Ignacio Zuloaga, *El Cristo de la Sangre* (The Christ of Blood), 1911. Reproduced courtesy of the heirs of Ignacio Zuloaga and Museo Nacional Centro de Arte Reina Sofía, Madrid.

green Oak, the Hawthorn, the Apple Tree, the Heather, the Rosemary Patch, the Holy Grotto, the Holy Fountain, the Spring, the Stream and so on. A special case that should be mentioned here is the Virgen del Pilar (Virgin of the Pillar), who is the icon of Zaragoza and in theory the national patroness of all Spain, a fact that would naturally be contested by the devotees of many other local Virgins. Numerous appellations refer to the Mater Dolorosa, the favored image of Mary in Spain, especially Andalusia: Our Lady of Tears, of Anguish, Succor, Pity, Mercy, Mercies, the Seven Griefs, the Greatest Grief and Pain, Solitude, the Greatest Grief in Her Solitude and so on. Many churches have icons of these Dolorosas, who wring their hands in grief as big tears well from their almond eyes and flow down their always-youthful faces. Innumerable Spanish girls have been baptized with the names of these Virgins, which reveal an expectation that a woman's life must be one of suffering: Angustias, Socorro, Amparo, Mercedes, Dolores, Soledad. Many more girls are baptized "María" alone (from Mary), or with combinations like María José (Mary Joseph); Spanish boys may be named for the Virgin in combinations like José María (Joseph Mary), etc. (Jesús is also a common Christian name for boys, and for girls in combinations like María Jesús.)

It is hard for outsiders to understand the sensual and erotic qualities of Spanish Virgins, so remote from the sexless pantheon of Protestant churches. Mary is decked out with more care than a bride; men are often forbidden to be present when the statue is disrobed and dressed. When she is paraded through the streets in procession, Andalusian men compliment her with *piropos* (see Chapter 1, "Languages"), while Castilians watch her pass in deep silence. Allen Josephs has described a typical procession in southern Spain:

A crush of people surrounds each Virgin chanting "Guapa y guapa, y guapa guapa guapa" [pretty and pretty, and pretty pretty pretty] while certain individuals make more direct remarks: "¡Que esto e divino! ¡Olé! ¡Viva! ¡Qué guapa ere, de verdá! ¡Qué guapa ere, hija! ¡Joé, qué guapa e!". . . . And "¡Viva nuestra mare!. . . . ¡Viva la má guapa de Andalucía!" and finally the incomprehensible adoration "¡Viva tu puta mare!"

He translates: "This is divine! *Olé! Viva!* How beautiful you are, really! How beautiful you are, daughter! Fuck, how beautiful you are!. . . . *Viva* our mother!. . . . *Viva* the most beautiful (Virgin) of Andalucía! *Viva* your whore mother!"? Clearly we are in a world completely foreign to Anglo-Saxon religious mentality. (See Chapter 1, "Languages," for cursing as a form of praise.)

Devotion to the Virgin is particularly strong in Andalusia, known popularly as *Tierra de María Santísima* (Land of the Most Blessed Virgin). This may surprise readers who remember that this region has one of the lowest rates of religious belief and practice in the Peninsula, along with one of the highest rates of anticlerical sentiment and politics. These facts do not disturb Andalusian men who proclaim with equal pride that they are atheists and fervent devotees of this or that local Virgin. (Women would be much less likely to be atheists.) Spanish popular religion, like anticlericalism, defies traditional categories. For many Spaniards, religion is a complex web of social customs more than a system of moral principles.

The most stupendous example of Marianism in Spain is the annual pilgrimage of the *Virgen del Rocío* (Our Lady of the Dew), celebrated at Pentecost in the province of Huelva and involving hundreds of thousands of Andalusians, other Spaniards and foreigners. People make the trip to the shrine in the village of Almonte from more than sixty points of departure, traveling for several days on foot, horseback, in ox-drawn carts, trucks, cars and trailers pulled by tractors across the marshy lands in this southwestern corner of Andalusia. Religious brotherhoods from all over the region take part in the rite, which includes more than enough singing, dancing, drinking and eating to scandalize a whole seminary-full of Protestants.

In the next chapter ("Fiestas") I will discuss some of the more secular features of the event (known simply as "El Rocío"), but I must admit that for the Andalusian, there is no separation between the festive and the devotional aspects. Let us listen to the moving words of Curro Camacho, a bullfighter from Sevilla who describes the culminating moment of the pilgrimage, when the men of Almonte carry the Virgin's float from her shrine into the streets, where thousands of people attempt to partake of the divine by touching her long white skirts. The *almonteños* say that the Virgin, their "Blanca Paloma" (White Dove) belongs to them alone, and that "only their shoulders should feel her weight" (a statement with clear sexual undertones).

Once I tried to push through those men so full of strength and wine to touch the Virgin. I wanted to ask her to let me triumph with the bulls that year. . . . By the time I had touched her skirts and pushed my way out of the crowd, my shirt was ripped, my shoulder was bruised from having been slugged and I had a big scratch on my face. But none of this makes any difference [when you feel] such devotion to the Virgin. The shouts of thousands of voices rang across the marshes: "¡Viva la Virgen del Rocío! ¡Viva la Blanca Paloma! ¡Viva la Reina de los Cielos! [The Queen of Heaven]!"

If anyone believes that Spain has become or will ever become a completely secularized nation, let him jump into the fray on Pentecost and try to touch the sacred robes of the Virgen del Rocío, the White Dove, Queen of the Marshes, Mother of Andalusia.

Marian visions have flourished in Spain and inspired passionate devotion. Seeing how Lourdes and Fatima revitalized piety in neighboring France and Portugal, Spanish Catholics have hoped for a sensational miracle that would galvanize popular religion and stem the tide of secularization. They almost had it in June of 1931, perhaps not by chance only two months after the declaration of the Second Republic. More than a million people flocked to the Basque town of Ezkioga where the Virgin was supposed to have appeared. The visionaries considered the apparition to be a summons to repentance and fervor in the tradition of Spanish mysticism. But the timing was wrong. The anticlerical spirit of the new Republic, which wanted to convert Spain into a secular, nonconfessional state, led to what William Christian has called "an open season in visionaries." The seers were suppressed by the state. When the movement threatened to revive after the Civil War, Franco cracked down on the pretense that the cult favored Basque nationalism. It is curious that the secular Republic and the pious dictator agreed in considering popular, visionary religion to be a threat to the state.

Seers have had an enduring presence in Spain, and they have often been accepted as agents of grace in contact with the divine. As Raymond Carr says, "Visionaries abound in Catholic countries, while Protestantism is a religion of self-help, each person having his own direct access to God, and few making use of intermediaries." Rural seers have been particularly successful in Spain; their visions usually involve the Virgin. One of the most publicized recent cases is Concepción López Soto—popularly known as "Conchi"—a married woman with three children who claims to have had repeated visions of Mary in the province of Sevilla since 1979. The Virgin's spiritual advice has been faithfully recorded on a tape recorder and transcribed. Some Spanish priests have commented on these messages in their sermons; they have found no contradictions of Catholic dogma. The messages can now be read on the World Wide Web.

Tracking the Virgin's apparitions has almost become a cottage industry in Spain. No doubt the country will continue to be one of the world centers of Mariolatry. Some Catholics describe the late twentieth century as a millennial "Age of Mary," but this is nothing new in the Iberian Peninsula.

The cult of the Virgin exceeds the worship of Jesus in most parts of Spain. Nevertheless there are icons of Christ that are venerated like the more numerous local Virgins. They too have their own appellations, like the Christ of Anguish, of the Five Wounds, the Expiration (nicknamed "*el Cachorro*" or the Cub), Humility, Mercy, Our Souls' Remedy, St. Peter, the True Cross (*Veracruz*), the Vegetable Gardeners, Our Father Jesus of the Death Sentence, the Great Power, Jesus the Nazarene, Jesus of Our Health, Redemption in Judas' Kiss and so forth, to name only a few Andalusian icons. Just as the Mater Dolorosa is the preferred image of the Virgin Mary, the crucified Man of Sorrows prevails over the risen Son of God. In Holy Week celebrations it is always Good Friday, not Easter Sunday, that forms the center of emotional significance. For centuries Spanish sculptors have made beautiful, multicolored images of bloody, twisted Christs on the cross that occupy cathedrals, chapels, shrines and museums throughout the country. The Baroque iconography of the crucifixion traveled with Spaniards to the New World where it can be seen in churches from New Mexico to Tierra del Fuego. It is also represented in the works of some of Spain's classic painters like El Greco, José de Ribera and Francisco de Zurbarán and in modern times, Goya, José Gutiérrez Solana and Ignacio Zuloaga (see again Photograph 1, *El Cristo de la Sangre*). The contemporary artist who has captured this solemn, penitential spirit of Spanish popular religion is not a painter but a photographer, Cristina García Rodero. She has taken many photos, usually in black and white, some of them showing the festive side of popular religion, but most depicting the dark, somber Spain that she calls "*España oculta*" (occult Spain). I remember in particular her startling shot of one of the famous *empalaos* (impaled men) of Valverde de la Vera (Cáceres), who commemorate Good Friday by having their arms tied to a rough-hewn beam slung across their shoulders, then wander through the streets in pain, barefoot.

Many foreigners and even some Spaniards have considered the worship of the crucified Christ to be unhealthy. The poet Antonio Machado, in verses based on the traditional Andalusian *saeta*—a song often addressed to Jesus on the cross during Holy Week—says

> Oh, you are not my song!
> I cannot sing or praise
> that Jesus on the cross,
> but him who walked on water!

Machado, an anticlerical socialist, missed the point. A later poet, Pedro Salinas, argued more objectively that the veneration of the crucified Christ does not represent a cult of death and a denial of life. On the contrary, it is precisely the acceptance and awareness of death, and the refusal to deny it, that creates the fullest and truest understanding of life for Spaniards. Salinas describes a Holy Week procession in Sevilla:

The images . . . that are kept in the churches go forth into the city in processions, carried on litters, and at a slow pace they pass through the streets, where they are admired by a large crowd. And one of those images, one of those splendid seventeenth-century wood carvings, is of Christ on the cross. It is impressive to see, over the heads of the people, the naked body of the dying Christ, proceeding step by step in the night. Anyone who might regard this spectacle as indelicate morbidity, as pleasure taken in the funereal symbol of a dying body, would be wrong. No, as far as the people are concerned, in the death of that God-man, everlasting life is actually being achieved.

The post–Vatican II Spanish Church has attempted to encourage a more modern, optimistic image of Jesus. These efforts have largely failed, notably in Sevilla, the city with the most massive Easter celebrations in all of Spain. One scholar says bluntly, "for the popular theology of Sevilla, the Resurrection has nothing to do with Holy Week." Timothy Mitchell concludes: "The plot line of the Passion according to Andalusia can be summarized as suffering, death, burial, and suffering without end. If the people do not wish to spoil this story with a joyous Resurrection, they must have some powerful reasons." These reasons have to do with the penitential nature of popular religion in southern Spain, with a fatalistic attitude and a pessimistic worldview engendered by centuries of socioeconomic injustice. Similar factors could be adduced for other parts of Spain.

The Spanish cult of *las ánimas*, the departed souls of the dead, particularly strong in the north of the Peninsula, is another aspect of this paradoxical mystery of Spanish religion. The dead are honored and propitiated for their active influence on the living in the course of All Saints' and All Souls' Days, as well as in funerals, wakes and novenas. In his classic study, *The Tragic Sense of Life*, the great Spanish writer Miguel de Unamuno captured the relationship between death and life in its philosophical dimension.

An important institution of popular Spanish religion, closely related to the cults of Christ and the Virgin, are the *cofradías* and *hermandades*, or civil-religious brotherhoods and confraternities. As their names would suggest, their members were once all male, but by the 1980s some women were allowed to participate in activities. The *cofradías* are especially numerous in Andalusia, the region of Spain where cults of local Virgins and Christs are generally most rabid. Each brotherhood is devoted to a particular icon of Mary, Jesus or a saint, which also gives the group its name: Brotherhood of the Virgin of Hope (Macarena), Brotherhood of Our Father Jesus of the Death Sentence and so on. In larger towns or cities, each may represent a particular *barrio* or neighborhood, profession (lawyers, for example) or social class.

The *cofradías* engage in charitable work and social gatherings throughout the year. In this they resemble Masonic orders, probably their closest cousins in the Anglo-Saxon world and elsewhere, in spite of vast cultural differences. The brotherhoods' activities culminate each spring in the rituals of Holy Week, particularly on Good Friday, the most important and widely celebrated holiday in the country. Throughout the evening and early morning, the brotherhoods bear their characteristic image on a *paso* or float through the streets of the village, town or city, as in the scene described by Salinas in Sevilla. The pasos are carried on the strong shoulders of *costaleros* (bearers) and flanked by caped, hooded *nazarenos* (penitents), wearing the unique garb of the particular *cofradía* and sometimes bearing heavy wooden crosses on their backs or walking barefoot in order to share in Christ's suffering. The poet Federico García Lorca evoked these mysterious, silent figures, who never fail to remind Americans of the Ku Klux Klan:

> Through the lanes
> come strange unicorns.
> From what fields,
> from what mythological forest?

The faithful may applaud, scream, weep and utter *piropos* or compliments to the passing Virgin or Christ. Strange as it may seem, they may also insult the icons of rival brotherhoods. In some Andalusian celebrations, singers located on a prominent corner or balcony sing moving *saetas* to the statue on the float. In the meantime, crowds line the routes of the procession, often taking swigs of beer, wine or brandy, diving into bars and cafés for more libations. As in the pilgrimage of El Rocío, there may also be dancing, singing and partying. There is always emotion, from the penitential to the festive. Holy Week is much more than religion: it is drama, costume, dance, song, ecstasy, myth, spectacle, wine, fiesta, rite of spring, rebirth. It is a kind of drunkenness of the senses, as evoked by Luis Maldonado in his description of the many physical elements of popular Spanish religion: "images, banners, insignias, emblems, coats of arms, precious objects, reliquaries, urns, tapers, lights, candles, lanterns, lamps, oil lamps, torches, candelabras, rockets, illuminations, palm leaves, branches, flowers, perfumes, incenses, costumes, ornaments, disguises, delicacies, drinks." All in a syncretistic whole with ancient roots in paganism as well as Christianity. It is without match anywhere in the world.

The brotherhoods offer a window on the two-tiered religion so typical of Andalusia and most other regions of Spain. Although they often possess enormous economic and social power, the *cofradías* might be said to represent the faith of the people in contrast to the doctrine of the Church. They have taken worship into their own hands by creating an elaborate series of rituals that often stray from official dogma and become heretical or blasphemous. The religious brotherhoods engage in a constant struggle with ecclesiastical authorities for control of the processions, pilgrimages and other practices carried out by the members, who consider these activities to be infinitely more important than attendance at Mass, confession and the sacraments. Isidoro Moreno-Navarro, the scholar who has studied popular Andalusian religion most extensively, says, "The people are not celebrating supernatural beings or forces as much as the *us*, the group. They celebrate *us* by fundamentally celebrating life and the sensuality of life, through collective rituals."

The brotherhoods also engage in rivalries with other *cofradías*. Marriage into the family of a competing group is discouraged: engagements have been broken—sometimes on the eve of the wedding—when a brother has violated his organization's endogamous prejudices. There are endless squabbles about which *cofradía* is the oldest, which has the right to leave its chapel first for a procession, which has more musicians, which explodes more rockets during a parade. In the town of Palma del Condado (Sevilla), for instance, two brotherhoods staged a fireworks battle in which one group launched a rocket onto the roof of its rival's chapel, starting a fire that wounded several people. To the consternation of the Church, celebrations may be canceled or interrupted because of wounded pride among the members of a particular *cofradía*. For these people, religion has more to do with social identity and prestige than with faith and worship.

Another aspect of popular religion in Spain, sometimes related to brotherhoods and confraternities, is *compadrazgo* or godparenthood. Since the rite of baptism continues to be almost universal, notwithstanding secularization and the decline of other sacraments, the role of godfathers and godmothers is very important. They are the witnesses of a newborn child's religious "birth" and have much more than the symbolic role common in other countries; they acquire a sort of spiritual kinship with the child's parents, who often address them forever after as *compadre* and *comadre*. Although these words are translated as "godfather" and "godmother," they actually mean "co-father" (*compadre*) or "co-mother" (*comadre*). For this reason I prefer to use the general term "co-parenthood" to refer to the institution of *compadrazgo* in all Hispanic countries, whether Spain or in the New World. These words have spawned a whole series of other nouns and verbs that disclose the pervasive social ties created by the institution. The words "*compadre*" and "*comadre*" themselves reveal so much affection that two good friends may use it as a nickname among themselves even if neither is actually a godfather or godmother of the other's child. In Andalusia and in other regions where religious brotherhoods are numerous, the members are often tied by relationships of *compadrazgo*, a fact that weaves the net of mutual relations even closer. Spanish society has certain primitive qualities that have disappeared from other Western countries. Ramón del Valle-Inclán, one of the country's greatest modern writers, said "Spain, in religious matters, is a tribe of central Africa."

Most of the customs mentioned so far have dealt with collective features of popular religion; there are many more that we cannot discuss here, such as the elaborate celebrations of Corpus Christi in late spring. We should also remember that Spain is a country that has nourished some of the greatest solitary expressions of faith. The Franciscan, Carmelite and Jesuit orders have followed various kinds of mystical and ascetic traditions, as seen in the lives and works of saints like Peter of Alcántara, Teresa of Avila, John of the Cross, Francis of Borja and many more. (Other less orthodox Spaniards were not canonized but persecuted, such as the *alumbrados* or "illuminated ones" in the sixteenth century.) These orders and others like the Trappists and Carthusians still encourage self-denial and meditation more than in most Catholic countries. A much newer and more secretive organization, *Opus Dei (Work of God), whose members include lay and clergy, men and women, also encourages certain forms of self-mortification.

Another form of solitary devotion is pilgrimage. It should be distinguished from *romerías*, which tend to be collective, shorter and more festive. Pilgrimage is normally but not always penitential. As in *romerías*, the goal is a shrine or sanctuary associated with the Virgin, Christ or a saint.

Pilgrims have been crisscrossing Spain for over a thousand years. In the Middle Ages, travel to a shrine was often carried out in fulfillment of a vow, a penance or a punishment. The rewards usually involved some kind of remission of sins—no laughing matter for people who believed this increased their chances of enjoying eternal life in heaven. Pilgrimage flourished for centuries and survived in Spain long after it had been denounced as pagan superstition by Erasmus and other Catholic reformers and by later critics such as Martin Luther. For most Protestants, travel to sanctuaries and shrines is unimportant, since contact with the divine is theoretically possible anywhere, anytime.

Like other examples of popular devotion, pilgrimage has undergone a revival in the late twentieth century in Spain. As I write these words, somebody is embarked on a trip to a sacred spot in the Peninsula. Instead of the medieval sandals, scrip and gourd, the modern pilgrim uses hiking boots, a backpack and a canteen. The goal may be the fulfillment of a vow or penance but could just as well be a break with routine, adventure or time alone in a natural setting.

There are many pilgrimages in Spain, but none is more famous or popular than the ancient Camino de Santiago, or Road of St. James across the northern part of the country, with branches deep into France. Since the ninth century, people from all over Europe have been heading toward the Spanish city of Santiago de Compostela, the cultural capital of Galicia in the northwest corner of the Peninsula, where the body of the apostle St. James (Santiago in Spanish) is believed to be buried. (Chaucer's Wife of Bath had been there.) Since the early 1980s, the Camino has soared in popularity and is now surpassed only by its two old rivals, Rome and Jerusalem, and by two modern upstarts, Lourdes and Fatima. In 1993 alone, a recent Holy Year or Jubilee, more than three million people visited St. James's tomb in Compostela, among them Pope John Paul II. Most of these traveled by air, sea, rail, car or bicycle, but thousands went the old way, on foot or horseback. Pilgrims came from Spain and countries all over the world. The Council of Europe named the Road the continent's "premier cultural route," while UNESCO baptized it "the universal heritage of mankind."

I have had the opportunity to walk the Camino de Santiago several times since the mid-1980s, and I have been able to experience this ancient custom firsthand. The rebirth of pilgrimage is one more example of the astounding resilience of popular religion in Spain. At the same time we should not forget that the Camino de Santiago, like el Rocío and Holy Week in Sevilla, have not escaped the ills of our time: commercialism, greed and exploitation.

Of course these ills also existed in former times, as did superstition and magic. While we should not ignore these phenomena, we should recall that they have often been exaggerated by the *leyenda negra* (Black Legend), the persistent vision of Spain as the country of backwardness, ignorance, popishness and cruelty—in a word, the Spain of the Inquisition. The legend originated among Protestants in northern Europe who were opposing Spanish power in war, politics and religion. It has prospered notably in the Anglo-Saxon world, for which Spain has been an enemy on repeated occasions, first for England from the late-fifteenth through the early nineteenth centuries, then for the United States in the Spanish-American War (1898).

Without falling into the trap of the Black Legend, we must recognize that superstition and magic form a part of Mediterranean culture, and Spain is no exception. The country's long history of invasions has created an amalgam of many influences, from the pagan to the Christian. The Catholic Church has combatted some of these tendencies but has assimilated those that could be reconciled with Christian belief. Thus there is a "saint for everyone's devotion," who can be invoked for any need, from a sore toe to a husband or a baby. Just as there is "good magic," so there is black magic, whose purpose is usually similar—to help the supplicant with supernatural powers. Caro Baroja has shown that the Spanish language and folklore evince the Manichean belief that there are animals of God and animals of the Devil, plants of God and the saints and diabolical plants, and so on in a system embracing the entire cosmos: "The course of life is thus a true drama in which all creatures are involved, from God and the Devil to animals and plants, the stars, men, the good and the bad."

Popular medicine is closely tied to the world of magic and superstition. In Spain, especially in the rural parts of the country, there has always been an alternative medicine practiced by *curanderos*, quacks or bonesetters; *saludadores*, men or women believed to possess a special gift for healing bodily ills and diseases; *emplasteros*, or specialists in plasters and poultices. A thin line separates these types from *ensalmadores* and *recitadores*, who claim to cure by reciting incantations. They deal with obscure ills like *mal de ojo* (evil eye), *mal de viento* or *los aires* (evil winds or airs), and general *daño* (injury). These characters have many regional and feminine variants, like the Andalusian *sabia* (wisewoman) and *echadora* (fortune-teller), the Galician *meiga* (sorceress) and the Basque *xorguiña* (witch). Their lore can be found not only in Spain, but also in Latin America, where it was transported by colonizers and mingled with native traditions.

Although many Spaniards have forsaken official religion, they have largely clung to their beliefs in certain areas that used to be governed by faith. A recent poll by Amando de Miguel shows that about three-quarters of the population believes in good or bad luck; more surprisingly, a third still believes in *gafes*, or people who are supposed to bring ill fortune. The percentages are even higher in certain regions like Andalusia. There these beliefs are not held mostly by peasants and the proletariat, as in other parts of Spain, but "vertically," by all classes. One researcher speaks of a "sincerely superstitious" middle class in southern Spain.

Some modern thinkers, like the philosopher Eugenio Trías, have tried to salvage the most positive aspects of popular magic in Spain. He argues that it is a healthy defense against our homogeneous, technological, capitalist world. Trías derives his "magical thinking" from anthropologists like Sir James Frazer and Lucien Lévy-Bruhl and sees it as the best way to cure the sterility of both official religions and secularization. This kind of thinking provoked a bitter reaction from Pope John Paul II when he visited Spain in 1991 and reproached the country's "new paganism."

Another phenomenon associated with superstition and magic is the spread of cults and sects, which of course were prohibited under the dictatorship. Many Spaniards still apply these terms indiscriminately to any kind of non-Catholic group with religious intentions, including Protestants. Here I will attempt to employ the words as they are generally used in other Western countries, in order to refer to small, esoteric, marginal groups that are relatively new. Available statistics in Spain unfortunately may reflect the old mentality, throwing Mormons, for example, into the same boat with people as radically different as Hare Krishnas. For this reason figures fluctuate wildly: estimates for the number of groups range from 27 to 300, with total membership between 76,000 and 500,000.

Most cults and sects in Spain come from the United States, Latin America or Asia, and a few from Europe. Some imports are Alpha Omega, Ananda Marga, Agora, Bhagwan Rajuesh, La Comunidad (The Community), Hare Krishna, Niños de Dios (Children of God), Mensajeros de Elohim (Messengers of Elohim or Raelian Movement), Nueva Acrópolis (New Acropolis), Rama, Unification Church (Moon). Those with native origins include Palmar de Troya (Trojan Palm Grove), founded in Sevilla, 1972; Rachimura, started in Barcelona, 1975; and Arco Iris (Rainbow), begun in Pamplona, 1978. The large cities, above all Madrid, Barcelona and Valencia, are the home for most of these groups.

One of the most controversial aspects of the cult craze has been the explosion of alleged sightings of unidentified flying objects and contacts with extraterrestrials. The Messengers of Elohim believe in semiangelic beings, called *"elohines"* in Spanish, who cloned humans and fly above the earth. The Rama group—considered to be a dangerous sect in Spain—speaks of "cosmic conspiracies" between extraterrestrials who battle each other; some of these beings threaten humankind, others protect us, and still others merely try to learn from us. As in many countries, some women, not necessarily members of these sects, have claimed to have sexual relations with visitors from other planets. The novelty here is not so much the sex—which recalls Inquisition trials of women who were supposed to have copulated with the Devil—but the willingness to reveal one's private life to millions of unknown listeners and spectators on radio and TV. As in other countries, a great part of the extraterrestrial vogue can be attributed to sensationalism by the media.

As we saw at the beginning of this chapter, no treatment of popular religion in Spain should forget its opposites, atheism, anticlericalism and iconoclasm. Let us take them in turn.

The oppression of dissent for centuries in Spain no doubt caused a reaction against official religion. Nonbelievers have had to be firm in their convictions in order to withstand the fervor of believers. On the other hand, many atheists and agnostics see no contradiction between their ideology and the acceptance of Catholicism as an integral part of Spanish life and culture. When it is a matter of baptism, marriage or burial, some communists, socialists and other leftists recur to the ceremonies of the Church. Manuel Azaña, prime minister of the Second Republic and the man who made the infamous statement that "Spain is no longer Catholic," had himself been married in the prestigious Church of the Jerónimos (Hieronymites) in Madrid. Many nonbelievers also accept the fact that religion and education have always been intertwined in Spain and do not mind sending their children to Catholic schools. Enrollment in private schools, most of which are religious, is highest in the two cities with the greatest incidence of nonbelief, Barcelona and Madrid. On the other hand, we should recall that religious education in southern Europe has probably produced more atheists than any other institution. Luis Buñuel, an even more fervent nonbeliever than Azaña, said that he wanted to send his sons to Catholic schools in order for them to have something to rebel against, as he had rebelled against his own Jesuit education. Victoria Abril, probably the most famous Spanish actress both at home and abroad, says, "An education at a school of nuns made me into a completely atheistic adult, like nearly all the women I know from my generation."

The religious oppression by the Franco regime caused a natural reaction among many Spaniards who equate agnosticism and atheism with freedom from ideological control. As we have seen earlier, about one-fifth of the population now considers itself to be atheist, agnostic or indifferent to religion. Indifference is perhaps the most significant word here, because in previous times it has been very hard for Spaniards to avoid taking a stand on religious matters. The country probably has a larger proportion of nonbelievers than any other in Europe except France, which has an even older history of iconoclasm and where approximately one-fourth of the populace are atheists.

The religious neutrality of many Spaniards suggests that anticlericalism may have moderated in recent years. For two centuries it almost amounted to a belief system of its own. Deep-seated anticlerical feelings are embedded in Spanish language and folklore. To judge by the *refranero* or corpus of Spanish proverbs, rare was the clergyman who did not have a mistress. "Don't ever make a monk's bed, nor give him your wife as maid"; "To live next door to a priest is grief"; "Not even for firewood can a young girl go safely to a priest's house." In Hispanic countries throughout the world, it is well known that when a clergyman refers to his "nephew" or "niece," he is employing a euphemism for his own child born out of wedlock.

Manuel Delgado, author of the best study on anti-religion in Spain, has shown that the language reveals a strange "cannibalistic obsession" with priests, monks and nuns. A curious word for "priest-baiter" in Spanish is *comecuras*, literally a "priest-eater." Many names for delicacies, especially sweets, associate food with religious figures: *huesos de santo* (saints' bones), *requesón de monja* (nuns' cottage cheese), *pedos de monja* (nuns' farts), *yemas de Santa Teresa* (St. Teresa's egg yolks) and so on. To describe something that is particularly tender and succulent, a Spanish man might compare it to "*una teta de novicia*" (a novice nun's tit). During periods of violence, like the Spanish Civil War, this obsession became macabre. In the Catalan town of Sant Adrià del Besós, in July of 1936, one could read the following mock menu: "Dish du jour: novice's tits with tomato sauce, friars' sausages, filets of bishop."

The religious indifference of many people might suggest that the old anticlericalism has disappeared forever. But we should remember that it is a recurring fetish of Mediterranean societies, always latent, merely waiting for a pretext to come to the surface. Some pretexts in recent times have been the national controversy on abortion, the debate on the use of condoms, the Church's campaign against the "paganization" of society, and the competition for public support between public and religious schools. Anticlerical feeling and blasphemy have also surfaced in isolated spots during Easter Week celebrations. Starting in 1986, a group of punk youths in the city of Vitoria performed a mock procession in which they carried an image resembling a punkie rather than the Virgin or Christ. In Cuenca in 1987, another procession of punks violently confronted the penitents of the Brotherhood of the Passion. In Pamplona in both 1987 and 1988, rebellious young men threw bottles at an image of the Virgin, screaming the motto of the rock group La Polla Records (Prick Records), "*¡Hay que quemar la Dolorosa!*" (The Mater Dolorosa must be burned!). In Zaragoza on Good Friday of 1988, a labor union and the Pagan Assembly also had a procession in which they yelled "*¡Virgen del Pilar, a trabajar!*" (Virgin of the Pillar, go to work!) and "*¡Religión, maldición!*" (To hell with religion!). It should be noted that these events occurred in cities, where anticlericalism finds its seedbed, and in some of the most devout regions of Spain—the Basque Country, Castile, Navarre and Aragón.

A very different kind of anticlericalism, mentioned earlier, is found not in cities but in rural areas, not among nonbelievers but the faithful. I am referring of course to pious rather than ideological anticlericalism, which does not see the Church as being too conservative, but too radical in adapting to changing conditions. Yet both groups employ the same language, proverbs and folklore, imbued with prejudices against priests, monks and nuns. Although Vatican II and the reconversion of the Spanish Church gave a new life to pious resistance, it has an ancient history in the Peninsula. The great Golden Age playwright Lope de Vega based his famous play, *Fuenteovejuna*, on a partly true story about a town that took power into its own hands when the local leaders lost their moral legitimacy. Throughout history Spanish peasants and workers have considered themselves more religious than the nobility and the clergy. They believe that the people, not the institution of the Church, are the bearers of true Christianity. The popular phrase for their spontaneous, naive devotion is significantly "*fe de carbonero*," or faith of the charcoal man. As more and more people abandon the countryside and migrate to the cities, this great conservative force in Spanish society will decline.

In spite of the relentless process of secularization, religion continues to be a weather vane of Spanish life. It points to nearly all the major categories of society: age, gender, politics, social class. Let us look at them in turn. Older people tend to be more religious than the young; while this may also be true in most Western countries, the gap between generations is much wider in Spain. In a recent survey by INJUVE (Institute of Spanish Youth), for the first time a majority of young Spaniards (between 15 and 29) declared themselves to be nonbelievers or indifferent to religious matters. Religion also highlights major differences between men and women. As in most Catholic nations, females in general show a higher incidence of belief and practice, but the tendency wanes with decreasing age. Thus older Spanish women are nearly twice as religious as their male companions, while younger people show virtually no variation by gender. As for politics, we have seen in several places that devotion rises predictably as we move farther right on the ideological scale. This dynamic may acquire new relevance under the conservative regime of the late 1990s. Lastly, religion is also related to social class, although the reconversion of the Catholic Church and democratic rule have made this factor less reliable. While the upper classes tended to support institutional religion from the middle of the nineteenth century until recent years, the latest figures show surprising developments. The old association among wealth, power and the Church remains largely intact in the poorest areas of the Peninsula, like Andalusia and Extremadura. But in most other regions, the balance has altered so much that the weathercock may now be pointing in the opposite direction. In other words, members of the upper classes have begun to be the least devout. This has been true in other countries for decades, but in Spain it is an entirely new phenomenon that demonstrates vast changes in the social fabric. A full two-thirds of the population believes that the Church is on the side of the poor and oppressed.

All of the above trends prove that anyone who follows Spanish life must keep an eye on religion. No matter what happens in the coming years, we can predict safely that it will continue to be a bellwether of change. Religion is too deeply ingrained in the Spanish people for it to be anything else. In the face of historical flux, the Catholic Church remains a potent force of unity and order, the oldest institution in the Western world. Its age is also its greatest liability: the crisis in vocations has created a body of priests (average age 56 and rising), monks and nuns that must be rejuvenated. In the new, pluralistic Spain, other Christian denominations and different faiths will also play a part. Recent emigration from northern Africa, for instance, has made the Muslim population of Spain higher than at any time since the expulsions of the early seventeenth century. A few Catholics have converted to Islam, seeing it as an integral part of the Peninsula's cultural past. Other Spanish families, aware of their Jewish ancestry, have begun to practice their old religion in synagogues, some of which have been officially blessed by the king and queen. Spain seems to be recuperating its multicultural heritage of three religions (Christian, Muslim and Jewish), a theme prominently emphasized in the country's pavilions at the Expo '92 (World's Fair) in Sevilla. Pluralism will also include the new paganism, manifested in esoteric cults that attract young Spaniards as alternatives to mainstream religion, with its heavy burden from the past.

Some scholars believe that the process of secularization has finally touched bottom in Spain. They see a sign of change in the overnight success of a compact disc of Gregorian chants by the monks of the monastery of Santo Domingo de Silos. Others adduce evidence such as the greater involvement by younger people in the Catholic Church, in evangelical denominations and sects of various kinds. Amando de Miguel, who is far from being a millennial fanatic and has often been accurate in his cautious predictions, foresees the possibility of a minor religious revival around the year 2000. Whether or not he is right, the memorable moment in Henry Adams's *Mont Saint Michel and Chartres*, when the Virgin and Child look down on a dead faith, will never occur in Spain. Popular Catholicism remains one of the most potent forces in the country—and Europe—at the end of the century.

To conclude I would like to imagine our two peasants again, recovering from their nearly fatal fall into the canyon. Along comes a third man or woman in a car, who finds the pair in the middle of the road, wounded and bloodied.

"Can I give you a ride to the village?" asks the newcomer.

"God must have sent you to help us!" exclaims the pious peasant.

"No, I drive by this spot every morning on my way to work," answers the driver, who has an image of the Virgin Mary on his dashboard.

"I refuse to ride in the same car with a priest-lover!" cries the skeptical peasant, pointing at the icon.

"She's the patroness of my hometown," says the driver.

The skeptic looks at his friend. Finally they nod to each other, get in the car and ride away with the newcomer.

RESOURCES

The Spanish search-engine "Olé" has dozens of religious websites, including Centro Bíblico (Biblical Center—evangelical), Conozca la Historia de su Santo (Know the Story of Your Saint), Diakonia (Orthodox), Estudio Teológico Agustiniano Tagaste (Tagaste Agustinian Theological Study), Grupos Bíblicos Universitarios (College Biblical Groups), Información sobre el Catolicismo (Information on Catholicism), Siempre Fiel (Always Faithful—Catholic), Religión, etc. On these and other sites, you can read everything from the Bible, biblical commentaries and theology to dictations by angels and the Virgin Mary.

BIBLIOGRAPHY

Adams, Henry. *Mont Saint Michel and Chartres*. 1904. Reprint. New York: Penguin, 1986.

Alaiz, Atilano. *Seducción de las sectas*. Madrid: San Pablo, 1997.

Alonso del Real, Carlos. *Superstición y supersticiones*. Madrid: Espasa-Calpe, 1971.

Alvarez Santaló, Carlos, María José Buxó, and Salvador Rodríguez Becerra, eds. *La religiosidad popular*. 3 vols. Barcelona: Anthropos, 1989.

Aranda Doncel, Juan. *Congreso de religiosidad popular en Andalucía*. Córdoba: Cajasur, 1994.

Aranguren, José Luis. *La crisis del catolicismo*. Madrid: Alianza, 1970.

Badone, Ellen. "Introduction." In *Religious Orthodoxy and Popular Faith in European Society*, edited by Ellen Badone, 3-22. Princeton, NJ: Princeton University Press, 1990.

Behar, Ruth. "The Struggle for the Church: Popular Anticlericalism and Religiosity in Post-Franco Spain." In *Religious Orthodoxy and Popular Faith in European Society*, edited by Ellen Badone, 76-112. Princeton, NJ: Princeton University Press, 1990.

Boissevain, Jeremy, ed. *Revitalizing European Rituals*. London: Routledge, 1992.

Brandes, Stanley. "Conclusion: Reflections on the Study of Religious Orthodoxy and Popular Faith in Europe." In *Religious Orthodoxy and Popular Faith in European Society*, edited by Ellen Badone, 185-200. Princeton, NJ: Princeton University Press, 1990.

———. *Metaphors of Masculinity: Sex and Status in Andalusian Folklore*. Philadelphia: University of Pennsylvania Press, 1980.

Bueno, Gustavo. "La influencia de la religión en la España democrática." In *La influencia de la religión en la sociedad española*, edited by Javier Sádaba and others, 37-80. Madrid: Libertarias, Prodhufi, 1994.

Burgos, Antonio. *Folklore de las cofradías de Sevilla: Acercamiento a una tradición popular*. 3d ed. Sevilla: Publicaciones de la Universidad de Sevilla, 1982.

Callahan, William J. *Church, Politics, and Society in Spain, 1750-1874*. Cambridge, MA: Harvard University Press, 1984.

Caro Baroja, Julio. *Inquisición, brujería y criptojudaísmo*. Barcelona: Ariel, 1970.

———. *Introducción a una historia contemporánea del anticlericalismo español*. Madrid: Istmo, 1980.

———. *Las formas complejas de la vida religiosa. Religión, sociedad y carácter en la España de los siglos XVI y XVII*. Madrid: Sarpe, 1985.

Carr, Raymond. "Homage from Catalonia." Review of *Visionaries: The Spanish Republic and the Reign of Christ*, by William A. Christian, Jr. *New York Review of Books* (28 November 1996): 56-58.

Christian, William A., Jr. "Folk Religion: An Overview. In *The Encyclopedia of Religion*, edited by Mircea Eliade, 5: 270-274. 16 vols. New York: Macmillan, 1987.

———. *Local Religion in Sixteenth-Century Spain*. Princeton, NJ: Princeton University Press, 1981.

———. *Moving Crucifixes in Modern Spain*. Princeton, NJ: Princeton University Press, 1992.

———. *Person and God in a Spanish Valley*. 1972. Revised ed. Princeton, NJ: Princeton University Press, 1989.

———. *Visionaries: The Spanish Republic and the Reign of Christ*. Berkeley: University of California Press, 1996.

Comelles, Josep María. "Los caminos del Rocío." In *Antropología cultural de Andalucía*, edited by S. Rodríguez Becerra, 425-445. Sevilla: Consejería de Cultura de la Junta de Andalucía, 1984.

Crain, Mary M. "Contested Territories: The Politics of Touristic Development at the Shrine of El Rocío in Southwestern Andalusia (Spain)." In *Coping with Tourists: European Reactions to Mass Tourism*, edited by Jeremy Boissevain, 27-55. Oxford: Berghahn Books (Europa Series), 1995.

———. "Pilgrims, Yuppies and Media-Men: The Transformation of an Andalusian Pilgrimage." In *Revitalizing European Rituals*, edited by Jeremy Boissevain, 95-112. London: Routledge, 1992.

Cruces, Francisco, and Angel Díaz de Rada. "Public Celebrations in a Spanish Valley." In *Revitalizing European Rituals*, edited by Jeremy Boissevain, 62-79. London: Routledge, 1992.

Delgado, Manuel. *La ira sagrada. Anticlericalismo, iconoclastia y antirritualismo en la España contemporánea*. Barcelona: Editorial Humanidades, 1992.

Díaz de la Serna Carrión, Angel, Antonio Salas Delgado, and Juan Mairena Valdayo. *El Rocío de siempre*. Córdoba: Publicaciones del Monte de Piedad y Caja de Ahorros de Córdoba, 1987.

Díaz-Salazar, Rafael. "La transición religiosa de los españoles." In *Religión y sociedad en España*, edited by Rafael Díaz-Salazar and Salvador Giner, 93–173. Madrid: Centro de Investigaciones Sociológicas, 1993.

Díaz-Salazar, Rafael, and Salvador Giner, "Prefacio." In *Religión y sociedad en España*, edited by Rafael Díaz-Salazar and Salvador Giner, xi–xvi. Madrid: Centro de Investigaciones Sociologicas, 1993.

———, eds. *Religión y sociedad en España*. Madrid: Centro de Investigaciones Sociológicas, 1993.

Driessen, Henk. "Celebration at Daybreak in Southern Spain." In *Revitalizing European Rituals*, edited by Jeremy Boissevain, 80–94. London: Routledge, 1992.

García Lorca, Federico. "Procession." From "Poem of the Saeta," *Poema del cante jondo* (1921). In *The Selected Poems of Federico García Lorca*, edited by Francisco García Lorca and Donald M. Allen, 21–22. Translated by Lysander Kemp. New York: New Directions, 1961.

García Rodero, Cristina. *España Oculta: Public Celebrations in Spain, 1974–1989*. Foreword by Julio Caro Baroja. Introduction by Mary M. Crain. Washington, DC: Smithsonian Institution Press, 1990.

Gilmore, David. "Andalusian Anti-Clericalism: An Eroticized Rural Protest." *Anthropology* 7 (1984): 31–42.

Giner, Salvador, and Sebastián Sarasa. "Religión y modernidad en España." In *Religión y sociedad en España*, edited by Rafael Díaz-Salazar and Salvador Giner, 51–91. Madrid: Centro de Investigaciones Sociológicas, 1993.

Gironella, José María. *Nuevos 100 españoles y Dios*. Barcelona: Planeta, 1994.

González Blasco, Pedro, and Juan González-Anleo. *Religión y sociedad en la España de los 90*. Madrid: Ediciones SM, 1992.

Hobsbawm, Eric, and Terence Ranger, eds. *The Invention of Tradition*. Cambridge: Cambridge University Press, 1983.

Hoinacki, Lee. *"El Camino": Walking to Santiago de Compostela*. University Park: Pennsylvania State University Press, 1996.

Josephs, Allen. *White Wall of Spain: The Mysteries of Andalusian Culture*. Ames: Iowa State University Press, 1983.

Lannon, Frances. "Catholicism and Social Change." In *Spanish Cultural Studies: An Introduction. The Struggle for Modernity*, edited by Helen Graham and Jo Labanyi, 276–282. Oxford: Oxford University Press, 1995.

———. *Privilege, Persecution, and Prophecy: The Catholic Church in Spain, 1875–1975*. Oxford: Clarendon Press, 1987.

———. "The Social Praxis and Cultural Politics of Spanish Catholicism." In *Spanish Cultural Studies: An Introduction. The Struggle for Modernity*, edited by Helen Graham and Jo Labanyi, 40–45. Oxford: Oxford University Press, 1995.

Linz, Juan J., and Alfred Stepan. *Problems of Democratic Transition and Consolidation: Southern Europe, South America and Post-Communist Europe*. Baltimore, MD: Johns Hopkins University Press, 1996.

———. "Religión y política en España." In *Religión y sociedad en España*, edited by Rafael Díaz-Salazar and Salvador Giner, 1–50. Madrid: Centro de Investigaciones Sociológicas, 1993.

Machado, Antonio. "La saeta." From *Campos de Castilla* (1907–1917). In *Poesías*, 149–150. Buenos Aires: Losada, 1973.

Madariaga, Salvador de. *Dios y los españoles*. Barcelona: Planeta, 1975.

Maldonado, Luis. *Para comprender el catolicismo popular*. Estella, Spain: Verbo Divino, 1990.

———. *Religiosidad popular. Nostalgia de lo mágico*. Madrid: Editorial Cristiandad, 1975.

Malo de Molina, Carlos A. *Los españoles y la sexualidad*. Madrid: Temas de Hoy, 1992.

Menéndez y Pelayo, Marcelino. *Historia de los heterodoxos españoles*. 1880–1882. Reprint. Mexico: Porrúa, 1982.

Miguel, Amando de. *La sociedad española, 1993–1994*. Madrid: Alianza, 1994.

———. *La sociedad española, 1996–1997*. Madrid: Complutense, 1997.

Mitchell, Timothy. *Betrayal of the Innocents. Desire, Power, and the Catholic Church in Spain*. Philadelphia: University of Pennsylvania Press, 1998.

———. *Passional Culture. Emotion, Religion and Society in Southern Spain*. Philadelphia: University of Pennsylvania Press, 1990.

———. *Violence and Piety in Spanish Folklore*. Philadelphia: University of Pennsylvania Press, 1988.

Mooney, Carolyn. "Blisters and Finding Saints on the Road to Santiago." *Chronicle of Higher Education* (19 July 1996): A47.

Moreno-Navarro, Isidoro. "Religiosité populaire andalouse et catholicisme." *Social Compass* 33, no. 4 (1986): 437–455.

———. *Cofradías y hermandades andaluzas: Estructura, simbolismo e identidad*. Sevilla: Editoriales Andaluzas Unidas, 1985.

Nesti, Arnaldo. "Introduction: le catholicisme espagnol dix ans après la mort de Franco." *Social Compass* 33, no. 4 (1986): 337–345.

Nooteboom, Cees. *Roads to Santiago: Detours and Riddles in the Lands and History of Spain*. Translated by Ina Rilke. New York: Harcourt Brace, 1997.

Olaizola, José Luis. *Guía de curas con encanto*. Barcelona: Plaza y Janés, 1996.

Payne, Stanley. *Spanish Catholicism: An Historical Overview*. Madison: University of Wisconsin Press, 1984.

Pereda, Carlos, and Miguel Angel de Prada. "Religious Debates in Spain in the 80's." *Social Compass* 33, no. 4 (1986): 347–362.

Puente Ojea, Gonzalo. *Ateísmo y religiosidad. Reflexiones sobre un debate*. Madrid: Siglo XXI, 1997.

———. "Del confesionalismo al criptoconfesionalismo. Una nueva forma de hegemonía de la Iglesia." In *La influencia de la religión en la sociedad española*, edited by Javier Sádaba et al., 81–146. Madrid: Libertarias, Prodhufi, 1994.

Riaza Ballesteros, José María. "La religiosité des jeunes espagnols." *Social Compass* 33, no. 4 (1986): 385–400.

Rodríguez Mateos, Joaquín. *La ciudad recreada. Estructuras, valores y símbolos de las hermandades y cofradías de Sevilla*. Sevilla: Diputación Provincial de Sevilla, 1997.

Sádaba, Javier, and others. *La influencia de la religion en la sociedad española*. Madrid: Libertarias, Prodhufi, 1994.

Salinas, Pedro. "Lorca and the Poetry of Death." In *Lorca: A Collection of Critical Essays*, edited by Manuel Durán, 100–107. Englewood Cliffs, NJ: Prentice-Hall, 1962.

Sánchez, José. *The Spanish Civil War as a Religious Tragedy*. South Bend, IN: University of Notre Dame Press, 1987.

Sellers, Jeff M. "Evangelicals Wary of Religious 'Cult' Label." *Christianity Today* 40, no. 11 (7 October 1996): 89.

Social Compass. International Review of Sociology and Religion 33, no. 4 (1986). Special issue on contemporary Catholicism in Spain.

Stanton, Edward F. *Road of Stars to Santiago*. Lexington: University Press of Kentucky, 1994.

Temas para el Debate, no. 32 (July 1997). Special issue on religious sects.

Thomas, Hugh. *The Spanish Civil War*. New York: Harper and Brothers, 1961.

Trías, Eugenio. *Metodología del pensamiento mágico*. Barcelona: Edhasa, 1970.

Turner, Victor, and Edith Turner. *Image and Pilgrimage in Christian Culture*. New York: Columbia University Press, 1978.

Unamuno, Miguel de. *The Tragic Sense of Life in Men and Nations*. 1913. Reprint. Princeton, NJ: Princeton University Press, 1972.

Urbina, Fernando, and José Sánchez. "Religion et societé dans l'histoire de l'Espagne." *Social Compass* 33, no. 4 (1986): 363–383.

Valle-Inclán, Ramón María del. *Luces de Bohemia*. 1924. Reprint. Madrid: Espasa-Calpe, 1968.

Vavra, Robert. *Curro: Reflections of a Spanish Youth*. Sevilla: Robert Vavra, 1975.

Vericat, José. "La veau d'Or. L'experience de la sécularisation et le labyrinthe religieux espagnol." *Social Compass* 33, no. 4 (1986): 401–418.

Walsh, Michael. *Opus Dei: An Investigation into the Secret Society Struggling for Power within the Roman Catholic Church*. New York: HarperCollins, 1992.

Zulaika, Joseba. *Basque Violence: Metaphor and Sacrament*. Reno: University of Nevada Press, 1988.

—— *Chapter 3* ——

Fiestas

There is reason to believe that the fiestas and celebrations described below, compared to most festivities today, are clearly superior. Although they follow rather rigid patterns, they always have an active character. Diversions today are passive. Men and women receive everything ready-made, whether it is on television or radio, in a cinema or a stadium. . . . There is no place for dramatic or poetic actions. The old dramas no longer stir us.

—Julio Caro Baroja

Caro Baroja, who has studied the annual cycle of Spanish fiestas more closely than anyone else, wrote this passage in the 1970s, at a time when it looked as if these ancient rituals were threatened by decay. Since that time many things have changed, including the nature of some traditional festivities. Not only have they not died out: often they are celebrated more than ever, perhaps too much for them to conserve their old power and purity.

Julio Caro Baroja spoke with great affection for the ageless cycles of rural life that he believed was endangered by modern forces: "The notion of the year or the seasons and months is fundamental for peasants and . . . gives a special meaning to their conception of the world: a cyclic conception, inexorable, within which move men, animals, plants and even the weather—heat and cold, rain and drought, storms and rainbows." Caro felt nostalgia for this kind of life because he was living in the midst of the greatest rural flight in the history of southern Europe. Between 1960 and 1975, in France, Italy, Spain and other Catholic countries, millions of people in small villages and towns fled to cities in search of a more prosperous life. Many villages remained empty or sparsely inhabited by a dwindling population of older people. Within two generations, two-thirds of Spaniards lived in towns of more than 20,000, while there were some fifty municipalities of more than 100,000. A mere 3.75 percent of the people had stayed on the land. As Caro said, it was not only a matter of certain customs or beliefs that were being lost within each rural community, but the community itself. Folklore was becoming an "archeological discipline" for studying customs that were dead or moribund.

Caro Baroja did not count on the great revival of popular culture that followed the rural flight. People left their villages but they returned for spring and summer festivals, driving cars with license plates from Madrid, Barcelona, Bilbao and Sevilla where they had migrated to find jobs. One August I happened to be passing through the almost-abandoned town of Rabanal del Camino (León) and saw it transformed by the arrival of its exiled sons and daughters who had come back for the celebration of their patron saint. Spaniards have a great loyalty to what is known as the *patria chica*, or small homeland, in contrast to the *patria grande*, the nation. It has been said many times that they are first and foremost members of a family, then inhabitants of a town and region, lastly citizens of a country. Although a majority live in cities now, many still talk about "*mi pueblo*" (my town) and the "*fiestas de mi pueblo*," which they try their best to catch during their summer vacation, usually in July, August or early September, not by chance the months of most patronal celebrations.

There is nothing like a Spanish fiesta. No country in the world celebrates as many so well. I remember seeing masked revelers dancing through the streets of Cádiz in Carnival, giant floats going up in flames during the springtime *fallas* in Valencia, young girls covered with flowers from head to toe during May festival in Almería, bonfires on the beach in Galicia for St. John's or Midsummer Night, the explosion of San Fermín that rocks Pamplona each year in the second week of July. Speaking of San Fermín, Hemingway said, "There is no other way to describe it."

The philosopher José Ortega y Gasset wrote about the "fiesta sense of life." He believed that it developed from the primitive Dionysian mysteries, combining dance, sacred orgy and feast—that is to say, fiesta. Many Spanish celebrations include bullfights (see Chapter 4), in Ortega's view the most authentic survival of the ancient rites. These fiestas, like the old mysteries, may also involve sacrifice, blood, wine, dance, revelry and feasting. In them there is a breakdown or reversal of everyday norms and inhibitions, a freeing of the senses, a renewed sense of fellowship and identity with local, regional and national dimensions. After a true fiesta, life is never the same.

In Spain a good time, like a good bar, is always nearby. Foreigners are often surprised by the number of holidays, most of them tied to the old Church calendar. In the seventeenth century more than a third of the year was dedicated to obligatory feasts in certain towns and dioceses. More recently the stretching of the *puente* or "bridge"—to make long weekends out of fiestas that fall on workdays—sometimes gives the impression that the situation has not changed all that much.

What has changed is the nature of Spanish fiestas. As part of the process of secularization discussed in Chapter 2 ("Religion"), many church festivals have declined or disappeared. On the other hand some sacred holidays have taken on an almost entirely secular character, like the world-famous San Fermín and other lesser-known patronal feasts. Large segments of the population, especially young people and women, traditionally confined to the house, now revel right along with the adult males who used to dominate public space. Political decentralization and the establishment of the country's seventeen autonomous regions in 1978 have also brought "festive escalation," as these young governing bodies attempt to preserve and revitalize old festivals or invent new ones. Finally, mass tourism has changed some Spanish fiestas, both by the presence of outsiders and the reaction of natives, some of whom have created counterrituals to protect themselves from contamination in a general movement that I would call the return to tradition. I will discuss all of these trends as well as others.

First I will describe the annual cycle of fiestas in Spain, from spring and summer when they rise to an explosive peak, through the fall and winter when they decline with the natural world. I will concentrate on certain rituals with a broad peninsular or even pan-European diffusion, such as May festivals, St. John's or Midsummer Night and Carnival. Since I discussed Holy Week and other religious rites in the last chapter, here I will concentrate on rituals with a marked secular tone, recognizing that it may not be possible to draw a line between the two. Finally I will explore some of the current trends signaled above: secularization, greater involvement by young people and especially women, festive escalation on the regional and local levels, commercialization, tourism, counterrituals and a return to tradition.

Before approaching the great annual cycle of fiestas, I should remind you of the indispensable book of photographs by Cristina García Rodero, *España Oculta* (see Chapter 2, "Religion," and the bibliography to this chapter), with a foreword by the ubiquitous Caro Baroja and introduction by Mary M. Crain. Unless you have the fortune to travel across the entire Peninsula for a whole year, living and observing the rituals that crowd the festive calendar, seeing this book is probably the best way to visualize the "magical whimsicality" of Spanish fiestas. Here is how Crain describes the collection:

The 126 photographs . . . depict festivals and rituals as practiced in contemporary Spain. These images range from solemn penitential processions, pilgrimages, and individual penitential acts, to popular fiestas, carnival, and romerías. Here we encounter both the pagan and the Christian, the ludic and the tragic, private faith and collective devotion as well as "the sacred in everyday life". . . . García Rodero captures those moments in which the streets, the plazas, the bullrings, the pilgrimage routes, and the backroads of Spain are brought to life through festive celebration. Her photographs highlight the creative power of individual men, women, and children who shape these events by . . . transforming the mundane space and time of everyday life into the magical act that is the fiesta.

Cristina García Rodero's photographs have won international prizes and been exhibited in many cities. They have carried unforgettable images of peninsular celebrations around the world.

Let us begin our tour through a typical year of Spanish fiestas. We will start in spring with the rebirth of nature after the winter cold. Here is how Caro Baroja introduces this fundamental time of the year, laden with symbolism in most cultures: "Turbulent and mysterious Carnival has passed, frost and snow have melted. The fields come to life again and the tender shoots of trees and bushes show new shades of green. Spring has arrived. Not only the poet, but even the simple people of the country feel its magic influence. Let us go, reader friend, into the fields with them."

This period begins toward the middle of April and extends to the end of June. Spanish folklore classifies these months as the time when the cuckoo sings. Those who have heard its haunting song will remember it always. (I had the fortune to hear it once in the former royal woods of Aranjuez.) It is a matter of dire concern if the cuckoo does not sing before a certain time in April, depending on the local climate:

> Se el pecu no canta
> *pal* veinte de abril
> o se ha muerto el pecu
> o viene la fin.
> (If the cuckoo doesn't sing
> by the 20th of April
> either the cuckoo is dead
> or the end is near.)

Plants, flowers and trees are celebrated during the spring in popular poetry, songs and fiestas. Even the dry plains of Castile and the reddish earth of Aragón may turn green, perhaps recalling the long-ago times when they were covered by virgin forests. From now until the fall and winter, many public celebrations include wreaths of flowers, bushes or trees. Young men adorn their girlfriends' houses with a *ramo* or wreath, which people also use to honor the Virgin or a patron saint, just as wine growers carry it in harvest festivals. Many of these rituals include a song that is called by the identical name, *ramo*. Caro Baroja notes that these and other rites are probably traces of primitive tree worship in the Peninsula.

Then comes May, the month of flowers, fiestas and love. Young men often plant the May tree, similar to the maypole of England and the *calendimaggio* of Italy, in the town square. They hang the houses of their girlfriends with wreaths. The boys are called *mayos* and the girls *mayas*, from whom the May Queen is chosen. A whole genre of love poetry has grown up around May songs. It is the month of love par excellence; Caro Baroja titles his book on spring festivals *The Season of Love*. In spite of this erotic association, there is a curious popular belief, held in ancient Rome as well as modern France, Italy and Spain, that it is bad luck to contract marriage during this month. We will return to May festivities later.

The weeks go by and one of the most important holidays in the annual cycle arrives, St. John or Midsummer Night (24 June). For millions of Spaniards and Spanish Americans, *San Juan* is a numinous time, related to the summer solstice, bonfires, bullfights, herbs and the plant world, water, fountains, rivers, fertility, sex and love. Thousands of traditional lyrics, ballads and songs ring with the magic of this date:

> Mañanita de San Juan,
> mañanita de primor . . .
> (Little morning of St. John,
> little morning of delight . . .)

Some of the vegetative rites that we have seen in the month of May are carried over into late June; thus there are also trees and bowers of St. John. All nature, including herbs, flowers, water and fire acquire unique virtues on this holiday, leading to endless superstitions.

It is not clear why the birth of St. John the Baptist has been associated with the summer solstice and a host of rituals and customs that obviously descend from the pagan world. Yet Caro Baroja reminds us that the summer solstice apparently did not have a great significance in the ancient religions. On the other hand San Juan has been one of the most uniformly celebrated holidays in Christianity for centuries, from one end of Europe to the other. During the Spanish Golden Age, in the sixteenth and seventeenth centuries, writers tell us that even Turks, Moors and other infidels celebrated the magical St. John or Midsummer Eve, a night when anything might happen and probably did. It is such an important time in popular Spanish culture that we must return to it later.

So we reach summer, the "festive season" itself. Between St. Peter's (29 June) and St. Michael's Day (29 September) and beyond, patronal feasts abound in Spain. In her useful handbook of popular fiestas in Spain, María Angeles Sánchez says, "After *San Juan* . . . until the arrival of autumn, our festive calendar hardly has a blank page and rare is the *pueblo*, however small, that does not honor its patron during these summer months." The main difference between these rites and all others is that they involve the whole village, town or city in a celebration of itself, rather than a mere part of the community such as a neighborhood, parish, guild, age group or gender. Although a town may have numerous festivals in a calendar year, the patronal event is always the longest. It is sometimes called the major feast (*fiesta mayor*) or the big feast (*fiesta grande*) to distinguish it from minor celebations.

In the new Spain the autonomous regions also have their patron saints. Galicia, for example, whose cultural capital is Santiago (St. James) de Compostela, has chosen this apostle's day, 25 July, as its holiday. St. James used to be the national patron, but no longer. Each region now chooses its own festivities and some prefer to honor a local figure. On 25 July 1997 I was in Pamplona, a city set squarely on the pilgrimage route to Santiago, and was surprised to learn that the autonomous region of Navarre had decided not to celebrate St. James's Day. Never fear: the local population of Galicians, a notably migrant people who have spread over the entire Peninsula and the whole Spanish-speaking world, were celebrating on the streets of Pamplona with bagpipes, flutes, parades, dancing, boiled octopus and bubbly Ribeiro wine.

It is not by chance that most patronal feasts coincide with the harvest season. In fact they have replaced old nature festivals in many cases. Scholars have seen a connection between this period of the year and certain rituals that seem to be related to fertility, such as tossing wheat on the bride at a wedding. Abundant food and drink, free spending, boundless generosity and lavish costumes all play a part in the patronal feasts of Spain and other Mediterranean countries. A common expression is "money flows" (*el dinero corre*) in these celebrations that are a veritable potlatch of consumption.

Patronal fiestas include dancing, music, parades, fireworks, ritual games and sports, bullfights or running of bulls and other activities. Each village, town, city and region is different, all showing common traits.

As fall sets in, the festive season gives way to more somber rituals. The happiness of patronal feasts turns into the sadness of All Saints and the Day of the Dead. The swing in moods continues in the wintertime when the family joy of Christmas is followed by the collective wildness of Carnival, usually considered to be the purest survival of pre-Christian rites. During forty years of Francoist dictatorship, this celebration was officially banned, at most replaced by "winter fiestas" that were a mere preamble to the rigors of Lent. With the new democracy and the secularization of Spanish society, Carnival has been reborn out of the lenten ashes and is once more an important part of the festive cycle. It is celebrated in hundreds of locales with hearty eating, heavy drinking, grotesque costumes, the persecution of animals, the blanketing of straw figures, the triumph and final death of a personage symbolizing Carnival itself. Lent follows, a prelude to the sadness of Holy Week and the joy of Easter, which is normally considered to be the beginning of the annual cycle of fiestas in Spain and other Catholic countries.

Now that we have seen the overall festive calendar, let us look at some of the most important celebrations in their rich complexity. It is impossible to do justice to all towns and all fiestas. I will speak of these rites in the present tense, although it is possible that some may have died out.

Let us start with springtime. May rituals and St. John's Day, the major fiestas of the "season of love," are pan-European festivities with many common elements: bonfires; customs involving water ("May water," "St. John's water") and trees ("May tree," "St. John's tree"); straw dummies; blessing of the fields. The two holidays are so similar that some scholars believe they could have common roots in pre-Christian beliefs and practices, whether Greco-Roman, Celtic or both. Caro Baroja notes that in Spain, both festivities celebrate a kind of spirit, vegetative or not, conceived in three forms with many variants: (1) human (a girl, boy, straw dummy or rag doll); (2) vegetal (a tree, branches, flowers); and (3) a combined human and vegetal form (a tree, branches or flowers with a dummy or person). The study of old texts reveals that Spaniards have often seen May festivals as a kind of preparation for St. John's and Midsummer. All three are celebrated in every region of the Peninsula, from Galicia, Asturias, the Basque Country and Catalonia to New and Old Castile, Valencia, Extremadura and Andalusia. In some areas, such as Galicia, they are particularly important.

May is the month of flowers and love:

> Que ha venido mayo
> con sus bellas flores.
> Ya los pajaritos
> cantan sus amores.
> (May is finally here
> with its lovely flowers.
> Now little birds
> sing songs of love.)

Popular fiestas during the month feature young people who adorn and dance around a tree or pole, sing songs, decorate each other's houses and celebrate mock weddings. In some towns unmarried men are even allowed to spend the night with nubile women, a custom that apparently does not stain the lasses' reputation in a rural culture that still values virginity. Caro Baroja associates these customs with primitive cults that celebrated the weddings of gods, goddesses or nature spirits. Although real marriages are often arranged in the course of May, many couples prefer not to hold the actual ceremony until later in the year. A Spanish proverb says "*bodas mayales, bodas mortales*" (May wedding, dead wedding).

The songs, dances and symbolic marriages of this month often scandalized ecclesiastical authorities. They condemned the customs time and again, as they did various rituals of St. John's Day. The people went on celebrating their age-old rites.

Another event in the annual round of spring festivities is the selection of "*la Maya*," the May Queen or May Girl. The competitors, decked out in jewelry, embroidered silk shawls and wildflowers, stand on an altar until a jury chooses the prettiest. La Maya is subjected to close public scrutiny: she must not move or speak while presiding on her throne, making the honor slightly less enviable than Miss America's. García Rodero has a telling photograph of a May Queen in Colmenar Viejo, north of Madrid (see Photograph 2, *La Maya*): this stern daughter looks weighed down by her duty. The custom of choosing the May Queen is found in many different regions of Spain and even in former Spanish Morocco as well as Tunisia.

The May tree or maypole has many variants. It is usually carried to the town square and decorated according to local custom. Sometimes this tree is substituted by a greased pole (*cucaña*) for young men to climb. Even if the tree or pole is used at another time of year, such as St. John's or the patronal feast, it is still known by the generic term that betrays its origins—"*mayo*."

In some towns a kind of straw dummy or rag doll is hung from the tree and adorned with leaves and branches. As we saw above, this figure, like the tree, pole and May Queen, represents the spirit of the season. Straw dummies also appear in celebrations of St. John's Day and Carnival, where they have an even more significant role.

Water plays a large part in the symbolism of May festivals. This is the month when most villages in Europe make petitions or prayers for the rain that is so beneficial to spring crops. The custom is widespread in Spain, where most regions have an arid or semiarid climate. At this time of year a brief shower can green a brown Castilian wheat field in a matter of hours. Popular sayings and proverbs reflect the common belief that May showers have unique properties. Gonzalo Correas's famous collection, dating from the early seventeenth century, already mentions rhyming saws like "*Agua de mayo, para todo el año*" (May water is good for the whole year) and "*Agua de mayo, vale un caballo*" (May water is precious as a horse).

The demonstrable value of May showers has created popular superstitions that extend their power to other domains. Young women in Spanish villages have long believed that the water of this month is particularly benevolent to their health and beauty. May water is used above all for skin care. Total immersion is also considered helpful.

The Church has opposed this kind of superstition as well as other profane customs in the season of love. While it has not been successful in stamping out these beliefs

2. *La Maya* (The May Girl), Colmenar Viejo (Madrid), 1989. Photo by Cristina García Rodero. Reproduced courtesy of Agence de Photographes.

and practices, it has been able to assimilate certain aspects of spring festivities. The tree or pole, for example, was turned into the Cross of May (*Cruz de mayo*) in some places; a saint, "*Santiago el Verde*" ("Jack in the Green" in English folklore) was created for the first day of the month; St. Gregory became the patron of May showers; the icon of a local saint was submerged in a pond, river or fountain in order to obtain showers for the crops; fields were blessed by priests; the Virgin Mary was made protectress of the whole month and the object of special worship. In some towns in the province of Teruel, for example, the symbolic weddings of boys and girls are still celebrated in such a way that Mary is considered to be a *maya* or May Girl herself. In Murcia the young men compete for the honor of trimming the door of the church with greenery and serenading the Virgin with songs, just as they do for their girlfriends.

In modern times the first of May is of course also celebrated as Labor Day. During its years in power (1982–1996) the Socialist government tried to secularize the very same holiday that the Church had been attempting to sanctify for centuries. Neither has been able to rob these celebrations of their perennial character as rites of spring.

If the Spanish Church and state have been unsuccessful in their attempts to steal May festivals, they have failed even more with respect to the other great fiesta of the season, St. John or Midsummer. It is the most popular of all. It too is a pan-European holiday with unique variants in the Iberian Peninsula (the bullfight, for example). It has preserved even more pre-Christian elements than May festivals—rites of love, nature worship, superstition and sorcery. Anyone who has been in a place where the "*sanjuanada*" is celebrated in all its intensity—such as Galicia or certain spots on the Mediterranean coast—knows the power of this holiday. In the Middle Ages its attraction was so irresistible that Moors apparently enjoyed it as much as Christians. In fact the fiesta acquires its greatest splendor in some regions where the Muslims were most established, like Alicante.

Even more than May, St. John is celebrated in word and music all over the Peninsula, in every language. The holiday has given rise to thousands of songs, poems and proverbs. Lope de Vega, the great Spanish playwright of the Golden Age, evoked it as well as anyone:

> Aquella hermosa mañana
> que todo el mundo celebra,
> porque parece que todo
> se alegra y se goza en ella.
> (That beautiful morning
> celebrated by all,
> when everything
> is a pleasure and joy.)

It is a mysterious night or morning when nothing is impossible. For heroes and heroines of innumerable songs and folktales, love and adventure begin on St. John's Day. What is probably the most famous ballad in all of Spanish literature opens with these verses:

> ¡Quién hubiera tal ventura
> sobre las aguas del mar,
> como hubo el infante Arnaldos
> la mañana de San Juan!
> (Who was ever as lucky
> by the shore of the sea
> as the king's son Arnaldos
> on the morning of St. John!)

Similar songs and ballads have spread all over the world with Spanish explorers, settlers and exiles. Caro Baroja says:

The fact that these poems have been preserved in the oral tradition with only minor changes from the sixteenth century to the present, from Smyrna to the altiplanos of Bolivia, can give us a pale idea of how many other more ancient elements of folklore, like superstitions, practices and rites have been saved . . . almost without variation not only over considerable stretches of time, but across such vast spaces.

The most obvious fact about St. John is that it falls very close to the summer solstice. Most scholars believe that it must have been related to sun worship in its origins. Early Christian writers pointed out that of all the Church's festivals, only two, Christmas and St. John—coinciding with the winter and summer solstices—honor a birth (saints and martyrs are normally venerated on the day of their death). This might explain in part the immense significance of midsummer rites in Spain and many other parts of Europe. It is well known, for instance, that early Christians celebrated the Nativity in order to compete with solstitial rites in other religions. We might speculate the same about St. John, but we do not have abundant evidence of a corresponding pagan ritual at the time of the summer solstice.

There are clear remnants of sun worship in modern festivities of San Juan. It is still the custom not to sleep on this night, 24 June, in order to climb a hill or mountain at dawn to see the sunrise on the longest day of the year. People say that one can observe the sun "dancing" as it rises above the eastern horizon. In towns like Herrera del Duque (Extremadura), the townsfolk watch for the break of dawn through a thin handkerchief, which exaggerates the wavering of the light. At many spots on the Spanish coast, people go to the beach to watch the sunrise above the ocean—on the Mediterranean—or over the land—on the Atlantic and along the Bay of Biscay. This contemplation may be followed by a swim in the sea, the custom in Lanzarote, one of the Canary Islands, for example. Here the two basic requirements of human and plant life, sun and water, are both worshiped on St. John's Day.

Midsummer festivals also involve the element of fire, related perhaps to its purifying power and to the warmth of the sun at the solstice. In fact bonfires may be the most immediate association that most Spaniards and some Spanish Americans would make with the *sanjuanada*. They are lit from one end of the Peninsula to the other on the night of 24 June. It is believed that their flames and smoke protect the good and scare away the evil in all orders of life. People jump over the fire (three times in some places), dance around it, breathe the smoke, pass children over the embers in order to have good luck. Meanwhile others eat, drink, yell, sing and walk through town and country with torches, lamps, lights and burning animal pelts, customs that resemble certain winter festivities, especially at Christmas and New Year.

Caro Baroja summarizes some of the supposed benefits of jumping over the flames on St. John's night:

1. Protection from certain illnesses (scabies, ringworm).
2. Curing of other ailments.
3. Expulsion of germs.
4. Protection from evil spells and the expulsion of both witches and thieves.
5. Protection against harm from animals (dog bites, snakebites, etc.).
6. Avoidance of all kinds of mishaps.
7. Certainty of marriage if a young woman leaps the flames in the right way.
8. Protection of animals against disease and spells if they are carried or walk over the dying embers.
9. Assurance of a good harvest if certain formulaic utterances are made while moving over the flames.
10. The ashes are protection against violent storms.
11. The smoke drives noxious animals from barns and corrals.

Here is a formula pronounced by the people of Garay (Vizcaya) while jumping over the flames of a bonfire at Midsummer (translated from Basque):

> St. John, St. John,
> I want nothing else
> but to burn, burn thieves and witches
> and to save, save the corn and wheat.

In folk tradition the night of San Juan is also dear to witches, who hold their most important sabbaths at this time of year, as the evil spirits of Walpurgis meet on the first of May in German folklore.

We have seen that midsummer celebrations often involve the cult of water. Both salt and fresh—streams, rivers, fountains and even the morning dew—are believed to have magical properties. A swim in the ocean is de rigueur on St. John's night in many parts of Spain and its former colonies. In Galicia there is a widespread custom of entering the surf to receive "*as nove olas*" (the nine waves), often at midnight and stark naked. Other people prefer to bathe themselves in a fountain or a river, or with the dew that falls on this magic evening or the next morning. A special cure for scabies and mange requires one to remove all clothes and hang them on an oak tree at midnight, to rub one's body against the bark, submerge oneself nine times in a river and dress again in new clothes. Similarly goiter is supposed to be cured by taking nine sips of water from nine fountains, also at the witching hour.

A cluster of beliefs relates to the surface of a pond or lake, perhaps covered by a light film of moss, known in Spanish by the lovely metaphor of "*la flor del agua*" (flower of the water). Whether in a salty or fresh body of water, a "*baño de San Juan*" (St. John's bath) is considered capable of curing many ailments, above all skin diseases (another similarity to May superstitions). Divination rites are also connected to water.

Some natural springs in Spain, once associated with a pre-Christian goddess or god, were renamed in honor of St. John, who of course is associated with baptism in the gospels. (Other springs were dedicated to the Virgin Mary.) Hispano-Roman inscriptions show that certain waters were dedicated to nymphs throughout the Peninsula, in widespread places such as Berzocana-Mérida, Baños de Salamanca, Montemayor, Talavera de la Reina, Orense, Baños de Bande, Caldas de Cuntis, Herrera del Río Pisuerga, Alcalá de Henares, Liria, Tarragona and Sevilla. Christian toponyms like Aguas Santas (Holy Waters), Fuen Santa (Holy Fountain) and Caldas (Hot Springs), as well as the names of San Juan or the Virgin, appropriated these pagan sources for the new religion. Churches, sanctuaries and hermitages were constructed on the sites of springs, wells and fountains believed to possess miraculous or medicinal powers. In some shrines priests aspersed the altar with St. John's water. Domestic animals were purified in a similar way. Both customs may have been practiced by the Romans too.

St. John and May festivities overlap in folklore having to do with vegetation as well as water. We have already seen that the May tree is sometimes erected as late as 24 June. In the Pyrenean Valle of Arán (Catalonia), the tree has a clear relation to fertility. In Asturias young men place a small ash or oak (called the "*ramu*") by their girlfriends' houses where they ask St. John to bless it. Then they sing

> Little morning of St. John
> rise early, girl, early
> to give your heart
> to the man who brought the tree.

Even more common than trees are entwined branches (*enramadas*), similar to those used for May festivals, decorated with flowers, garlands, wafers and colored ribbons. Once more the young men carry them to their girlfriends' houses. In Santander they leave flowers and green branches with white and blue ribbons at the houses of pretty girls, while they reserve thistle, thorns, fig leaves and ashes for the less attractive young ladies, willow branches and moss for eligible widows. These rites can be both amorous and superstitious; sometimes the branches are hung over beds where they are supposed to protect the family against evil for the entire year.

The importance of vegetation at Midsummer is also revealed by other customs. In many Basque and Navarrese towns, one is not supposed to climb a tree on St. John's or St. Peter's (29 June). Caro Baroja remembers how his young friends in Vera de Bidasoa (Basque Country) threatened severe harm to anyone who failed to observe this superstition. Many stories are told about those who ignored the taboo and were punished for their temerity. In Extremadura some even more curious beliefs exist about trees that sing on the night of St. John. In Alcuéscar, for example, on the western edge of the town, people say there is an enchanted orchard where fruits on the trees wail in the night.

A complicated folklore also surrounds herbs that grow in Midsummer. From time immemorial it has been a custom to pick flowers and herbs for St. John. A popular saying goes "*Mañana de San Juan, mozas, vámonos a coger flores*" (On St. John's morning, young girls, let's go pick flowers), parodied by young men who reply, "*Mañana de San Juan, mozas, a mi casa todas*" (On St. John's morning, young girls, all of you come to my house). Flowers and herbs are supposed to have a double power at this time of year, both amatory and medicinal. Certain plants, such as clover, ferns, sweet basil and vervain are preferred for their special properties. A famous song says

> A coger el trébole, el trébole, el trébole,
> a coger el trébole la noche de San Juan.
> (Let's go pick the four-leaf clover, the clover,
> go pick the clover on the night of St. John.)

From northern to southern Spain, ferns are believed to flower on the night or morning of 24 June. In the forest of Chicoteros near Cañete (New Castile), people say that whoever picks flowering ferns will achieve happiness, but such terrifying noises are heard that only the intrepid dare to try their luck. As in many superstitions at this time of year, there is a kind of Manichean struggle between the forces of light and dark: while good people may be protected by beneficent herbs, witches know that the magic of the season will make their own spells more potent. Thus in Extremadura the fern is said to flower between the sixth and seventh bell at midnight, when a battle royal begins between devils and fairies to see who can pick it first.

In Spain the midsummer herb par excellence is the verbena or vervain with its showy spikes of white, red, pink or blue flowers. In Asturias and other regions it is supposed to protect people from harmful animals:

> El que coja la verbena
> la mañana de San Juan
> no le picará culiebra
> ni bicho que le haga mal.
> (He who picks verbena
> on the morning of St. John
> will not be bitten by a snake
> or any other creature.)

This flower is so abundant and characteristic of Midsummer that it gave its name to rural fiestas and pilgrimages long ago. Later it became synonymous with open-air celebrations of local saints in towns or cities. These usually occur at night and are sometimes called *veladas* or evening parties. For most urban Spaniards, verbena has lost its original meaning and refers only to these neighborhood events in the spring and summer. More than a traditional Spanish fiesta, they resemble a local fair in the United States—with dances, games, prizes, hawkers, rides, stands for drinks and food and so on. *Verbenas* are characteristic of Old and New Castile and Andalusia. In Catalonia and Valencia the equivalent is the *enramada*, a local fair whose name comes from the typical entwined branches of St. John.

The Church has tried to make the cult of midsummer herbs and flowers more respectable by creating certain rituals. Plants are blessed by priests. This custom has its origin in pre-Christian rites, whose purpose was to protect the harvest. Because it falls at a crucial time in the agricultural calendar, St. John has become the patron of farmers in many parts of the old kingdom of Valencia. Some towns have brotherhoods dedicated to his worship. They perform a procession on 24 June, hanging the saint's image with the first fruits of the harvest. Then there is a dance followed by a special Mass for the souls of the dead members of the brotherhood. In some places Masses are celebrated at sowing and harvest season in a small church dedicated to St. John, as in the village of Masías de Ahillas or Aquillas.

Midsummer herbs have special uses in funeral rites. In some Basque towns the people burn elderberry flowers that have been blessed on St. John's Day in the dead person's room. The cadaver may be washed with an infusion of herbs and flowers of the season.

Medicinal lore of Midsummer is often related to the curing of hernias in children. A man named Juan (not hard to find in Spain) and a woman named María (even less so), or two Juans, carry the child through the branches of a tree with a double trunk, or through a split trunk. The oak, ash and osier are the preferred trees for this rite, which has variants in other European countries.

Finally we will look at the divination and sorcery that are associated with St. John, always related to water and plants. Midsummer night is believed to be propitious for guessing the future. Andalusian women, for example, claim that they can see the face of their future beau in a large pan filled with clear water. Another way to see into the future is for a girl to throw water out the window as she pronounces a prayer to St. John, then to ask the name of the first man to step on the wet street: that will also be the name of her suitor. A young woman in Madrid breaks a fresh egg in a bowl filled with water on Midsummer Eve; the figure that emerges will indicate her boyfriend's occupation. If she perceives the shape of a boat, the man will be a sailor; if she makes out a hammer or saw, he will be a carpenter. Another custom in Madrid is for a girl to place two branches beneath her bed, giving one her name and the other that of her boyfriend. The one that flowers the next morning will tell whether she or her beau loves more truly. The rite is explained by the belief that plants flower on the day or night of St. John.

To end the discussion of this most important holiday, I would like to point out that many of the rituals described here are celebrated with astounding uniformity throughout the Peninsula. There are innumerable variations to be sure, but the essential elements exist in all major regions. In Catalonia, for example, with all of its linguistic and cultural differences from Castile and other areas, we see rites very similar to the ones we have studied above: trees (*maigs*) and entwined branches, bonfires, the cult of water and plants, the superstition regarding hernias and so on. I believe that this kind of consistency gives us the right to speak of "Spanish popular culture," not merely "Castilian," "Basque" or "Catalan."

We now reach full summer, the festive season almost by definition. Virtually every village, town and city in Spain has a patron saint who is honored during the warm weather. Sometimes individual quarters and neighborhoods celebrate, or even a single street, as in the little town of Nules in the province of Castellón.

The patron can be a male or female saint. Under her varied appellations, the Virgin Mary is patroness of numerous Spanish *pueblos*, many of whose feasts fall in the late summer for two important Marian dates (the Assumption on 15 August and the Birth on 8 September). The variety and richness of patronal feasts makes it impossible to give more than a general treatment in our limited space.

A fiesta is the main expression of a people's identity. As anthropologists have shown, the presence of outsiders (*forasteros* in Spanish) is absolutely necessary for a *pueblo* to define itself in relation to others. For this reason a town may organize a fair at the same time as its fiesta, an event that will encourage attendance by the neighboring population. The glory of a celebration is measured by the number of visitors; there is often a lively competition between rival towns. The Mediterranean code of hospitality requires that people be generous to outsiders, but hostility is never far from the surface. Sometimes it is declared openly, as in the case of a *pueblo* in La Rioja that unfurled a banner declaring "A warm welcome to our fiesta to all outsiders except those from X" (the nearest town).

Common meals express the sense of unity among townsfolk during festivities. In the case of villages the whole population may be invited to eat together on the patron saint's day. In larger towns the meal may be limited to public employees or members of the municipal government. Parishioners of a church may also have their own repast. In the old days meals called *caridades* (charities) were given to the poor, a traditional snack of bread, wine and cheese. Finally, the meat of bulls slain in patronal *corridas* (bullfights) may be consumed by the people, as in the Fiesta de las Calderas (Festivity of the Kettles) in Soria (Old Castile).

Other activities at patronal feasts may include bullfights and running of bulls (see Chapter 4), dancing, music, parades, fireworks, ritual games, sports and other competitions. Let us look at each of these.

Dancing at patronal feasts shows the richness of folklore in the various regions of the Peninsula. Sword (*espadas*) and stick (*paloteados*) dances, performed in many places, probably have their origins in primitive agrarian rites. We should recall that patronal fiestas have often replaced an earlier harvest festival that used to be celebrated at the same time of year.

Dancers usually turn out in elaborate local costumes. There is enormous variety in different parts of the country. Some areas have sumptuous popular costumes. The getup in rural Salamanca, transported to the New World, for example, would become the inspiration for the fancy *charro* outfit of the Mexican *ranchero*. In the province of Toledo, popular costumes are known for their elaborate fretwork, embroidery and silver buttons. Luxurious materials like silk are used in the Valencian region. By way of contrast, costumes in the north are known for their severity, while archaic styles are favored in remote areas of the Pyrenees in Navarre and Alto Aragón.

It has been said that folkwear more or less imitates the clothes of the aristocracy; this is the case in some regions of Spain. More notable are the exceptions, in which the popular costumes of certain regions, like Andalusia, became the fashion for the privileged classes. The bullfighter, *majo* or *maja* of the eighteenth century, captured lovingly in the paintings and drawings of Goya, set the style for the aristocracy of the times. In this and so many other areas, popular culture has dominated the national life in Spain.

A Spanish fiesta would not be complete without "*gigantes y cabezudos*," giants and fatheads or Carnival-like figures normally made of varnished papier mâché over a wooden frame. Some scholars have tried to connect these festive characters to Celtic rites of spring and summer, without too much success. The giants are tall (some twelve feet) and may be dressed like royalty. The *cabezudos* are of human size except for their enormous heads; they tend to be satirical or grotesque. They serve as buffoons and tricksters, smacking children and adults with animal bladders or foam-rubber sticks. Caro Baroja associates this playful custom with the expulsion of evil spirits. We will see similar rites during Carnival.

The giants and fatheads of Pamplona are probably the most famous in the country. *Gigantes* appeared at the fiesta of San Fermín from the sixteenth to the eighteenth century but then disappeared until 1860, when the present figures were constructed. The eight characters are dressed in long, bright-colored robes and represent four races of human beings and four continents (before Australia and Antarctica). Each is manipulated by a single man who can make the huge figures move and dance with dreamlike grace. My friends in Pamplona, who have grown up with the giants, refer to them with affectionate nicknames. The fatheads are also familiar characters with names like Potato, Vinegar-Face and Pigtail. If you ever see the giants perform their circling, floating dance along the cobblestoned streets of the old quarter of Pamplona as a band plays a waltz during fiesta, you will understand why people feel so much fondness for these characters.

In the same ludic spirit as the *gigantes y cabezudos*, games also have a function in patronal feasts. We should differentiate them from modern sports, discussed in Chapter 5. We also need to distinguish them from trivialized modern games: festive play is always collective and ritual, inscribing the participant in the unique space and time of celebration. An example would be the poetic competition between *bertsolariak*, the folk poets in the Basque Country (see Chapter 10, "Popular Literature"). Some games may have a religious or symbolic meaning, perhaps lost in the mists of time. This would be true of many traditional rites involving animals—donkeys, roosters, ducks and geese—some very cruel, many modified in recent years.

At this point we should look at some specific patronal feasts. Here is the schedule of events for one day in the town of Mojados (Castile-León) for their fiesta in 1996:

8:00	"Dawn Bull" with garlic soup for participants
11:00	Solemn Mass in the Church of San Juan
12:15	*Encierro* or running of bulls
17:00	Bullfight
20:30	*Verbena* with music
24:00	Festivities in bullring

Here is the program for the patronal feast of San Fermín (St. Firmin) in a much larger town, Pamplona, on 11 July 1986:

6:45	Music, *dianas* (reveille)
8:00	*Encierro*
8:30	*Encierro* for children
9:30	Parade of giants and fatheads
10:30	Mass of San Fermín
12:00	Concert of regional music
12:30	Parade of bands
17:30	Parade of caparisoned mules to bullring
18:00	*Corrida*
18:30	Children's theater festival
20:00	Children's party
21:00	Regional music
22:00	*Toro de fuego* ("Fire bull")
24:00	Parade of bands
24:30	Popular dance

This program hardly gives an idea of the real life of a patronal feast. In fact those who live the fiesta to the fullest may only participate in a few of these officially scheduled activities, leaving most of their time to chance and spontaneous play. Even so there is never enough time and most of these brave souls hardly sleep more than a few hours a night.

Neither do statistics supply an accurate impression of the inner life of the fiesta. But they can give us an idea. During the week-long celebration of San Fermín in Pamplona, hotels are always full, the population of the city triples and more than 70,000 people sleep in the streets and parks. Some three million liters of alcoholic beverages are consumed, leaving 160,000 kilos of glass. The fiesta produces 650,000 kilos of garbage and more than 2,000 cubic meters of water are needed to wash down the streets. Suffice it to say that it's the world's greatest party, a Mardi Gras and Kentucky Derby to the tenth power. Perhaps only the Carnival of Rio de Janeiro can be compared to San Fermín in its primal power, its freedom from everyday inhibitions, its sheer Dionysian revelry. (See Photograph 3, Fiesta of San Fermín.)

3. Fiesta of San Fermín, Pamplona, 6 July 1995. Reproduced courtesy of Rafa Rivas, *El Mundo del País Vasco.*

The best way to evoke the fiesta from the inside would be to describe a day in the life of a celebrant during the *sanfermines*. I have been fortunate enough to be in Pamplona several times in the second week of July, so what follows is based on my own experience and that of friends, local as well as foreign. The day could begin—or the night could end—with a free *caldico* or warm broth in the Plaza del Castillo, the main square with its trees, central kiosk and bars under the arcades. Then you might dance in the streets to the *dianas* or reveille played to the thin, plaintive sound of the Basque flute or *txistu* accompanied by drums. It is the best way to clear out your head after a night at private parties, in cafés and bars or on the town. It is also a good warmup for the *encierro*, an event that is now televised all over the world every morning between 7–14 July. This is the heart of the fiesta, what gives it an edge of danger and death, the necessary counterpoint to the celebration and joy. Assuming that you survive the running of the bulls, you could reward yourself with a traditional breakfast of *magras con tomate y huevos*, fried eggs with rashers of lean ham in a spicy tomato sauce; eaten preferably at the famous Casa Marceliano, this meal will supply the protein and calories needed for the next twenty-four hours. More delicate souls would prefer a thick hot chocolate with *churros* on Mañueta Street. At this point, if you are clever enough, you might escape from your "*cuadrilla*" or team of fellow revellers and grab a few hours of sleep after the emotional drain of a night of partying and running the *encierro*. If not, you could return to the bullring to see competitions of Basque sports or *recortadores* (bulldodgers; see Chapter 4, "Bulls"). At the hour of the prelunch *vermú* or cocktail, you can take a walk along Estafeta, Comedias, San Nicolás and San Gregorio and drop into some of the liveliest bars with the best *tapas*, like Roch, Monasterio, Sixto, Fitero or La Granja. Around two or three o'clock you should have a hearty lunch, the main meal in Spain; typical dishes for this time of year are *pochas* or fresh white beans; *ajo-arriero*, codfish cooked with oil, garlic, tomatoes and eggs; beef stew (*estofado de toro*), prepared with the meat of the bulls who ran the *encierro* and were killed the previous afternoon in the bullfight—if you know the right people, that is. Rounding off the meal with a demitasse of espresso and a snifter of *pacharán*, a liqueur made from berries picked in the nearby Pyrenees, followed by a Cuban cigar, you are ready to make your way to the bullring for the *corrida*, which starts at 6:30. There you will have more snacks: by now you have discovered that eating constantly and abundantly is one of the secrets for staying alert for some twenty hours a day over the course of a whole week. After the bullfight you can file out of the ring with the *peñas* or youth clubs, white banners surging over their heads, bands playing under the trees, chanting deep-voiced songs, dancing down the hill in the early evening where the bars already have their lights on inside. Before beginning the night, a visit to the Gaztelu Leku gastronomic society on the Plaza del Castillo, where they serve a justly famous lemon sherbet, is a good way to clean the palate for a night of more eating, drinking, dancing and singing. You can choose your own atmosphere: for the bravest, the wild spots on Jarauta and Navarrería; Latin rhythms in the Plaza de San Francisco; fireworks and concerts in the city parks and gardens; rides and attractions at the fair on the edge of town.

Every year people die during San Fermín. The same happens at Mardi Gras in New Orleans or Carnival in Rio. They do not necessarily die in the *encierro*, where only thirteen people have perished in the last seventy years. (Of course thousands have been wounded, some seriously.) People die mostly in accidents or falls, rarely in fights. People die because in the fiesta, death is also a part of life, not merely its end. This is one of the great lessons you will learn; it will give fullness and depth to your experience.

Sometimes I think that Spaniards need the slow season of fall and winter to recover from their patronal feasts. The next explosion does not come until late winter, when Carnival is celebrated. As we saw earlier, this event has grown in popularity and has been restored to a place in the annual festive cycle. In the process, however, it has changed beyond recognition in some towns. Although Carnival has always been known, both by the Church and its enemies, as the most pagan event of the festive year, we must remember that Christianity gave meaning to the final fling before Lent. With the secularization of Spanish society, penitence and fasting are no longer practiced by most people. An intense celebration before Lent has lost its appeal. Spaniards can now revel all year around, so why make a big fuss about a few days? A common expression is "There aren't fiestas anymore because we're in fiesta every day." The contrast between work-time and feast-time was much stronger in the past, when the hard conditions of life seemed to enhance small pleasures—in food, drink or entertainment. Older people often argue that in comparison to the current proliferation of leisure opportunities, the old celebrations were "more of a fiesta" because they were practically the only release from grinding work and routine.

Julio Caro Baroja says that the decline of Carnival began in the eighteenth and nineteenth centuries when the middle and upper classes in the cities began to imitate the habits and costumes of France and Italy with luxurious balls, mounted processions and elegant masquerades—substitutes for the simpler festivities of the people in the country. By the early 1900s Carnival was already on the wane. After the Civil War, nearly forty years of the Francoist regime (1939–1975), which identified this celebration with its secular enemies, almost gave the coup de grace. In the last twenty years Carnival has undergone a revival as a kind of winter fiesta, a warmup for the other great feasts of spring and summer. The new regionalism and festive escalation have also contributed to its growing popularity. Yet its traditional nature as a pre-Lenten festival has probably gone forever.

Carnival has always represented a mockery and reversal of the social order, a time to right the wrongs committed during the rest of the year. Old engraved broadsides (*aleluyas*) show "the world upside down." Women dress as men and the other way around, civilians masquerade as politicians, transvestites openly show their identities. Authorities and celebrities are often subjected to ridicule.

Other transgressions are called "Carnival grievances" (*agravios de carnaval*). These include public satire, ritual abuse, insults to passersby and breaking, stealing or hiding everyday objects. It is a time of year when almost anything is permitted. In García Rodero's photographs, for example, one sees a man peeing in the street, a woman dancing at the front of a parade with bare breasts.

As in nearly all Spanish fiestas, animals play a role in these winter celebrations. Unfortunately their role is usually that of scapegoats. For centuries they were chased, blanketed or beheaded to the amusement of the populace. Roosters always played a special part as symbols of dawn whose morning song traditionally expelled witches, demons and other evil spirits. *Corridas de gallos* or running of cocks are still performed in many places, with the rooster being chased and often decapitated.

Straw dummies or rag dolls are even more common at Carnival than during May rites and Midsummer. In fact the word for these figures in Spanish, *pelele*, is still defined in the dictionary of the Royal Spanish Academy as "A human figure of straw or rag that is customarily hung on balconies or is blanketed by the people at Shrovetide" (the three days before Ash Wednesday). One of Goya's most poignant paintings, simply called *El Pelele* (1791, Prado Museum, Madrid), shows a dummy being tossed in a blanket by young women. Tossing and hitting the straw figure allows the release of pent-up anger and frustrations. It is clearly a scapegoat connected to the ritual expulsion of evil, like the Judases and other figures who are struck or burned at this time of year and during Holy Week, May festivals and St. John's.

I have left a characteristic feature of Carnival—costumes and masks—for the end. If one travels to villages and small towns, especially in the northern parts of the Peninsula, one will see an almost endless variety of large, colorful, imaginative, humorous, grotesque and terrifying masks worn by revelers. Some tip the scales at ten pounds or more, measuring as much as five feet in height. Those who wear them are known by many different names in the local language or dialect. They are called *foliones* in the town of Buxián and *peliqueiros* in Laza (both in Galicia), *guirrios* in Llamas de la Ribera (León), *ziripot* and *zaldiko* in Lanz (Navarre). Some masks and costumes have been around for centuries. In the Leonese town of Llamas de la Ribera, where Carnival languished until recent times, people are attempting to recover their tradition by making new masks according to the descriptions of the old-timers.

Carnival of course has always been a time to gorge and imbibe before the rigors of Lent. Since abstinence is hardly practiced in the country now, this part of the celebration has lost some of its notoriety. It is simply another occasion for Spaniards to eat and drink heartily as they do many other times during the year, with or without fiestas.

Carnival normally culminates with the victory and death of a symbolic figure. The triumphant part of the ritual occupies the time between Saturday or Sunday and Mardi Gras. The death often takes place on Ash Wednesday. The most common rite in Spain is called the "Burial of the Sardine," a custom that everyone knows but nobody can explain. Why should a poor man's fish, which used to make up the diet of many devout Catholics during Lent, be buried at the end of Carnival, a celebration still known by its old name of *Carnestolendas* ("removal of meat")? No matter; the symbolic rite is a pretext for still another parade, more music, dancing, eating and drinking.

The idiosyncracies of Carnival can only be understood by looking at specific places where it is celebrated. The most famous festivity is held in Santa Cruz on the island of Tenerife in the Canaries. Spanish explorers brought Carnival and other fiestas to the island when they landed there in the middle of the fifteenth century. It continued to be celebrated, with the usual disapproval and countermeasures by Church and state, until it was prohibited by the Nationalists at the beginning of the Civil War

(1936–1939). By 1945 *tinerfeños* had begun to celebrate the old-style Carnival clandestinely in their homes. Twenty years later "winter fiestas" were permitted and this title lasted until the year after General Franco's death, 1976, when the ancient name of Carnival was restored. By 1980 it had become so well known that it was named a Fiesta of International Tourist Interest by the national government. Now the people of Santa Cruz claim to have the second most famous Carnival in the world, after Rio de Janeiro. (The inhabitants of Cádiz and certain other cities might not agree.) It is characterized by flashy parades, dances, processions and masquerades; *murgas* or bands of street musicians with instruments made from sugarcane and cardboard, who sing satirical songs; and *rondallas*, also groups of musicians, who perform traditional Spanish songs and opera.

The Catalonian town of Centelles can serve as an example of a modern "winter festival" that has lost most of its ritual significance. This holiday was organized in 1980 by a group of young people and has been celebrated each year since then. The first festivity included clowns, drum majorettes and rock concerts. In 1986 a heavy snowfall convinced the organizers to postpone the party. By 1989 they had recovered and now included an official proclamation or *pregón*, a children's spectacle, a parade, a costume ball and dirty dancing. The following year the organizers were arrested by the Civil Guard at the beginning of the fiesta for reasons that I have been unable to determine. By 1997 the kitty had been enriched so that 200,000 pesetas (about $1,500) were thrown into the streets during the parade. For 1998 the organizers planned a "witches' eve" with a parade and all-night music, inspired by a local tradition that attributes supernatural powers to women born in the town and in other Catalonian localities like Altafulla and Vallgorguina. The Centelles website proclaims: "Come to the first Carnival anywhere, we do it before anyone else; exactly a week before it is marked on the calendar." Here we might say that Carnival has become a carnival.

In contrast the fiesta in the Pyrenean town of Bielsa (Aragón), celebrated according to the church calendar, has preserved its traditional character in spite of depopulation in the region. Many of the former residents return faithfully for this and other holidays. The main protagonists of Carnival are masculine figures called *trangas*; they wear a bull's head whose snout has been smeared with tar, carry bells on their back, dress in checked shirts, animal skins and long skirts. They wield an enormous wooden cudgel and strike the ground with it in order to wake up the sleeping earth, chase away evil spirits and announce their sexual power. The erotic element is made clear when they rub the bells, make masturbatory movements and playfully caress the bodies of young women. The female figures who contrast with the *trangas* are called *madamas* (revealing the influence of nearby France), whose white dresses can be worn only by the nubile girls in town. These skimpy outfits, hardly appropriate for the mountain climate, fit the girls' bodies so snugly that they must be torn off after the festivities. Together the *trangas* and *madamas* celebrate the principal event of Carnival in Bielsa, a sort of procession called the *ronda*. At five in the afternoon the male figures meet in the main square and then parade through the town to the accompaniment of a band of street musicians or *charanga*, stopping at every house where a *madama* is waiting for them. Then they all go together to the plaza where everyone is regaled with a glass of *poncho* (a kind of sangría) and food. A dance begins there and later moves to the town's social club. Another characteristic figure of Carnival in Bielsa is the Amontato, an old woman who carries a male figure on her back. She is interpreted as a satire of the local men who underestimate the value of women's labor in this region that has been described as matriarchal. The fascinating Carnival of Bielsa ends with the burning of still another traditional character, Cornelio (also known as Peropalo or Marquitos), the scapegoat for all misfortunes, who then hangs for three days from a window of City Hall.

With Carnival we reach the end of the annual festive cycle, which of course begins anew with spring and Easter. We are ready to conclude with a summary of recent trends in Spanish fiestas, announced earlier: secularization, the greater role of young people and women, festive escalation, regional variants, commercialization, tourism, counterrituals and a return to tradition.

As part of the overall movement away from liturgical celebrations, many public rituals have acquired a mostly profane character. Already in 1925, Hemingway had to remind his readers in *The Sun Also Rises*, amidst all the rockets, eating, drinking, running and fighting of bulls at San Fermín, that this "is also a religious festival." Some of my friends in Pamplona have deep devotion for the patron saint whose fiesta has become a great party; yet many locals and nearly all outsiders consider it a non-religious event. The same occurs in many other celebrations, notably Carnival, as we have seen in detail. In a democratic society, local and regional governments have been forced to heed the voice of less-privileged classes and minorities to be included in public festivities. In response they have provided subsidies for *verbenas* and carnivals, fairs, pop music and ethnic festivals that now compete with traditional fiestas. These too have changed in character, deemphasizing their ritual elements and highlighting their playful aspects. As explained by Jeremy Boissevain, ritual has to do with a celebration's structured, formal events, characterized by "rules, hierarchy, and constraints of time and place." In comparison, play thrives in the absence of ritual and is unstructured, informal, spontaneous, egalitarian and ludic. "If ritual is serious and solemn, play is joyful and silly." Those who have observed or lived through a Spanish fiesta will realize how the two forces, ritual and play, can work against each other. One example is the famous *riau-riau* on the afternoon of 6 July at San Fermín, when the *mozos* or young men dance ahead of the municipal authorities, doing everything in their power to keep them from reaching the church of San Lorenzo where the statue of St. Fermín is kept. It is a perfect example of what anthropologists call a ritual of rebellion. The longer the dance, the more time the *mozos* have to raise hell along the way. What would normally be a five-minute walk takes three to five hours. The *riau-riau* is a matter of establishing right from the start who is in charge of the fiesta, the people or the officials. In Pamplona the people have won the battle for the street and the authorities hardly stand a chance.

Spanish festivities used to embody a privileged space and time for adult males, while their wives and daughters stayed home, cooking the food and washing the clothes that enabled the men to celebrate for days on end. Under the new democracy, young people of both sexes and especially women challenged this situation, demanding and winning access to festive space in the streets as both participants and observers. Vociferous public debates took place in villages, regional capitals and Madrid. The resulting change has been so dramatic that some fiestas now seem to be dominated by young males and females more than by adult men. Festive celebration for them has become a rite of passage in which they can break family rules regarding dress, curfews and alcohol, enjoy greater freedom and achieve sexual initiation. As Julian Pitt-Rivers has said, "The fiesta is always a rite of passage. . . . It marks the passage from one season to another, one year to another, and in order to effect this passage, it always tends to decree an inversion of conceptions and conducts in daily life from which one escapes in the fiesta in order to re-enter it renewed and changed."

The patriarchal rules associated with rural life have worn away as a result of exodus to the cities and changing family patterns. Young women now hang out at bars and cafés—the traditional meeting place of men—in both small towns and large cities. During fiesta they join the men in *peñas* and may even organize their own clubs. If public celebrations seem to be more popular in recent times, it is because more than half of the Spanish populace has been freed to participate.

Another trend is festive escalation, an increase in the number and popularity of local and regional celebrations; it goes hand in hand with the drastic decline of strictly religious holidays (see Chapter 2). Contrary to received wisdom, the rural flight, increased secularization, consumerism and the mass media have not taken their toll of public rituals. On the contrary, all of these forces have created a nostalgia for rural roots and traditions, especially among the upwardly mobile classes, in Spain and other countries. Some towns have expanded their patronal feasts from one to several days, or even a long week.

The devolution of power from Madrid to the autonomous regions has also strengthened local festivities and led to the proliferation of new ones. There has been a call for decentralization and a revival of "authentic" fiestas distinct from those exalted under Francoist and Castilian hegemony. In Andalusia, for example, the regional council and provincial and municipal governments have poured money into both secular and religious fiestas in villages, towns and cities. Power elites have sprouted to absorb the new largesse. Elected officials, intellectuals and religious authorities all benefit from the new cultural politics. Vested interests are now committed to diversity as much as the Francoists were devoted to uniformity.

A related trend is the commercialization of the fiesta. Some towns earn more income during a week of patronal feasts than in the remaining fifty-one weeks of the year. The local population may swell with the presence of visitors, journalists, folklorists, anthropologists, and above all, tourists. Unlike recreational tourism—"sun, sand, sea and sex"—cultural tourism is not limited to the summer months and the seaside or mountains. For this reason it helps alleviate the industry's endemic seasonal unemployment and benefits areas far from the coast. This trend was revealed in 1992, a key year for Spain that included the 500th anniversary of Columbus's arrival in the New World, the summer Olympics in Barcelona and the Expo '92 World's Fair in Sevilla. Preparing for an unprecedented invasion by foreigners, the government decided to change its former tourist slogan from "Spain: Everything Under the Sun" to "Spain: Passion for Life."

Cultural tourism is called *turismo integral* by the state. It is exemplified by a large billboard on the highway extending from the village of Almonte (Huelva) to the hamlet of El Rocío, site of the famous Virgin of the Dew pilgrimage at Pentecost (see Chapter 2, "Religion"). The sign beckons the motorist with the following message: "You have just entered the paradise of your dreams: The National Park of Doñana [one of Europe's largest nature reserves], the beach resort of Matalascañas, and the shrine of the Virgin of El Rocío all await you." What more could a visitor want? Ecological tourism and recreation as well as colorful ritual are all offered in a package.

The "touristification" of the fiesta, a word as ugly as the phenomenon it describes, can have an effect on the event itself and on the people who celebrate it. Some outsiders or foreigners have been known to desecrate Spanish rituals, often incurring the wrath of the local population. The press has been guilty of its usual hunger for a story. At two o'clock on Monday morning, 15 May 1989, when the statue of the Virgen del Rocío was being carried out of the church by the townsmen, this climactic moment was interrupted by television cameramen who interposed themselves between the icon and the crowd. They had committed the unpardonable sin of violating sacred space and preventing the people's access to it. When the cameras panned across the tightly packed onlookers, one woman raised her hand and shouted in disgust, "This is not the movies, this is El Rocío!" Like San Fermín, Holy Week and the fair of Sevilla, this celebration can now be viewed on commercial videotapes for home consumption.

The excesses of tourism have created a curious reaction in several countries, above all in Spain, where fiestas are a way of life. Increasing irritation with foreigners has led some communities to move existing rites to places and times that may discourage outsiders. These are "insider-only" celebrations that Boissevain has compared to cast parties held by actors and the stage crew to celebrate the end of a performance, well out of view of the audience. Similarly the inhabitants of tourist destinations withdraw to celebrate without the presence of strangers. This trend has been called "hiding from the tourist gaze." It has been studied brilliantly by anthropologists. Mary Crain describes how the villagers of Almonte, the sight of the desecration by TV cameramen in 1989, have given new vigor to a counterpilgrimage in mid-August, when tourists would wilt in the Andalusian heat (sometimes as high as 110 degrees F). This event, known as *el traslado* or the removal, since it involves carrying the statue of the Virgin from the shrine in El Rocío to Almonte, has acquired greater importance for the local population precisely at a time when the Pentecost pilgrimage has been partly expropriated by the media and outsiders. A spirit of solidarity reigns that would be impossible in the crowded confusion of the main festival. The alternative ritual regenerates an old tradition while restoring a sense of identity and intimacy to the members of the local community. Once more they reside "at the moral center of the universe" (Caro Baroja).

Some Spanish *pueblos* have not only reinforced existing fiestas but created new ones in response to cultural tourism. Antonio Miguel Nogués Pedregal describes how the inhabitants of the tiny coastal village of Zahara de los Atunes in the province of Cádiz (population 1,183 in 1991) have invented their own fiesta called the *Castañá* (Chestnut-roast) in the fall, when most outsiders have departed and the residents' pockets are full of money earned during the tourist season. It is a completely new event, organized for the first time in 1990 by the Neighbors' Association. Although it is held on All Saints Day (1 November), it is not a religious rite or a commemorative feast. Nogués Pedregal describes the *Castañá*: "It is a purely communal celebration for 'insiders' only, meaning what could be called the nuclear community—its permanent residents. This excludes emigrants on holiday, visitors from nearby communities and tourists, whether national or foreign, and those who have moved from elsewhere." The people simply meet in a courtyard, roast chestnuts over coals and drink sherry, sweet wine and soft drinks. Nogués Pedregal has attended twice and on each occasion was the sole outsider. "There is nothing to do but eat toasted chestnuts while talking with companions," he tells us. But for the inhabitants, harried by foreigners and too busy working during the long tourist season to enjoy themselves, it is an opportunity to relax and revitalize their sense of community.

The well-known British historian Eric Hobsbawm has spoken of the "invention of tradition," a term that could easily be applied to Zahara de los Atunes and other Spanish towns. Two more anthropologists, Francisco Cruces and Angel Díaz de Rada, have analyzed a related trend that they call "the return to tradition." Using as their model the public celebrations in the Jerte Valley in northern Extremadura (province of Cáceres), they show how *pueblos* in the region have been able to maintain and revitalize traditional fiestas in the face of social and economic change. Since the life of the valley now depends on its cherry orchards, which require intense labor in the spring and early summer, the villagers tend to neglect minor religious rituals during this season in favor of festivities later in the year. Even in towns that have suffered depopulation, the return of emigrants who departed in search of jobs has enabled the most popular fiestas to be celebrated without interruption. These people live most of the year in large cities like Barcelona, Bilbao and Madrid but go back faithfully to their *pueblos* on holiday, especially for patronal feasts. They may still own small plots of land and a house. The villagers know who they are, who is the son or daughter of whom, and continue calling them by their old nicknames. In many ways the immigrants consider themselves to be members of the local community. During the summer months there is a "reconstitution of families that is the reconstitution of the community as well."

Emigration, changing demographic trends and other social factors cause certain problems in maintaining the continuity of public festivals. The younger people may have to be taught by their seniors how to dress, dance, sing and perform in traditional celebrations. In the town of Casas del Castañar (Cáceres), for example, also studied by Cruces and Díaz de Rada, the girls who sing the saints' canticles for the patronal feast have to learn them from married women. In neighboring Piornal a popular instructor from the provincial capital gives lessons in traditional dance to the girls in town. In Navaconcejo children must learn the songs and dances of their grandparents at school. Cruces and Díaz de Rada refer to this trend as "retraditionalizing."

Another significant development analyzed by these two anthropologists is the simultaneous presence of old and new festivities. Juxtaposed to patronal feasts, with their ancient rituals, songs, dances, games and communal meals, are activities like disco dancing, sports, marathons, card championships and soccer matches. In one town a "cultural week" preceded the patronal fiesta and included an ecological bicycle ride around the valley and a "day of the elderly" promoted by the village council. These events celebrate levels of identity beyond family and village, the anchors of traditional festivities. The result is "a continuous negotiation between modernity and tradition," in which all interests and activities need not be shared by the whole *pueblo*. People enjoy a greater diversity of ways to express their sense of belonging to the community, consistent with the fragmentation of contemporary society. Cruces and Díaz de Rada conclude that the persistence and continuous re-creation of public festivities can be regarded as a refutation of the predicted death of ritual in postindustrial countries. Boissevain goes even farther, foreseeing a greater flourishing of public rituals in Spain and other countries as an effective antidote to the increased homogenization of the European Union, the mass media and the global economy.

After writing these pages, I have the feeling that I have not been able to communicate in words, in a book of this kind, the stunning intensity and power of Spanish fiestas. My best advice is that you go to see for yourself.

RESOURCES

See the search engine Olé, *Cultura: España: Folklore*, for an enormous list of Spanish towns, cities and regions with their local fiestas: <http://www.ole.es/Paginas/Cultura/Espa@na/Folklore/. For the famous Carnival in Santa Cruz de Tenerife (Canary Islands), see <http://www.arrakis.es/~fiesta97/historia.htm>. For the interesting Carnival in the small Pyrenean village of Bielsa, see <http://www.ctv.es/USERS/pyrene/carnaval.htm>. For an example of a nontraditional and commercialized Carnival in the Catalonian village of Centelles, see <http://www.redestb.es/personal/jterns/carna_e.htm>. For an example of an official program for the fiesta in a Spanish town, see <http://www.vites.es/vites/fiestas/mojados/programa.htm>.

The new Getty Center for the History of Art and the Humanities in Los Angeles has more than 6,000 of Cristina García Rodero's photographs in its files, which are available for consultation by scholars. As stated in the text of this chapter, seeing her work is the best way to visualize public celebrations in Spain, unless you can go there yourself.

In Madrid, the Ethnological and Anthropological Museum is located at Alfonso XII, 68; telephone 011-34-91-539-5995, fax 011-34-91-467-7098. The Museo del Pueblo Español is now closed to the public, but its archives are still open at Avenida Juan de Herrera, 2; telephone 011-34-91-549-2290, fax 011-34-91-544-6970.

BIBLIOGRAPHY

Alonso Ponga, José Luis, and Antonio Sánchez del Barrio. *Teatro popular. Danzas de palos.* Valladolid: Castilla Ediciones, 1996.

Boissevain, Jeremy, ed. *Coping with Tourists: European Reactions to Mass Tourism.* Providence, RI: Berghahn Books, 1996.

———. ed. *Revitalizing European Rituals.* New York: Routledge, 1992.

Brandes, Stanley. *Metaphors of Masculinity.* Philadelphia: University of Pennsylvania Press, 1980.

Caro Baroja, Julio. *El Carnaval: análisis histórico-cultural.* Madrid: Taurus, 1965.

———. *El estío festivo (Fiestas populares del verano).* Madrid: Taurus, 1984.

———. *Ensayos sobre la cultura popular española.* Madrid: Editorial Dosbe, 1979.

———. *La estación de Amor (Fiestas populares de mayo a San Juan).* Madrid: Taurus, 1979.

———. *Estudios sobre la cultura popular española.* Madrid: Editorial Dosbe, 1979.

———. *Los pueblos de España.* 2 vols. Madrid: Istmo, 1985.

Correas, Gonzalo. *Vocabulario de refranes y frases proverbiales y otras fórmulas comunes de la lengua castellana.* 1627. Reprint. Madrid: Edición Mir, 1924.

Crain, Mary. "Contested Territories: The Politics of Touristic Development at the Shrine of El Rocío in Southwestern Andalusia (Spain)." In *Coping with Tourists: European Reactions to Mass Tourism,* edited by Jeremy Boissevain, 27–55. Providence, RI: Berghahn Books, 1996.

———. "Pilgrims, 'Yuppies,' and Media Men. The Transformation of an Andalusian Pilgrimage." In *Revitalizing European Rituals,* edited by Jeremy Boissevain, 95–112. New York: Routledge, 1992.

Cruces, Francisco, and Angel Díaz de Rada. "Public Celebrations in a Spanish Valley." In *Revitalizing European Rituals,* edited by Jeremy Boissevain, 62–79. New York: Routledge, 1992.

De la Fuente, Gloria. "Las jóvenes rurales en la encrucijada (el caso castellano)." *Agricultura y Sociedad,* no. 42 (January–March 1987): 47–71.

Douglass, Carrie B. *Bulls, Bullfighting, and Spanish Identities.* Tucson: University of Arizona Press, 1997.

Fraguas Fraguas, Antonio. *A festa popular en Galicia.* La Coruña: Ediciós do Castro, 1995.

García Rodero, Cristina. *España Oculta. Public Celebrations in Spain, 1974–1989.* Foreword by Julio Caro Baroja. Introduction by Mary M. Crain. Washington, DC: Smithsonian Institution Press, 1990.

Hanbury-Tension, Robin. "The Last Great Migration" [on *transhumancia* or "cattle drives" in Spain]. *Geographical Magazine* 68, no. 10 (October 1996): 53.

Hemingway, Ernest. *The Sun Also Rises.* 1926. Reprint. New York: Scribner's, 1970.

Hobsbawm, Eric, and Terence Ranger, eds. *The Invention of Tradition.* Cambridge: Cambridge University Press, 1983.

Lisón-Tolosana, Carmelo. *Invitación a la antropologia cultural de Espana.* Madrid: Akal, 1980.

Martí, Josep. *El folklorismo. Uso y abuso de la tradición.* Barcelona: Ronsel, 1996.

Nogués Pedregal, Antonio Miguel. "Tourism and Self-Consciousness in a South Spanish Coastal Community." In *Coping With Tourists: European Reactions to Mass Tourism,* edited by Jeremy Boissevain, 56–83. Providence, RI: Berghahn Books, 1996.

Ortega y Gasset, José. "Idea del teatro (una abreviatura)." In *Obras completas,* 7: 439–501. 9 vols. Madrid: Revista de Occidente, 1964.

Pitt-Rivers, Julian. "L'identité vue à travers la 'fiesta.'" In *Culturas populares: Diferencias, divergencias, conflictos,* edited by Yves-René Fonquerne and Alfonso Esteban, 11–23. Madrid: Casa de Velázquez, Universidad Complutense, 1986.

————. *The People of the Sierra*. Chicago: University of Chicago Press, 1974.

Rubio, Cristina. "Carnaval. La España rural saca a la calle las máscaras y viejas tradiciones." *Tribuna de Actualidad* 9, no. 459 (10 February 1997): 102–105. Contains impressive photographs of Carnival costumes and masks in small Spanish towns.

Sampedro Gallego, María del Rosario. "Mujer y ruralidad: un análisis de las relaciones de género desde la perspectiva del hábitat." In *Sociología de las mujeres españolas*, edited by María Antonia García de León, Marisa García de Cortázar and Félix Ortega, 137–157. Madrid: Editorial Complutense, 1996.

Sánchez, María Angeles. *El bien y el mal en la tradición festiva española*. Salamanca: Centro de Cultura Tradicional, Diputación de Salamanca, 1995.

————. *Guía de fiestas populares de España*. Madrid: Tania, 1982.

Turner, Victor, ed. *Celebration: Studies in Festivity and Ritual*. Washington, DC: Smithsonian Institution Press, 1982.

————. *Dramas, Fields, and Metaphors: Symbolic Action in Human Society*. Ithaca, NY: Cornell University Press, 1974.

Weisman, Alan. "The Rites of Spring: A Visit to Carnival to Contemplate the Enduring Rituals of Rural Spain." *Los Angeles Times Magazine* (11 April 1993): 12–16.

Chapter 4

Bulls

In Spain, from its centuries-old tradition to its very geographical shape in the form of a bull's hide; from its ethnic virtues to the joyous impudence of its language, almost everything is connected . . . to the attributes and figure of the bull. There is no other totem that grips us so tightly.

—Antonio Gala

A recent count showed 4,228 works on bullfighting in the Spanish National Library. The list excludes many works in English and other languages. What can I hope to add to this avalanche of words? How can I maintain the "freshness of soul and mind" that the philosopher Ortega y Gasset recommended for anyone who broached the subject?

The best answer to this question, and to others relating to bulls and bullfighting, was given by Ernest Hemingway in his classic work, *Death in the Afternoon*. The American writer put all future commentators on guard by warning them against "unsoundness in an abstract conversation or, indeed, any overmetaphysical tendency in speech," which he called "horseshit." I will heed his warning. Here the reader will find no mystical theories attempting to trace the origins of bullfighting to prehistoric cave paintings, sacrificial cults, fertility rites, labyrinths and minotaurs in ancient Crete, gladiators in Roman circuses. Nor will the reader find Freudian notions of the *corrida* as a symbolic killing of the father, a struggle between life and death, eros and thanatos, male and female, ego and id. There are too many practical things to be said. "Nobody knows anything about it," Hemingway said in his book, and the situation has not changed too much since he wrote these words.

On the first page of *Death in the Afternoon*, the novelist also says that he will not try to defend bullfighting, "only to tell honestly the things I have found true about it." I will do the same. I discovered bullfighting in a public library when I was a teenager, have read about it on and off ever since, and have attended *corridas* all over Mexico and Spain for the last forty years. I will try to tell honestly here what I have found true about it.

Bulls and bullfights are interwoven in all aspects of Spanish life. Let us begin by seeing how they are connected to the other chapters in this book. Beginning with language (Chapter 1), we can say that Castilian and the other languages of the Iberian Peninsula are shot through with references to brave bulls and the *corrida*. Taurine vocabulary is so extensive that there are several dictionaries in print, none of them complete. Spanish speakers may have as many words for designating the color and markings of a brave bull as Eskimos have for describing snow. Proverbs are so common that many people use them without ever having attended a *corrida*. "*No hay quinto malo*" (There is no bad fifth bull), for example, says a well-known saw referring to the next-to-last *toro bravo* in a regulation *corrida* of six animals. The expression is routinely used when couples have four children and are thinking of having another, and in similar situations. Another case would be the expression "¡*Vaya trapío!*" (What a build!), used to describe a large, strong fighting bull, easily transferable to a woman as a *piropo* or flirtatious compliment. This comparison shows us the close relationship between bulls, the *corrida*, sex and love. For centuries the bull was worshiped by many cultures in the Mediterranean basin as the embodiment of masculine power. The matador Luis Miguel Dominguín used to say that he always performed for the women in the crowd. In 1976 it became legal for females to be professional bullfighters in Spain; twenty years later Cristina Sánchez received her *alternativa* or confirmation as a *matadora de toros*, only one of two in the country today (Mari Paz Vega is the other). There are several *novilleras* or women who are apprentices.

Bullfighting is also closely related to religion (Chapter 2). Most bullfights are held on Sundays or on sacred holidays. Both the *corrida* and the Catholic Mass involve a sacrifice. With the exception of the liturgy, in fact, there is probably no spectacle in Western life as formal and hierarchic as the *corrida*. If there are few atheists in the trenches during warfare, there are even fewer in bullrings during *corridas*. All major rings contain a chapel where toreros invariably pray before stepping onto the sand. The *corrida* could only have developed in a Catholic country, where a clear distinction is maintained between human beings with immortal souls and soulless animals. Since bulls do not have souls according to the Church, it is not wrong for humans to kill them.

The connection between bullfighting and fiestas (Chapter 3) is also related to religion. The major cycles of *corridas* occur during patronal feasts: San Isidro in Madrid (May and June), San Fermín in Pamplona (July), the Virgen de Begoña in Bilbao (August), the Virgen del Pilar in Zaragoza (October). The apparent exception would be the annual fair of Sevilla, but it is a moveable feast that takes place two weeks after Easter, always depending on the Church calendar. Many phrases used to describe bullfighting employ the term *fiesta: la fiesta brava, la fiesta taurina, la fiesta del toro, fiesta de toros*. The best-known expression of all, *la fiesta nacional*—loosely, "the national pastime"—was used without dispute for decades. It has been criticized in recent years by people in regions like Galicia, Asturias and Catalonia, where the *corrida* has never been as firmly rooted as in the central and southern parts of the Peninsula. They see bullfighting as still another expression of Castilian hegemony imposing itself on the rest of the country.

Chapter 5 ("Sports and Games") is the only section of this book in which the bull-fight should *not* be discussed. One of the most common misconceptions of foreigners is that the *corrida* is supposed to be a fair competition between a human being and animal. Nothing could be further from the truth. Bullfighting cannot be judged by the notions of sport and fair play—in large part creations of the Anglo-Saxon world. One *plays* a game but one *celebrates* a *corrida*. Sports do not deal with death but with victory; they replace the bullfight's avoidance of death with the avoidance of defeat. The *corrida* must be seen as a tragedy in which the bull, and perhaps the man, must die. The French writer Michel Leiris has expressed beautifully the difference between sport and *toreo*:

Contrary to the rules of sport, which specify a great number of permissible plays and a limited number of forbidden plays, the bullfighting code allows the "player" only a very small number of permissible "plays" in relation to the considerable number of forbidden ones; hence, one might imagine one was watching not a sporting event, whose rules merely constitute a loose framework, but a magical operation with a meticulously calculated development, in which questions of etiquette and style take precedence over immediate effectiveness.

The very word "bullfight" is of course a misnomer, implying an adversarial relationship between torero and bull rather than a mutual participation in a prescribed ritual, or as some have suggested, a kind of sublimated lovemaking. For all these reasons, I will not abuse the terms bullfight and bullfighter, preferring from here on *corrida*, torero or matador, in addition to *toreo*, the only word that describes the complete art. I see no good alternative to the term "fighting bull," however, since in fact it is one of the few animals on the face of the earth that will attack without provocation or hunger. I will also employ the Spanish expression *toro bravo* (brave bull), which has a ring unmatched in any other language.

There is not a separate chapter on food and wine in this book, but if there were, in it we would find many connections with bulls. The libation of wine forms part of the *apartado* or sorting of *toros bravos* in corrals at the ring as well as in gatherings of aficionados before and after the *corrida*. The meat of fighting bulls is routinely slaughtered and sold after the performance. Both it and the animals' blood are considered to have extraordinary powers. The writer Eugenio Noel, the most famous enemy of *toreo* before Brigitte Bardot, admitted, "Whoever eats of that meat will live for a long time, they tell me." The bulls' testicles are a prized delicacy in many places and not surprisingly are considered to be a potent aphrodisiac.

As for bulls and music (Chapter 6), who does not recognize a pasodoble or two-step, many of which have been dedicated to legendary bulls, toreros or aficionados? The martial strains of "La Virgen de la Macarena" or "España Cañí" stir the blood of fans from Spain, Portugal and France to Mexico, Venezuela, Colombia, Ecuador and Peru—the major countries in which *corridas* are celebrated on a regular basis.

Film (Chapter 7) is another area of popular Spanish culture that has explored the esthetic and social dimensions of the *corrida*. The best-known movies are the many versions of *Sangre y arena* (*Blood and Sand*), based on Vicente Blasco Ibáñez's best-selling novel. The writer himself did a film in 1916 for a Catalan production company; this was followed in 1922 by the Rodolfo Valentino version, in 1941 by the Tyrone Power–Rita Hayworth classic, and in 1989 by the international blockbuster with Sharon Stone, directed by Javier Elorrieta. We should not forget the parodies like *Mud and Sand* (1922) by Hal Roach with Laurel and Hardy and *Bull and Sand* (1924) by Mack Sennett, because they reveal the Anglo-Saxon opposition to *toreo*. The great Mexican comic Mario "Cantinflas" Moreno starred in a Mexican parody in 1941, *Ni sangre ni arena* (Neither Blood nor Sand, 1941). Other, more serious Spanish films have also treated bulls, toreros and related themes, such as Jorge Grau's *El espontáneo* (The Amateur, 1964), Luis G. Berlanga's *La vaquilla* (The Fighting Cow, 1985) and Pedro Almodóvar's *Matador* (1986—discussed in Chapter 7).

Just as there have been taurine films, many television and radio programs in Spain feature toreros, *ganaderos* or breeders, critics, writers and aficionados (Chapter 8). The series *Juncal*, by the well-known movie director Jaime de Armiñán, starred the superb Spanish actor Francisco Rabal and enjoyed a great success in the late 1980s. Now nearly every Spanish TV channel transmits one or more taurine programs. Some examples are *Tendido Cero*, with Fernando Fernández Román and Federico Arnás, Matías Prats's program on Antena 3 and Miguel Angel Moncholi's spot on Telecinco.

The Spanish press (Chapter 9) spills a lot of ink covering toreros, *corridas* and related matters. Most major newspapers have a bullfight critic, such as Joaquín Vidal for *El País* and Vicente Zabala, Jr. for *ABC*. Taurine magazines are often lost among the myriads of soccer publications but one can still run across issues of *El Redondel*, *Claridades* and *El Ruedo*. You won't see them on the newsstands, but glossy journals such as *Clarín Taurino* and *Taurología* can be found in good bookstores. On the other hand there is no dearth of scandals and rumors about toreros and their lovers, wives and former wives in the yellow press.

Finally, popular literature (Chapter 10), like almost every other area of Spanish culture, has thrived on *toreo* ever since the late eighteenth century when the spectacle acquired its modern form. There are endless popular ballads and songs, broadsides, plays, pulp novels and comic books about famous toreros and *corridas*.

This rapid trip through the other chapters of our book reveals how deeply bulls and bullfighting are rooted in Spanish life. They and religion are the most widely spread and characteristic phenomena in the country.

The classic way to approach *toreo* is to begin with the bull, to continue with the torero and finish with the public. Since we are discussing the most orthodox of all arts, I will follow this prescribed order. Another advantage of this method is that it gives priority to the animal rather than the man, avoiding hero worship and rumor-mongering—major defects of Hemingway's *Death in the Afternoon* and other books on the subject. It will also enable us to examine from the start other taurine activities besides the formal *corrida*, such as *capeas* or informal capings in towns and villages, *encierros* or driving of animals through the streets, and *recortadores* or runners who dodge brave bulls and cows.

El señor toro, the bull. How is it possible to describe in words the rippling muscle, the powerful, sinewy build, the death-dealing horns that hook and jab like a good boxer's fists? (See Photograph 4.) The Spanish fighting bull, *Bos taurus Africanus*, is the only surviving descendant of the *Bos primigenius*, the wild urus or auroch that once roamed the primeval plains and forests of Europe and was hunted by Julius Caesar. As Hemingway said better than anyone before or since, this animal is as different from an ordinary bull as a wolf is different from a dog. In bullbaiting and other barbarous spectacles, the *toro bravo* used to be pitted against bears, lions, tigers and even elephants, all of which it usually eviscerated with its deadly horns. In this sense, and in the common sense of most Spaniards, the fighting bull is the true king of beasts. It has survived only in Spain, where its ancient bloodlines have been maintained and passed onto animals exported to southern France, Portugal and Spanish America, the other places in the world where *corridas* are celebrated. If it were not for *toreo*, fighting bulls would not have survived our pragmatic modern age, since they have no other economic use and are not as docile as domesticated stock.

I cannot stress enough the absolute, primary importance of the *toro bravo* in the *corrida*. Without him there is no danger, no dignity, no ritual, no sacrifice, no art, no catharsis, no emotion. *Nada.*

In addition to being the center of the *corrida*, the fighting bull is the most recognizable symbol of Spain. As far back as the first century, the Iberian Peninsula was described by the Greek geographer Strabo as a dried, stretched bull's hide, and this metaphor has stuck. It is enough for someone to pronounce the phrase (*la piel de toro*) for listeners to understand the reference to Spain. The bull is a more universal symbol than the Spanish flag, which must compete with the banners of the semiautonomous regions. (At the Barcelona Olympics in 1992, the Catalan flag enjoyed equal status with the Spanish tricolor.) The bull means Spain; for this very reason anti-Castilian independence movements have opposed the bullfight as well as the central government.

The Spanish countryside is marked with immense, black billboards in the shape of a fighting bull, testicles and all; they crown hills, promontories and other strategic spots on the horizon. They appear so lifelike that some foreigners believe they are real animals, though no fighting bull has ever been known to measure twenty feet in height. Originally signs for Soberano ("Sovereign") brandy manufactured by the Osborne company, they were prohibited along with all other advertising on highways in the country. The opposition to their removal was so violent that the government was forced to declare the billboards as national artistic monuments. Some observers compared the event to the public's rejection of new Coca-Cola in the United States, although it is hard to equate a fighting bull with a soda pop.

Other companies have also used the fighting bull as a logo for products as diverse as sherry wine, sunflower seeds, copying machines and books. A *toro bravo* was the official emblem of the 1982 World Cup Soccer Championships and the 1986 World Swimming Championships, both held in Spain of course. Celebrated in Madrid, the second event sported a bull in a Speedo swimming suit (*Pepe el toro*) as its mascot. The opening ceremonies included a bloodless exhibition of bullfighting on horseback (*rejoneo*). The reaction of the people and the press was scandal and outrage. One person suggested that a *corrida de toros* on inner tubes should be part of the ceremonies. A journalist recommended filling the *plaza de toros* with water and having a

4. *Matador* Juan Serrano ("Finito de Córdoba") executes a *verónica* with a bull from the ranch of Lamamié de Clairac, Bilbao, August 1992. The bull's horns have probably been shaved. Reproduced courtesy of Miguel Calvo, *El Mundo del País Vasco*.

frogman-torero confront a whale. These comments were facetious, but they were right on the mark: *toreo* is a ritual and a tragedy and should not be used as a symbol of a mere sport like swimming or soccer.

When the country joined the European Economic Community in 1985, Salvador Dalí, the most famous living Spanish artist at the time, offered an original pen and ink drawing to each of the seventeen ministers who signed the treaty. The work portrayed the rape of Europa, the Greek myth according to which Zeus, in the form of a bull, ravished a beautiful woman and carried her to Crete, where European civilization was born. Dalí explained that an Iberian *toro* held onto Europe and that the continent therefore owed its very being to his country. It was not Spain that was joining the EEC, he claimed with his usual panache, but the EEC that was joining Spain.

Like a true totem, the bull is ultimately eaten. It is butchered within the precincts of the *plaza* immediately after the *corrida* and sold or given to the local market. As we have seen in the last chapter ("Fiestas"), its meat and organs are also consumed in patronal feasts throughout the country. Some of these include the fiesta of St. John in Soria, St. James in Guadalaviar (Teruel), St. Augustine in Bujalaroz (Zaragoza), the Virgin Mary in Jerez del Marquesado (Granada), St. Otilia in Vellel (Teruel), and the Virgin of Mercy in Herencia (Ciudad Real).

It has been said that the fighting bull leads the life for which all Spaniards secretly long. He grazes freely in the country for some five years, enjoying the best pastures, food and water. Instead of ending his life in a dank slaughterhouse, he dies in the sun, displaying the bravery for which he has been bred. "That blind arrogance, that instinctive audacity, that growing bolder the more he is punished . . . That readiness for death. Ah! All that is ours." Who wrote these words? An admiring critic, torero, rancher, aficionado? No. Eugenio Noel, the most eloquent and prolific enemy of the bullfight.

Out of some 7,595 taurine events celebrated in Spain in 1985, only 485 were formal *corridas de toros* regulated by the national government. Similar figures could be cited for later years. Related spectacles include *becerradas* for one-year-old calves, *novilladas* for three- or four-year-old bulls, festivals for charity. These activities are all more or less formal and follow the prescribed ritual whose model is the *corrida*; together they still make up only a small part of the total number of events involving brave bulls, calves or cows.

The great bulk of taurine events in Spain are local, loosely regulated by town authorities or sometimes by the people themselves. In this sense they are closer to popular Spanish culture than the formal *corrida de toros*. Some Spaniards who reject the classic bullfight are enthusiastic supporters of the taurine events in their hometowns, usually celebrated during patronal fiestas. They see no contradiction between these two opposing attitudes.

Let us look at some of the more common taurine activities that take place outside of the bullring. We will begin with *capeas*, the caping of brave animals that has taken place during fiestas in thousands of small pueblos for centuries, as they are depicted by Goya. In the old days a temporary arena was created by drawing carts and wagons together in a circle around the town square, rather like the defensive ring of stagecoaches in cowboy-and-Indian movies. Nowadays the main square may be blocked off, a small *plaza de toros* may be used or a temporary ring may be hauled in and set up. Once a brave calf, bull or cow has been released, young boys and men run around the *plaza* trying to cape, touch, push, pull or tease the animal. Many wounds and deaths have occurred in these events throughout the years. The animal is rarely killed in the *plaza*. If it is to die, it is dispatched outside the ring by a professional torero or by a butcher in the local slaughterhouse.

Many *capeas* used to be extremely cruel. If the *pueblo* could afford to purchase the bull, it might be "killed by the populace swarming over him with rocks, sticks, daggers, and knives until he sways and goes down" (*Death in the Afternoon*). Time, pressures from animal-rights supporters and the European Union have slowly eliminated most of the worst abuses. Spaniards do not take easily to outsiders meddling in their age-old local customs. Some who oppose any use of animals in fiestas, for example, also resist any prohibitions that do not derive from the people themselves.

Eugenio Noel, the greatest portrayer of Spanish *capeas* and patronal feasts in general, says: "Just as there is no bull like another bull, you can be sure that no two *capeas* are alike. . . . I don't know what sort of devilish creativity towns employ in conceiving and developing them, but with the forced participation of a little *toro*, or a cow, or an ox, they devise skits, epic theater, comedies and farces that are admirable for their novelty." One example of these inventive variations is the *toro del aguardiente*, or "brandy bull," a *capea* in which a makeshift stand is set up somewhere in the ring to dispense the local firewater to the participants, making them braver but also more foolhardy. In the town of Soto del Real (Madrid), the brandy bull was outlawed for the first time during the patronal feasts in August 1997, owing to a new regulation by the regional government. Most politicians supported the change but many townspeople were opposed. Fulgencio Fernández, a municipal employee and sweeper in the bullring, told a reporter that "everything used to be more fun. This is the fault of some idiot who went too far." Anselmo, a man of 81 who did not wish to give his last name, lamented: "In my day the young people enjoyed themselves with the *torito del aguardiente*. But now the custom is to get drunk instead of enjoying oneself. And for that reason the bulls didn't used to gore us and now they do."

Other changes are making *capeas* less primitive than they were in Hemingway's time. Local officials control the events more than ever before. In general both the animals and the people are treated better. Mobile units that specialize in taurine surgery are usually on call. (Horn wounds typically have several "trajectories," all of which must be carefully cleaned and medicated before a dressing is applied.)

Capeas have many different forms. The animals may be released two or three at a time. Their horns may be covered or padded. When more than one animal occupies the *plaza*, there is too much mayhem for individuals to cape them. This common variant of the *capea* is sometimes called *vaquillas* in reference to the brave cows that are used in place of *toros bravos*.

The best-known taurine activity outside the bullring is the *encierro* or running of brave bulls, calves or cows through the streets. This event has come to the attention of people throughout the world as a result of Hemingway's *The Sun Also Rises* and the movies based on the novel. The early-morning run is televised in Spain and many other countries each day of San Fermín between 7–14 July in Pamplona (see Chapter 3, "Fiestas"). Before the time when fighting bulls were transported by truck directly to the *plaza de toros*, the original purpose of the *encierro* was to drive them into the ring for the *corrida*. This tradition continues in some small towns and villages.

Pamplona is the only large city with an *encierro*. The streets are barricaded and storefronts are protected by slabs of wood or iron bars along the nine hundred yards from the corrals to the bullring. Local men and foreigners gather along the course, many of them carrying a rolled-up newspaper in order to "measure" their distance from the running bulls, to throw it as a decoy in case of an emergency, or simply not to feel completely naked. Waiting for the animals' release, they raise the paper in their right hands while singing the traditional prayer to St. Firmin, slightly ungrammatical in Spanish but highly moving in the early-morning streets after a night of carousing:

> A San Fermín pedimos
> por ser nuestro patrón,
> nos guíe en el encierro,
> dándonos su bendición.
> ¡San Fermín, viva!
> ¡San Fermín, gora!
> (We pray to San Fermín,
> our patron saint,
> may he grant us his blessing
> and guide us in the run.
> Long live San Fermín!)

The resonant, man-voiced song will put goose pimples on your arms. Where else in the world can you hear thousands of males singing a prayer in unison, a prayer they believe in truly? I say men because the *encierro* is one of the few masculine prerogatives left in Spain or anywhere else. Most of the runners are young and unmarried, although I have known men who have run well into their forties. Women are not forbidden from the streets in Pamplona, but I have never seen one actually run close to the bulls. (Females are more active in the *encierros* of other Navarrese towns like Puente la Reina and Estella.) The police remove children, drunks and others they consider to be unfit to defend themselves.

At eight o'clock the first rocket explodes to signal the opening of the corrals. A few seconds later another explosion warns that the bulls have passed through the gates and are now running up the streets toward the *plaza de toros*. Chaos ensues for the following two or three minutes, the average length of an *encierro* in Pamplona. During that time, which may seem endless to a participant in the event, thousands of slips, falls, spills, accidents, woundings and near-misses occur. It is impossible to evoke the confusion and excitement unless you can imagine six freight trains and thousands of people on streets that are no more than fifteen feet wide.

The goal is to run as long as possible in the magical space in front of the bulls' horns. Since a four-legged bovine can outrun a human being except for a short stretch, this goal can only be achieved for a few unforgettable seconds. Some believe that proximity to the animal brings health, good luck or sexual potency. If there were not good reasons to risk one's life, there would not be so many runners. Of course some people, both Spaniards and foreigners, run because it is "the thing to do."

For decades the *encierro* was celebrated in Pamplona without anyone realizing that it had become a kind of popular art form. In recent years the phenomenon has been studied brilliantly by Javier Echeverría, a professor of logic and philosophy at the University of the Basque Country. In books, articles and lectures he has shown that running the *encierro* is a "secret art" known only to a few insiders who perform day after day during San Fermín, year after year. In some ways it is an art as demanding and beautiful as *toreo*. Other towns with *encierros* have different styles of running, such as Tafalla (also in Navarre), Soria and Cuéllar (Segovia).

Good runners in Pamplona attempt to perform the following actions, which can be compared to the *suertes* or prescribed maneuvers of the formal *corrida de toros*: (1) spot a bull in the herd, which is composed of six *toros bravos* and several oxen; (2) enter the herd from the front, side or rear; (3) run at the same speed as the chosen animal in order; (4) to "mark the time" or rhythm of the bull's pace (*marcar el paso*), moving forward while keeping the animal at just the right distance to the rear, one hand holding the newspaper extended back toward the horns, attempting to separate the bull slightly from the others, leading it toward the *plaza*, the man and the animal having achieved a kind of harmony; but sooner or later this supreme stage must end, followed by the runner's effort; (5) to leave the herd, either by moving toward the barricade or a wall on the side of the street or square or perhaps even "passing on" the bull to another expert runner, much as a baton is passed from one team member to another in a relay.

While these actions may sound simple on paper, there are only a handful of men who have the speed, agility, experience, courage and presence of mind to carry them out in a few seconds, surrounded by unpredictable people, animals, weather and street conditions. More than the bulls themselves, the greatest danger is in fact other runners, especially those who do not know the unwritten rules of the game, such as never running diagonally or in front of another man. Although the authorities give a detailed report of each *encierro*—its exact length, the number of dead, wounded, hospitalized and so forth—never are the most important facts mentioned: those that we have just enumerated, those that transform the *encierro* from a sporting event into a popular art, an ephemeral dance between a fighting bull and a human being. These truths are known only to a few participants in the ritual, who may not even mention them to others, or perhaps limit themselves to a few words like "X ran well today." These men live for the *encierro*. For them nothing is more satisfying or exhilarating than running the bulls.

Echeverría makes the point that it is just as difficult to run the *encierro* of Pamplona well as it is to perform well in the bullring during the *corrida* with the very same bulls in the afternoon. The difference is that the streets are open to all—that is all who possess the bravery, speed, agility and clearheadedness to run the right way. It should not surprise us that many of the best runners—known as *los divinos* ("the divine ones") in Pamplona—consider the brave bulls to "belong to them" as much as to the professional toreros who are paid to kill them in the bullring. The runners are the first to jeer and whistle at the *matadores* if they abuse the *toros bravos* in the *plaza*: they have earned the right to be critical by exposing themselves to the animals before they have been punished with pike and sword, when they still possess their morning freshness and power. For this and other reasons the public of Pamplona is known to be one of the most demanding in the country, one feared and avoided by some toreros.

There are many variants of the *encierro* throughout the Peninsula. While in Pamplona the course makes two turns—they often produce spectacular slides and skids by bulls and men—in Manzanares (Madrid) the route is quite straight. In Segorbe (Castellón) the men and boys are mounted on horseback. In Falces (Navarre) brave cows are used instead of bulls.

Several other taurine games are related to the *encierro*. Sometimes a huge rope is tied around a bull's horns and young men pull on the animal (*toro enmaromado* or *ensogado*). In the town of Grazalema (Cádiz) the people drag the *toro* to the neighborhoods of competing factions. In Benavente (Zamora) the rope measures 250 meters in length, weighs a thousand kilos and may be pulled by as many as two thousand men. These figures give an idea of what Hemingway calls the fighting bull's "unearthly" bravery and strength.

Another variant of the *encierro* is the *toro embolado* or bull whose horns are capped with burning balls of tar. This event is typical of the eastern regions of Spain, especially the province of Valencia. At midnight during patronal fiestas, torches are screwed to the *toro's* horns, they are lit and the animal is released in the streets, where the young men chase, slap and run away from it. In most localities the law requires the sacrifice of the bull or brave cow, but this regulation is often ignored so that the creature can be used in another town to the benefit of its owner. These activities have various names according to the place: *bou emboulat* in Valencia and Catalonia, *toro jubilo* in Medinaceli (Soria), *toro de ronda* in Cariñena (Zaragoza), *toro de los hachos* in Navalcarnero (Madrid). In the province of Valencia alone, there were over 1,200 fiestas of this kind in 1985. As we will see later, this kind of spectacle has understandably been a prime object of protests by advocates of animal rights and has been restricted in certain areas of the country.

A related custom is the "fire bull" (*toro de fuego*), which in fact is really a man disguised as an animal. It always takes place at night during patronal feasts. The man hides beneath a long, rectangular wooden box that is shaped like a bull and crowned with real horns. Firecrackers are attached to the back, they are ignited and the *toro de fuego* runs through the streets, scaring the children and spreading mayhem.

In the morning of a patronal fiesta there is sometimes a competition among *recortadores* or bull-dodgers (see Photograph 5). As can be perceived in the photograph, the man swerves in front of the animal's horns at the last instant, just as it turns to gore him; the two figures are almost joined in one (like their shadows on the sand). This kind of close shave is possible because a man can turn (*recortar*) more quickly on two legs than an animal on four. The photo actually shows not a fighting bull but a

5. *Recortador* (bull-dodger), San Sebastián de los Reyes (Madrid), February 1996. Copyright © Fernando Manuel Durán Blázquez.

brave cow. She reveals no visible signs of cowhood and no evidence of femininity: "it is in the female of the fighting bull that you can see most plainly the difference between the savage and the domestic animal" (Hemingway).

Recortadores supposedly practice an old custom that has reappeared in patronal feasts. It probably began as a spontaneous activity and has been formalized in recent times. Unlike most of the taurine events described above (with the exception of the formal *corrida*), it is not free; the public pays to attend. Yet the dodgers themselves are amateurs. They make up two-men teams who have one minute in the arena to dodge or jump over the animal, which is nearly always a brave cow rather than a fighting bull: a *toro bravo* would be spoiled for a *corrida* by being exposed to men on foot. Each swerve or dodge is rated artistically by three judges. Working in tandem, the teammates next have two minutes to place three-inch rings over the brave cow's horns. The judges award prizes for the best dodge and for the highest number of rings.

As we have seen, the formal *corrida de toros* constitutes only a small part of the many activities involving brave bulls, cows and calves in Spain. When the *toro bravo* is called a totem of the country and its culture, it is because for centuries so many Spaniards have lived and worked closely with animals that bear brave blood, both inside and outside the *plaza de toros*. As Caro Baroja says, bulls are "the most familiar animal for Iberian man."

Like any activity involving humans, animals and money, the *corrida de toros* and other taurine activities are subject to exploitation and dishonesty. Fraud, graft and bribery have usually been as common as in horse racing, which is probably the best reference point for a non-Spanish speaker. Just as thoroughbreds have been doped, over- or underfed and tampered with in every imaginable way, fighting bulls have also been abused in many forms. While the adulteration of horse racing is carried out solely for profit, in bullfighting there is the additional motivation of lessening the danger to the man. For this reason *toros bravos* have been drugged, sandbagged on the neck, overfed to make them slower and underfed to make them weaker. The most common abuse of all goes straight to the source of danger—the bulls' only weapons, their horns.

Horn shaving is the most pernicious form of corruption in the *corrida de toros* and in other taurine events like *capeas*. When a few centimeters are filed from the tips of its horns, the animal loses its precise sense of distance. If the nerves are exposed, it will be less willing to charge a man or horse, or to ram the *barrera*—the red painted wooden fence that encloses the arena—or the *burladeros*, the shelters placed at intervals around the ring where the toreros seek refuge.

Horn shaving is clearly beneficial to the men who must confront *toros bravos*. One might think that it would not be beneficial to *ganaderos* or breeders of fighting bulls, who should be concerned with maintaining the reputation of their stock. But in the incestuous world of the *corrida*, toreros are often related to breeders by blood or marriage, or they are breeders themselves. Both bullfighters and *ganaderos* depend on promoters or impresarios for their livelihood, who may also connive in the shameful crime of horn shaving. In fact all three—toreros, breeders and promoters—belong to the same syndicate, the Confederation of Bullfighting Professionals. This organization went on a three-day strike in March 1997 to protest the national government's new rules for post-mortem inspections of the bulls' horns. The event was strategically timed to coincide with the opening of the season in early spring, as in a baseball strike at the same time of year. The Confederation managed to secure a moratorium on the new rules in the key region of Valencia, where the first important *corridas* are celebrated in March. The state declared its determination to control the abuse, but it is outweighed by the economic power of the bullfight industry, which provides subsistence to thousands of Spaniards and wields enormous amounts of capital and political influence. As Carrie Douglass asks, "What other national government is in charge of keeping a spectacle dangerous?"

Corruption does not stop with horn shaving. Toreros routinely pay off newspaper critics in order to receive favorable reviews of their performances. This custom is sometimes called the "disease of the envelope," a reference to the custom of delivering a bribe to a journalist in a sealed envelope. The practice is so common that newspapers often consider taurine criticism to be a form of paid publicity.

Students of Spanish history will recognize many of these abuses. The bribery, fraud and favoritism that plague the *corrida* have scourged other areas of national life for centuries. In his book *Blood Sport*, Timothy Mitchell argues that the corruption of *toreo* is simply a reflection of the society as a whole. He summarizes:

I am prepared to assert that bullfighting has been nothing less than a microcosm of the Spanish social order. I affirm that to an uncanny degree it has replicated almost every feature of the Spanish political system. . . : (1) corruption and fraud in bullfighting; (2) the internal patronage system of bullfighting; (3) the matador as padrino [godfather; see Chapter 2, "Religion"]; (4) the matador as demagogue; and (5) the distorted notions of power, authority, and democracy that were derived from or reinforced through public behavior at bullrings.

If *toreo* is so rife with deceit, scam and chicanery, how can it be justified? Of course the same question could be asked about horse racing, but it is merely a sport, not a ritual tragedy involving life and death; it is probably less racked by corruption than the bullfight too. This is a dilemma that has irked the conscience of many aficionados. Most resolve it by saying that the emotion of a good *corrida* is so strong and so beautiful that it is worth putting up with all the rest. Referring to the *faena* or last part of the ritual, Hemingway said "It is impossible to believe the emotional and spiritual intensity and the pure, classic beauty than can be produced by a man, an animal and a piece of scarlet serge." It is also a rare emotion; in order to feel it, you will probably have to see many bad *corridas* and many abuses.

Before moving our gaze to the men who fight bulls, we should mention the current state of brave animals in Spain. Hundreds of *ganaderías* or ranches breed the bulls, calves and cows that are fought in *plazas* and used in local taurine events throughout the country. Most of the ranches are located in the central and southern parts of the Peninsula, which are also the areas where *corridas*, *encierros* and other taurine activities are most popular. Modern-day fighting bulls descend from only five *castas* or bloodlines. They are purebreds in the sense that they must come from an accredited ranch that can attest to their genetic purity. Like a race horse, each *toro bravo* has a genealogy that is sometimes printed in the program at a *corrida*.

Aficionados often go to the bullring to see the bulls of a specific *ganadería*. The legendary bulls of Miura were known for decades as being the most dangerous; many toreros died on their horns. At present the most prestigious ranches are probably the Buendía, Herederos (Heirs) de Celestino Cuadri, Moreno Silva and Victorino Martín in Spain, and Murteira Grave in Portugal. When one attends a *corrida* with these animals, the whole atmosphere changes. From the moment the *toro* explodes into the ring through the gate of the *toril* to the moment it is dragged dead across the sand by a team of mules, often to the standing applause of the crowd—everything becomes charged with danger and excitement. I've had the fortune to witness *corridas* of Victorino Martín during several San Isidro fiestas in Madrid, and it was like a different spectacle. Unfortunately these outstanding *ganaderías* are the exception to the rule of ranches run by men who are merchants more than true breeders, who try to produce a "light" and easy bull for the convenience of toreros.

For several years fighting bulls have been afflicted by a tendency to be weak in the front legs and to fall down easily, especially after punishment by the lance of the *picador*. Entire books have been written about the syndrome of the "falling bull." Some attribute it to overfeeding by breeders who are more concerned with their animals' weight than strength and bravery. Others claim that there may be more serious, genetic causes. No matter what the explanation, I do not know of a single aficionado or critic who believes that today's animals are superior to those of the past. Yet one can still see occasional *corridas* of truly brave bulls.

The *toro bravo* is the center of all taurine spectacles, from the formal bullfight to the local fiesta. We must never lose sight of this fact as we turn our attention to the men who face brave bulls for a livelihood. Ever since the development of modern *toreo* in the eighteenth century, its practitioners have come from the lower classes, like those *majos* painted so brilliantly by Goya in the late-eighteenth and early-nineteenth centuries. Many toreros had rags-to-riches careers, made and lost colossal fortunes, led turbulent lives and engaged in scandalous love affairs. The most marginal ethnic group in all of Spain, the gypsies, have made up a disproportionate percentage of *matadores* in the twentieth century. Some famous bullfighters with gypsy blood include Rafael el Gallo, Joselito, Chicuelo, Cagancho, Gitanillo de Triana, Antonio Ordóñez, Curro Romero, and Rafael de Paula. Although most toreros have come from poor and uneducated families, there have always been exceptions. The matador Ignacio Sánchez Mejías, whose death by goring was sung by the poet García Lorca, was a playwright and a man of great culture. With the advent of democracy and the economic miracle, social classes have been blurred in Spain and some toreros now come from the bourgeoisie. It is no longer necessary for aspiring *novilleros* to go through a poverty-ridden, dangerous apprenticeship in small-town *capeas*, in which they used to pay for the right to perform. The old proverb may no longer hold true: "Hunger is more painful than a goring" (*Más cornadas da el hambre*).

Nowadays many toreros are trained in formal bullfighting schools. Ten were founded in the 1980s, two of them in France. (There is now one in San Diego, California.) In 1990 the Escuela Nacional de Tauromaquia de Madrid (National School of Bullfighting) had about one hundred students. Critics say that these institutions do not turn out true artists, but mere technicians. The argument is similar to those made about creative writing programs in American schools. The comparison may seem far-fetched, but both bullfighters and poets are born as well as made.

Although the social extraction of toreros has been changing in recent times, many of their attitudes have not. Nearly all are devout Catholics. Most are superstitious. The constant threat of wounding and death makes them sensitive to good or bad omens. At a table where bullfighters are eating, for example, one would never pass a saltshaker to someone else's hands; it must be placed on the table first, then picked up by the second person. In a study carried out by a team of doctors in Pamplona in the 1960s, many toreros were found to have phobic and obsessive-compulsive traits, undoubtedly related to their many rituals and superstitions.

In spite of the fact that bullfighters have clearly lost some of their heroic aura, some are still worshipped. After all, they risk not only their reputations with every performance—like any other artist—but also their physical integrity and their lives. When the popular matador Paquirri was gored by a bull in the third-rate *plaza* of Pozoblanco (Córdoba) in September 1984, dying a few hours later, an outpouring of grief revealed once again that toreros may be the last mythic figures in modern life as well as cult heroes of mass culture. An estimated one million people attended Paquirri's funeral, which showed the reservoir of delirium beneath the surface of modern Spanish society.

After looking first at the bull and then the torero, we should now turn our attention to the public. The very word "aficionado" has become an international term for any kind of fan, whether of the bullfight, gardening or stamp collecting. Here we use it only in its pristine sense. An aficionado is one who feels *afición* for bulls and *toreo*. Although this word derives from the Latin for "affection," it means much more. It refers to the quality of passionate understanding that is rare even in Spain and the Spanish American countries where *corridas* are celebrated. Many aficionados belong to a bullfighting club (*peña taurina* or *club taurino*) or gather regularly to discuss their common passion (*tertulia taurina*). The Club Cocherito de Bilbao, at eighty-five years, is the oldest such group in the country. Some matadors enjoy the support of fan clubs that bear their names, such as the Peña Taurina Curro Romero.

It is a common misconception that an overwhelming majority of the Spanish population are aficionados. An example of this error is Paul Theroux's grand tour of the Mediterranean, *The Pillars of Hercules*: "Spaniards, not a people noted for finding common agreement on anything, are almost unanimous in their enthusiasm for bullfighting." He is so right about the first point that he is wrong about the second. No modern poll has ever found more than half of the population to be interested in *toreo*, and no more than a third who actually attend *corridas* or *novilladas*. As Table 1 shows, interest remained fairly stable between 1971 and 1986—a period embracing Francoism, the dictator's death, transition to democracy and election of the Socialists. Perhaps what is most interesting about this survey is that no more than 2 percent of the sample ever refused to reply. There is probably no other aspect of Spanish life

Table 1
Bullfighting Surveys over Time

Gallup	1971	1977	1985	1986
Interest in corridas				
Much	22%	17%	19%	18%
Some	32%	28%	30%	31%
None	43%	54%	50%	51%
No answer, don't know	2%	1%	1%	1%

Source: From *Bulls, Bullfighting, and Spanish Identities* by Carrie B. Douglass. Copyright © 1997 by The Arizona Board of Regents. Reprinted by permission of the University of Arizona Press.

that evinces less indifference than bullfighting: almost everyone has an opinion, whether for or against, often passionately held.

As Carrie Douglass has argued, these figures may have little to do with behavior and everything to do with beliefs. The bull is such a totem in Spain that accepting or rejecting it is an expression of individual or collective identity. To be in favor of *corridas* implies a centrist Castilian ideology, while to be against them indicates a tendency to support regional autonomy or independence. To be an aficionado suggests that one is "Spanish" and "traditional," and to be against *toreo* intimates that one is "European" (or "Basque," "Galician," "Catalan") and "modern." In short, most bullfight fans fall somewhere to the right of center along the political spectrum, while the opponents of *toreo* fall to the left. In a 1985 Gallup poll, 32 percent of the conservative party (Acción Popular) showed "much interest" in *corridas*, while only about 20 percent of the Socialists and a mere 4 percent of the Communists considered themselves to be aficionados. Of course there are exceptions.

The bullfight has many political dimensions. Queen María Cristina told her son, later King Alfonso XIII of Spain, that one must go to the *plaza de toros* in order to understand the Spanish people. He apparently did not go often enough, because he was deposed in 1931 at the age of 45. Yet his mother's advice was probably sound. The bullfight in many ways is a bellwether of the current political situation. It was supported by Franco, who saw it as an expression of traditional, Catholic Spain. The regime's critics recalled the satirist Juvenal's famous phrase about Roman blood sports: "*panem et circenses*" (bread and circuses). The sharp rise in the number of *corridas* and attendance that occurred during the 1960s was a direct result of the government's policy of fomenting tourism. The number of bullfights leaped from 150 in 1950, before the tourist boom, to 645 in 1970, when it was still near its height. A decline followed the death of the dictator and the demise of his regime in the late 1970s, as special *corridas* for the benefit of foreigners were eliminated and other European countries competed for tourists. With the democratic elections of the 1980s and 1990s, more people went to the bullring as a result of increasing prosperity and a nostalgia for the old, traditional Spain. Villages and towns resurrected or invented taurine activities as part of their patronal fiestas. Attendance at formal *corridas* is now at an all-time high, with thousands of people filling *plazas de toros* and millions watching on television. Bullfighting has become a phenomenon of mass culture. The critic Alfonso Carlos Saiz Valdivielso has complained: "This reality has a decisive and negative influence on the values that used to protect a mystery: bullrings plagued by microphonic journalists, television cameras that invade privacy, crowds of photographers violating the ritual of the *corrida*."

Many politicians have attempted to reform the bullfight. Few have succeeded because they know that any change would be unpopular. The dichotomy between ideology and practice is best revealed by a famous declaration made by the writer Ramón Pérez de Ayala: "If I were dictator of Spain, I would suppress the bullfight with one stroke of my pen. But until then, as long as there are *corridas*, I will continue to attend." A more recent author, Antonio Gala, tells the story of having coffee with a female politician who was also president of the Spanish Animal Protection Society. The lady excused herself because she had to go to the bullring, where she would be the honorary president of the *corrida* that day. Gala is a living contradiction himself: although he is honorary president of several animal societies, he has written eloquently about the fundamental role of *toreo* in Spanish life (see the epigraph to this chapter).

The beloved former mayor of Madrid, Enrique Tierno Galván, was a sociologist who loved to attend *corridas*. He believed that *toreo* embodies a conception of the world that a Spaniard must either accept or reject; it is impossible to remain indifferent because it makes up the people's "common psychological subsoil." If bullfighting ever becomes a mere form of entertainment, like the movies, for example, he predicted that this would imply a change in the very foundations of national identity. He said that all social classes attend *corridas*: artisans, businessmen, members of the liberal professions, priests, the nobility. The *plaza de toros* itself, especially in small towns, is the space in which the people live together through a common experience like no other. In this sense Tierno affirmed that bullfighting has "educated" more Spaniards than any other single institution. The very form of the *plaza*, round and structured in concentric circles that gravitate toward the center, makes the spectators feel themselves to be part of a storm whose eye is a torero and a fighting bull. Unlike a racetrack or a soccer stadium, a *plaza de toros* does not have straight lines or perspectives: its physical geometry and its psychological projection are round, manifesting themselves in circles like the swirls of the bullfighters' capes. Even the *faena* or final stage of a *corrida*, in which the matador replaces the large cape with the smaller *muleta*, tends to be circular. The artist leads the bull in a series of passes with a smaller and smaller circumference until the moment of truth, the kill, which in theory could be said to occur in the center of an imaginary circle created by the movements of man and animal.

Other writers have opined that true Spanish democracy is in the bullring. The public in a *corrida* makes up a kind of chorus that constantly accompanies and comments on the action of the tragedy being performed in the arena. If a torero has performed well, he may be granted one or both of the dead animal's ears by popular acclamation, signalled by the waving of white handkerchiefs. In the case of the first ear, the president in the authorities' box merely has to decide whether more than half of the public wants the reward to be granted. The regulations determine that the awarding of a second ear is in the power of the president, who is always advised by an expert. Nevertheless it is difficult for the authorities to ignore the people's reaction, which usually ends up carrying the day.

The democracy of the bullring may turn into demagoguery. In the most famous taurine novel ever written, *Blood and Sand*, Vicente Blasco Ibáñez has his main character, the *matador de toros* Juan Gallardo, die from a horn wound in the infirmary while the public continues to roar in the *plaza*. The book ends with these words: "The beast roared: the true beast, the only one." Some critics agree that the public drives toreros to take unnecessary risks that may lead to wounding, maiming or death.

An example of modern demagoguery is the notorious Tendido (Section) 7 in the Ventas bullring of Madrid. In these seats sit some of the most severe aficionados in the world. They perpetually criticize bulls, *matadores* and their *picadores* (horsemen with lances), *banderilleros* (assistants), the president and his advisors, who they believe are too lenient. It takes almost a miracle on the sand for these men (there are few women among them) to applaud or even approve a torero's performance. Throughout every major *corrida* they constantly kibbitz and scream advice such as "*¡Bájale la mano, muchacho!*" (Keep your hand lower, kid!) and "*¡Sácalo a los medios!*" (Take him to the center of the ring!), not to mention other less discreet utterances. Anyone who has attended *corridas* in Madrid remembers the sight of a torero taking a lap of the ring to the applause of the crowd, carrying trophies—one or two ears of the bull, on rare occasions a tail—while the men seated in Tendido 7 stand on their feet and wave their arms back and forth like windshield wipers on a car to show their disapproval: "No."

While these aficionados are impossibly demanding, most fans nowadays are in fact too permissive. Because so many Spaniards can afford to attend bullfights, the *plazas* are being filled with people who do not have experience or knowledge. They tend to applaud what is showy and easy, not what is subtle and hard to perform. If they disapproved more strongly of inferior bulls, breeders would be forced to present only the very best stock in the ring. Most of all, these new fans—like the thousands of tourists who attend *corridas* every year—want a fast death for the animal, which encourages toreros to make unsightly *estocadas* or sword thrusts, exposing themselves as little as possible as long as the animal expires quickly. The act loses its solemnity when a noble animal is not killed according to precise laws, but slaughtered for convenience.

Like religion, bullfighting is a weather vane of Spanish life (see Chapter 2). It points to many other categories besides politics: age, gender, demographics, regionalism. Children under fourteen years of age are not allowed to attend *corridas*. Yet like many laws in Spain, this one is rarely enforced. When my son was eight years old, I took him to a bullfight in Madrid, and I believe that few experiences at his age could have been more instructive. Until a few years ago, most aficionados tended to be older adults; only in recent years have young people begun to compete with their seniors in *afición*. This may be another example of the neoconservatism in Spanish and Western society as a whole.

Most fans were of course male until quite recently, but now many Spanish females—especially younger women—consider themselves to be *aficionadas*. This tendency may have reached its climax in a *corrida* celebrated in the third-class bullring of Aranjuez in October 1994, televised on closed circuit and featuring the flashy young sensation Jesulín de Ubrique, a popular singer and media personality as well as a bullfighter. Instead of regaling the torero with the customary bouquets of flowers or leather wineskins, the female public (men were not allowed to attend) threw panties, brassieres and nylon stockings to their idol. Here is the reaction of the bullfight critic Saiz Valdivielso, whose voice is typical of those aficionados who want to maintain tradition in the *corrida*: "This phenomenon . . . is an expression of the tastes and pleasures of a Spain in the midst of an identity crisis, a depersonalized, computerized, homogenized, televised, consumerist, directionless, unthinking country; a frivolous and blind Spain, intoxicated by the media that compete for audiences with contests, comedians, karaoke, talk shows." The tone of this passage shows that aficionados do not take change lightly, to say the least.

Bullfighting preferences also reflect certain demographic patterns. Most *corridas*— 363 out of 495 in 1984–1985—take place in cities. Cost is no doubt a determining factor; few *pueblos* could afford to buy six brave bulls or calves and pay for three toreros to perform in a regulation *corrida*. Yet inhabitants of the countryside or small towns tend to be more interested in *toreo* than city dwellers. Many of them have direct experience with brave bulls, calves and cows and participate in local events like *capeas*, *encierros* and *toros embolados* during their patronal feasts.

As we saw above, attitudes toward the bullfight also follow certain regional lines. More *corridas* are generally celebrated in Andalusia than in any other area of the country. Yet a 1983 survey indicated that there was more *afición* in Castile-La Mancha (49.8%), La Rioja (45.1%), Castile-León (45%) and Aragón (43.6%) than in the south (42.9%), followed closely by Navarre (42.6%). As far as attendance, there were higher rates in Navarre (27.3%), La Rioja (26.1%), Castile-La Mancha (24.8%), the Basque Country (24.7%), Madrid-province (22.2%), Galicia (20.6%) and Extremadura (20%) than in Andalusia (19.3%). The figure dropped even lower in two northern regions, Catalonia (18.4%) and Asturias (16.6%). Of course other factors may be involved besides pure devotion to *toreo*. Many of the people who fill *plazas de toros* in the south are tourists in search of beaches and sun. It is expensive to attend bullfights in Spain: Andalusia is one of the poorest regions in the country and many aficionados no doubt are unable to buy tickets as often as they would like. A good seat in the shade at a major *feria* nowadays is worth $75 or more. At the 1998 Feria de San Isidro in Madrid, with twenty-six *corridas* and six *novilladas*, prices for an *abono* or subscription ticket ranged from $90 for a seat in the sunny grandstands to a cool $2,833 for a spot in the shade.

Before concluding our discussion of the public, we should remember the opponents of bullfighting. If there are many true aficionados, there are also many convinced detractors. For centuries the Catholic Church opposed *toreo*, associating it with the barbarous spectacles of pagan times. The first theological description of the devil, made by the Council of Toledo in the year 447, evoked a strangely familiar creature: "a large, black, monstrous apparition with horns on his head, cloven hoofs, hair, fiery eyes, terrible teeth, an immense phallus, and a sulphurous smell." The Church expressed concern for the danger to the men who faced bulls, not the animals, who after all were soulless and unredeemable. Two popes attempted to outlaw taurine spectacles in the sixteenth century. Threats of excommunication and denial of Christian burial were not enough to keep aficionados (including priests) away from the bullring. With the decline of Church power and the ascendance of the modern nation-state, the government became the leading enemy of the bullfight. Between 1750 and 1808, Spanish monarchs attempted to prohibit the bulls, obviously without success since the bans had to be repeated. Beginning in the eighteenth century, the enemies of the spectacle were assumed to be influenced by foreign ideas. The terms of discourse that were established in the Enlightenment have remained identical to the present day: for aficionados, bullfighting represents the essence of Spain, and opposition to it derives from European ideas; for its detractors, *toreo* stands for cultural backwardness, and resistance to it implies a liberal way of thinking.

The most famous enemy of *corridas* was the indefatigable writer Eugenio Noel, who crisscrossed the Peninsula for decades in a futile anti-taurine campaign. I am going to transcribe here his most powerful condemnation of *toreo*, in which the author's words ring with the same passion shown by aficionados. The passage is very long, but indispensable in any discussion of the subject. Noel saw bullfighting as a social disease:

From the bullrings come the following features of our race: most crimes committed with a knife; the pimp; the man who puts himself above any moral considerations; swearing; bad manners; the pasodoble and its derivatives; flamenco and the baseness of the gypsy dance whose accomplice is the guitar; disrespect for the law; thievery; that strange conception of courage expressed by the word "kidneys" [perhaps a euphemism for "testicles"] and that has been and will continue to be the cause of all our misfortunes; the delirious laughter, partying and idleness that plague our people; the worship of physical valor and disdain for anything except duels, fights, arrogance, pride, pomp, irreverence; the liberty to do whatever one pleases; the vomiting of slang and the basest words in the language; the narrow-mindedness of the *zarzuela [Spanish light opera]; pornography without voluptuousness, art or conscience; political corruption; all, absolutely all abuses of petty tyranny and nepotism; the complete lack of respect for a pure idea; the outbursts of sensual, vulgar and ambiguous sentimentality that gnaw away at the very bowels of our nation; the disastrous fact that it is the only completely national event in our country, since only *afición* for bullfighting unites the different regions and turns a Basque into an Andalusian, and a Catalan into an Extremeñan; the cruelty of our feelings; the desire to make war; our ridiculous Don Juanism with its two extremes, white slavery and orgies, and, in short, whatever has to do with enthusiasm, grace, self-respect, splendor, is all, all spoiled, defiled, adulterated, bastardized by those emanations that come from the bullrings to the city and from there to the countryside.

We have seen that Noel knew his material and was the Spanish writer who best described *capeas* and patronal feasts. Some of his respected contemporaries, authors like Azorín (José Martínez Ruiz) and Ramón Gómez de la Serna, pointed out that in his writings and lectures he was like a torero, fighting the "bull" of a hostile public and employing a vast repertoire of taurine details and expressions. One might also envision him as a modern Don Quixote, risking his life and tilting at windmills in a utopian campaign that was doomed to defeat. Eugenio Noel was a man born in the wrong century.

Recent opposition to the bullfight has come from animal rights supporters rather than cultural critics. Unlike the Church and state in earlier times, these people express concern for the suffering of the animals—*toros bravos* and the horses mounted by *picadores*—and not for the dangers to human life. On the walls of bullrings they write graffiti such as "*Toreros—asesinos*" (Bullfighters—assassins). They buy space in newspapers and magazines to publicize their campaigns. One ad shows a dying bull lanced by the Spanish flag, with the words "Torture is neither art nor culture. The national shame" (a play on the "national spectacle"). Another, sponsored by the Asociación para la Defensa de los Derechos del Animal (Association for the Defense of Animal Rights), appeared in various newspapers the week before St. John's day in 1985, which is celebrated with bullfights all over Spain (see Chapter 3, "Fiestas"): "SOS to the authorities of Extremadura, the Spanish government, all of Spain. A bull, atrociously martyrized by the whole town, with the cutting off of its testicles as trophies, while it was still alive."

Some organizations outside of Spain also engage in active anti-taurine activities. In this way they nourish the old *Black Legend, according to which Spaniards are a backward, violent people. In the spring of 1985, after the negotiations for Spain's entry into the European Economic Community, but before the signing of the treaty in June, a British member of the European Parliament submitted an amendment that would have banned the country's entry into the EEC until bullfights were prohibited. The measure was also supported by German and Italian animal protection societies, and was based on the EEC ban on degrading treatment and unnecessary cruelty to animals. This and similar amendments have failed to be approved. Rather than mobilizing support in Spain, foreign initiatives to outlaw the bullfight have probably encouraged many Spaniards to cling to their national customs. Even a well-known opponent of *toreo*, the ethnologist Julio Caro Baroja, retorted: "These gentlemen of the North have a puritanical attitude about *corridas*; meanwhile they fill their bellies with steaks and roasts." This is the same man who liked to tell the anecdote about an anti-taurine friend who once asked, "Do you believe it makes sense for a man to move his butt with elegance in front of Death?"

If attempts at foreign intervention in the *corrida* have failed, some of the autonomous regional governments in Spain have passed legislation that clearly responds to European initiatives. They also oppose the Spanish state's official control of the *corrida* under the most recent ordinances, Law 10 (1991) on administrative powers and Royal Decree 145 (1996) on the regulation of taurine spectacles. Thus the Parliament of Catalonia has approved a law for protecting animals in accordance with international treaties and the norms of other European countries. This legislation bans taurine spectacles like *encierros* (*corre-bous* in Catalan) except in those localities where they have been celebrated as a tradition, but even in these cases forbidding the animals' death.

As I reach the end of this chapter, I feel that something is missing. Most of the discussion of bulls has necessarily been quite general. I would like to make it more concrete by portraying three Spanish friends, two men and one woman, who come from different areas of the Peninsula, belong to three generations, and have very distinct views of the *corrida*. In this way the meaning of *toreo* in Spanish popular culture may become more human to the reader.

Fernando Claramunt was born in the Mediterranean city of Alicante in 1929, the son of a doctor who was also the attending physician at the local bullring. In the Plaza de Gabriel Miró where he was born, the region's first *corridas* on foot had been celebrated. Fernando was brought up with close contacts in the "planet of the bulls," following his father around the *callejón*, the passageway between the barrera and the first row of seats in bullrings. He received his medical degree from the prestigious University of Salamanca; the subject of his thesis was animal disorders. He continued his studies in Paris, Switzerland and in the United States at Northwestern University. In the College of Medicine and Psychology at the Complutense University in Madrid, he taught classes while maintaining a private practice. He is the author of medical monographs, essays, and books on literature, psychopathology and above all, *toreo*. His important essay, "Bullfighting and Psychology," appears in volume 7 of the taurine Bible, José María de Cossío's famous *Los toros* (see chapter bibliography). Fernando's best-known book, *Historia ilustrada de la tauromaquia* (Illustrated History of Bullfighting) is a valuable reference work. He appears frequently on radio and television programs devoted to bullfighting, and in the off season hosts a taurine **tertulia* or informal gathering in his elegant Madrid flat.

Although he is an extremely cultured man who speaks five languages and has a broad range of interests, Fernando's true life is the bulls. An English nobleman once said, "All time not devoted to hunting is wasted"; Fernando says the same about bullfighting, with only a little irony. "The *corrida* is not a sport or a hobby but a major event of our existence," he has written; "it is a way of life." Fernando is a subscription ticket holder for the great San Isidro festival in Madrid, a yearly feria that celebrates a *corrida* nearly every day for almost a month. Not a mere armchair torero, at the age of sixty-five he was still facing brave calves and cows in private *plazas* in the countryside. He has small, white, immaculate hands that have never seen a dust rag or a dishcloth, but they are hands that have fought bulls with cape, *muleta* and sword. I can attest from personal experience that he knows *toros bravos* in practice as well as theory. At Cortijo Bravo, a private ring in Navacerrada, north of Madrid, he once saved me from the charges of a brave-blooded calf who wanted to make this book a posthumous one.

I have spent many summer hours talking of men and bulls in Fernando's book-lined study overlooking the Paseo de la Castellana, Madrid's Park Avenue. Among the books are interspersed objets d'art, mostly statues of fighting bulls in cast iron, marble and bronze. The walls display sketches, oils and watercolors of bullfighting scenes, many of them by Fernando himself, who is also an accomplished artist. While we talk, his charming wife Pura brings us tall glasses of *paloma*—anisette with ice and water. We watch the ice change the clear liqueur, clouding, slowly turning it the color of a white dove.

When the sun sets and the evening begins to cool, Fernando leads me to a place in his house known fondly as the Toricuarto or Bull Room. It is covered from floor to ceiling with paintings, photographs, posters, sculptures and memorabilia: reproductions of cave paintings with ancient bulls and bisons; statues of sacred bulls from Crete and Mallorca; women's fans made of silk, tortoise shell or mother-of-pearl, hand-painted with scenes from bullrings; bright-colored pairs of *banderillas* with their small steel barbs; *monteras*, black toreros' caps; broad-brimmed beaver-skin hats worn by *picadores*; unfurled capes and *muletas*; paintings of bullfight scenes by Francisco Bayeu, Goya, Mariano Fortuny, Zuloaga, Julio Romero de Torres, Daniel Vázquez Díaz, Pablo Picasso; portraits of *matadores*—the founding father Pedro Romero; the mythical figures of Pepe Illo, Paquiro, Lagartijo, Frascuelo, *Guerrita*; the creators of modern *toreo*, Joselito and Belmonte; the great Mexicans Rodolfo Gaona and Silverio Pérez; Marcial Lalanda, Nicanor Villalta, Ignacio Sánchez Mejías who died "at five o'clock in the afternoon"; the long-faced Manolete; huge yellowing posters with oil paintings by Ruano Llopis, Roberto Domingo and Navarrete, announcing long-ago *corridas* in the *plazas* of Madrid, Sevilla, Valencia, Alicante, Murcia, Pamplona, Bilbao. Presiding over the room is the stuffed head of a fighting bull, mounted on the wall furthest from the door: glassy eyes and thick, bossed, up-turned horns. In a place of honor on the wall opposite the bull's head is a glass niche containing a ticket from the *plaza de toros* of Talavera de la Reina, dated 16 May 1920 and another from Linares, dated 28 August 1947—the two most infamous days in the history of modern bullfighting, when the great Joselito and Manolete were gored to death. The Toricuarto resembles a shrine with the bull as godhead, Joselito and Belmonte as his prophets, the other toreros as the community of saints. The whole room is a monument to the pagan, Celtiberian, Hispano-Arabic, Roman Catholic, Baroque, Goyesque, Romantic, gypsy, Andalusian, folkloric, picturesque, tragic apotheosis of life, death and the bullfight.

Fernando sips from his glass, looks up at the ceiling covered with bullfight posters, speaks: "Without *toros bravos*, Spain would be like any other place in the world. They are modern man's last connection to the ancient, heroic past."

It would be hard to imagine an aficionado more different from Fernando Claramunt than Alberto Flores. He is about ten years younger, hails from a small town in the province of Sevilla and has very little formal education. He comes from a large family; in the black years after the Civil War (1936–1939), he saw some of his twelve brothers and sisters die of hunger and remembers eating almond blossoms and the bark of trees. In spite of hard times, Alberto and some of his friends would secretly climb through the fences of local *ganaderías* on moonlit nights and take passes at the fighting bulls with a cape and *muleta*, risking their lives both with the animals and the watchmen who would shoot trespassers: it is an illegal action because the *toros bravos* remember any exposure to human beings and become more dangerous in the bullring.

As soon as he was old enough to leave home, Alberto worked at odd jobs and finally joined the Spanish merchant marine. He sailed all over the world and lived in France, Austria, Germany and Australia before ending up in San Francisco, California. There he worked in a body shop, saved enough money to buy the business himself, then opened a restaurant on Fisherman's Wharf. He ran it for seven years, sold it and with the proceeds bought a bar on Calle Arlabán in downtown Madrid, El Patio.

When we met, Alberto was in his early forties, with a dark mustache and a build like a Miura bull. He was tending bar at El Patio and we struck up a conversation. After he told me his story, I asked him why he had left America.

"The heart it call me back," he answered in his thick accent with the palm of one hand on his chest. Then he pointed to the underside of his wrist: "The blood she Espanish. Like his." He indicated a large photograph of Curro Romero, the famous matador from Sevilla, displayed on the wall in a prominent spot behind the bar that was like a miniature altar. Silently I read the dedication: "*Para Alberto Flores, mi amigo sevillano de 'El Patio.' Curro Romero.*"

"You know Curro?" he asked me.

"I've seen him in three *corridas*. He was a coward the first two times and divine with one bull the last time."

"That's right," he said, "that how Curro fight. He either sink in earth or he touch stars."

Nowadays Alberto enjoys playing golf more than going to the bullfight. But if his compatriot Curro Romero is appearing in Madrid, Sevilla or anywhere else in the country, he hops in his car or an airplane and attends the *corrida*. Curro is still going strong in his late sixties, a phenomenon unparalleled in the history of *toreo*, as if Mikhail Baryshnikov were dancing in the world's best theaters at a similar age. But Baryshnikov is barely fifty and does not risk his life when he dances.

On my last trip to Madrid I dropped into El Patio for my usual drink and to say hello to Alberto and his wife Evelyn. I told him that I was writing a book on Spanish popular culture with a chapter on bulls.

"Do you think bullfighting will ever disappear in Spain?" I asked him.

"*Nunca jamás*, never," he answered. "Not as long as there be young boys with *afición*, boys who don't care risk lives to fight bulls. I know."

Mari-Cruz Rodríguez was born in 1972 in the Basque city of San Sebastián, an elegant beach resort that is the Spanish Biarritz. Her parents emigrated there from the province of Cáceres in Extremadura, in search of work like thousands of other Spaniards. She has never attended a bullfight but has gone to the feria of San Fermín in Pamplona three times, once with her parents and twice with friends. "For us the most important thing was not the bulls," she says, "but the dancing, the fun, the fiesta."

For a long time Mari-Cruz's family has spent part of the summer in the town of Haro in the heart of La Rioja, the Spanish Bordeaux. In June the people celebrate the "Batalla del Vino" (Battle of Wine) and in September the fiesta of the wine harvest; both include *vaquillas* and *encierros*. Mari-Cruz has always enjoyed these events. When *novilladas* or *corridas* were celebrated in the local bullring during her childhood, she and her friends would peek at the *desolladero* or slaughterhouse next to the bullring. The sight of the immense carcasses of the bulls hanging from steel hooks (like Rembrandt's *Flayed Ox*), their heads already decapitated, their blood flowing on the cement floors, impressed Mari-Cruz so much that she has never forgotten it.

"I know that *toreo* is an art," she says, "and you have to understand it from the inside, like my grandfather who would always watch *corridas* on television. But to kill an animal—any animal—is cruel. I don't understand it."

"Would you like to attend a bullfight someday?"

"It doesn't appeal to me."

"What if someone offered you two free tickets?"

"*Hombre*, man, I'd probably say yes, but could I trade them for free tickets to the movies or a concert? I just can't see myself seated for two hours watching a *corrida*, when I could be reading a book or watching a movie."

"Are you against bullfighting?"

"I'm not for it or against it. Anyhow I know that it would be impossible to get rid of it. Not as long as there are aficionados like my grandfather. I think it's good that we have *vaquillas* and *encierros* in our local fiestas. What I don't like is the death of the bull in *corridas*. Maybe there could be some way to keep the art of *toreo* without the killing, some way to respect the animal's life and dignity while still allowing men to show their bravery—or women, because look at Cristina Sánchez."

"I know, she is very brave. Do you have any friends who are aficionados?"

"Not really. Here in the Basque Country everything is politicized, and bullfighting is associated with conservative politics, Castile and the state. To give you an idea, my friends like to get together to eat and drink. If we found a worm in our salad, we are the kind of people who would get up from the table and take the worm to the garden so it could live."

Will bullfighting survive in Spain? For many Spaniards, including my three friends—for all their differences in age, origins and education—it would be impossible to do away with *toreo*. Tierno Galván imagined a situation in which the *corrida* degenerated into a popular entertainment like any other, like the movies. In that case, he said, there would have to be an epitaph at the Spanish border in the Pyrenees, declaring, "Here lies Tauridia" (Land of the Bulls). The poet and playwright Lorca asked, "What would become of the Spanish springtime, of our blood and our language, if the dramatic trumpets of the *corrida* failed to sound?" The writer Antonio Gala is much more broad-minded than these two illustrious aficionados. His words open this chapter, and they will also close it. Recognizing that the bullfight serves as a catalyst for all of Spanish culture and all Spaniards, for aficionados and their opponents alike, he said: "Take away the bull and we'll see what's left. Would we recognize ourselves without the passion for and against the bull?"

SOURCES

In the United States, the main branch of the Los Angeles Public Library probably has the country's most extensive collection of modern books on bullfighting, mostly as a result of a bequest from George B. Smith, who donated some 5,000 volumes.

The main branch of the New York Public Library also has a large number of books on the subject. The Hispanic Society of America (Broadway and 155th Street, New York, NY 10032) houses the collection of Luis Carmena y Millán, an erudite collector from Spain who has been considered one of the fathers of taurine bibliography. The Taurine Bibliophiles of America, founded in 1964 by Robert Archibald, has some 120 members. It publishes a quarterly newsletter called *El Clarín de la Busca*, as well as the semiannual journal *La Busca*. Membership can be obtained through the Secretary-Treasurer, Glen Greer, 18950 Joaquín Court, Salinas, CA 93908.

A useful taurine bibliography, compiled by Rosario Cambria, can be found in Timothy Mitchell, *Blood Sport: A Social History of Spanish Bullfighting* (see Bibliography).

On the World Wide Web: *Glosario de términos taurinos* (Glossary of Bullfighting Terms), prepared by El Toro Association of Madrid, can be located online: <http://www.eltoro.org/glosaidx.htm>. "Los toros desde la barrera," a supplement of La Guía Raquelin, is located at <http://www.ctv.es/user/eledi/la fiesta.htm> and gives access to *PcToros*, advertised as the first encyclopedia of bullfighting on Windows 95; *El Web de PcToros*; *Mundo Taurino (Internet)*, maintained by Stanley Conrad from San Diego, CA; *Tauromaquia*, maintained by former matador Mario Carrión; *Torero, Torero*, maintained by Rosa Jaramillo; <http://mundo-taurino.org> has a "Rough Guide to Bullfighting."

A moderate treatment of cruelty to brave bulls and cows in popular festival in eastern Spain can be found in *Toros, ¿tradición o barbarie?*: <http://www.cgt.es/~aitana/jrtoro.htm>.

Two anti-bullfighting groups, The World Society for the Protection of Animals (WSPA) and the Humane Society International (HSI), have websites specifically devoted to the issue of bullfighting: <http://www.way.net/wspa/zzbull.html> and <http://www.way.net/wspa/bullfact.html>.

Spain's animal-rights organization, Asociación Nacional para la Defensa de los Animales (ANDA) has its headquarters at Gran Vía, 31, 28013 Madrid.

BIBLIOGRAPHY

Agenda taurina 1998: España, América y Francia. Prologue by José Serrano Carvajal. Madrid: Temple, 1997.

Alvarez de Miranda, Angel. *Ritos y juegos del toro*. Madrid: Taurus, 1962.

Amorós, Andrés. *La lidia: diccionario de tauromaquia*. Madrid: Temas de Hoy, 1996.

Arauz de Robles, Santiago. *Sociología del toreo*. Madrid: Prensa Española, 1978.

Barga, Ramón. *El toro de lidia*. Madrid: Alianza, 1996.

Baylón, José. *Tarde de toros*. Madrid: Mauricio D'Ors, 1996.

Beltrán, Pedro. *Términos taurinos*. Madrid: Siruela, 1995.

Benítez Reyes, Felipe. *Palco de sombra (escritos taurinos, 1985–1991)*. Sevilla: Renacimiento, 1996.

Bergamín, José. *La claridad del toreo*. Madrid: Turner, 1985.

Blasco Ibáñez, Vicente. *Sangre y arena*. 1908. Reprint, Barcelona: Luis de Caralt, 1962.

Boada, Emilia, and Fermín Cebolla, *Las señoritas toreras. Historia, erótica y política del toreo femenino*. Madrid: Felmar, 1976.

Cambria, Rosario. "Bullfighting and the Intellectuals." In Timothy Mitchell, *Blood Sport*, 199–230. Philadelphia: University of Pennsylvania Press, 1991.

———. *Los toros: tema polémico en el ensayo español del siglo XX*. Madrid: Gredos, 1974.

Caro Baroja, Julio. *El estío festivo (Fiestas populares del verano)*. Madrid: Taurus, 1984.

———. "Toros y hombres . . . sin toreros." *Revista de Occidente* 36 (1984): 7–26.

Claramunt, Fernando. *Del prado a la arena*. Prólogo de Angel Luis Bienvenida. Madrid: Egartorre, 1995.

———. *Historia ilustrada de la tauromaquia. (Aproximación a una pasión ibérica)*. 2 vols. Madrid: Espasa Calpe, 1989.

———. "Los toros desde la psicología." In José María de Cossío, *Los toros*, 7: 1–181. 9 vols. Madrid: Espasa Calpe, 1982.

Clarín Taurino (Bilbao). A beautiful journal, edited by the bullfight critic Alfonso Carlos Saiz Valdivielso, that has appeared since 1969, with some interruptions.

Cossío, José María. *Los toros: tratado técnico e histórico*. 12 vols. Madrid: Espasa-Calpe, 1943–1997. The Bible of bullfighting.

Del Campo, Luis. *Historia del encierro de los toros en Pamplona*. Pamplona: n.p., 1980.

———. *Psicología del corredor del encierro de los toros en Pamplona*. Barcelona: Talleres Gráficos SET, n.d.

Delgado Ruiz, Manuel. *De la muerte de un dios: la fiesta de los toros en el universo simbólico de la cultura popular*. Barcelona: Nexos, 1986.

———. "El toreo como arte o cómo se desactiva un rito." *Taurología* 1 (Fall 1989): 32–38.

Douglass, Carrie B. *Bulls, Bullfighting, and Spanish Identities*. Tucson: University of Arizona Press, 1997.

Durán, L. F. "'Ley seca' en los encierros." *El País* (4 August 1997): 16.

Echeverría, Javier. "Correr toros en el encierro de Pamplona." *Taurología* 1 (Fall 1989): 41–46.

———. "Del arte de correr toros a pie: el encierro de Pamplona." In *Arte y tauromaquia*, edited by Universidad Internacional Menéndez Pelayo, 127–185. Madrid: Ediciones Turner, 1983.

Estado actual de la fiesta de los toros. Sevilla: Fundación El Monte, 1996.

Feiner, Muriel. *La mujer en el mundo del toro*. Madrid: Alianza, 1995.

Fulton, John. *Bullfighting*. New York: Dial Press, 1971.

Gala, Antonio. *Charlas con Troylo*. Madrid: Espasa-Calpe, 1981.

———. "Piel de toro." *Club Taurino-Pamplona* 6 (1985): 7–9.

García Lorca, Federico. "Teoría y juego del duende." In *Obras completas*, edited by Arturo del Hoyo, 1: 1097–1109. 2 vols. Madrid: Aguilar, 1977.

Gómez Castañeda, Juan. *Tauromaquia y sociedad: escritos desde el tendido*. Ciudad Real: Diputación de Ciudad Real, 1996.

Hemingway, Ernest. *Death in the Afternoon*. 1932. Reprint. New York: Scribner's, 1960.

Jiménez Martos, L. *Tientos de los toros y su gente*. Madrid: Rialp, 1981.

Josephs, Allen. *White Wall of Spain: The Mysteries of Andalusian Culture*. Ames: Iowa State University Press, 1983.

Leiris, Michel. *Manhood: A Journey from Childhood into the Fierce Order of Virility*. Chicago: University of Chicago Press, 1984.

López Izquierdo, Francisco. *Fiesta nacional: calendario de los toros tradicionales y populares*. Madrid: Agualarga, 1996.

Machado, Antonio. "Juan de Mairena (1936)." In *Obras completas: Manuel y Antonio Machado*. 5th ed., edited by Heliodoro Carpintero, 1136. Madrid: Editorial Plenitud, 1967.

McCormick, John, with Mario Sevilla Mascareñas. *The Complete Aficionado*. Cleveland: World, 1967.

Macnab, Angus. *Fighting Bulls*. New York: Harcourt Brace, 1959.

Marvin, Gary R. *Bullfight*. Cambridge: Basil Blackwell, 1988.

Mata y Martín, César. *Ritos populares del toro en Castilla y León*. Salamanca: Junta de Castilla y León, 1996.

Mitchell, Timothy. *Blood Sport: A Social History of Bullfighting*. Philadelphia: University of Pennsylvania Press, 1991.

———. "Bullfighting." In *Encyclopedia of World Sport*. New Haven, CT: Yale University Press, 1996.

———. "Bullfighting: The Ritual Origin of Scholarly Myths." *Journal of American Folklore* 99 (October 1986): 394–414.

Noel, Eugenio. *Escritos antitaurinos*. 1914. Reprint. Madrid: Taurus, 1967.

———. *Nervios de la raza*. Madrid: Sáez Hermanos, 1915.

Ortega y Gasset, José. "Enviando a Domingo Ortega el retrato del primer toro." In *Obras completas*, 7: 25–31. 9 vols. Madrid: Revista de Occidente, 1962.

———. "Goya." In *Obras completas*, 7: 503–573.

———. "La caza y los toros." In *Obras completas*, 9: 447–473.

———. "Velázquez." In *Obras completas*, 8: 451–661.

———. "Una interpretación de la historia universal." In *Obras completas*, 9: 11–242.

Pedraza, Felipe B. *Iniciación a la fiesta de los toros*. Madrid: Edaf, 1997.

Pérez de Ayala, Ramón. "Política y toros." In *Obras completas*, 3: 810–814. 3 vols. Madrid: Aguilar, 1963.

Roda, María Antonia. Letter. *El País* (27 August 1986): 7.

Saiz Valdivielso, Alfonso Carlos. "El toreo." In *Estado actual de la fiesta de toros*, pp. 31–40. Sevilla: Fundación El Monte, 1995.

Sánchez, María Angeles. *Guía de fiestas populares de España*. Salamanca: Centro de Cultura Tradicional, Diputación de Salamanca, 1995.

Sánchez Dragó, Fernando. *Volapié: toros y tauromaquia*. Madrid: Espasa-Calpe, 1987.

Santa Cecilia, Carlos G. "Dalí dibuja el rapto de Europa." *El País* (12 June 1985): 30.

Serrán Pagán, Ginés. "El ritual del toro en España." *Revista de Estudios Sociales* 20 (1977): 87–100.

Taurología. A beautiful journal published in Madrid.

Theroux, Paul. *The Pillars of Hercules: A Grand Tour of the Mediterranean*. New York: Putnam's, 1995.

Tierno Galván, Enrique. *Desde el espectáculo a la trivialización*. Madrid: Taurus, 1961.

———. *Los toros, acontecimiento nacional*. Madrid: Turner, 1988.

Vázquez Montalbán, Manuel. "Paella." *El País* (26 August 1986): 32.

————— *Chapter 5* —————

Sports and Games

The world is surely a ball, but with more than air inside.

> —José Ortega y Gasset

Work consists of whatever a body is *obliged* to do. . . . Play consists of whatever a body is not obliged to do.

> —Mark Twain

Readers may be surprised that several of the previous chapters have dealt with "what a body is not obliged to do": religious festivals, patronal feasts, bullfights. This chapter will deal with more unobliged activities of the body, from traditional games to professional sports. Popular culture in general tends to be ludic, especially in the Peninsula, sometimes at the expense of workaday life. If Spain ever created a pantheon of gods and goddesses, they would probably be like the Greek divinities—indolent and playful.

Most anthropologists believe that sports and games grew out of religious celebrations, perhaps involving music and dance, and also as a sublimation of war and aggression. We remember that the Greeks declared a sacred truce during the Olympian festivals every four years. But in the modern period, as sports have become an integral part of mass, secular society, festive time has been replaced by the calendar and clock. In this and other ways the bullfight, frequently celebrated during Catholic festivals, remains much closer to its sacred roots. As we have seen in Chapter 4 ("Bulls"), *toreo* should not be considered a sport, but a tragedy.

There are traces of religion in sports throughout the world, such as athletes who make the sign of the cross on the playing field. These vestiges are more common in Spain than in most other countries. New stadiums are routinely blessed by the Church, for example, and teams have patron saints to whom they offer thanksgiving after a winning match. On the seventy-fifth anniversary of the Fútbol Club de Barcelona in 1974, the coach took the team on an official visit to Montserrat, site of an ancient monastery and the spiritual home of Catalonia, where the abbot blessed the players. Such an act would be hard to imagine in the Protestant world.

As one of the most tradition-bound countries in Europe, Spain fostered folk games until recent times. Modern sports and exercise, on the other hand, developed slowly. Their backwardness reflected the preindustrial nature of the society. Until the early 1900s, "sport" in Spain meant hunting and fishing. By the 1930s, Ernest Hemingway noted that "Madrileños whose only exercise used to be walking to the cafe are all going in for sports, for picnics in the country and for walking trips in the Sierras." The Civil War of 1936–1939 halted this trend. Then the authoritarian regime of General Franco placed sports in the hands of generals and the Falangist Party. The sociologist Manuel García Ferrando has called this the "blue" period of Spanish sports, alluding to the color of the shirt worn by the Falangists. Others have spoken of Spanish soccer in the postwar years as "National Footballism," with a pun on National Socialism: like the Nazis, Francoists manipulated athletics for propaganda. As sports became part of mass culture in the 1960s and Franco hired young technocrats to renovate his stale regime, Spain entered a "gray" period, or rather "bluish gray," says García Ferrando, since the Falangists maintained control. In the 1970s, with the death of Franco, the rebirth of democracy and the decentralization of power, the "multicolored" stage began; it has endured to the present. The Constitution of 1978 gave the country's seventeen semiautonomous regions the responsibility for promoting leisure, physical education and sports. The Olympic Games of 1992, celebrated in Barcelona, showed the multicolored, pluralistic stage in action. Three flags waved in the air—those of Catalonia, Spain and the International Olympic Commission, whose president was a Catalan Spaniard, Juan Antonio Samaranch.

In this chapter I will start with traditional games that have managed to survive in modern times. Some ancestral competitions, such as Basque *pelota* or jai-alai, have become professional, and will serve as a bridge to our discussion of soccer, tennis and other mass spectator sports that dominate the media in Spain and every other country in the world. In all cases I will attempt to isolate what is unique in Spanish sports and games.

TRADITIONAL GAMES

"It can be said that the notion of 'play' has become trivial or banal in modern societies," says Julio Caro Baroja in his study of Spanish festivals. In some rural communities, however, play still preserves a festive character, usually associated with religion. Ancestral games are played as part of patronal feasts, as we have seen in Chapter 3 ("Fiestas"). Here are three examples from the Castilian town of Briviesca (Valladolid): *chapas* or "coins," similar to the game of marbles, most commonly seen during Holy Week when the authorities turn a blind eye to illegal betting; *taba* or knucklebones, played around the feast of St. Casilda in May; a primitive form of bowling called *calva*, observed around the feast of St. Anthony in June. This game, which uses a horn and stones, was traditionally played as part of a festival but now has become popular at any time of year. *Chapas* has been even more successful, spreading from the country to towns and cities. (My son played it with bottletops at his school in Madrid, 1980.) These forms of traditional play have lost their collective, ritual nature as part of the sacred calendar. This will also be true of the games discussed below. I will use Old Castile as a model, both because it is fairly typical of central Spain and because it has been the subject of careful research.

Traditional games have variants not only in different areas of the Peninsula, but in particular towns. For this reason they are hard to classify. Some scholars believe that the degree of a game's popularity is inversely proportional to its degree of regulation, which tends to kill its uniqueness and spontaneity.

Bowling, in its many varieties, is probably the most common popular game in Spain and most of southern Europe. Of course I am not referring to the standardized modern sport played in commercial bowling alleys. In central Spain *bolos* is played in the open air, usually on dirt, with a hemispherical ball about 6″ in diameter that weighs no more than a kilo (2.2 pounds), used to strike wooden pins—nine tall and one short. A person designated as "counter" declares the number of points of each toss and keeps a running score. If you travel in the Spanish countryside, it is a nice sight to see old men, usually dressed in black and wearing *boinas* or berets, playing the sport in a dusty park or vacant lot, always surrounded by onlookers. Traditional games are communal in the sense that they are virtually inconceivable without observers and kibitzers.

Petanca is another bowling game that is not quite as primitive and unique as *bolos*. Many people are surprised to learn that this sport is played in Spain, since the French *pétanque* and Italian *boccie* balls are better known. The participants try to throw their steel balls around a smaller wooden ball made from the trunk of an olive tree—a tipoff on the game's Mediterranean origins.

Calva is also known by other names such as *chana* and *morrillo*. It originally involved throwing a rock at the horn of an ox or goat that had been placed on the ground at a short distance; it probably arose from shepherds practicing their aim in order to keep their flocks from wandering. The game is still played this way in the towns of Santa Elena de Jamuz and Villanueva de Jamuz (León). In its more modern version, an L-shaped wooden *calva* replaces the horn while an iron cylinder, about 7″ long, 2½″ in diameter and weighing about three pounds, is used instead of a rock or stone. One of the interesting aspects of this game is that many towns in Old Castile have their own version, and some have even created their own schools and styles of play. The men of Castrodeza and Medina del Campo (Valladolid), for example, are known for their prowess and belong to *calva* clubs that hold regular competitions.

Tanga is another throwing sport. A metallic disc of about 4″ in diameter is tossed at a wooden stake (*tanga*) topped by a 50-peseta coin. The object is for the disc to land closer to the stake than to the coin. In parts of Old Castile this traditional game is making a sort of comeback. Like *bolos* and *calva*, the equipment is cheap and just about any flat surface will serve as a playing field, which is usually the dry, beaten earth on the outskirts of a town.

Monterilla (little cap) is another throwing game with pastoral beginnings. The only equipment are a *boina* and a shepherd's staff. The players attempt to throw the staff and make it land on the cap from a distance of some thirty meters. A related game is *cachava* (staff), in which competitors use the stick to hit balls into holes in the ground—a kind of ancient golf.

Barra castellana (Castilian pole) is quite different from all the other throwing contests described above; it is practiced in parts of Navarre and Aragón as well as Old Castile. It could be described as a cross between the javelin and the discus in which the competitor throws an iron pole (about a yard long and weighing some ten pounds) for distance from a trapezoidal pit that is dug in the ground.

A final throwing game is *taba*, mentioned earlier. It is unique among all the other contests described here in that it is played only by girls or women. It is an ancient practice that has been known in various parts of Europe for some two thousand years. In the Spanish version, the metatarsus or metacarpus bone of a sheep is tossed into the air and the thrower wins or loses according to how the object lands on the ground. There are many variants. The most basic form is for girls to sit in a circle and toss the bone in the air. In older, crueler times, the loser's wrists were lashed by her mates with a leather belt.

Chirumba (stick) is a curious game that could be described as a primitive form of baseball. Players hit a short, narrow stick back and forth with a board or club. The player who initiates this exchange stands in a circle called *casa* ("home").

Sporting pigeons is an interesting popular sport that has enjoyed a revival in certain areas of Spain, notably Old Castile. In the province of Valladolid alone it is estimated that there are some 4,000 of these birds. The sport involves a competition between numerous male pigeons—as many as fifty at a time—to entice a lone female from a tree to her cage. The birds are quite different from those that are fed by old ladies in public parks: they have a larger maw, a thicker and shapelier beak, redder and stronger claws and a more colorful ring around their eyes. The female always has a white feather, which allows her to be distinguished by the judges; she remains in heat all year around, allowing the sport to be played in any season. The males are kept in strict celibacy until they are released for competition; they surround the female in the foliage and try to win her in the most varied ways. One writer notes that many familiar human types can be recognized among the cock pigeons:

there are the bothersome ones and the irritable ones who fight their competitors with beak, wings and pushing. Others are more correct and ceremonious and do no more than caress the female. But the most abundant are the annoying ones who use louder and louder calls to intimidate both their rivals and the female, who, in spite of her coyness and playfulness, uses a thousand tricks to get rid of so many boring suitors.

Although I have never seen this traditional sport, it seems to bring together so many aspects of Spanish life that its popularity is not surprising: a close relationship between humans and animals, the obsession with sexuality, chance and the unknown.

The Basque region in northern Spain is a fertile area for traditional sports and games. They all betray the basically rural nature of the society. Most of these activities still occur in conjunction with patronal feasts. Many also involve some form of betting—a passion among these people.

While the Olympics emerged from a tradition that was essentially military, Basque sports and games are mostly agricultural. Men compete in chopping down beech trees with an axe; in lifting bales of hay, wooden carts or stones as heavy as 650 pounds; in pulling oxen or bulls with a rope. Farm animals have their own contests: dogs herd sheep, oxen pull stones weighing up to 3,300 pounds. The importance of the sea in Basque life is revealed by other events that involve rowing boats of different sizes with crews of four to thirteen men. Needless to say, these sports are for males alone. The wonderful, unpronounceable names that refer to the burly competitors seem to evoke their power: *aizkolariak* (woodcutters), *harrijasotzaileak* (weight lifters), *estropadak* (rowers).

Michael Shearer describes one of these Basque competitions:

These agricultural athletes pulled and hefted, lifted and pushed, demonstrated their prowess in shifting awkward things about; like hay bales and farm carts. The finale involved lifting one end of a heavy cart and walking around in a circle with it. Muscles ruled here, and the emphasis was on efficient bulk and tensile sinew. Biceps bulged . . . and veins stood out like pods of runner-beans, and the crowd of lesser men, plus maidens, potential wives, loved it.

Of all Basque sports, only *pelota* or jai alai has been professionalized and exported to other parts of the world. With a bare hand, stick or net used to hit a hard little rubber ball, it is performed all year around in nearly every hamlet, town and city of Euzkadi. *Pelota* is the generic name for a family of similar games. It is a unique example of a traditional contest, developed in the Basque areas of both Spain and France, that has spread to many parts of the world and become a highly popular and lucrative sport. From an informal, loose series of games played according to archaic rules and the honor system, it has developed into a formal, regulated sport governed by an international body, with large sums of money at stake. In both ancient and modern forms it has been characterized by complicated betting that continues throughout the match as the odds change constantly.

Pelota might be called the most Spanish of all sports for several reasons: it has become more professionalized on the southern side of the Pyrenees than on the northern; most of the best players also come from the south, where three-quarters of all Basques live; most countries where the sport is played are Spanish-speaking (Spain, Mexico, Argentina, Uruguay); the international headquarters is located in Madrid.

Some speculate that *pelota* may have its roots in early Greek and Roman games, or in Mesoamerican competitions observed by Spanish chroniclers. Although the Basques like to claim that it has existed from the time of Adam, there is no direct evidence of its being played in the Peninsula before 1755. However, autopsies of skeletons from the early sixteenth century show the deformation of the phalanges that marks players' hands.

Courts were usually built near the center of towns, not more than a stone's throw from the parish church. Thus priests became involved as players (*cura-pelotaris*). In fact playing the game was considered a calling second only to the priesthood itself. Increasing professionalism caused the demise of the player-priest, but clerics continued to be recruited as judges, both for their reputed honesty and their knowledge of the game.

Witnesses describe matches with as many as 12,000 spectators in the nineteenth century. Those lacking liquid assets wagered pigs, oxen or a herd of goats, or a promise of their next harvest. People not fortunate enough to attend could learn the results by carrier pigeon. By mid-century a rubber-cored ball replaced the primitive sphere made from animal hair and skin. The sport began to shed its parochial character and spread to Argentina, Uruguay, Brazil, Bolivia, Mexico, Cuba, Florida and California—all places with communities of Basque émigrés. In 1921 the Fédération Française de Pelote Basque was formed; it codified the various games and recorded rules from the oral tradition. Spain and several Latin American countries followed suit by creating their own national federations. In 1924 the game was played at the Olympic Games in Paris, and five years later the Federación Internacional de Pelota Vasca was founded in Madrid. All that remained was for an appropriate patron saint to be chosen—a Basque if possible. The best candidate was the Jesuit St. Francis Xavier (1506–1552), born in Navarre; an autopsy of his corpse showed the telltale deformation of the phalanges, a kind of stigmata that qualified him to be named the sport's new patron. In 1952 the Federación organized the first world championship in San Sebastián. Since then the organization has continued to grow and the championships are held every four years in Spain, France or Latin America.

Pelota is played on a three-sided court, the fourth side being a tiered terrace for spectators. The name of the court is sometimes used to refer to the game itself: *frontón*. It measures some fifty meters in length and is also known as a *jai alai* (Basque for the "sprightly" or "lively" game). The term has become synonymous with *pelota's* flashiest offspring, *cesta punta*, developed in Havana around 1900, in which a pointed wicker basket is tied to the player's hand; he catches the ball in it and propels it at lightning speeds. I have seen jai alai in Bilbao, Buenos Aires and Mexico City; I have never seen a more exciting or faster game. It requires a keen eye and great agility; the players perform graceful leaps and bounds to catch and hurl the ball. Other versions involve from two to ten players, bare hand or a basket-glove of varying shapes and sizes, and different systems of scoring.

Most commentators forget that some form of *pelota* is played in other parts of Spain besides the Basque region. It ranks eleventh among all participant sports in the country, practiced by about 3.6 percent of the population. In 1987 there were more courts in Castilla-León (1,422) and Valencia (891) than in the Basque Country (616) and Navarre (483), but of course the population of those regions is much larger (6.2 versus 2.4 million). It is also true that the less spectacular forms of the game, such as handball, are more common in these regions than jai alai. *Pelota* may be the closest thing to an original "national" sport in Spain.

SPORTS

With the exception of traditional games and *pelota*, sporting activities of Spaniards are similar to those of other people in the Western world. But this statement ignores that fact that the country has undergone an athletic revolution in the last third of the twentieth century. The poverty and hunger of the post-Civil War period made competition a luxury for the privileged elite. Women were excluded as participants because physical effort was not considered proper for females. The Sección Femenina of the Falangist Party made sure that delicate señoritas were not "masculinized" by unnecessary exertion and perspiration, since their main object in life was supposed to be marriage and childbearing, activities that involved enough effort of their own. What saved both men and women from total sedentariness was the inveterate Spanish *paseo* or stroll, in which males and females walked, usually in opposite directions, around the town square in the early evening hours. This custom continues to be the most popular physical activity in the country, with no less than 90 percent of the population—slightly more men than women—doing it daily or several times a week. (Now the sexes usually walk in the same direction.)

The *paseo* is related to a general characteristic of exercise in Spain: sociability. Just as Spaniards tend to eat and drink, watch television and listen to the radio in groups, they also practice sports in the company of friends more than people in most other countries. While a mere 17 percent of the population plays sports in solitude, 56 percent participate with friends. Another interesting fact is that a full quarter of those interviewed in one poll considered "meeting one's friends" to be the most important motivation for competing in the first place, more than those who thought that "staying in good shape" was paramount. As we might expect, Spaniards also love to talk about sports. One study showed that 18 percent spoke with friends about sports more than about work, politics, cultural matters, education, money, health or religion; only "social life and events" was a more popular topic of conversation. The sporting press is correspondingly abundant: in 1993 the daily *Marca* was the third most popular newspaper in the country, while its competitors, *As* and *Sport*, were in seventh and thirteenth place. These figures reveal the collective, social character of sports in Spain, in contrast to their more solitary, utilitarian nature in northern Europe and the United States.

The tourist boom of the late 1950s and early 1960s had an influence on athletics as well as most other areas of life. Spaniards saw that foreigners exercised routinely, even while on vacation. Anyone who jogged in Spain in those years could be easily classified as a visitor. Then Spaniards began to imitate the tourists in dress, donning the warmup suits that were popular at the time. Soon a few brave souls decided to actually exercise in the new attire. Around the same time, "Sports for Everyone" campaigns started in some European countries and soon reached Spain: marathons, soccer games and bicycle races were organized by neighborhood associations or municipal governments, sometimes as part of local fiestas. The Spanish sports revolution had begun.

After the death of Franco in 1975, sports began to occupy a much more important place in Spanish life. Some of the causes for the change were the dismantling of the quasi-military administration of leisure, the Constitution of 1978 with its decentralization of power, the general prosperity, the media's greater role and the country's entrance in the European Union. The Socialist government of Prime Minister Felipe González (1982–1996) created more facilities and promoted athletics as an integral part of physical and mental health in the modern welfare state. In many ways the

1992 Olympic Games in Barcelona were the culmination of twenty years of revolution in sports. The media barrage and the phenomenal success of Spanish competitors, who won thirteen gold medals that summer, created an awareness of sports that was unparalleled in the country's history.

Although the situation has changed radically, Spain still lags behind other European nations. As far as general interest, for example, sports (31%) ranks behind family (79%), friends (54%), radio (53%), television (52%), music (40%), movies (35%) and trips to the country (34%), but ahead of "shows" (21%), dating (17%), manual work (17%) and "nothing in particular" (16%). On the level of performance, only 46 percent of Spaniards regularly play some kind of sport, compared to about 60 percent in France, Belgium and Denmark, 75 percent in Sweden and 84 percent in the United Kingdom. In general the most prosperous regions of Spain, such as Catalonia, the Basque Country and Madrid, show the highest levels of participation. However these figures should not be taken too literally since other polls show results that are quite different.

As in so many countries, men are more active than women in all aspects of sport: interest, participation, attendance, following events on radio or television. In the first survey ever conducted on the subject in Spain, in 1968, only 7 percent of women played sports, compared to 18 percent of men. By 1975 the figure for females had risen to 12 percent and by 1985, to 23 percent, exactly one-half the rate for men. In more recent times there have been encouraging trends: women, mostly from the urban middle classes, have begun to join health clubs and gyms where they perform aerobics, ballet, yoga and *sevillanas* (see Chapter 6, "Music"). Yet housewives remain the single sector of society, comprising no less than ten million women, with the lowest participation in physical activities outside the home. No wonder: they spend an average of nine hours a day in domestic work. There are clear signs that this is changing, but reliable statistics are unavailable.

After sex, the largest variable is education: one poll showed that only 6 percent of Spaniards with a primary school education competed regularly in sports, compared to 59 percent of those with a university background. Not surprisingly, age is also a factor. The younger the person, the more likely that he or she will participate in sports. Spaniards seem to have a bad conscience about their lack of physical activities; a survey showed that sports was the one area of their lives to which most people would like to dedicate more time. These are indications that the population of the future will be more physically fit than their elders. The sports revolution is more than a passing trend.

Swimming is probably the most popular participant sport in the country: 43 percent of Spaniards practiced it in 1986, although allowance should be made for the fact that it is a seasonal sport that cannot be practiced all year around in most parts of the Peninsula. Soccer was second (28%), followed by jogging (22%), basketball (11%), cycling (10%) and tennis (9.5%).

It should be noted that Spain has excelled in some of these sports on an international level. The popularity of a superstar like the Navarrese cyclist Miguel Indurain, winner of five Tour de France, two Giro d'Italia, one Vuelta a España, an Olympic medal and many other prizes, has no doubt inspired many young Spaniards. Known as "Miguelón" or "Michelone" (Big Mike), "El Rey Miguel" (King Michael), "El Navarro de Oro" (The Golden Navarrese), "El Dios Navarro" (The Navarrese God) and even "El Extraterrestre" (The Alien), Indurain has been called the greatest Spanish athlete of all time. Other international stars such as the tennis players Arantxa Sánchez Vicario, Conchita Martínez and Sergi Bruguera have also created greater interest in this sport, to which the Spanish climate lends itself very well. A whole new crop of young players has arisen in recent years—Julián Alonzo, Alex Corretja, Albert Costa, Jacobo Díaz, Gala León, Félix Mantilla, Carlos Moya, Vivi Ruano, María Antonia Sánchez, Magüi Serna, Cristina Torrens. In May 1998, Spain, a country roughly the size of Montana, had an amazing sixteen men ranked among the world's top one hundred singles players. No wonder that some journalists are speaking of a new "Spanish Armada" at Wimbledon and other international matches.

Cultural anthropologists have suggested that it is possible to divide the world into those people who play baseball and those who play football (soccer). Spain clearly belongs to the latter group. Just as a knowledge of baseball can help us penetrate the hearts and minds of Americans, soccer is a key to understanding Spaniards.

Bullfighting and football could be seen as the flipsides of Spanish life. Fans of the two activities normally do not overlap; many aficionados of the bulls ignore soccer, while many *hinchas* (football fanatics) return the favor. Bullfight fans tend to be more conservative in politics and traditional in their values: soccer buffs associate *toreo* with old-fashioned mores and a stale past. It is not by chance that the seasons occupy different parts of the calendar: bullfighting takes place from spring to early fall, while football is played from fall to late spring. More importantly, as we suggested early in the chapter, *toreo*, a tragedy and ritual rather than a sport, usually occurs during sacred festivals and patronal feasts, while soccer games are scheduled according to the secular calendar, like basketball, tennis and other modern sports. If football matches occur on Sundays, it is not because of the sabbath, but because people are off work. In Spain, where the sport is so popular that we could speak of soccer widows as well as soccer moms, the clergy has been careful not to attempt to uphold the sabbath, knowing that they would be accused of national treason.

Like most other sports in the Peninsula, football is a male prerogative. A higher percentage of girls play the sport in the United States than in Spain. The mood before a soccer match is definitely masculine and in this alone resembles the ambience of a *corrida*: cigars are sold outside the stadium, along with beer, soft drinks, *bocadillos* (Spanish submarine sandwiches), sunflower seeds, pine nuts, popcorn and peanuts.

Football reached Spain and the rest of the world through British commerce and colonialism. The first major teams were established rather late, after those in some Latin American countries, for example. The names of some soccer clubs reflected their British origins: Athletic of Bilbao, Sporting of Gijón. During the period of isolation and retrenchment in the post–Civil War period, the Francoist government eliminated these vestiges of decadent foreign influence and hispanized the names: Atlético de Bilbao, Deportivo Gijón. It has been shown clearly that the regime exploited football—the most lucrative and popular sport in the country—to distract the population from social problems, to create a sense of patriotism and to fill the state coffers. The historians Raymond Carr and Juan Pablo Fusi believe that soccer was part of the "culture of evasion" during the years of Franco rule (1939–1975). In his prologue to Duncan Shaw's book on football and Francoism, Paul Preston calls Spanish soccer of the time "a social drug . . . part of the . . . political fabric of the dictatorship." Vázquez Montalbán states: "Sports replaced the Circus, because in fact, from the point of view of those in power, they were simply its extension: bread and Circus, bread and Sport." The regime systematically scheduled important matches on the eve of 30 April, in order to keep workers away from May Day rallies. Victories of the Spanish team in the European Cup between 1956 and 1960 were seen as national triumphs. Defeats of Britain ("perfidious Albion") and the USSR were propaganda successes for the state, no less than the German medals in the Berlin Olympics of 1936 were prizes for the Nazis. With his usual humor, Vázquez Montalbán refers to Spain's 1964 triumph over the Soviet Union in the European Cup as "our most important milestone since the last victories of our soldiers in the Thirty Years' War." The famous announcer Matías Prats thrilled the nation with dramatic radio commentaries that made no pretense to impartiality; in 1967 he was named a member of the Cortes or Parliament. Meanwhile soccer singlehandedly supplied the national sports budget through a system of *quinielas* or betting pools. The pools still exist but the national government and the semiautonomous regions have had separate funding for sports and leisure since 1988. The *quinielas* continue to be generous: the pot for 10 February 1998, for example, was 228,028,340 pesetas ($1,520,188), with seven lucky Spaniards pocketing $325,755 each, not to mention many smaller winners.

The successes of Spanish football helped Franco improve the dictatorship's poor image abroad. In the dark years after World War II, Ireland and Portugal were two of the only countries that accepted matches with Spain. As Franco's hatred of communism made him a strategic ally of the West in the Cold War, Spanish teams played in more international competitions. The country participated in the 1950 World Cup in Brazil, carrying away a respectable fourth place. Soon the United Nations lifted its boycott and Spain was once again admitted to the family of nations.

The soccer team that played the major role as Spanish ambassador was Real Madrid, whose coat of arms was capped by the crown of the monarchy. When the team won the Latin Cup in Paris in 1955, each player was awarded the Medal of the Imperial Order of the Yoke and Arrows—symbol of the ruling Falangist Party. The club's monthly bulletin stated with typical fascist rhetoric: "Real Madrid represents . . . a style of sportsmanship and the team knows how to carry the name of Spain around the world with the utmost decorum. Its players behave like authentic ambassadors, contributing with their performance to the prestige of the fatherland."

Two well-known sports sociologists have developed the theory that soccer serves as an important mechanism for social integration in some countries. In her book *Soccer Madness*, Janet Lever argues that the sport "helps complex modern societies cohere." For his part, Roberto Da Matta proposes that football teaches players and fans to live by standardized rules and to accept winning or losing in a disciplined way, thereby laying the groundwork for a democratic society. These theories may work for young countries like Brazil and Argentina, but they fail to account for the complex regional tensions of an ancient country like Spain, as we will see.

It is ironical that Franco's attempt to manipulate soccer for evasion and propaganda exploded in his face on the home front, encouraging political conflict and separatism. The great competition between the major teams of Madrid, Barcelona and Bilbao, for example, mirrored the perpetual friction between the capital and the Catalan and Basque regions. More ink has probably been spilled on this subject than any other in Spanish soccer. I will concentrate here on the historical rivalry between El Real Madrid Club de Fútbol and El Fútbol Club Barcelona (see Photograph 6, "El Duelo Eterno"), by far the two most powerful sporting institutions in Spain.

As the winningest teams in the country's two major cities, the teams have a long history of opposition. The historic resentment harbored by Catalonia against Castile since the fifteenth century has often revealed itself on the playing field. When Franco won the Civil War, he punished Barcelona for its support of the Republic in many ways, even in sports. Teams were purged of players, coaches and administrators who had opposed the Generalissimo's revolt against the legitimate national government. The severity of the regime kept Catalonian separatism at bay until the 1960s, when the tourist boom, a late industrial revolution and the spirit of the times created a more permissive atmosphere. "Barça," as the team is affectionately called, began to recover the use of Catalan in official acts and in the stadium, where fans carried banners written in the regions's language. Even before Franco's death in 1975, the *senyera*, the Catalan flag, with four red stripes against a yellow field, could sometimes be spotted waving in the stands. After the Generalissimo's demise, Josep Taradellas, president of the Catalan government in exile during the dictatorship, addressed 100,000 spectators in Camp Nou, the largest sports stadium in Europe. "Our club is great because it has always remained faithful to Catalonia. . . . I am sure that you will all keep this Catalan spirit and that will make possible a Catalonia that will be richer, stronger, freer than ever. And for this reason I give you my profoundest gratitude. *Visca el Barça y visca Catalunya!*" (Long live Barça and long live Catalonia!). The crowd then broke out in "Els segadors," the Catalan hymn. The impossibility of an event like this in the United States points up the cultural uniqueness of soccer in Spanish life.

Everything else is politicized in Spain, so why not football? The Real (= Royal) Madrid team, with its seat in the national capital and its Bernabéu Stadium on the Paseo de la Castellana, the city's Park Avenue, has long been associated with the Spanish monarchy, aristocracy and ruling elite. Its coat of arms has a purple stripe—the royal color and also that of Old Castile—on a white field, with the team's initials in gold, surmounted by a crown and cross. In contrast, Barça has usually been associated with the more democratic traditions of Catalonia, and its coat of arms shows a soccer ball and the team colors of blue and red, in addition to the *senyera*. (The *azulgrana* or "blue-red" is another nickname for the team.)

Each club has some 100,000 members. Joking about them, Vázquez Montalbán—a Barça fan himself—says that parents "make their babies members while they are still

6. "El Duelo Eterno" (The Eternal Duel) between Barcelona (left) and Real Madrid (right). From *Todo el arte de* El Mundo (February 1991). Reproduced courtesy of *El Mundo del País Vasco*.

hanging from their umbilical cords." Composers and *cantautores* have dedicated songs to the teams. Sports publications are not above the rivalry and usually declare themselves to be either *madridista* (supporters of Real Madrid) or *barcelonista* (supporters of Barcelona); sales fluctuate with the ups and downs of their respective teams.

The mystical rapture of Barça's fanatics usually surpasses that of Madrid's followers, because the team is so closely related to Catalan identity. For this reason writers, artists and intellectuals in Catalonia have declared themselves to be aficionados more readily than their peers in the capital city. The famous painter Salvador Dalí did a drawing and a painting in honor of Catalan soccer. On the occasion of Barça's platinum anniversary, the painter Joan Miró designed the official banner, while other artists like Antoni Tàpies and Josep Maria Subirachs also participated. Agustín Montal, president of Fútbol Club Barcelona like his father, declared "One must admit that [the team] is the most representative entity of Catalonia. . . . Love is the word that unites us around our Barça."

Both Real Madrid and F. C. Barcelona are powerful organizations that sponsor other sports as well as soccer. In the past they have fielded teams in basketball, handball, track and field, rugby, field and ice hockey, volleyball, tennis, gymnastics, judo, baseball and ping-pong. But in recent years, after soccer they have concentrated on basketball—the other great rivalry between the two clubs—as well as handball and tennis. There are more than two thousand *peñas* or fan clubs of the two teams, mostly in Spain but also in places as far-flung as the Central African Republic, China and the United States.

Most Spaniards admit that Barça and Real Madrid will always be enemies, because the two cities and the two regions they represent are so different and maybe incompatible. Only on a few occasions have they suspended their rivalry. The most memorable truce occurred on the last evening of the 1992 Olympic Games in Barcelona, when the Spanish team—fielding players from both clubs—beat Poland for the gold medal in the Camp Nou. Many Catalans were astonished to find themselves waving Spanish flags and cheering "¡España! ¡España!" while Castilians were equally surprised to be rooting for the same team as their habitual rivals.

Although F. C. Barcelona is the most famous opponent of Real, we should not forget that other teams have also had bitter rivalries with Madrid. Athlétic of Bilbao and Real Sociedad of San Sebastián, the two most powerful clubs from Euzkadi, also earned their stars as anti-Franco teams. Like the Catalan *senyera*, the Basque flag, the *ikurriña*, was a subversive symbol when it made an appearance in a football stadium. While most players for F. C. Barcelona have been Spaniards from outside of Catalonia or foreigners, the Basques have fielded squads whose ranks are filled with natives of the region. Their resistance to Real Madrid was more violent than Barça's—including coordinated bombings by the terrorist organization *ETA—while the Catalan opposition tended to be more refined and intellectual.

I will conclude with a passage from the sports sociologist Joseph L. Arbena in reference to Latin American soccer, which can be applied to the sport in Spain too: "It seems obvious . . . that any activity that can repeatedly attract up to . . . [120,000]

spectators in many places at about the same time, support multimillion dollar betting pools, sustain profitable daily and weekly newspapers, fill hours of radio and television programming, justify significant governmental budgets, provide the theme for speeches by politicians from mayors to presidents . . . and more—such an activity merits serious analysis."

RESOURCES

In addition to the website "Sí, Spain" from the Spanish Embassy in Ottawa, the Iberian Studies Web from Brigham Young University gives access to information on sports in Spain: <http://www.lib.byu.edu/~rdh/wess/iber/index.html>. After reaching this site, click "*Spain Links*" to reach Miguel Indurain's personal web page, another on the Spanish Soccer League, etc. The daily newspaper (including Sundays) *Sport* can be reached through the Iberian Studies Web or directly at <http://ns.bon.servicom.es/sport>. Another site is <http://www.cybermundi.es/deportes.htm>.

BIBLIOGRAPHY

Arbena, Joseph L. "Sport and the Study of Latin American Society: An Overview." In *Sport and Society in Latin America. Diffusion, Dependency, and the Rise of Mass Culture*, edited by Joseph L. Arbena, 1-14. Westport, CT: Greenwood Press, 1988.

Arlott, John, ed. *The Oxford Companion to Sports and Games*. London: Oxford University Press, 1975.

Blanco Alvaro, Carlos. "Juegos populares." *Cuadernos Vallisoletanos* 11 (1986): 3-31. This special number of the journal is devoted to traditional games of Old Castile, which are played with many variants in other parts of the Peninsula.

Boletín del Real Madrid C.F. Madrid, no. 128 (January 1961).

Broughton, Hugh. "Athletic Madrid." *The Architectural Review* 198, no. 1186 (December 1995): 34. About a new soccer stadium in Madrid.

Cagigal, José María. *El deporte en la sociedad actual*. Madrid: Editora Nacional, 1975.

————. *¡Oh Deporte! Anatomía de un gigante*. Valladolid: Editorial Miñón, 1981.

Caro Baroja, Julio. *El estío festivo (Fiestas populares del verano)*. Madrid: Taurus, 1984.

Carr, Raymond, and Juan Pablo Fusi. *Spain: Dictatorship to Democracy*. London: George Allen & Unwin, 1979.

Coca, Santiago. *El hombre deportivo*. Madrid: Alianza, 1993.

Da Matta, Roberto. "Esporte na sociedade: um ensaio sobre o futebol brasileiro." In *Universo do futebol: esporte e sociedade brasileira*, edited by Roberto Da Matta and others, 19-42. Rio de Janeiro: Edições Pinakotheke, 1982.

Durán, María Angeles. "La práctica del ejercicio físico del ama de casa española. Un estudio sociológico." In *Mujer y deporte*, 91-102. Madrid: Instituto de la Mujer, Ministerio de Cultura, 1987.

España 1994. Una interpretación de su realidad social. Madrid: Centro de Estudios del Cambio Social, Fundación Encuentro, 1995.

Fisis: monografías sobre ciencias del deporte. Madrid: Consejo Superior de Deportes, 1994.

La función del deporte en la sociedad: salud, socialización, economía. Madrid: Consejo Superior de Deportes, 1996.

García Candau, Julián. *Madrid-Barça. Historia de un desamor.* Madrid: El País, Aguilar, 1996.

García Ferrando, Manuel. *Aspectos sociales del deporte. Una reflexión sociológica.* Madrid: Alianza, 1990.

———. *Hábitos deportivos de los españoles.* Madrid: Ministerio de Cultura, Consejo Superior de Deportes, 1986.

———. "Popular Sport and Sociocultural Change in the Spain of the 80s." *International Review of Sport Sociology* 3 (1982): 5–26.

Hemingway, Ernest. "The Friend of Spain: A Spanish Letter." *Esquire* 1, no. 2 (February 1934): 22, 156. Reprinted in *By-Line: Ernest Hemingway,* edited by William White, 144–152. New York: Scribner's, 1967.

Hughes, Robert. *Barcelona.* New York: Knopf, 1992.

International Review of Sport Sociology.

Journal of Popular Culture.

Letra Internacional (Madrid), no. 44 (May–June 1996): 35–55. Special issue on soccer with contributions by Spanish and foreign authors.

Lever, Janet. *Soccer Madness.* Chicago: University of Chicago Press, 1982.

Levinson, David, and Karen Christensen, eds. *Encyclopedia of World Sport. From Ancient Times to the Present.* 3 vols. Santa Barbara, CA: ABC-Clio, 1996.

London, John. "The Ideology and Practice of Sport." In *Spanish Cultural Studies: An Introduction. The Struggle for Modernity,* edited by Helen Graham and Jo Labanyi, 204–207. Oxford: Oxford University Press, 1995.

Lüschen, Günther R. F., and George H. Sage, eds. *Handbook of Social Science of Sport.* Champaign, IL: Stipes Publishing Company, 1981.

Moreno Palos, Cristóbal. *Aspectos recreativos de los juegos y deportes tradicionales en España.* Madrid: Gymnos Editorial, 1993.

Ortega y Gasset, José. "Juventud." In *Obras completas,* 3: 463–471. 9 vols. Madrid: Revista de Occidente, 1962.

Puig, Núria. "El proceso de incorporación al deporte por parte de la mujer española." In *Mujer y deporte,* 83–90. Madrid: Instituto de la Mujer, Ministerio de Cultura, 1987.

Shaw, Duncan. *Fútbol y franquismo.* Prologue by Paul Preston. Madrid: Alianza, 1979.

Shearer, Michael. Unpublished manuscript on the Camino de Santiago (Way of St. James).

Sherrow, Victoria. *Encyclopedia of Women and Sports.* Santa Barbara, CA: ABC-Clio: 1996.

Sociology of Leisure and Sport Abstracts.

Twain, Mark. *The Adventures of Tom Sawyer.* 1876. Reprint. *The Family Mark Twain.* New York: Harper & Brothers, 1935.

Vázquez Montalbán, Manuel, Andrés Mercé Varela, and Joaquín Ibarz Melet. *Cien años de deporte. Del esfuerzo individual al espectáculo de masas.* 2 vols. Barcelona: Difusora Internacional, 1972.

———. *Crónica sentimental de España.* 1971. Reprint. Madrid: Espasa-Calpe, 1986.

—————— *Chapter 6* ——————

Music

Quien canta sus males espanta (Whoever sings has a heart that rings).
—Spanish proverb

Until the middle of the twentieth century, the term *música popular* usually meant traditional or folk music. With the depopulation of the Spanish countryside and the growth of urban, mass culture in the last twenty-five years, the term has come to refer more often to commercial music on record, tape, compact disc, radio and television. I will look at both kinds of music in this chapter. To describe folk music transmitted orally, I will use the term "traditional," while I will call commercial music "popular." Of course there are crossovers between these two vast fields, which combine elements of both.

As I have done earlier, I must stress again how much my subject is related to material treated in other chapters, especially those on religion (2) and fiestas (3). Most of the songs and dances in the huge repertory of traditional music are performed at sacred events and secular festivities. They have influenced liturgical music and been influenced by it in turn. A classic example would be the thirteenth-century *Cantigas de Santa María*, attributed to King Alfonso X the Wise, which contain both liturgical melodies and folksongs that were still being sung in recent times. The *Misterio de Elche* (Mystery of Elche), a sacred drama celebrated for centuries in honor of the Virgin Mary's death and Assumption, fuses Renaissance polyphony with ancient folk melodies, blended in a powerful synthesis. A final example is the dance of the *seises* (choirboys) in the cathedral of Sevilla, executed to the accompaniment of instruments and their own castanets during Corpus Christi. We have seen that this combination of high and low art is one of the recurrent tendencies of Spanish culture in general and a source of its great vitality and strength.

I will begin by looking at traditional music: folksong and dance in the major regions of the Peninsula. Then I will consider the curious phenomenon of *la canción española* ("the Spanish song")—also called *cuplé, tonadilla* or "the national song"—a unique hybrid of high and low art. Next I will discuss the *zarzuela or Spanish light opera, another crossover genre with one foot in the palace and the other in the street. I will end by glancing at certain types of pop music, some still linked to traditional genres (like flamenco), others belonging entirely to the world of mass culture: *cantautores* or singer-songwriters; *la nova cançó* or the Catalan New Song; rock; fusion, *mestizaje* or "crossbreeding" and other recent trends. Throughout the chapter I will be stressing the elements that distinguish Spanish music from that of other countries. What gives it such an unusual character and unmistakable ring?

TRADITIONAL MUSIC

In his classic study, *The Music of Spain*, Gilbert Chase declared: "It is generally agreed that Spanish folk music is the richest in the world." He attributed his belief in part to the many cultures that have lived in the Peninsula: Iberian, Phoenician, Greek, Carthaginian, Roman, Muslim, Jewish and Christian. He did not even count the influence of peoples ruled under the Spanish Empire, like the Italians, Sicilians, Dutch and Flemish, as well as the indigenous peoples of Latin America. Delighted to have an Anglo-Saxon music historian state what they themselves already believe, Spanish scholars have echoed Chase's sentence. For our purposes it is enough to say that traditional music in Spain can be extraordinarily beautiful, varied and moving.

The *romance* ("ro-mán-ce") or ballad has been studied more exhaustively than any other genre of the oral tradition in the Peninsula. Its name derives from the fact that it was sung in the common tongue—Castilian, a Romance language—and not in Latin. Indeed it became a part of the national identity; the Romantics called Spain "the country of the *Romancero*"—a term that refers to the whole corpus of balladry. Its origins go back to the earliest expressions of Castilian literature, the great medieval epic poems that extolled the deeds of heroes like Bernardo del Carpio, El Cid and Fernán González. Ramón Menéndez Pidal and other scholars have shown that *romances* were often based upon fragments of these lengthy compositions, learned by heart, sung and diffused by *juglares* (minstrels). Border ballads told stories of the many skirmishes and truces between Moors and Christians during the so-called reconquest (actually centuries-long wars of attrition); Moorish ballads expressed a more heroic view of the Arabs; later artistic *romances* blurred the boundaries between narrative and lyric poetry. When the Jews were expelled from Spain in 1492, they carried with them archaic Spanish ballads (and other genres) that can still be heard in many places of the Sephardic diaspora, from North Africa, the Middle East and the Balkans to North and South America. During the age of discovery, Spanish soldiers and sailors carried their music across the seas. Gradually the typical *romance* form—eight-syllable lines with assonance or vowel rhyme in the even verses—was applied to songs based on events in the New World. As it spread throughout the Americas, the ballad became the model for the *corrido* in countries like Mexico, Peru and Argentina. It remains the most widespread poetic form in the Hispanic world.

With the invention of the printing press, ballads were transcribed and published. Their most common form of transmission was *literatura de cordel*—"string literature" or "colportage" in English: cheaply printed broadside sheets of four or eight pages, sometimes more, containing ballads and other poems, saints' lives and miracles, *aleluyas* or doggerel with Easter prints, *cartelones de feria* or signs and banners for popular festivals. In Spain these sheets were often sold and distributed by the blind; thus the term *romance de ciego*, or blind-man's ballad. Goya made several poignant paintings of these singers.[1] It is a well-known fact that the blind, unable to depend on sight as a mnemonic crutch, develop a much stronger memory than people blessed with vision. Sometimes the blind themselves composed ballads; other times they merely memorized and recited or sang them. Julio Caro Baroja, the leading authority on the subject in Spain, recalled hearing *romances de ciego* in his own childhood in Madrid during the teens and twenties; he also remembered a woman who played the guitar and sang popular songs in his neighborhood every Thursday, seated on an ox-cart loaded with fresh, fragrant herbs.

We could not imagine that scene in Madrid today; yet the ballad tradition has not died out. Scholars continue to collect *romances* in many parts of the Peninsula. Most of the informants are female. Older women preserve the tradition much more than their daughters and granddaughters—a clear sign that the tradition is on the verge of distinction. The ballads are sung. Each has its own melody, which helps to preserve the text. The modern corpus comprises the old traditional pieces; "vulgar ballads" surviving from printed sheets or colportage, containing tales of smugglers and robbers from the eighteenth and nineteenth centuries, *causes célèbres* involving horrible crimes, unhappy lovers, abandoned children; religious poems usually devoted to the Virgin Mary; bullfighter ballads; gypsy songs and so on.

The *romance* verse is the archetypal form of traditional poetry in Spain; some believe that the eight-syllable utterance is the most natural to the language. Many folk styles in fact possess a similar verse structure, like the widespread *copla* or song, which has been imitated by later, educated poets and musicians. The *villancico* or pastoral song often hovers around eight syllables, but unlike the ballad, it always has a refrain. In modern times the term has become almost synonymous with the Christmas carol and is known by various names throughout the Peninsula: *villancet* or *nadal* in Catalonia; *ator-ator* in the Basque Country; *nadal*, *panxoliña* or *navidá* in Galicia. *Villancicos* have spread to the New World where they are sung as *posadas* in Mexico and the southwestern United States.

The Spanish people have songs and dances for almost every occasion. They include music for childbirth, lullabies, children's games, fiestas and funerals; street cries; songs of courtship, the land, work at home, in the field and town. The musicologist Josep Crivillé i Bargalló divides Spain's traditional music into four categories: (1) collective songs, (2) individual songs, (3) instrumental pieces, and (4) dances. Let us look at each.

Some of the better-known collective styles celebrate May rituals, St. John's or Midsummer Day, weddings, patronal feasts, Christmas, Carnival, Easter, Pentecost. This music is related to the customs we have discussed in Chapters 2 ("Religion") and 3 ("Fiestas"). It may encompass folkdances of obscure ritual origins, like the sword and stick dances that have counterparts in other areas of the Iberian Peninsula, including Portugal.

One important group of collective songs comprises *canciones de ronda* or serenades, always performed by a group of musicians who roam the streets of a village, town or city. Some of the more typical instruments include various members of the guitar and lute family (many without English translation), such as the *guitarrillo* (four-stringed) and the mandolin-like *bandurria* (twelve-stringed), perhaps with the addition of tambourines, castanets and more primitive percussion like pieces of iron and large spoons. The musicians, usually male, perform May tunes, *alboradas* or early-morning wedding songs, Christmas carols and *pasacalles* (literally "passing through the streets") in addition to other styles. Serenade music is played by *tunas*, groups of young men, often college students, who perform romantic songs, usually in honor of women—a sweetheart, a mother or the Virgin Mary. Nowadays their repertory also contains *pasodobles*, waltzes, rumbas and boleros. The origins of this music are often linked to medieval troubadours, goliards and wandering minstrels, but the first *tunas* probably did not appear until the sixteenth century. The musicians are traditionally rewarded with food and drink, which inspires more songs and revelry. For this reason, large wooden forks and spoons make up part of their attire, along with long black capes and colored ribbons that supposedly are gifts from their ladyloves. In the streets and plazas of many Spanish towns, songs of the *tuna* can be heard into the wee hours.

One of the oddest groups of individual songs are *pregones* or street cries, which have survived in Spain longer than in other Western countries. Towns used to have their own *pregonero* or town crier who would make public announcements and hawk commercial wares. Although the profession has largely disappeared, one can still hear remnants of these songs in markets and town squares. Another profession with its own repertory of public cries was that of the *sereno* or night watchman, whose pounding of a wooden club on the sidewalk and plaintive cries announced the watches of the night: "*La una ha da—do y nu—blaa-do!*" (One A.M. and cloudy!), "*Las tres han da-do y se-ree-no!*" (Three A.M. and all clear!). Unfortunately the *serenos* have disappeared in the last two decades.

One of the richest veins of individual song is the lullaby, still very much alive throughout the country. Its many appellations give an idea of its diffusion and variety: *canción de cuna, nana, arrorro, arrolo, añada, berçe, lo kantak, bressol, vou-veri-vou.* The occult origin of the lullaby as an exorcism of evil spirits is still evident in some of the lyrics. What distinguishes Spanish lullabies from others is their realism, even cruelty. The poet and playwright García Lorca noted that most European cradle songs are gentle and monotonous, while those in his country often distill a "sharp sadness." Here is one of the examples he cites:

> Este galapaguito
> no tiene mare,
> lo parió una gitana,
> lo echó a la calle.
> (This little tortoise
> has no mother,
> a gypsy gave birth to him
> and left him on the street.)

As in other cultures, the baby is reminded of the dark forces that lurk outside the home, like the *coco* or bogeyman. The bull and the "Moorish queen" are the most common threats in Andalusia, while in Castile it is the *loba* (she-wolf) or *gitana* (gypsy woman). In Salamanca:

> Por aquella calle a la larga
> hay un gavilán perdío
> que dicen que va a llevarse
> la paloma de su nío.
> (Along that street
> there is a stray sparrowhawk
> who is going to steal
> the dove from her nest.)

Many of these lullabies are of extraordinary beauty in both their words and music.

Worksongs survive in all areas of the Peninsula. They are usually sung by individuals but may extend to several people. They include songs for ploughing, reaping, threshing (probably the most common), gleaning, olive picking, grape harvesting, shepherding, hunting and fishing. Certain varieties, like the Galician *alalá*, are sung to ease hard work or feelings of loneliness. Many trades used to have their own repertory of worksongs: charcoal-men, quarrymen, muleteers, carters, wheelwrights, millers. Most of these styles have disappeared along with their jobs. Among the women's songs, often performed by two or more people, are those of spinners, embroiderers and lace-makers. (For a nice modern example see the end of Pedro Almodóvar's film, *La flor de mi secreto* [The Flower of My Secret, 1995].) In Andalusia and bordering areas, several primitive worksongs, unaccompanied by instruments, may be the most archaic forms of *cante jondo* (deep song) or flamenco: the *toná* and the *martinete*, the latter sung to the rhythm of a blacksmith's hammer. Like so many of the folksongs we have mentioned, they often have stanzas of four octosyllabic lines and may in fact be ancient ballads that were assimilated to traditional Andalusian tunes. We will return to flamenco later in this chapter.

Instrumental music, played alone or to accompany dancing, typically expresses a regional style. Among the most common stringed instruments are the guitar, the lute and their many relatives. In addition to the *guitarrillo* and *bandurria* mentioned earlier, there is the *requinto*, a descendant of the medieval Spanish *vihuela*, an early form of the guitar. The *rabel*, probably of Arabic descent, is a kind of primitive viola. Among the wind instruments, the most widespread seem to be the *dulzaina* and *chirimía*, similar to wooden clarinets or oboes, and the *gaita* or bagpipe with its air bag, drones and melody pipes, characteristic of the two Celtic regions of Spain, Galicia and Asturias. These are quite different from the bagpipes of Great Britain and Ireland, with a unique tone that can be appreciated by listening to jams between pipers from the three countries, not uncommon in the current Celtic revival. Although some people claim that they can distinguish the sound of the Galician and Asturian pipes, to my ears they sound almost identical. Neither is ever accompanied by any instrument other than a small drum, often played by a young boy. In the Basque Country and Navarre, the delicate *txistu*, a kind of reedy flute, is the most representative wind instrument. It has three finger holes for the left hand; the right hand is free for the player to accompany himself on a drum that hangs over his shoulder. An instrument with a venerable history, the *txistu* is mentioned in documents as early as the eighth century A.D. and probably existed much earlier. It can be heard at most ritual celebrations: baptisms, weddings, patronal feasts, burials, processions, religious ceremonies. The musicians, known as *txistularis*, tended to be shepherds, millers, carpenters, cabinetmakers, cobblers and other artisans. Nowadays they can belong to any social class and deservedly command respect as the bearers of an ancient musical culture. Associations of *txistularis* have become important social institutions, serving as models for preserving traditional music in modern times. The plaintive sound of a *txistu* will pull at your heart, even if you are not Basque or Navarrese. (See Photograph 7.)

The final category of traditional music comprises songs to accompany dances, nearly always with instrumental backing. These include typical regional forms, some of them famous beyond the Spanish frontier: the *jota* of Aragón and Navarre; the *fandango* from points north and south; the *bolero* of Andalusia (not to be confused with the Latin American song of the same name); the *seguidilla* of Castile and León, especially from the area of La Mancha, with its popular southern variant, *sevillanas*; the *muiñeira* of Galicia; the *zortzico* of the Basque Country; the *sardana* of Catalonia. We will look at each in turn.

The *jota* is probably the closest thing to a national dance in Spain, although it belongs first and foremost to Aragón, the old kingdom that lies between the Basque provinces and Catalonia. It continues to be very popular in Navarre, where it has its own regional character. To a lesser extent, the *jota* can also be found in parts of Castile and Valencia. In spite of the fact that the *jota* is much more widespread than flamenco in the Peninsula, it has not been exported successfully. It is less tragic or joyous than *cante jondo*, hovering around the middle range of the emotional spectrum rather than the extremes; it sings of courtship, love, devotion to the Virgin or Christ and to the local town or region. The lyrics tend to be moralistic, no match for the wrenching poetry of some flamenco songs. Like so many other traditional forms, the *jota* consists of octosyllabic quatrains, as illustrated by the following examples:

> Me páices por comparanza
> manzanita sanjuanera,
> que ya sabes tú que son
> pequeñicas pero buenas.
> (You remind me
> of a spring apple,
> which you know are small
> but always tasty.)

Or:

> Olivera bien plantada
> siempre parece olivera;

7. Basque or Navarrese musicians with *txistu* (flute) and drums, c. 1920. Photo by Kurt Hielscher. Courtesy of The Hispanic Society of America, New York.

> y una dama bien casada
> siempre parece doncella.
> (A well-planted olive grove
> always looks like what it is;
> and a well-married woman
> always looks like a maiden.)

Nobody knows where or when the *jota* originated. The Aragonese style has quick triple time with harmonic shifts between the dominant and tonic. The principal accompanying instruments are guitars of various shapes and sizes and the *bandurria*. The dance is never solitary, always involving one or more couples, male and female. Although it represents the perennial theme of courtship, the *jota* lacks the erotic power of flamenco: it is athletic and playful, demanding great agility in the feet. Its steps look fast, firm and vigorous. I find it hard to describe the *jota*'s peculiar strident quality and appeal. It does not seem to "travel" or record well; without the presence of singers and dancers, it loses much of its charm. On the spot it can be very enjoyable, creating a warm sense of well-being among performers and audience. Like so many other traditional Spanish dances, it was imitated by nineteenth-century composers in Europe and Spain itself, notably in the *zarzuela* or light opera.

The same could be said of the *fandango*, an elusive form that is even harder to pin down than the *jota*. It too is sung in the inevitable eight-syllable quatrain of the *copla*, but its lyrics have been overwhelmed by the dance for the last two centuries. Crivillé i Bargalló does not exaggerate when he says of the *fandango*: "total uncertainty surrounds both the word and its origins." All we know is that it took root in most regions of the country sometime in the eighteenth century. Its characteristic ternary rhythm apparently started very slow, then became more rapid and energetic. Both the song and dance vary according to the region. The northern styles contrast so markedly with the Andalusian forms—*granadinas*, *malagueñas*, *murcianas* and *fandanguillos*—that they do not seem to belong to the same genre, with more differences than similarities between them.

The *bolero* is another style of traditional Spanish music that is difficult to classify. Like the *fandango*, it developed in the eighteenth century. We do know that it first appeared as a dance in the Andalusian city of Cádiz around 1780. It was performed by either one or two dancers, in triple meter with slow, majestic movements. Chase points out two distinctive features of the *bolero*, the "*paseo*" and the "*bien parado*." The first refers to a sort of promenade that precedes the dance itself:

The dancers merely walk around—but what beauty and fascination there is in the mere walk of a good Spanish dancer! Pride and nobility of bearing are united to the utmost gracefulness of carriage. The greatest of the modern Spanish flamenco dancers, Pastora Imperio, walked in such a way that it was said she had received this gift from God and out of it had made a new art—that of walking.

The second feature of the *bolero*, the *bien parado*, will also help us understand flamenco dance. The term refers to an abrupt pause at the end of a musical phrase, during which the dancer assumes an absolutely still pose, placing one leg slightly forward, bent at the knee and turned outward, the body somewhat twisted and thrown back upon the support of the other leg, while one arm is held arched over the head and the other is crossed in front of the chest. When this figure is skillfully executed, the spectators cry out *Bien parado!*—which means literally "well stopped!" (Chase)

Both distinctive features of the *bolero* could also be applied to other flamenco styles. The fact that they involve mere walking and the cessation of movement, rather than movement itself, gives us a hint of the expressive power of the body. We should end our discussion of the *bolero* by warning the reader that nowadays most Spanish speakers would associate the word not with the venerable genre of traditional music, but with the modern Latin American songs: pieces with extremely romantic and sentimental lyrics whose relation with the classic *bolero* remains unclear. They have become famous throughout Latin America and Spain, not to mention other countries, and belong to the world of popular rather than traditional music. (Good examples can be heard on the sound track of films by Pedro Almodóvar.)

Some musicologists consider the true, classic, Spanish *bolero* to be an offshoot of the *seguidilla*, a dance and song found all over the Peninsula with many regional variants. Its verses have a tripping meter in quatrains of seven- and five-syllable lines, with catchy tunes on the usual topics of courtship and love. The *seguidilla* is often associated with the region of La Mancha in southern New Castile, where it has been performed continuously since the sixteenth century. There it is called a *castellana* or *manchega*, while in Murcia it is known as a *parranda* or *murciana*, in the Canary Islands as a *saltona* ("jumper"), in various parts of Andalusia as a *gitana* ("gypsy"), *playera*, *chamberga*, *torrá* or *sevillanas*, the best-known variety of all. This last style has received international press during the famous annual spring *feria* in Sevilla, where you cannot avoid the dance even if you want to. Although *sevillanas* may be performed a cappella or to the accompaniment of guitar, cello, drums and other percussion instruments, even piano, they usually provide a mere background to a dance involving one or more couples. The dance always represents a stylized relationship between a male and female, in which she always "conquers" him in four stages: courtship, a fight, reconciliation and ultimate bliss. In recent years it has become common to see people of all ages dancing *sevillanas* in any part of the country. Spaniards take group lessons at their local dance studios or recreation centers in much the same way that Americans enroll in ballroom dancing or aerobics classes.

The most typical dance of Galicia is the *muiñeira* (from *muiño*, mill), sung and danced in 6/8 time to the accompaniment of the *gaita gallega*, the region's bagpipe, together with a drum and tambourine. It can be danced either alone or in couples, often six in a circle. Like so many folk dances, it represents courtship: the man shows off his grace and agility in front of the woman, who demurely receives his offering as she keeps her gaze on her partner's feet. The *muiñeira* often has a melancholy tone—especially when it is sung without dancers—and is best heard while you are walking along a street in a Galician town and hear the music coming from a local tavern. Another common folk dance from this region is the *pandeirada* (from *pandeiro*, tambourine), sung by a single voice and a chorus of women. It has a binary rhythm and is accompanied by percussion like seashells and pieces of iron.

The principal dance in the Basque Country is the *aurresku*, a communal form with eight sections, one of which is the famous *zortzico* in 5/8 time. Chase compares this section to the hornpipe, a lively folkdance from the British Isles. The *ezpata-dantza* or sword-dance is also well known in the Basque provinces; one person, Chase says, represents a corpse while the others "express a desire to avenge his death in their choreographic pantomime."

When we think of Catalonia, the *sardana* comes to mind. Throughout the entire Iberian Peninsula there is probably no dance more closely associated with regional identity. In fact it is a symbol of unity among the Catalans, virtually their national hymn. The first mention of the dance dates from the eighteenth century. In its present form the *sardana* is a more recent development both in its music and choreography, created by known artists beginning in the nineteenth century. Although it is strongly rooted in traditional forms, in the strictest sense it cannot be called a folk dance. The *sardana* is always collective and may be performed by any number of people, often ranging from the very young to the very old; others join at will without the slightest ruffling of its fluidity. The dancers form a circle, usually alternating males and females, hold each other's hands above shoulder height and move to one side then to the other, while executing a series of deceptively simple steps. The musical accompaniment is performed by a *cobla*, a small band consisting of a kind of flute and drum (played by a single musician), two pairs of wind instruments resembling the oboe or *dulzaina*, two cornets, two bugles, a double bass and maybe one or two trombones. In contrast to the *jota* of Catalonia's southern and western neighbor, Aragón, the *sardana* never makes a display of virtuosity; rather, according to Chase, it "expresses the satisfaction of communal participation in a traditional pastime." Few sights are more moving in this part of the world than spotting a group of Catalans, arms raised, performing their graceful, lilting dance. While the *sardana* holds center stage, Catalonia has other traditional dances like the *bolanguera* and the *ball rodó*.

By this time it should be clear that the folk dances in northern Spain are usually collective, while those in the south, particularly flamenco, tend to be solitary. There are so many different kinds of folkdances in the Peninsula that this general rule has many exceptions, like the *sevillanas* described above.

Other regional dances include the *danza prima* and *giraldilla* of Asturias, the *rueda* or "wheel dance" of Castile, the *charrada* of León (especially Salamanca), the *son* of Extremadura (unrelated to the better-known Cuban dance), the *mateixa* of Mallorca, the *isa* and *folía* of the Canary Islands.

What are the characteristic rhythms, melodies and harmonies of the abundant traditional music in Spain? What makes it possible to distinguish these songs and dances from those of other European countries? In very general terms we could say that two basic musical styles are at work, which can exist either in isolation or in hybrid form. First, the songs that employ symmetric structure, regular rhythm, the diatonic scale, major or minor modes and harmony can be called syllabic—one note is sung for each syllable of the lyrics. They resemble the folk music of most European countries, from which classical composers probably took their thematic material. This style can be found in all parts of Spain but prevails in the north. Second, the songs that use irregular or free rhythm, asymmetric structure, chromatic elements and non-Western modes can be called melismatic—multiple notes are sung for each syllable of text. This style employs a scale found "in an uninterrupted line from India to the westernmost part of Morocco, all across northern Africa" (Crivillé i Bargalló). It appears in all regions of Spain but dominates in the center and south. Its most characteristic embodiment is the stunningly rich repertory of flamenco but can also be found in other regional styles, notably in worksongs, lullabies and improvisations. With its changing rhythms and microintervals, this music may be too complex to be represented in standard notation. It, and its combination in various degrees with the first kind of music, give folk songs their unique, unmistakable sound, recognizable to all—what has been called "the Spanish idiom" (Chase). National composers like Pablo Sarasate, Isaac Albéniz and Enrique Granados have absorbed this idiom in their creations, as have foreign composers—notably the French—like Georges Bizet, Emmanuel Chabrier, Claude Debussy, and Maurice Ravel.

Beyond technical matters, we might also say that traditional music in Spain often appears to be far more emotive than in northern Europe. The poet Antonio Martínez Sarrión says: "To white Anglo-Saxon Protestants it seems sappy, shameless and in bad taste to reveal the depths of the soul," which is precisely the goal of many Spanish folksingers. He uses Frank Sinatra as an example, contrasting him with a famous Argentine tango singer, whom we could easily substitute with a flamenco *cantaor* without violating the spirit of the comparison. Old Blue Eyes's cool, relaxed delivery would be considered cold and frivolous by Spanish aficionados of *cante jondo* and other forms of traditional music. By way of contrast, the American scholar Timothy Mitchell notes that "a typical first impression of deep song [*cante jondo*] is that it is a combination of singing and weeping," not to say screaming, hiccuping or vomiting. The contrast between Anglo-Saxon restraint and Hispanic effusion may also help us understand some of the different genres discussed below. Emotiveness is another defining element of the Spanish idiom in music.

LA CANCIÓN ESPAÑOLA ("THE SPANISH SONG")

During the final years of the nineteenth century and the first three decades of the twentieth, a sort of musical chaos reigned in the world of popular culture. This was the great period of the *café chantant*, the music hall, *varietés* (related to vaudeville) and the *zarzuela* (see "Zarzuela" section, pp. 140–141). Most of these spectacles disappeared, but out of the confusion emerged a new style of song, usually called the *cuplé* (from French *couplet* or cabaret song). It is a light, short piece that shows some of the characteristic verse forms of traditional Spanish poetry and music, such as the eight-syllable quatrain, like the *copla*. It also draws on the vast repertoire of *zarzuelas* and *tonadillas* (lightweight theatrical songs). The *cuplé* is a hybrid that fuses elements of both musical styles discussed above: while it has a symmetrical form and a refrain—typical of traditional songs in the northern part of the Peninsula—it also makes abundant use of melisma and ornamentation—more common in the southern and central regions. The *cuplé* became so widespread in the first half of the twentieth century that people began to call it the *canción española* (Spanish song) or even the *canción nacional* (national song). It is impossible to understand popular culture in Spain without taking this song into consideration.

While cabaret singers in France and other countries could be male or female, in the Peninsula they were nearly always women; the men worked behind the scenes as composers, arrangers and impresarios. Some of the *cupletistas* acquired immense wealth and fame as both singers and dancers. The invention of the long-play record and radio allowed their music to reach an unheard-of multitude of listeners. Artistes like Raquel Meller, Pastora Imperio, Concha Piquer, Lola Flores and Sara Montiel were as well-known as the best bullfighters, with whom they often married or had liaisons. The stage names of other, less famous singers will give us an idea of their personalities: *Preciosilla* (The Precious Little One), *La Sultanita* (The Little Sultaness), *La Africanita* (The Little African Girl), *La Venus Moderna* (The Modern Venus). Indeed some *cupletistas* were prostitutes as well as singers, especially during the earlier period. In some of the shadier cabarets, they were known as "*señoritas de alterne*" because they alternated singing and dancing with sexual favors. (The term was later extended to prostitutes in general.)

After the devastation of the Spanish Civil War (1936–1939), the *cuplé* was reborn in a much different world. In an effort to exclude foreign influences, the Francoist regime allowed this music to flood the air waves, where censorship ruled for some forty years (see Chapter 8, "Radio and Television"). *Cuplé* lyrics avoided any explicit mention of social or economic problems while offering the listener contagious tunes about love, local color (especially Andalusia) and national virtues:

> Tiene un tesoro mi España
> que nadie puede igualar,
> tiene un tesoro mi España
> con su sol y sus mujeres
> con su vino y su cantar . . .
> ¡Mujeres como las de España
> jamás las he visto yo! . . .
> (My Spain has a treasure
> that nobody can match,
> Spain has a treasure
> with its sun and its women,
> with its wine and songs . . .
> Women like those in Spain
> I have never seen anywhere!)

The patriotic, sentimental, conservative tone of these songs mirrored the ideology of the Franco regime. The portrayal of woman in the *cuplé* also reflected official values: she appeared either as saint or sinner, a selfless victim of masculine deceit or a perfidious femme fatale. Here is how Serge Salaün, the leading authority on this music, describes the role of women: "The two categories of women who dominate in the *cuplé*, the erring prostitute and the unyielding virgin, maintain the traditional Spanish stereotype—girlfriend or slut; the contrast does not allow gradations. They are two sides of the same false social coin, embodied in the singer who alternates between the two caricatures, on the stage and, many times, in her own life."

Foreign musical styles like the bolero, rumba, cha-cha and mambo entered Spain like stowaways through the *cuplé*, which had earlier adopted elements of the cakewalk, the fox-trot, the shimmy and other international dance rhythms during the pre-war period. This flexibility is one of the main reasons for the genre's staying power.

Several scholars, including Salaün, have revindicated *cuplés* in recent years, seeing them as a necessary emotional release during the terrible years of isolation, hunger and repression. "They were songs for survival," says one woman in Basilio Martín Patino's brilliant film, *Canciones para después de una guerra* (Songs for after a War, 1971—see Chapter 7, "Film"). Feminist critics have read *cuplés* and other popular songs of the period as "a form of female cultural resistance" to Francoist gender norms and the material misery inflicted upon women (Helen Graham). One memorable song, "Tatuaje" (Tattoo), has received much attention from cultural gurus like the writer Manuel Vázquez Montalbán and the director Pedro Almodóvar. It relates the story of a woman who seeks a lost sailor-lover whose name is tattooed on her arm. The longings of a whole generation of Spanish women seemed to crystallize in the figure of the tall, blond, foreign sailor.

The *cuplé* helped to form popular consciousness and memory for two decades after the Civil War. While Spaniards may laugh at the absurdity of its lyrics, they cannot forget the contagious melodies or the voices of the singers who filled the air of their youth and adulthood. In one of the most famous of all *cuplés*, a bullfighter falls in love at first sight with a young lady and puts his cape on the ground for her to walk on it. Next thing we know, she attends a corrida in which the same torero is performing. Naturally he is mortally wounded by a bull, falls to the ground "inert," takes a reliquary from his chest and "in his delirium utters this":

> Pisa morena, pisa con garbo,
> que un relicario, que un relicario
> me voy a hacer
> con el trocito de mi capote
> que haya pisado, que haya pisado
> tan lindo pie.
> (Step, dark lady, step with grace,
> because a reliquary, because a reliquary
> I am going to make
> with the little piece of my cape
> that has been trodden, trodden,
> by such a lovely foot.)

The song does not tell us how an unconscious bullfighter manages to make himself heard by the lady in the crowd, nor how he will construct a reliquary from beyond the grave; yet its tune is irresistible. Salaün says of this piece, "El relicario": "I can lament the ineptitude of the lyrics . . . , grind my teeth at the voice and affectations of Raquel Meller [the *cupletista*], and still accept without the slightest guilt that I like this song, that it gives me pleasure, that I know the words by heart and that I can sing it whenever I feel like it . . . Melodrama can produce excellent songs." Some *cuplés* are also redeemed by their humor and ingenious word play, as in "Paca la Peque" (Little Paca), "El perro chico" (The Little Dog) and "Idiomas" (Languages).

With the advent of democracy in Spain, these songs underwent a predictable decline, since they appeared to symbolize the worst qualities of the fallen regime. Yet the *cuplé* made a startling comeback in the 1980s that has endured in the neoconservative atmosphere of Spanish society. The most recent star, Isabel Pantoja, has combined the hallmarks of so many *cupletistas*—a meteoric career with a sensational private life (she was married to the matador Paquirri, killed by a bull). In addition to her many records, tapes and compact discs, she has starred in movies, following the example of the *folklóricas* in the history of Spanish cinema (see Chapter 7, "Film"). Other symptoms of rebirth are numerous books dedicated to the genre, serial articles in popular magazines, programs for radio and television. Almodóvar, the most popular Spanish director in history, has used the song both in his stage appearances and films. Meanwhile its style has continued to adapt to changing times by incorporating elements of jazz and pop music. As Salaün says, "The *cuplé* is a compendium of the contradictions that make up Spanish modernity, harnessing tradition and innovation."

ZARZUELA

The wittiest and most concise definition of the Spanish light opera is Vázquez Montalbán's: "a total music spectacle, spoken and sung, much closer to the popular reality and the real sentimentality of the people than the opera, in which tenors are prevented from asking for a glass of water because they have to do it by singing." Arias from the *zarzuela* are closely related to the *cuplés*, particularly those that have been excerpted from the vast operatic genre, performed and popularized as individual creations. Salaün suggests that many *cuplés* can be defined as *zarzuela* songs in reduced form, without the staging, dramatic plots and large casts. Both forms subscribe to the same ideology, based on a reactionary vision of Spain as the country with the most beautiful women, the most dashing *caballeros*, the best wine, the sunniest climate and in general the best life in the world.

Songs from the *zarzuelas* cannot be classified technically as folk music, since they are written by composers and performed by professionals. Yet some of its songs and dances derive from traditional forms like *jotas*, *fandangos*, *boleros*, *seguidillas*, *sardanas* and *zortzicos*. The settings, the characters and the atmosphere are always decidedly popular.

The *zarzuela* grew out of the lyric theater in the mid-seventeenth century, during the so-called Golden Age of Spanish literature. It was roughly equivalent to the English masque: a spectacle containing lyrics, music and dances. The word *zarzuela*—not to be confused with the fish and shellfish stew of the same name—derived from the Palacio Real de la Zarzuela, just north of Madrid, where entertainments of this kind were first held (and where the royal family now resides). From the beginning they have been an urban form, both in the settings of their librettos and in the public that has formed their audience. They did not acquire their current form until the eighteenth century when the bullfight, flamenco and other expressions of popular Spanish culture also emerged. No sooner had native operetta begun to take root when it was swept off the stage by the tidal wave of Italian opera. While the foreign import flourished among the wealthy, the people continued following the *tonadilla escénica*, a spectacle containing humorous types from everyday life, popular songs and dances. When the Italian fever subsided, the *zarzuela*, with remnants of the *tonadilla*, acquired a permanent hold on the public, as did Jacques Offenbach's French *opérette*. In the nineteenth century alone, no less than 1,500 *zarzuelas* were composed, out of a total of 8,000—most of them deservedly forgotten. The core of the standard repertoire was created by a constellation of talented musicians from the second half of the 1800s: Francisco Barbieri with *Pan y toros* (Bread and Bullfights, 1864) and *El barberillo de Lavapiés* (The Little Barber of Lavapiés, 1874), Federico Chueca with *La Gran Vía* (Main Street, 1886), Tomás Bretón with *La Verbena de la Paloma* (The Feast of Our Lady of the Dove, 1893), Ruperto Chapí with *La Revoltosa* (The Unruly Lass, 1897). The last musician to compose popular *zarzuelas* was Federico Moreno Torroba, who died in 1982.

Like the *cuplé*, Spanish light opera has had a checkered history. After the Civil War it was nurtured by the Franco regime as another expression of picturesque, folkloric Spain. When the country began to come out of its cocoon in the early 1950s, people abandoned the *zarzuela* as a symbol of the past. But in the conservative atmosphere of the 1990s, a dose of nostalgia and, let's face it, the irrepressible catchiness of the tunes, have brought about a small renaissance. As in the case of the *cuplé*, there are more books and television programs about this music than ever before, and performances at the Teatro de la Zarzuela in Madrid are often sold out. While it is difficult to imagine a new generation of Spanish composers returning to the genre, it is equally difficult to imagine night life in Madrid without *zarzuelas* (where the most famous composers have been enshrined in the city's street names and plazas). The fame of Spanish opera singers like Montserrat Caballé, José Carreras, Victoria de los Angeles and Plácido Domingo, who regularly include *zarzuela* arias in their repertory—even on American television—has given a new international exposure to the genre.

POP MUSIC

It would be impossible to write a history of pop music in Spain within the limits of this chapter. For this reason I will restrict myself to the most original expressions of pop music in the last quarter-century, particularly those that are not mere imitations of international movements: music by *cantautores* (singer-songwriters), the Catalan New Song (*la nova cançó*), new flamenco (sometimes called neoflamenco), and several recent trends in rock and other styles.

The changes that shook Spanish society in the 1950s and 1960s, mentioned in many parts of this book, did not spare the music industry. The winds of novelty blew from foreign countries and brought new melodies into the country. With the opening of the borders through commerce and tourism, the Franco regime could no longer keep international music off the air waves. Songs by Frank Sinatra, Connie Francis, Paul Anka, Elvis Presley, Domenico Mondugno, Edith Piaf and Charles Aznavour could be heard on the radio along with *cuplés*, flamenco and *zarzuelas*. Imitating European festivals like Italy's San Remo, a Barcelona radio station organized the first Gran Premio de la Canción (Grand Prize of Song) in 1962. Other, more successful events followed: festivals in Benidorm and Mallorca. It was no coincidence that the location of these festivals became popular venues for tourists, who brought their musical tastes and portable radios on their trips to Spanish beaches. New personalities like Raphael and Julio Iglesias made their reputation along with European stars. These singers enjoyed the support of the general public and the Francoist regime, which considered them as safe, nonpolitical exponents of the new taste.

At the same time, a group of talented young singer-songwriters (*cantautores*) began to make themselves heard. Nearly all of them espoused liberal politics, regional autonomy and opposition to the regime. Just as people spoke of the "new song" in other European countries and Latin America, critics used the term in Catalonia, the Basque Country, Galicia and Castile. Although the majority of the *cantautores* performed their own music and lyrics, some used verses by famous poets like Antonio Machado, Federico García Lorca, Rafael Alberti, Miguel Hernández, Gabriel Celaya and Blas de Otero, all of whom had suffered from Francoist repression (some with their lives). Paco Ibáñez, for example, enjoyed commercial successes with poems by Alberti ("Balada del que nunca fue a Granada"), Hernández ("Andaluces de Jaén") and Otero ("Me queda la palabra"). Raimon used verses by classical Catalan poets like Ausias March or a modern writer like Salvador Espriu. Joan Manuel Serrat devoted two of his best-selling LPs to the poetry of Machado and Hernández. Here was a new phenomenon in Spain: beautiful lyrics set to a new style of international music, energized by an implicit opposition to the regime both by the lyricists and the singer-songwriters.

More than anywhere else in the Peninsula, the new pop style took root in Catalonia, where it was baptized with the name of *nova cançó*. Some of the best *cantautores*, like Raimon and Serrat, were also leading exponents of the new Catalan song. The trend emerged around a group of writers and artists who called themselves "El Setze Jutges" (The Sixteen Judges); the fact that they were actually fewer in number gives an idea of their playful and irreverent attitude. Their aims were to rescue Catalan language and culture from domination by Spanish on the one hand, and on the other to create a musical alternative to commercialized foreign imports, mostly in English. Els Setze Jutges looked to the modern French *chanson* as a model, particularly to singers like Georges Brassens and Léo Ferré, while they also established contacts with Latin American artists who were developing their own *nueva canción* under much graver persecution. This highlights the crucial point that the Catalan movement was marginalized in Spain but not abroad, where it formed part of an international trend in favor of music accessible to all social classes, extolling basic human rights and solidarity among all repressed peoples. Some of the songs that embodied these values were Ovidi Montllor's "Als Compays" (To My Companions), María del Mar Bonet's "Que volen aquesta gent" (What Do These People Want), Serrat's "La, La, La" and

Luís Llach's "L'Estaca" (The Stake). The lyrics of this song will give us an idea of its message: a young man asks his grandfather how people tied to a stake can free themselves, and the older man responds "If I pull hard this way / and you pull hard that / the stake will surely fall / and we will all be free."

The Franco regime did everything possible to repress the exponents of the *nova cançó*: their music was pronounced "*no radiable*" (unfit for radio transmission), they were required to submit a program before each concert, prohibited from singing in Catalan at international festivals, forbidden to appear in certain cities or even banned from the country. But times had changed and the government's actions were in vain, as shown by the ludicrous situation in which concert audiences chanted the same songs that the artists themselves were prohibited from performing.

The movement's success was also the greatest threat to its survival: purists feared that too much popularity would convert it into another trivial expression of the "establishment"—a word they loved to use. When Els Setze Jutges disbanded in the late 1960s, the *nova cançó* in effect died as a collective phenomenon, but individual singers continued performing in the teeth of government repression until after Franco's death in 1975. In the climate of political disenchantment in the 1980s, resistance music waned and only a few of the Catalan *cantautores* managed to survive, assimilating their style to the new times. Serrat sang in Castilian as well as Catalan, while Llach, after being banned from performing in Spain for five years, made a comeback with songs in both languages that dealt with individual feelings more than collective problems—a characteristic of nearly all pop lyrics in the last two decades.

Unlike so many other passing trends, the *nova cançó* did not disappear without leaving a trace. It helped to develop a new awareness among a generation of younger Catalans who would become the leaders of the region in the period of political and cultural revival of the 1980s and 1990s. It helped lay the foundation for the international movement of protest music that flourished in the late 1960s and the 1970s, especially in nations that suffered brutal dictatorships in Spanish America, such as Chile, Uruguay and Argentina. It was also related to the Cuban Nueva Trova, embodied by its most famous singer, Silvio Rodríguez, who had his share of trouble from the establishment in that country. Most of all, the *nova cançó* left behind a repertory of inventive melodies and lyrics that have aged much less than other styles of popular music. For those who attended concerts in Catalonia at the height of the movement, in which thousands of people would light candles, matches and cigarette lighters in the darkness—a fitting symbol of the regime—these songs are simply unforgettable, a part of their lives and their collective memory.

A perceptive reader will notice that I have skirted flamenco until now, mentioning it only in passing. I despair of being able to say anything new about a music that has been analyzed and interpreted to near death, and I am afraid of adding fuel to the perennial stereotype of Spain as an exotic, southern country peopled by passionate guitarists, singers and dancers with castanets. There is an abundant bibliography of very few good and mostly worthless books on the subject. Here I will limit myself to general comments about this controversial music, before attempting to make some sense out of its most recent tendencies.

We have already mentioned flamenco styles in that part of the chapter on traditional music—particularly worksongs like the *toná* and *martinete*. Lullabies can also be sung in the style of *cante jondo* or deep song, the term normally used for the most complex, archaic and authentic forms of flamenco. This music has the flavor of "the Spanish idiom" described by Chase, with its use of irregular rhythm, asymmetric structure, melisma and the chromatic scale. We have seen that this style is found mostly in the southern and central regions of the Peninsula, which are more or less the areas where flamenco developed: Andalusia, parts of Extremadura and New Castile, Murcia, Alicante and Valencia. Modern migration patterns have complicated this geographical distribution, with a general northerly movement creating pockets of Andalusian music in places as distant as Barcelona and Bilbao, not to mention France (home of Tino de Geraldo, José el Francés and the Gipsy Kings, all performers of Spanish origin). In a curious way, the foreign stereotype of flamenco as the "typical" music of all Spain has become partly true in the last twenty years.

There are other signs that flamenco has been adopted by Spaniards from areas beyond Andalusia and its adjoining provinces. When José Monge Cruz, "Camarón de la Isla," the most famous singer of *cante jondo* in the 1980s, died of a drug overdose in 1992, he had become a kind of folk hero, called the "king of flamenco." His death shocked the country in a way that had not been felt since the mortal goring of the matador Paquirri in 1984 (see Chapter 4, "Bulls"). Something similar, if not as unexpected, occurred at the death of the older dancer Antonio in 1996: tens of thousands of fans bade him farewell in a funeral chapel installed in the City Hall of Sevilla, and the national press was full of eulogies.

The comparison between a *cantaor* (singer) or *bailaor* (dancer) and a bullfighter should not be taken lightly: there has always been a kind of symbiosis between the arts of flamenco and *toreo*. It was not by chance that Eugenio Noel, the nineteenth-century crusader against the *corrida*, also broke his lance against flamenco, which he considered to be equally nonproductive, unedifying and plagued by corruption (see Chapter 4). A few years later, the philosopher José Ortega y Gasset spoke of the "vegetative ideal" of Andalusian culture, characterized by an abhorrence of work, hedonism and a culture of leisure, not to mention indolence. The endless imbibing of wine, especially sherry—whose name derives from *Jerez* de la Frontera in southwestern Andalusia—forms a ritual part of this complex. In the more prosperous Spain of the European Union, whisky, gin and vodka have been added. Finally, the ubiquitous presence of gypsies in both flamenco and *toreo* provides further evidence of mutual influence. Ever since the second half of the eighteenth century, when the two arts acquired their modern form, a few select gypsy families have spawned stars in both fields.

Flamenco styles show great diversity in form. Our old friend, the basic eight-syllable line, appears in many combinations, including fragments of the ballad and the *copla*. The language of *cante jondo* is Andalusian Spanish with some vocabulary from *caló* (the gypsy dialect of southern Spain), and a few terms of *germanía* or criminal slang. The lyrics can be visceral; they have been admired and imitated by the best poets in the country.

> Si mi corazón tuviera
> birieritas e cristar,
> te asomaras y lo vieras
> gotas de sangre llorar.
> (If my heart were made
> of little pieces of glass,
> you would look and see it
> crying tears of blood.)

Singers, led by the superb Enrique Morente, now use verses by well-known poets in their songs—following the example of the *nova cançó*—rather than the anonymous lyrics that make up most of the repertory. Sometimes the feeling becomes so intense that the words end abruptly, turning into a cry of anguish—"*ay*"—especially in the most serious forms, like *soleares* and *siguiriyas* (the Andalusian pronunciation of *seguidillas*). Utilizing the technique known as *jipío*, the singer vocalizes on a high tone, similar to a prolonged "*ay*," at the beginning or the end of a musical phrase. These and other passages are so complex that they cannot be transcribed in standard musical notation.

Emotiveness and intensity are the hallmarks of flamenco. The desired vocal quality is not mellifluous, but harsh and grating—what Roland Barthes has called "the body in the voice as it sings." This quality is called "*afillá*" from the nickname of the famous nineteenth-century *cantaor* El Fillo. (Nicknames comprise another link between flamenco and *toreo*.) Singers with forcefulness and depth are said to have "*rajo*" ("splitting" and "tearing"), and if they are really good, "*duende*" ("demon" or "inspiration"). Lorca described this as "a mysterious power which everyone feels but no philosopher can explain." The impact on the listener is called "*pellizco*," literally a "pinching," perhaps comparable to e. e. cummings's definition of good poetry: it makes your hair stand on end. The listener feels an emotional release similar to the one experienced by aficionados at a good *corrida*. Allen Josephs says that the two arts, flamenco and *toreo*, offer "the only true catharsis left in Western culture." Old-timers tell stories about spectators who wept during performances, tore their clothes and squeezed their wineglasses until they shattered.

We have been emphasizing the vocal realm of flamenco until now, but of course it is a composite art form that also involves dance and accompaniment by guitar, as well as complicated snapping of fingers (*pitos*), clapping of palms (*palmadas*) and stamping of heels (*taconeo*). True "*jondos*" scorn castanets, which are employed only in the most frivolous forms, like danceable *alegrías* and *bulerías*.

Perhaps the best way for an American to understand the modern development of flamenco is to compare it to jazz or the blues, with which it shares many features: ties to rural and folk music, blending of influences from various ethnic sources, improvisation, emotiveness and a tragic vision. One of the many modern trends of flamenco is in fact a fusion with jazz, called "jazzmenco." Like the blues, *cante jondo* was considered a lowlife phenomenon before it began to be admired by writers, artists and musicians in the early decades of the twentieth century. Its latest revival began around 1950 and has not abated since. Now there are more recordings, books, concerts and festivals than ever before. The Andalusian Center of Flamenco, run by the regional Council of Culture and the Environment, occupies a lovely old palace in Jerez de la Frontera, with archives, recordings and videotapes for researchers.

Flamenco festivals began to grow like mushrooms in the 1960s and 1970s. Some have been celebrated for more than thirty consecutive years. The locations for 1996 were Sevilla, Caracolá de Lebrija, Mairena de Alcor, Marchena, Morón, Puebla de Cazalla, Córdoba, Puente Genil, Jerez de la Frontera, Los Ogíjares, Jódar, Linares, Pegalajar, Almería, La Unión, Valencia. Festivals are even held in Ceuta (the Spanish enclave in Morocco) and in southern France (Mont de Marsan and Pau). For anybody who wants to hear and see good flamenco, attending a festival is probably the best way to start. Entrée to a private *juerga* or party is not easy to obtain without good contacts or a small fortune, and flamenco clubs (*tablaos*) in the major cities tend to charge high prices for stale talent.

More than any other form of traditional music in Spain, flamenco has shown a remarkable resilience to change. Alone among all the genres studied above, it has thrived in the new world of mass culture. A form like *bulerías*, for example, has absorbed styles as diverse as those of the Spanish *cuplés* and Mexican *rancheras*. One critic says that even the telephone book could be set to *bulerías*. Other international genres have also been blended with Andalusian music, such as rock, salsa, bossa nova, Peruvian, Moroccan and other ethnic songs. Let us look briefly at some of these trends, generally known as neoflamenco, fusion or *mestizaje* (crossbreeding or mixing).

Lionel Hampton made the initial connection between jazz and flamenco in the 1950s, followed by Miles Davis and Gil Evans. The brilliant guitarist Paco de Lucía was the first Spanish artist to mix jazz with Andalusian music in a more or less systematic way: he has recorded with American musicians like Chick Corea, John McLaughlin and Al De Meola, as well as Carlos Santana, Rubem Dantas and other international stars. His sextet, varying in members over the years, has been performing all over the world for almost three decades. More than any other artist, Paco de Lucía has proved that it is possible to remain faithful to flamenco roots while at the same time searching for constant change. The poet Félix Grande, one of the leading writers on *cante jondo*, evokes the guitarist with passionate words that could apply to all of the best new flamenco: "Paco de Lucía is one of the few beings who are both inheritors and inventors of a language; one of those necessary madmen whose respect for his roots and his freedom are equally intense, and who for that very reason deserves the privilege and the curse of opening new paths, gathering into his forge new metal and greater heat for that hot alloy that we call music." Younger guitarists like Tomatito and Rafael Riqueni have followed his example, striding "between two waters" ("Entre dos aguas," title of Paco's first hit): tradition and innovation.

Paco de Lucía's career has alternated from playing solo guitar and accompanying singers or dancers to participating in combos like his sextet. This movement characterizes neoflamenco in general, in which the group has tended to replace the solitary performer, or in which one virtuoso singer or guitarist plays with another, sometimes for no more than a single concert, other times for months or years. The *cantaor* Enrique Morente has been a tireless experimenter, combining his classic, moving voice with styles as diverse as symphonic music and trash-metal rock. The group Ketama is another pioneer. Its members belong to gypsy families from the flamenco demimonde. They have not been afraid to move "between the waters"—in their case between flamenco and rock, pop or salsa. Their concerts fill basketball and soccer stadiums. Ketama has performed all over the world, including Japan and the United States—at the Palladium in New York with Camarón de la Isla and the group El Ultimo de la Fila (The Last One in Line) in 1990. The Gipsy Kings also belong to the crossover genre, variously known as "new flamenco," "flamenco pop," "flamenco rock," "gypsy rock" or "Andalusian rock." Though their monotonous, propulsive style resembles a kind of flamenco Musak, they have evidently satisfied a worldwide demand for a more accessible version of Andalusian song. Another group, Pata Negra (Black Paw), has made more interesting experiments, recording with the blues guitarist B. B. King and doing other blends of flamenco with rock, rumba and tango.

Overshadowing all of these interesting experiments is the "Macarena" phenomenon, the only case of an Andalusian song reaching the top of the international hit parade. A duo from Sevilla, Los Del Río, cut this song in April 1993; it became the summer hit in Spain, then spread to Latin America, Europe and the United States, where it sold some 300,000 copies (one million worldwide). In its numerous remix versions, synthesized percussion accompanies the original guitars in a combination characteristic of flamenco pop. Like the Cuban mambo and cha-cha of the 1950s, or the Brazilian *lambada* of the 1980s, the "Macarena" is both a dance and a vocal style. Its name derives from the famous Virgen de la Macarena of Sevilla; some have even interpreted its lyrics as an elaborate *piropo* or amorous compliment to the Virgin Mary (see Chapter 1, "Languages"). But for most listeners, Macarena is simply the name of a flirtatious young woman who likes dancing and shopping. The piece was still going strong at the 1996 Olympics, where it was performed by the American women's gymnastic team, and penetrated the ultimate terrain of cultural style, the wedding reception, where it was danced along with the conga, the hokeypokey, the alley cat and the electric slide. It could also be heard at office parties, beauty pageants and bar mitzvahs, in restaurants, shopping malls and baseball stadiums. Couples named their baby girls "Macarena." The song itself may not be much weightier than "The Itsy Bitsy Teenie Weenie Yellow Polka Dot Bikini," but it has shown that pop flamenco is capable of reaching an international audience.

Nothing could be more different from the simple-minded, Simon-says "Macarena" than orthodox flamenco dancing. While we have concentrated on singing and instrumental music, we should remember that there is a whole new generation of dancers who have also created new styles. They have mastered the classic genres but engage in experiments as innovative as those of singers and guitarists. The best example is probably Joaquín Cortés, a former member of Spain's National Ballet, who employs the term "flamenco fusion" to describe his choreography, which incorporates classical dance, pop and jazz, with musical accompaniment by bongo drums, violin, flute and double bass. Although Andalusian dancing is solitary almost by definition, his show involves fourteen dancers, five singers and nine musicians in a kind of extravaganza that resembles a Broadway show more than a traditional *tablao*. Cortés's "flamenco fusion" combines traditional dance and music with the high-tech paraphernalia of pop concerts: computers, spotlights, lasers. The critic Clive Barnes, who saw Cortés on the stage of Radio City Music Hall in 1996, wrote that the appeal of his show "is for the mass audiences that would be no more likely to attend an art-dance performance—be it classic or modern dance—than devotees of pop and rock would the Philharmonic."

Flamenco has proven itself to be the most persistent traditional music in Spain, as well as the most innovative. Its quality ranges from the sublime to the trivial. From a few provinces in the south and east of the Peninsula, it has spread to the whole country and the rest of the world with a seemingly endless capacity for change. A music that was once extremely local and regional—almost clannish and private—has become quasi-national and global. The question remains: how far can traditional music stray from its origins without losing its unique identity?

The rock scene may be even more ephemeral in Spain than in other countries. Imitation of American and British fads sometimes makes it hard to judge if a band is Spanish or foreign. In spite of the fact that the two most popular radio networks, Dial and Radiolé, have a Spanish-only policy, many performers continue to use English or French. Dover, for example, is a group that has sold more than 300,000 discs sung in English; critics now speak of "the Dover spin" to refer to the phenomenon. Australian Blonde, whose members are neither light-haired nor Aussies, but dark-complexioned Spaniards, are based in the Asturian city of Gijón, whose busy alternative scene has earned it the nickname "the Seattle of Spain." This band's sound has been described as punk influenced, postgrunge noise-pop.

In rap music, fans tended to prefer American recordings until a few years ago, often without a clue of what the lyrics were about. At the same time, they rejected Spanish bands that used English. Lately the situation has changed somewhat. Groups like Mission Hispana add a political edge to their songs. In order to underline their multicultural message, they perform in Spanish, French and English. Another band, Negu Gorriak (Red Winter), could serve as an example of contemporary music in the minority regions of Spain. These radical rockers from the Basque Country, who support regional independence, play a blend of hardcore, punk, rap, ska and hip-hop.

As long as international companies control the recording industry, foreign music will probably continue to dominate the pop scene. In the mid-1990s, five multinationals controlled some 85 percent of sales. The results can be seen in the hit parades. On *Billboard*'s pop chart for Spain in December 1997, nine of the top ten singles and seven of the top ten albums were foreign—all in English. As in film, radio, television and the press, Spaniards will have to struggle to maintain their independence in an increasingly global electronic culture.

One encouraging trend in recent years is the growth of independent studios and labels. Their biggest success has been a spinoff of Europe's disco-dancing craze during the last decade. The companies, located mostly in Barcelona and points south, have created a kind of Mediterranean dance style in remixes that contain techno-pop, light rave, house and Eurotrance. This music can be heard all summer from dusk to dawn in Spanish, Portuguese, French, Italian and North African discotheques.

One of the few indigenous movements in Spanish rock is related to the dance craze. Called *bakalao*—a pop spelling for "codfish," a staple in Spain for centuries—it denotes a style resembling hip-hop, very loud, mostly instrumental, with few lyrics beyond occasional screams. This sound is the basis of a phenomenon of the 1990s dubbed "*La ruta del bakalao*" (Kodfish Route). The term refers to the road between Madrid and Valencia, which young people drive on weekends, stopping at discos along the way to dance, snort drugs and drink booze. Some never reach Valencia or return to Madrid.

The word of the moment in Spanish pop-rock seems to be *mestizaje*—crossbreeding, blend or fusion. In recent times the "Cuban connection" has been the most fertile. One pioneer has been Santiago Auserón, leader of Spain's most influential pop-rock band of the 1980s, Radio Futura (Radio of the Future). He visited Cuba to study the traditional *son* and now mixes Spanish guitar with Afro-Cuban rhythms. As would be expected, several flamenco artists have also experimented with Cuban sounds. A very different kind of artist, the Galician Carlos Nunez, is a virtuoso of the *gaita* who leads an exciting band with Latin American influences, but which also embraces Irish, Scottish and flamenco elements. Another talented musician from northwestern Spain, Emilio Cao, composes and sings enchanting, original music based on Galician folk influences, other Celtic and classical sounds. There seems to be no end to the possibilities for mixing different musical traditions.

The "crossbreeding" with Latin American rhythms is repeating, on a musical plane, the experience of the Spanish discovery of the Americas; the difference is that now the influences are two-way. Recent contacts between the Peninsula and Northern Africa have reopened another centuries-old cultural bridge. With its place in the European Union finally established, Spain has a unique opportunity to create a dynamic popular music based on its historic relations to the Old and New Worlds.

NOTE

1. See "The Blind Guitarist," "El Ciego de la Guitarra" and "The Blind Singer," in Pierre and Juliet Wilson, *The Life and Complete Works of Francisco Goya* (New York: Reynal, 1971), 48, 86, 370.

RESOURCES

Billboard magazine prints the pop charts in Spain and runs occasional pieces on Spanish popular music (see "Bibliography").

The Centro Andaluz de Flamenco, administered by the Consejo de Cultura y Medio Ambiente of the semiautonomous regional government of Andalusia, has archives, recordings and videotapes available to qualified researchers. The address is Palacio Pemartín, Plaza de San Juan 1, 11403 Jerez de la Frontera, tel. 011-34-956-34 92 65, fax 011-34-956-32 11 27.

The only store dedicated entirely to flamenco is located in downtown Madrid. At El Flamenco Vive (La Unión 4, 28013 Madrid, tel. 011-34-91-547 39 17) you can find almost everything that has been recorded and published on the subject, including musical scores, instruments, videos, books, magazines and so on. A bookstore that specializes in flamenco is Cultura Andaluza (San Pablo, s/n [= no number], 14002 Córdoba, tel. 011-34-957-48 58 66).

Una de Música is the "Hispanic center of music on the web. Lessons, concerts, lyrics and links to the most important musical sites." Its URL is <http://www.musica.org>.

There are many websites on Spanish music. For zarzuela, see <http://www.ciudadfutura.com/madrid>.

On flamenco: <http://www.flamenco-world.com/>. This website allows fans to join a flamenco "cyberclub."

On Spanish pop music in general, see <http://www.ole.es/Paginas/Imagen_y_Sonido/M@usica/>.

BIBLIOGRAPHY

Adorno, Theodor. "On Popular Music." In *Cultural Theory and Popular Culture: A Reader*, edited by John Storey, 202-214. London: Harvester Wheatsheaf, 1994.

Alvar, Manuel. *El romancero en la tradición oral moderna*. Madrid: Gredos, 1972.

Alvarez Caballero, Angel. *El cante flamenco*. Madrid: Alianza, 1994.

Apel, Willi. *Harvard Dictionary of Music*. Cambridge, MA: Harvard University Press, 1969.

Arrebola, Alfredo. *La saeta: el canto hecho oración*. Málaga: Algazara, 1995.

Barce, Ramón, ed. *Actualidad y futuro de la zarzuela*. Madrid: Alpuerto, 1994.

Barnes, Clive. "New Pop Dance and Its Audiences." *Dance Magazine* 70 (December 1996): 130.

Barthes, Roland. *Image—Music—Text*. London: Routledge, 1977.

Billboard. Has a permanent correspondent in Madrid and does occasional pieces on Spanish pop music. See vol. 107, no. 27 (8 July 1995): 40-51, 55; vol. 108, no. 30 (27 July 1996): 1, 60-70, 84.

Blas Vega, José, and Manuel Ríos Ruiz. *Diccionario enciclopédico e ilustrado del flamenco*. 2 vols. Madrid: Cintero, 1988.

Boyle, Catherine. "The Politics of Popular Music: On the Dynamics of New Song." In *Spanish Cultural Studies. An Introduction. The Struggle for Modernity*, edited by Helen Graham and Jo Labanyi, 291-294. Oxford: Oxford University Press, 1995.

Bustamante, Enrique. "The Mass Media: A Problematic Modernization." In *Spanish Cultural Studies. An Introduction. The Struggle for Modernity*, edited by Helen Graham and Jo Labanyi, 356-361. Oxford: Oxford University Press, 1995.

Canciones para después de una guerra (film, 1971). Directed by Basilio Martín Patino, this movie is a good introduction to the popular music and culture of post–Civil War Spain.

Caro Baroja, Julio. *Ensayo sobre la literatura de cordel*. Madrid: Revista de Occidente, 1969.

———. *Romances de ciego (Antología)*. Madrid: Taurus, 1966.

Chase, Gilbert. *The Music of Spain*. 2nd ed. New York: Dover, 1959.

Crivillé i Bargalló, Josep. *El folklore musical*. Vol. 7 of *Historia de la música española*, directed by Pablo López de Osaba. 7 vols. Madrid: Alianza, 1988.

Demófilo. Revista de Cultura Tradicional. Fundación Machado, Sevilla.

Douglass, Carrie B. *Bulls, Bullfighting, and Spanish Identities.* Tucson: University of Arizona Press, 1997.

Estudios de Artes y Costumbres Populares. A journal published by the Universidad Autónoma of Madrid.

Fairley, Jan. "The New Flamenco." *Folk Roots* 14, no. 4 (October 1992): 22–23, 25.

"Flamenco." *El País Semanal*, no. 1032 (7 July 1996): 27–67. An excellent introduction with superb photographs, discography and texts by Angel Alvarez Caballero, José Manuel Gamboa and other well-known authors.

Gamboa, José Manuel, and Pedro Calvo. *Historia-guía del nuevo flamenco.* Madrid: Antonio de Miguel, 1994.

Gammond, Peter. *The Oxford Companion to Popular Music.* Oxford: Oxford University Press, 1991.

García Lorca, Federico. *Deep Song and Other Prose.* Edited and translated by Christopher Maurer. New York: New Directions, 1980.

———. "Las nanas infantiles." In Federico García Lorca, *Prosa*, 141–168. Madrid: Alianza, 1972.

Graham, Helen. "Gender and the State: Women in the 1940s." In *Spanish Cultural Studies. An Introduction. The Struggle for Modernity*, edited by Helen Graham and Jo Labanyi, 182–195. Oxford: Oxford University Press, 1995.

———. "Popular Culture in the 'Years of Hunger.'" In *Spanish Cultural Studies. An Introduction. The Struggle for Modernity*, edited by Helen Graham and Jo Labanyi, 237–245. Oxford: Oxford University Press, 1995.

Grande, Félix. "Almoraima." Record jacket for this album by Paco de Lucía.

———. *García Lorca y el flamenco.* Madrid: Grijalbo Mondadori, 1992.

Herrero, Germán, *De Jerez a Nueva Orleans: Análisis comparativo del flamenco y del jazz.* Granada: Editorial Don Quijote, 1991.

Irles, Gerardo. *¡Sólo para fans! La música ye-ye y pop española de los años 60.* Madrid: Alianza, 1997.

Josephs, Allen. *White Wall of Spain: The Mysteries of Andalusian Culture.* Ames: Iowa State University Press, 1983.

Katz, Israel J. "The Traditional Folk Music of Spain: Explorations and Perspectives." *Yearbook of the International Folk Music Council* 6 (1974): 64–85.

Larkin, Colin, ed. *The Guinness Encyclopedia of Popular Music.* 4 vols. Chester, CT: New England Pub. Associates, 1992.

Ling, Jan. *A History of European Folk Music.* Rochester: University of Rochester Press, 1997.

López Chávarri, Eduardo. *Música popular española.* 2nd ed. Barcelona: Editorial Labor, 1940.

Manuel, Peter. "Andalusian Gypsy and Class Identity in the Contemporary Flamenco Complex." *Ethnomusicology* 33, no. 1 (1989): 47–66.

Marín, Enrique. *Música en nuestro tiempo.* Barcelona: Teorema, 1984.

Martí, Josep. "Folk Music Studies and Ethnomusicology in Spain." *Yearbook for Traditional Music* 29 (1997): 107–140.

Martín Herrero, José Antonio. *Manual de antropología de la música.* Salamanca: Amarú, 1997.

Martínez Sarrión, Antonio. *Cargar la suerte (Diarios 1968–1992).* Madrid: Alfaguara, 1994.

Menéndez Pidal, Ramón. *Romancero hispánico (Hispano-portugués, americano y sefardí).* 2 vols. Madrid: Espasa-Calpe, 1953.

Merino, Luis, ed. *Anuario de la música.* Madrid: Ediciones El País, 1995.

Mitchell, Timothy. *Flamenco Deep Song.* New Haven, CT: Yale University Press, 1994. The best study in English.

Museo Español de Arte Contemporáneo. *Tradición y danza en España*. Madrid: Ministerio de Cultura, 1992.

Navarro García, José Luis, and Miguel Ropero Núñez, eds. *Historia del flamenco*. 4 vols. Sevilla: Editorial Tartessos, 1996. Includes compact discs.

Noel, Eugenio. *Escenas y andanzas de la campaña antiflamenca*. Valencia: F. Sempere, 1914.

Ordovás, Jesús. "Cuarenta años de música popular en España." In *España hoy*, edited by Antonio Ramos Gascón, 2: 351–375. 2 vols. Madrid: Cátedra, 1991.

———. *Historia de la música pop española*. Madrid: Alianza, 1987.

Pohren, Don. *The Art of Flamenco*. Madrid: Musical New Services, 1962. The author is an American guitarist who has lived in Spain for years.

———. *Lives and Legends of Flamenco: A Biographical History*. Madrid: Society of Spanish Studies, 1980.

———. *A Way of Life*. Madrid: Society of Spanish Studies, 1980.

Regidor Arribas, Ramón. *Aquellas zarzuelas*. Madrid: Alianza, 1996.

Retana, Alvaro. *Historia de la canción española*. Madrid: Tesoro, 1967.

Revista de Folklore (Valladolid).

Revista de Musicología. Sociedad Española de Musicología, Madrid.

Rey García, Emilio. *Bibliografía de folklore musical*. Madrid: Sociedad Española de Musicología, 1994.

Román, Manuel. *Memoria de la copla. La canción española de Conchita Piquer a Isabel Pantoja*. Madrid: Alianza, 1993.

Sadie, Stanley. *The New Grove Dictionary of Music*. 6th ed. 20 vols. London: Macmillan, 1980. The author is also the editor of the forthcoming *New Revised Grove Dictionary of Music*.

Salaün, Serge. *El cuplé (1900–1936)*. Madrid: Espasa-Calpe, 1990.

———. "The *Cuplé*: Modernity and Mass Culture." In *Spanish Cultural Studies. An Introduction. The Struggle for Modernity*, edited by Helen Graham and Jo Labanyi, 90-94. Oxford: Oxford University Press, 1995.

Stanton, Edward F. *The Tragic Myth: Lorca and Cante Jondo*. Lexington: University Press of Kentucky, 1978.

Storey, John. "Popular Music." In *Cultural Studies and the Study of Popular Culture: Theories and Methods*, by John Storey, 93-112. Athens: University of Georgia Press, 1996.

Vázquez Montalbán, Manuel. *Cancionero general 1939-71*. 2 vols. Barcelona: Lumen, 1974.

———. *Cien años de canción y music-hall*. Barcelona: Seix Barral, 1974.

White, Julian. "Music and the Limits of Cultural Nationalism." In *Spanish Cultural Studies. An Introduction. The Struggle for Modernity*, edited by Helen Graham and Jo Labanyi, 225-228. Oxford: Oxford University Press, 1995.

Zurita, Marciano. *Historia del género chico*. Madrid: Prensa Popular, 1920.

— Chapter 7 —

Film

In today's world, just as in former times we spoke of the style of French and Italian cinema, now we can speak, and with good reason, of German and Spanish cinema.

—José Luis Aranguren

One man beats another to death with a hock of ham. Most of a feature film is shot in the semidarkness of a monk's cell. A woman makes love to a man and murders him by plunging a long hairpin into his back as she is about to come. A nun masturbates with a crucifix.[1]

These are all examples of Spanish films made in the last twenty years. It would be hard to find a similar group of scenes in movies from any other country. After years of isolation, Spanish cinema is finally being recognized in international markets and festivals. Yet the same industry that has produced brilliant work has turned out too much trash, suffers deadly competition from Hollywood, television and videos, and often seems to be on the verge of financial breakdown. In some ways Spanish cinema has always been hostage: yesterday to Franco and censorship, today to democracy and the free market. "The same dogs with different collars," as the Castilian proverb has it.

We must look at the birth and growth of Spanish cinema in order to understand what it is today. Although it is sometimes hard to distinguish between artistic and commercial movies, between *auteur* and entertainment, I will try to keep my lens focused on those aspects of Spanish film that draw their inspiration from popular culture.

SILENT FILM (1896–1930)

Only six weeks after the Lumière brothers showed the first motion picture in the Grand Café de Paris in late 1895, one of their cameramen projected a movie in the basement of a hotel in downtown Madrid. Soon he would make new films in Spain: *Llegada de los toreros* (Arrival of the Toreros), *Maniobras de la artillería en Vicálvaro* (Artillery Maneuvers in Vicálvaro) and *Salida de los alumnos del Colegio de San Luis de los Franceses* (The Exit of Students from the School of St. Louis). The cameraman had revealed a sure instinct for choosing his subjects—three of the most conservative and powerful institutions in Spanish life: bullfighting, the military and the Church. While early French directors filmed workers leaving factories, Spaniards showed the faithful coming out of Mass. This became the first subgenre in Spanish cinema, one that would hardly change the history of film.

From the beginning Barcelona and Madrid were the centers of moviemaking in the Peninsula. The real founder of Spanish cinema was Fructuoso Gelabert, a Catalan photographer. He was followed by Segundo de Chomón, an almost mythic name in the early days of Spanish film. Chomón worked for a while in Barcelona, was contracted by Pathé in Paris, then returned to Spain where he directed the first movie based on a *zarzuela or light opera. In doing so he created a genre that would have a long history in Spain.

It did not take long for the great nemesis of Spanish film to raise its hydra head: a royal decree of 1913 established the first law of censorship. The state would try to enlist the support of filmmakers to improve its image at home and abroad, especially during the dictatorship of General Primo de Rivera (1923–1930). More than any other Western country, Spain would be plagued by government meddling in movies for most of the twentieth century.

Like other Europeans with a long theatrical tradition, Spaniards tended to see early cinema as an extension of the stage. Endless adaptations of plays filled the screens while actresses and actors went back and forth from the theater to the studio. But movies had already become the most popular form of entertainment: by the eve of World War I there were already 900 motion picture houses in Spain. It has never ceased to be one of the most lucrative markets in Europe.

The gold rush was on. Production firms formed overnight. They filmed one or two pictures then dissolved, to be replaced by new companies. Investment in the cinema was like a roll of the roulette wheel, more of an adventure than a long-term commitment to a growing industry. Competition with Hollywood and other European countries turned fiercer. By the mid-1920s more than 90 percent of screen time was taken up by foreign films.

In 1928 the angry young Spaniard Luis Buñuel, in collaboration with the brilliant Catalan painter Salvador Dalí, shot *Un chien andalou* (Andalusian Dog) in Paris. The film opened with one of the most disturbing sequences in all cinema: a straight razor slits a woman's eyeball and a thin stratus cloud slices the moon. With those images and others purportedly derived from Buñuel's and Dalí's dreams, the true history of Spanish movies was born. Physical violence and the surreal became constants of Buñuel's career for the next half-century. Like *Un chien andalou*, most of his later films would be shot in exile from Spain—in France and Mexico—yet he always drew on his memories of childhood and youth in the Peninsula and remained haunted by obsessions that we find often in Spanish art, like religion, sex and mortality.

In the same year Buñuel and Ernesto Giménez Caballero, director of the magazine *La Gaceta Literaria*, founded the Cineclub Español in Madrid. The writer Guillermo Díaz-Plaja and Josep Palau created the Cineclub Mirador in the other capital of Spanish movies, Barcelona. The involvement of men of letters in the founding of the country's first two film clubs suggests that cinema was still seen as an offshoot of the traditional arts, above all the theater. In fact most writers and intellectuals in Spain would not take the nation's film seriously for almost fifty years.

The introduction of talkies in 1929 coincided with the international economic crisis and the crumbling of Primo de Rivera's regime. The need for sound studios and more complex equipment made conditions even more tenuous for homespun Spanish moviemakers. When *The Jazz Singer* premiered in Madrid, it had to be shown as a silent film because there was not a single theater with a sound system.

The output of feature films plummeted. Confirming the old Spanish resistance to technological change, producers either continued shooting silent movies or sent their films to foreign studios for the addition of a sound track. In Spain the sound revolution was not a gradual transition but a violent rupture that forced a new industry to be born from the ashes of silent film.

THE REPUBLIC (1931–1936)

The creation of the Second Republic caused the first great convulsion of Spanish life in the twentieth century. It overlapped with the economic depression of the 1930s and the polarization of political life in the Western world. Although literature and theater received generous support from the Republican government, cinema remained confined to the ghetto of escapist spectacles.

In 1932 the first sound studio was built in Barcelona, capital of the most industrialized region in the Peninsula. Foreign movies began to be dubbed in Spanish at home rather than abroad. Filmmakers in Madrid and Barcelona finally turned talkies to their advantage by exporting movies to the immense market of Spanish-speaking countries in the New World. The Americans did not take long to get into the action, producing Spanish-language movies on their own sets in Los Angeles and Paris (Paramount).

In this way, by pure chance, the period of the Republic became the one and only golden age of Spanish film in Hollywood. Spanish-language versions of movies by superb directors like Howard Hawks and Raoul Walsh were shot on the heels of their original English versions, before the sets had even been dismantled. Believe it or not, great Hollywood comedians like Buster Keaton, Stan Laurel and Oliver Hardy, Harry Langdon and Charley Chase all made movies in Spanish. Buñuel and other skilled Spanish directors and screenwriters—Enrique Jardiel Poncela, José López Rubio, Gregorio Martínez Sierra, Edgar Neville, Eduardo Ugarte (most of them playwrights)—worked for American studios. In his memoirs Buñuel tells how the Spaniards used to gather for parties at Charlie Chaplin's house. This Hollywood interlude is a mostly forgotten chapter in the history of Spanish cinema.

Meanwhile screens at home were dominated by two types of film that reflected the structure of society. On the one hand the educated public in the cities preferred foreign cinema or cosmopolitan movies made by Spanish filmmakers. On the other hand the illiterate people in the provinces flocked to see native products: still more celluloid versions of *zarzuelas*, now with music; movies featuring priests, monks or nuns; and *españoladas*—one of the most enduring genres of Spanish film. The critic Román Gubern describes it:

The *españolada* . . . originated in France, during the period of Romanticism with works like *Carmen* (1845), by Mérimée, which cultivated the exotic nature and the local color of an underdeveloped part of southern Europe. . . . Spanish filmmakers willingly accepted this colonization and exaltation of a *different* Spain, that is to say an agrarian and underdeveloped Spain dominated by religious superstitions, large feudal estates, hunger, the cult of masculinity and bullfighters.

The *españolada*, usually set in Andalusia, had already been a genre of silent film in Spain. With the invention of sound, folk music—especially flamenco—was added to the other ingredients to make a recipe that would intoxicate audiences for the next sixty years. Any study of film and popular culture in Spain must take the *españolada* into account.

Spanish cinema did not escape censorship even during the five years of the Republic. When Luis Buñuel shot *Las Hurdes* or *Tierra sin pan* (Las Hurdes, or Land Without Bread, 1933), a withering documentary on one of the most backward regions of the Peninsula, the Republican government banned the film because it did not present the progressive image of the country fostered by official propaganda. Although he made movies in Mexico, Buñuel would not direct another film in Spain until 1961.

THE CIVIL WAR (1936-1939)

The number of movie houses in Spain had grown to 3,000; there were now eleven studios in the country, eighteen sound laboratories and more than twenty production companies. With the explosion of the war in July 1936, the film industry would fall apart almost overnight. Both Madrid and Barcelona, always the twin capitals of Spanish cinema, remained in the hands of the legal Republican government. The rebel Nationalists had few facilities in their territory but soon began making movies in the safety of studios located in other fascist countries—Germany, Italy and Portugal.

On both sides the production of feature-length movies declined in favor of documentaries and propaganda. The Republicans tried to follow the model of avant-garde Soviet cinema: a movie like Eisenstein's *Battleship Potemkin* had won more communists than a thousand political speeches. In the last great age of ideology, the Spanish liberals, socialists, communists and anarchists all tried to carry their platforms to the screen. *Aurora de esperanza* (Dawn of Hope, 1937), shot in Barcelona under the auspices of the Anarcho-Syndicalists, may be the best film made by Spaniards on either side during the Civil War. It showed the life of a worker in a large metropolis, anticipating in some ways the neorealist movies of the post–World War II period. For their part the Nationalists had the example of Leni Riefenstahl's magnificent propaganda movies made for the Nazis, *Triumph of the Will* and *Olympia* (1935 and 1936). Although he won the war on the battlefields, Franco lost the campaign to win supporters through film, mainly because he lacked a cohesive ideology. What he did not lack was a severe censorship: the chief of rebel propaganda, the poet Dionisio Ridruejo, was not even allowed to see films made by the enemy.

The most interesting movies of the Spanish Civil War were shot by foreigners on the government side. With the aid of American writers like Ernest Hemingway and John Dos Passos, the Dutch director Joris Ivens made *The Spanish Earth*, one of the most forceful propaganda movies ever filmed. The French novelist André Malraux, who had flown missions for the Republic early in the war, filmed a feature titled *Sierra de Teruel* based on his novel *Man's Hope*. The movie could stand as a symbol of the legal government's fate: after initial shooting in Spain it had to be finished in Paris because Franco's forces were advancing and the Republican cause was already doomed.

FILM UNDER FRANCO (1939-1975)

The Big Sleep in the history of Spanish film began with the victory of General Franco's forces in March 1939. The Great Dictator applied to peacetime the same model of censorship and propaganda he had used during the hostilities. The result was an insipid movie industry that followed the rules of the game imposed from above. Scripts had to be submitted to the censors before shooting.

The world of Spanish film became even more artificial than Hollywood's. Cinema was one of the cornerstones of what has been called the "culture of evasion" in the Francoist period. Subjects like the Civil War, the country's poverty and lack of freedom were taboos violated at the filmmaker's risk.

After 1941 all foreign movies were dubbed, a process that gave the censors the power to rewrite scripts according to their whim. Sometimes the cure was worse than the disease: in John Ford's *Mogambo* (1953), the dubbers turned Grace Kelly and her husband into siblings in order to conceal her affair with Clark Gable, creating an incestuous subplot that was far more shocking than the adultery in the original version. In other movies, as Raymond Carr and Juan Pablo Fusi have said, "sinners were mysteriously devoured by tigers; 'voices off' assured the audience that, contrary to what it had seen on the screen, the criminals did not escape punishment."

The culture of evasion fed on imports. Between 1939 and 1961, 4,277 foreign movies were shown in Madrid, half of them American, compared to 879 Spanish films. The imports also tended to run twice as long as local products. Carr and Fusi have noted: "The culture of evasion was double-edged. If foreign films allowed Spaniards to escape into fantasy, at the same time they could point a painful contrast to the poverty of the forties and fifties. . . . In Spain foreign films . . . undermined the official view of life. Esther Williams and Betty Grable could not be ingested into the official culture or the morals of continence and austerity."

The movie house was the only place where Spaniards could escape fleetingly from the poverty and oppression around them. Spain had more cinema seats per capita than any other European country; it was a nation of movie addicts. The writer Manuel Vázquez Montalbán evokes the lively atmosphere of Spanish theaters: "the neighborhood movie-houses with two flicks and a musical show for two, three, four pesetas. . . . After the clowns came the acrobats who did somersaults; old women dancing flamenco, with varicose veins . . . and curly hair, with an odor of vinegar that you could smell from the sixth row."

Meanwhile the Spanish dream machine created a new genre, the patriotic and historic movie, which attempted to rewrite the past by linking the current regime to the imperial, Catholic Spain of the sixteenth and seventeenth centuries. In later years writers would evoke the torpid atmosphere of the cinemas that showed these modern epics. The novelist and critic Carmen Martín Gaite says, "All you had to do was look at the movie posters, where one saw virile and austere countenances adorned by a stiff collar or a military cap, smiling gypsy women wearing ornamental combs and mantillas, queens on horseback or saccharine bourgeois girls with a well-concealed décolletage, and the adventure of going to the movies was instantly deflated and turned into a kind of compulsory visit to a member of your family."

Popular genres of the prewar period—the *españolada* and the religious drama—were favored by the state because they glossed over the country's festering problems. Producers churned out more films based on *zarzuelas* and folk music. What mattered in those melodramas was not the director or the screenwriter, but the female lead who was at once protagonist, singer and dancer. Names like Conchita Piquer, Nati Mistral, Lola Flores and Carmen Sevilla became as well-known as those of Pastora Imperio and Imperio Argentina in the Republican years. Called "*folklóricas*" in Castilian, these actresses embodied a stereotype of the ideal Spanish woman of the time, sweet but spirited, affectionate but pure, loved by all but surrendering to none, unless it was to the man of her dreams. The writer Terençi Moix called these women "the missionaries of optimism." They sing and dance their way through mechanical plots to the accompaniment of flamenco guitars, heel stomping and castanets. A good study of their movies, a genre that endured from the 1920s to the 1980s, is waiting to be written.

The continuing fascination that Spaniards feel with these popular musicals is shown by more recent works that recreate the world of the *folklóricas*. Basilio Martín Patino's *Canciones para después de una guerra* (Songs for after a War, 1971) is a semi-documentary work on the formation of popular memory after the Civil War, while Jaime Chávarri's *Las cosas del querer* (This Business of Love, 1989) is a nostalgic homage to the world of the female singers of the late 1930s and the 1940s.

In 1947 the government created the Instituto de Investigaciones y Experiencias Cinematográficas (IIEC) in order to train students in the art of filmmaking. In spite of the control exercised over its activities, the Institute stood out as a tiny oasis in the vast desert of Spanish cinema. Its fruits began to appear in the early 1950s. One of the first graduates, Luis García Berlanga, shot *¡Bienvenido, Mr. Marshall!* (Welcome, Mr. Marshall!, 1952), a work that would be one of the milestones in the history of Spanish cinema. The inhabitants of a poor Castilian town dress up as Andalusians in order to impress the Americans and be included in the Marshall Plan. Neither the fictional town nor Spain itself was ever included in the Plan, but the American and Spanish governments were in fact already negotiating a military and economic agreement that would be signed the year after the movie appeared. The promotional materials for the film emphasized the political context (see Photograph 8). *¡Bienvenido,*

8. Hollywood in Spain: Luis García Berlanga, *¡Bienvenido, Mr. Marshall!* (Welcome, Mr. Marshall!), 1952. The promotional materials for the movie included these fake dollar bills, with the actors' faces substituting for the symbols on the reverse side of a greenback. Reproduced courtesy of UNINCI.

Mr. Marshall! demonstrated a process that has characterized every major change in peninsular art: the blending of foreign and domestic influences to create new forms of expression. Combining elements of the *españolada* with others from Italian neorealism and the Hollywood western, Berlanga created an original work that opened a new path for the country's cinema. It was the first "Trojan horse" that a Spanish director managed to slip into the fortress of the Francoist state (Méndez-Leite).

In 1951 the director Cesare Zavattini had participated in an Italian film week in Madrid. The same year José Antonio Nieves Conde came out with a movie that showed the impact of the neorealist movement that was transforming Italian cinema. Unlike previous movies in Spain, *Surcos* (Furrows) dealt with a real social problem, the migration of peasants to the metropolis. Although the work was not intentionally subversive like *¡Bienvenido, Mr. Marshall!*, its use of cinematic images to portray the slums of Madrid also chipped away at the monolithic edifice of Francoist ideology.

In 1953 Juan Antonio Bardem, a classmate of Berlanga's at the IIEC who had written part of the screenplay for *Bienvenido*, joined other left-wingers to found the film journal *Objetivo* (= camera lens). The first issue devoted eighteen pages to Zavattini; the journal became the spokesman for Italian neorealism in Spain. One of the major achievements of *Objetivo* was to help organize and document the First National Conversations on Film, held in the university city of Salamanca in May 1955. The participants, who came from all sides of the political spectrum, denounced Hollywood and established Italian neorealism as the main esthetic model for Spanish film. Bardem read a provocative paper whose lapidary words are often quoted: "After sixty years, Spanish cinema is politically useless, socially false, intellectually vile, artistically nonexistent and industrially crippled."

One of the first fruits of the Conversations on Film was Bardem's own *Muerte de un ciclista* (Death of a Cyclist, 1955). Like his and Berlanga's *¡Bienvenido, Mr. Marshall!*, it fused foreign and native elements to forge a new critical language for Spanish movies. Bardem adapted the conventions of the classic film noir, as well as Italian neorealism, to tell the story of Juan and María José, a bourgeois man and woman who are having an adulterous affair; their car accidentally kills a poor man on a bike. The event leads to a crisis of conscience in Juan about the injustices of the social structure, and eventually to his own murder by María José. The censors insisted that the woman also be punished: after all she was both an adulteress and a murderer. It was one of those fortuitous cases in which government meddling actually improved the finished product. The fatal crash of María José in the final scene—in the same car that had killed both the cyclist and Juan—completes a perfect narrative and ends the film on a note of poetic justice.

Bardem's *Calle Mayor* (Main Street, 1956) continued in the critical vein of *Muerte de un ciclista*. It offered a ferocious view of Spanish provincial life and machismo. The following year it won the Critics Prize at the Venice Film Festival. European critics had begun to notice Spanish movies for the first time since Buñuel's silent films.

In 1960 Buñuel himself returned to Spain to film *Viridiana*, considered by many critics as his best work. The movie renewed many of the director's old obsessions—sex, religion, death, social change—with greater craft and a critical view of Spain emerging from the ruins of the past. *Viridiana* managed to get through the censors more or less unscarred. When it became the first Spanish film to win the Golden Palm at the Cannes Festival in 1961 and was condemned the next day by the Vatican's *L'Osservatore Romano*, Franco banned not only the movie but the very mention of its name. It would not be shown in Spain for seventeen years.

The "spirit of Salamanca" lived on into the 1960s, when it helped to foment the so-called New Spanish Cinema. The name of the movement was not created by its exponents or the critics, but by the government's new general director of cinema. José María García Escudero was a reformed Catholic who had participated in the Salamanca conference; he believed that a more realistic cinema would help Spain improve its image abroad. With his official blessing, a group of younger filmmakers would shoot a series of works that attracted attention from foreign critics, won prizes in international festivals and revealed more cracks in the wall that had sealed off the country from the rest of the world. The New Spanish Cinema coincided to a certain extent with other movements such as the French *Nouvelle Vague*, the new Italian cinema by directors like Federico Fellini and Michelangelo Antonioni, the Brazilian *Cinema Nôvo* and the American underground. It enjoyed a greater freedom of expression, showed a new technical brilliance and dared to present a more critical view of society.

Carlos Saura, like Buñuel a filmmaker from Aragón, had studied at IIEC and debuted with *Los golfos* (Hooligans, 1959), a movie about an aspiring young bullfighter in the slums of Madrid. The work showed influences of Buñuel, the Italian neorealists and American film noir. Six years later Saura would shoot one of the most brilliant works of the New Spanish Cinema, perhaps its most representative film. *La caza* (The Hunt, 1965) told the story of a group of veterans of the Spanish Civil War who hunt for rabbits on a former battlefield. The arid landscape scarred by bombs and memories of the war, the blinding Castilian sun, the tension of the hunt explode with a violence that shocked Spanish and foreign spectators. Marsha Kinder notes that Saura expanded the "language of cinematic violence and its effectiveness for political ends." When he saw *La caza*, the American director Sam Peckinpah reportedly said that it changed his life.

Saura became the most prolific director in Spain, shooting an uninterrupted string of movies both before and after Franco's death. With Bardem and Berlanga, he was the third man of postwar Spanish cinema. Like them he had constant struggles with the censors. "Anything but sex, politics and religion," they told him, as if filmmaking followed the same rules as polite conversation. Yet Saura was able to push all of these subjects to their farthest possible limits under the prevailing conditions, in the meantime becoming the first Spanish director since Buñuel to achieve an international reputation.

Other young filmmakers, most of them in their thirties and alumni of IIEC, shot films that have been associated with the New Spanish Cinema: Miguel Picazo, with *La tía Tula* (Aunt Tula, 1964); Basilio Martín Patino, with *Nueve cartas a Berta* (Nine Letters to Berta, 1965); Manuel Summers, with *El juego de la oca* (The Game of the Goose, 1965). Luis Buñuel returned once more to film *Tristana* (1970), his last movie in Spanish, with an international cast starring Catherine Deneuve and Fernando Rey.

In addition to fomenting the New Spanish Cinema, the government took other measures that were part of the *apertura*, the cultural opening of the 1960s. The rules for censorship were made less fuzzy, the state formalized its system of subventions, and the IIEC was reformed under the new title of Escuela Oficial de Cine (EOC, Official School of Cinematography).

While the New Spanish Cinema was flourishing in the late 1960s, a group of film-makers in Catalonia was shooting a different kind of movie. Directors like Vicente Aranda, Carlos Durán, Jacinto Esteva, Jordi Grau, Joaquín Jordá and Gonzalo Suárez came to be known loosely as the School of Barcelona. In general their films were less dependent on the Madrid-based system of state support and more concerned with style than social content. The group was still another embodiment of the ancient Catalan resistance to Castilian control. It considered the Madrid directors to be provincial; it tended to draw its inspiration from contemporary European cinema. The fact is that the School of Barcelona, if it existed at all, produced some interesting films but never achieved full independence and failed to achieve national or international recognition.

By the early 1970s most Spaniards believed that the New Spanish Cinema had run its course. But during these years of the *dictablanda, or "soft" dictatorship, film-makers made new inroads against the remaining limits of government censorship and won still greater respect abroad. Saura's *La prima Angélica* (Cousin Angelica, 1973) was the first Spanish movie to mock the Falangists openly and to treat the losing side in the Civil War with sympathy. In the same year Víctor Erice came out with his first feature film, *El espíritu de la colmena* (Spirit of the Beehive), one of the most hauntingly beautiful works ever filmed in Spain. It was financed by Elías Querejeta, the producer most frequently associated with the New Spanish Cinema. *El espíritu de la colmena* tells the story of a family in a small Castilian village around 1940. The mother's and father's lives have been sundered by the Civil War; they live in a kind of inner exile. The movie focuses on their younger daughter, who is entranced by the movie *Frankenstein* when it arrives at the makeshift town cinema. In the child's imagination the kind monster becomes confused with a Republican fugitive who is captured and killed by the Fascist authorities. The film shows how an entire generation of Spanish children had a mixed relationship of love and fear for patriarchal figures (Franco-Frankenstein), a combination that caused distorted fantasies of patriotism or rebellion. Using slow, hypnotic movements of the camera and soft, filtered light, the camera creates a visual surface and a desolate atmosphere that fulfill the prophecy of true cinema: they are impossible to describe in words.

On the eve of Franco's death, José Luis Borau, another director from Aragón (like Buñuel and Saura), came out with a work that is considered a turning point in the history of Spanish film as well as one of its top-grossing movies of all time. The release of *Furtivos* (Poachers, 1975) had been delayed for months by the censors; it was the first movie shown in Spain without an official license. A rural drama filmed to perfection, it exposed the violence lurking beneath the peaceful surface of Spanish life.

While artists like Borau, Erice and Saura were making serious works acclaimed at home and abroad, other directors were exploiting the relaxed rules of censorship in order to shoot films with mass appeal. Many of these movies depended on a female star who was also a singer, in the vein of the *folklóricas*—Sara Montiel, Carmen Sevilla, Marisol, Ana Belén. The main interest of these films was that their female leads were not simply the objects of the camera's gaze, like previous cinematic heroines in Spain: they could also be erotic subjects with their own desires, whose sexual needs often drove the action.

The whole country seemed ready to burst out of the corset that had been confining it for almost forty years. When Bertoldo Bertolucci's *Last Tango in Paris* premiered in the southern French city of Perpignan in 1973, 110,000 Spaniards streamed across the border to see it. (The population of Perpignan was 100,000.) Travel agencies organized "cinematographic weekends" in French cities so that curious Spaniards could see the movies that were banned in their own country. Another tactic to avoid censorship was for Spanish directors to film two versions of the same film: a discreet one for domestic consumption and a livelier one for export, with partial nudity and longer, wetter kisses. When the foreign version of one film was shown by mistake in Santiago de Compostela, crowds overflowed the theater and people in the surrounding villages chartered buses to see the movie before the censors realized their mistake.

A whole series of cheap, popular, erotic flicks flooded the local market. Their titles speak for themselves: *Lo verde empieza en los Pirineos* (The Fun Starts on the Other Side of the Pyrenees), *No desearás al vecino del quinto* (Thou Shalt Not Covet the Neighbor on the Fifth Floor), *Mi mujer es muy decente, dentro de lo que cabe* (My Wife Is Very Decent, Up to a Certain Point). This was largely the state of Spanish filmmaking when Franco lay on his deathbed.

TRANSITION AND DEMOCRACY (1975–   )

A Castilian proverb says "When the dog dies, the rabies dies with him." But when Francisco Franco died on 20 November 1975, repression did not vanish overnight. Saura went through still another battle with the censors, this time to have his *Cría cuervos* (Cría, 1975) released. Jaime Chávarri's *El desencanto* (The Disenchantment), a work resembling cinema vérité, was filmed before the Generalissimo's death but not exhibited until the following year. Borau, who had collaborated with Manuel Gutiérrez Aragón in *Furtivos*, codirected *Camada negra* (Black Brood, 1977) with him; it is a satirical portrait of a family of fascist brothers who are choirboys by day and terrorists by night. The film displeased the censors; theaters were threatened with bombings.

Besides these political works, the other novelty of the transition was pornography. Spaniards discovered it like a new toy. It was everywhere—on the newsstands, in the bookstores, theaters, moviehouses. By 1979, 20 out of 105 feature films produced in Spain were pornographic; in 1980, 11 out of 88. I happened to be in the country at the time and went to a lot of movies. At the seedy old Cine Carretas near the Puerta del Sol in Madrid, I remember soft-porno flicks like *La dudosa virilidad de Cristóbal* (Cristóbal's Dubious Virility) and *Bacanal en directo* (Live Orgy). They were far less explicit than European or American films of the time, revealing that in truth little had changed. The female characters are still much more interested in marriage and motherhood than in the new sexual experiences they were supposed to be enjoying. *La dudosa virilidad de Cristóbal* portrays Spanish housewives who go to all extremes to beg, buy or steal a baby. In *Bacanal en directo* the main character is a young woman who attends a wild party in Madrid where she is terrified of losing her virginity, which is her only guarantee for finding a respectable husband with whom she can have children.

After the euphoria that followed Franco's death and the end of political censorship, the period known as the *desencanto, the disenchantment or "crisis" started in Spanish film and society as a whole. (It had been anticipated by Chávarri's film of the same name in 1976.) Production costs spiraled; local movies now had to compete with foreign films that were formerly banned, as well as the usual Hollywood blockbusters; television and videos were taking viewers away from cinemas. The total number of spectators who attended movies sank from 331 million in 1970 to 101 million in 1985. Berlanga observed: "Instead of the political and ideological censorship that we used to have, we are now feeling the effects of what one might call economic censorship."

The state broadcasting corporation, Radio Televisión Española, began to subsidize movies in the period of transition. It provided a new source of funding for filmmakers, granting production costs in exchange for TV rights two years after a movie's release. Spanish cinema has depended on RTE for its survival ever since.

Once the novelty had worn off political and pornographic movies, filmmakers were hard pressed to find subjects worthy of their new freedom. With the enemy dead, Saura turned to popular culture in his flamenco trilogy, *Bodas de Sangre* (Blood Wedding, 1980), *Carmen* (1983) and *El amor brujo* (Love, the Magician, 1986). In other directors the obsessions of the Franco era spilled over into the period of transition and democracy. The Children of Franco continued to make most of the best movies in Spain: in addition to Saura, filmmakers like Erice, Borau, Gutiérrez Aragón and Chávarri, all of whom had grown up during the Civil War or the 1940s. The phrase comes from a statement by Borau in an interview with the American critic Marsha Kinder. She describes the phenomenon:

It refers to that generation of Spanish filmmakers who grew up under the repressive Francoist regime and who first worked with the paternalistic film industry, a condition which led them always to define themselves and their films in opposition to Franco, both before and after his death. Thus, they tended to see themselves as emotionally and politically stunted children who were no longer young; who because of the imposed role as "silent witnesses" to a tragic war that had divided country, family, and self, had never been innocent, and who, because of the oppressive domination of the previous generation, were obsessed with the past and might never be willing to accept responsibility for changing the future. Many of their films are populated with precocious children who are both murderous monsters and poignant victims, and with infantilized adults who are obsessed with distorted visions of the past.

In her brilliant book *Blood Cinema: The Reconstruction of National Identity in Spain*—the most important work on Spanish film in any language—Kinder explores the master themes that recur in the works of the Children of Franco and other directors. They include Oedipal narratives whose main figure tends to be a dominant male, but who may be substituted by a woman who takes on the lost patriarchal power; sacrifice, massacre and other forms of violence that are often related to the struggle against repression and which have a special meaning in the context of Spanish history and culture; exile and diaspora, the legacy of a Civil War that created "two Spains," the "winners" at home and the "losers" abroad who defined themselves in opposition to the Francoist regime, and whose prototype was Luis Buñuel.

Some of the younger Spanish directors have attempted to deny the bugaboos that hound the Children of Franco. They have not always been able to erase a half-century of conflict, oppression and pain from the collective memory.

When the Socialists won the elections of 1982, they named Pilar Miró as director-general of cinema. She was the first filmmaker and the first woman to head the country's film program. A graduate of the EOC, she had been one of the most prominent victims of continued government interventionism after Franco's death: her *El crimen de Cuenca* (The Crime in Cuenca, 1979) was banned but it later turned into a box-office success. Soon after her appointment as director-general of cinema and almost as a reward for the democratic elections, a Spanish film was given an Oscar for the first time: José Luis Garci's well-intentioned but schmaltzy work about a Civil War veteran and poet, *Volver a empezar* (To Begin Again) won the trophy for the best foreign movie.

Miró's appointment signaled the end of censorship but not of favoritism. If Franco had used cinema and television to promote his regime, the Socialists did the same with a much lighter hand and a little more taste. Miró's measures to protect Spanish movies from foreign competition failed and were eventually suspended. In the meantime she had given a push to the careers of several young filmmakers who were going to create a different kind of Spanish cinema for the 1980s and 1990s.

The well-publicized movement known as the *movida, based in Madrid, was connected with the new style. The leading representative of the trend turned out to be a self-taught filmmaker from rural La Mancha named Pedro Almodóvar. Just as Federico Fellini, born in the provinces, made Rome his own city in his films, Almodóvar made Madrid his own. Born in 1949, he belonged to a generation that had not lived through the Civil War, that did not look at the past with either remorse or nostalgia, that did not accept the Socialist blueprint for the future and was simply trying to live in the present with as much intensity as possible. In the period of a few years he went from being an underground director of Super-8 shorts to the most famous Spaniard in the world, a prize-winning director, a celebrity and head of the most successful production company in Spain's history.

Almodóvar draws constantly from popular culture in his movies: advertising, radio, television, music, photonovels, sentimental romances, pornography, previous films from the *españolada* to European cinema and Hollywood. His work has been judged frivolous by many critics. But as Paul Julian Smith says, Almodóvar "not only sees the seriousness in vulgarity; he also sees the vulgarity in seriousness." He laughs at the pieties of both Left and Right. Although he is often cited as the symbol of post-

Franco Spain, his postmodern melodramas blithely avoid the debates on regional autonomy and terrorism that have convulsed the nation in the last twenty years.

Almodóvar's movies have a look and feel that are unmistakable. As the writer G. Cabrera Infante says, they resemble nothing so much as another film by Almodóvar: "That is called, in other spheres of art, style." The Spaniard's style is total, involving all the senses, even nonsense. It has been called kitsch, camp, a "cult of surface," a "cinema of saturation." Color, costume, makeup, mise-en-scène and music may bear as much meaning as narrative and dialogue, which tend to be comical, melodramatic, zany, absurd and outrageous. In *Matador* (1986), for example, the prime Almodóvarian color of red links the two protagonists who will be fatalistically drawn together in love and death: María's exaggerated red lipstick and Diego's red bullfighter's cape. In the film that secured the director's reputation, *Mujeres al borde de un ataque de nervios* (Women on the Verge of a Nervous Breakdown, 1988), the soundtrack of boleros and other romantic music anticipates the happy conclusion of a story that could have ended in murder. In one of his more recent and best works, *La flor de mi secreto* (The Flower of My Secret, 1995), the female lead wears a royal blue coat that heralds the hopeful ending of a plot that is almost cut short by suicide.

Pedro Almodóvar's movies are more disturbing for Anglo-Saxon audiences than for Spaniards, who can see them in a cultural context that has often embraced extremes, obsessions with love and death, surrealism. His protagonists are usually on the fringe—punk-rock musicians, porno queens, a lesbian nun, serial killers, a homosexual filmmaker, a sex-changed actress, a drag artist-judge, a writer of popular romances. Almodóvar defies our sense of hierarchy by placing these characters center-frame in his movies; the marginal becomes the norm. He steadily turns traditional categories upside down and inside out—high and low, serious and comic, male and female, straight and gay or lesbian. His Spain is more feminine than patriarchal, more motherly than machista. Cinematic techniques like crosscutting, fragmentation, staggering of dialogue or effects in scene changes, conflict between soundtrack and image all tend to disorient us, to challenge our sense of order, to make us see the screen and the world in unusual ways. These films embody the schizophrenia of modern Spanish culture.

The Almodóvar phenomenon has cleared the way for other Spanish films abroad. It is as if audiences now expect all Spanish exports to be stylish, erotic and crazy. Films like Fernando Trueba's *Belle Epoque* (1991) and José Juan Bigas Luna's *Jamón, Jamón* (Ham, Ham, 1992) have benefited from the frame of reference offered by Almodóvar's works. At the same time the older generation of Spanish *auteurs* has continued shooting films unaffected by the new vogue: Carlos Saura's *¡Ay, Carmela!* (1990), a brilliant tragicomedy of the Civil War and the year's biggest box-office success; Vicente Aranda's *Amantes* (Lovers, 1990), a powerful treatment of sexual roles and national identity under the dictatorship; Victor Erice's *El sol del membrillo* (The Sun of the Quince Tree, 1992), a documentary that won two prizes at the Cannes film festival and might be the best Spanish film of the decade; Luis G. Berlanga's *Todos a la cárcel* (Everyone to Jail, 1993), a successful comedy based on the political situation at the time.

Another major trend of the democratic period has been the production of movies by Spain's regional governments. Semiautonomous television networks have subsidized films in the País Vasco, Catalonia and other areas. At the same time Spanish producers have participated in more joint ventures with other member states of the European Community. Of forty-two feature films released in the country in 1990, ten were international coproductions. Attempting to recapture the huge Spanish-speaking audience abroad, Radio Televisión Española financed a series of movies shot in Latin America and directed by local filmmakers. Some were flops but others showed the possibilities for cooperation between Spain and its former colonies, like Nicolás Echeverría's *Cabeza de Vaca* (1993) and María Novaro's *Danzón* (1991), both coproductions with Mexico. By 1995, total production had reached fifty-six films, twenty-three of which were international. When Spanish film celebrated its one-hundredth anniversary that year, it was clear that its future would depend, perhaps more than that of any other European cinema, on a special interplay of regional and international forces.

Most filmmakers and critics are gloomy about the situation. Approximately 87 percent of viewers see film chiefly on television, 10 percent on videocassette and less than 3 percent in moviehouses. To sound the alarm about the crisis, in 1992 Spanish filmmakers organized Audiovisual Español 93 in Madrid. Like the famous Salamanca conference in 1955, it considered the social, economic and political aspects of Spanish film and made an even more apocalyptic prophecy for the future. The president of Audiovisual Español 93, the outstanding theorist and critic Román Gubern, made this diagnosis for a dying patient: "Metastasis of television, gangrene from the American enemy and paralysis of the central neuropolitics."

The outgoing Socialist government responded to the crisis by initiating new subsidies for both television and motion picture producers. It remains to be seen whether the Partido Popular (conservatives), elected to power in 1996 on a platform of privatization, will allow these programs to die. Contrary to most predictions, they increased government funding for the movie industry in the first years of their mandate.

In spite of these dire warnings, more Spaniards are going to movies all the time. Box-office admissions have grown steadily, from 69 million in 1988 to 89 million in 1994. The number of movie screens—many of them now multiplex—has grown to nearly 1,800. Clearly the people are more sanguine about cinema than the professionals. The problem is that the movies they see are mostly American (72% in 1994), not Spanish (less than 10%). In spite of screen quotas requiring theaters to show a certain number of Spanish (or European Union) films, the public continues to prefer Yankee blockbusters. Part of the blame must rest on Spain's so-called film industry, whose byzantine web of subsidies, intrigue and corruption squashes most good projects before they reach the production stage.

The media giant PRISA (Productora de Informaciones, S.A.), publisher of Spain's leading newspaper *El País* and owner of radio and TV stations, recently negotiated a deal with producer Andrés Vicente Gómez to make between twenty-four and thirty feature movies. If the plan is carried through, some 135 million dollars will be spent on new films. This will account for almost half of the national production. It remains to be seen if the deal will produce better results than previous efforts.

With a population of less than 40 million, less than Britain, France, Italy or Germany, Spain does not have the demographic base for anything more than a modest movie production. Pressures from TV, video and the marketplace do not show signs of waning. The health of Spanish film will depend on a more enlightened policy in Madrid, vitality in the regional governments, cooperation with other European states and appeal to an international audience, especially in the Spanish-speaking countries of Latin America and in the world's largest movie market, the United States.

NOTE

1. The four examples are from José Juan Bigas Luna's *Jamón, jamón* (Ham, Ham, 1992), Carlos Saura's *La noche oscura* (Dark Night, 1988), Pedro Almodóvar's *Matador* (1986) and Jordi Grau's *Cartas de amor de una monja* (Love Letters of a Nun, 1978).

RESOURCES

The best resource for the study of Spanish film in the United States is the Instituto Cervantes, 122 East 42nd Street, Suite #807, New York, NY 10168; telephone (212) 689–4232, fax (212) 545–8837, e-mail <cervanny@class.org>. For a reasonable annual membership fee, you can borrow videos by mail from a large catalogue of Spanish feature films, documentaries and television programs. The Museum of Modern Art in New York, the Library of Congress in Washington, and the University of California at Los Angeles (UCLA) Film and Television Archive house collections of Spanish cinema, with viewing facilities for researchers. The Museum of Modern Art's Film Study Center and Library has a good collection of print materials. Spanish and other European movies can be rented or purchased from Facets Video, 1517 West Fullerton Avenue, Chicago, IL 60614.

For the student who is able to travel to Spain, the Filmoteca Española has the world's most complete collection of Spanish films and related documents: Carretera de la Villa s/n [= no street number], 28040 Madrid, Spain. The Filmoteca also has its own theater, the Cine Doré, which runs constant film cycles and festivals: Calle Santa Isabel 3, 28012 Madrid. The Center for Cinematic Research FILM-HISTORIA is based at the University of Barcelona. For information, you can write José M. Caparrós-Lera c/o FILM HISTORIA, Centre for Cinematic Research, P.O. Box 12109, 08080 Barcelona, Spain; e-mail <filmhist@trivium.gh.ub.es/>; or Carl J. Mora, Cinema Research and Consulting, 8 Canyon Lane, Cedar Crest, NM 87008; e-mail <cmora@swcp.com>. Every other year the Center holds an international seminar at the University of Barcelona. The next seminar is scheduled for 1999.

Several sites on the World Wide Web can be helpful to students of Spanish film. The most relevant is Cinema Studies at the University of Barcelona: <http://www. swcp.com/~cmora/cine.html/>.

BIBLIOGRAPHY

Amell, Samuel, ed. *Literature, the Arts, and Democracy: Spain in the Eighties*. Toronto: Associated University Presses, 1990.

Aranguren, José Luis. "Prólogo." In *Cine español 1896-1983*, edited by Augusto M. Torres, 9-12. Madrid: Ministerio de Cultura, 1984.

Asenjo, Frutos. *Indice del cine español*. Madrid: JC, 1998.

Bacarisse, Pamela, ed. *Carnal Knowledge: Essays on the Flesh, Sex and Sexuality in Hispanic Letters and Film*. Pittsburgh: Ediciones Tres Ríos, 1991.

Bardem, Juan Antonio. "Informe sobre la situación actual de nuestra cinematografía." *Objetivo*, no. 6 (junio 1955): 7-8.

Besas, Peter. *Behind the Spanish Lens: Spanish Cinema under Fascism and Democracy*. Denver: Arden Press, 1985.

———. "The Financial Structure of Spanish Cinema." In *Refiguring Spain: Cinema/Media/Representation*, edited by Marsha Kinder, 241-259. Durham, NC: Duke University Press, 1997.

Buñuel, Luis. *My Last Sigh*. Translated by Abigail Israel. New York: Vintage Books, 1984.

Cabrera Infante, G. "El indiscreto secreto de Pedro Almodóvar." *La Nación*, Culture Section (10 December 1995): 1-2.

Caparrós Lera, J. M. *El cine español bajo el régimen de Franco (1936-1975)*. Barcelona: Edicions de la Universitat de Barcelona, 1983.

———. *El cine español de la democracia. De la muerte de Franco al "cambio" socialista*. Barcelona: Anthropos, 1992.

Carr, Raymond. *Modern Spain, 1875-1980*. New York: Oxford University Press, 1980.

Carr, Raymond, and Juan Pablo Fusi. *Spain: Dictatorship to Democracy*. 1979. Reprint. London: George Allen & Unwin, 1981.

David, Yasha, ed. *¡Buñuel! La mirada del siglo*. Madrid and Mexico City: Ministerio de Educación y Cultura, Consejo Nacional para la Cultura y las Artes, 1996-1997. Catalogue of the exhibit held at the Museo Nacional Centro de Arte Reina Sofía (Madrid) and the Museo del Palacio de Bellas Artes (Mexico).

D'Lugo, Marvin. *Carlos Saura: The Practice of Seeing*. Princeton, NJ: Princeton University Press, 1991.

Edwards, Gwynne. *The Discreet Art of Luis Buñuel: A Reading of His Films*. London, New York: Marion Boyars, 1985.

Evans, Peter. "Back to the Future: Cinema and Democracy." In *Spanish Cultural Studies. An Introduction. The Struggle for Modernity*, edited by Helen Graham and Jo Labanyi, 326-331. Oxford: Oxford University Press, 1995.

———. "Cifesa: Cinema and Authoritarian Aesthetics." In *Spanish Cultural Studies. An Introduction. The Struggle for Modernity*, edited by Helen Graham and Jo Labanyi, 215-222. Oxford: Oxford University Press, 1995.

———. "Cinema, Memory, and the Unconscious." In *Spanish Cultural Studies. An Introduction. The Struggle for Modernity*, edited by Helen Graham and Jo Labanyi, 304-310. Oxford: Oxford University Press, 1995.

Fiddian, Robert W., and Peter W. Evans. *Challenges to Authority: Fiction and Film in Contemporary Spain*. London: Támesis Books, 1988.

Gasca, Luis. *Un siglo de cine español*. Barcelona: Planeta, 1998.

Grau, Jorge. *El actor y el cine*. Madrid: Rialp, 1962.

Gubern, Román. *Cine español en el exilio, 1936-1939*. Barcelona: Editorial Lumen, 1976.

————. *Melodrama en el cine español (1930-1960)*. Barcelona, 1991.

————. *1936-1939: La guerra de España en la pantalla*. Madrid: Filmoteca Española, 1986.

Higginbotham, Virginia. *Spanish Film under Franco*. Austin: University of Texas Press, 1988.

Hopewell, John. *Out of the Past: Spanish Cinema after Franco*. London: British Film Institute, 1986.

Kinder, Marsha. *Blood Cinema. The Reconstruction of National Identity in Spain*. Berkeley: University of California Press, 1993.

————. "The Children of Franco in the New Spanish Cinema." *Quarterly Review of Film Studies* 8, no. 2 (Spring 1983): 57-76.

————, ed. *Refiguring Spain: Cinema/Media/Representation*. Durham, NC: Duke University Press, 1997.

————, ed. Special issue, "Remapping the Post-Franco Cinema." *Quarterly Review of Film and Video* 13, no. 4 (1991).

Kovács, Katherine S. "Berlanga Life Size: An Interview with Luis García Berlanga." *Quarterly Review of Film Studies* 8, no. 2 (Spring 1983): 7-13.

————, ed. Special issue, "The New Spanish Cinema." *Quarterly Review of Film Studies* 8, no. 2 (Spring 1983).

Llorens, Antonio. *El cine negro español*. Valladolid: Semana de Cine de Valladolid, 1988.

Martín Gaite, Carmen. *Usos amorosos de la postguerra española*. Barcelona: Anagrama, 1987.

Méndez-Leite, Fernando. *Historia del cine español*. 2 vols. Madrid: Rialp, 1965.

Moix, Terença. "El filón del 'Osú.'" *Nuevas Fotogramas* (10 May 1974): n.p.

Mora, Carl J., Jr. Entry on cinema in *Historical Dictionary of Modern Spain, 1700-1988*, edited by Robert Kern and Meredith Dodge, 141-143. Westport, CT: Greenwood Press, 1990.

Morris, Cyril Brian. *This Loving Darkness*. Oxford: Oxford University Press, 1980.

Neroni, Hilary L. "Annotated Bibliography of English-language Works on Spanish Films." In *Refiguring Spain: Cinema/Media/Representation*, edited by Marsha Kinder, 327-346. Durham, NC: Duke University Press, 1997. Extremely useful for students who do not read Spanish.

Pineda Novo, Daniel. *Las folklóricas y el cine*. Huelva: Festival de Cine Iberoamericano, 1991.

Pozo, Santiago. *La industria del cine en España*. Barcelona: Publicacions i Edicions de la Universitat de Barcelona, 1984.

Puente, David. "Turnstiles Show Steady Climb (Growing Number of Multiplex Movie Theaters in Spain)." *Variety* 360, no. 8 (25 September 1995): 78.

Rodríguez Lafuente, Fernando. "Cine español: 1939-1990." In *España hoy*, edited by Antonio Ramos Gascón, 2: 241-279. 2 vols. Madrid: Cátedra, 1991.

Sánchez Vidal, Agustín. *Borau*. Zaragoza: Caja de Ahorros de la Inmaculada, 1990.

————. *El cine de Carlos Saura*. Zaragoza: Caja de Ahorros de la Inmaculada, 1988.

————. *Luis Buñuel: Obra cinematográfica*. Madrid: Ediciones J.C., 1984.

Schwartz, Ronald. *The Great Spanish Films, 1950-1990*. Metuchen, NJ: Scarecrow Press, 1991.

————. *Spanish Film Directors, 1950-1985: 21 Profiles*. Metuchen, NJ: Scarecrow Press, 1986.

Smith, Paul Julian. *Desire Unlimited. The Cinema of Pedro Almodóvar*. New York: Verso, 1994.

————. *Laws of Desire: Questions of Homosexuality in Spanish Writing and Film, 1960-1990*. Oxford: Clarendon Press, 1992.

Torres, Augusto M., ed. *Cine español 1896-1983*. Madrid: Ministerio de Cultura, 1984.

————. *Diccionario del cine español*. Madrid: Espasa-Calpe, 1994.

————. *Diccionario Espasa Cine*. Prologue by Guillermo Cabrera Infante. 2nd ed. Madrid: Espasa Calpe, 1997.

————. "The Film Industry: Under Pressure from the State and Television." In *Spanish Cultural Studies. An Introduction. The Struggle for Modernity*, edited by Helen Graham and Jo Labanyi, 369–373. Oxford: Oxford University Press, 1995.

Vázquez Montalbán, Manuel. *Crónica sentimental de España*. 1971. Reprint. Madrid: Espasa-Calpe, 1986.

Vidal, Nuria. *The Films of Pedro Almodóvar*. Madrid: Ministerio de Cultura, 1988.

Chapter 8

Radio and Television

In Spain, radio is something more than just radio.
—Manuel Vázquez Montalbán

Television has always been the great den of power.
—Juan Felipe Vila San Juan

Both radio and television had slow starts in Spain. By the 1990s the nation had been enjoying a long love affair with radio that was unequalled in Europe; at the same time Spaniards were watching more television than most of their neighbors. Both media are well suited to the Spanish culture of leisure.

RADIO

The philosopher Miguel de Unamuno believed that Spaniards do not like to read, but "to be read to or recited to." Years later the media guru Marshall McLuhan said that Spain is an auditory culture more than a visual one. Perhaps for these reasons, and contrary to popular belief and expectations, radio has survived the competition with TV in Spain—even thrived. It played a unique role in the transition to democracy after Franco's death in 1975. It is now a prosperous industry with a vast audience and a healthy mix of private and public stations. More than half the population listens to the radio every day. It seems to be the most natural form of expression in a country that is one of the final bastions of oral culture in the Western world.

Like sound movies and television years later, radio did not catch on easily in Spain. The first stations began to operate in 1924 but did not reach a large audience until the time of the Civil War (1936–1939). Both factions used it in the "war of the airwaves." On the Nationalist side the nightly broadcasts of General Queipo de Llano from Sevilla were eagerly awaited by his supporters and equally feared by his enemies. "The Marxists are ferocious beasts . . . but we are gentlemen" the general screamed into the microphone. "Señor Companys [head of the Catalan government] deserves to have his throat slit like a pig's." The most famous broadcaster for the Republic was the Communist Dolores Ibarrruri, known as "La Pasionaria," who engaged in her own kind of rhetoric: "In our country there are no acts of vandalism except the ones carried out by the rebel generals. . . . Long live great and prosperous Spain, united to all the democratic peoples of the world! Long live the democratic Republic!" It was the first time radio had been used as a propaganda weapon. Spaniards discovered the new medium because of the war.

The journalist Domingo de Fuenmayor explained what the radio meant to the sympathizers of General Franco who were caught in government-controlled territory and tuned in on Nationalist stations: "Anyone who has not lived in the Red Zone during the Muscovite domination would find it hard to comprehend how our tormented lives were relieved only by listening to the radio. We acted like robots in everything else and our only spiritual activity consisted of placing ourselves in front of the speaker, to free our souls from the surrounding degradation." Of course many similar tales were told by Republican sympathizers who were forced to live in rebel zones.

When the Civil War ended in 1939, the battle of the airwaves continued in a different way. The government confiscated radio stations on the Republican side. The Falange, official party of the Franco state, controlled broadcasting as well as other media. The government would stay "on military alert against all domestic and foreign enemies." The main role of broadcasting was still information and propaganda. It is significant that the word for a military dispatch in Spanish, *el parte*, continued to be used by Spaniards for years after the Civil War to refer to the official news reports on the main government network, Radio Nacional de España (RNE). Every station in the country, public or private, was legally required to broadcast them simultaneously: all over Peninsula the cries of "*¡Viva Franco! ¡Arriba España!*" opened and closed each news report.

Just as in wartime, radio continued to be the best source of news, censored or not. Spaniards with shortwave sets could tune in Radio Andorra, Radio París, Radio Moscú (Moscow), Radio España Independiente and Radio Euzkadi, which transmitted from the Basque country on the French side of the border. Anyone suspected of listening to these subversive stations could be denounced to the authorities.

The great Spanish scholar of Renaissance manuscripts, José Labrador, has told me how his family secretly listened to shortwave broadcasts in their house in the small Castilian town of Cobeta (Guadalajara) in the late 1940s and early 1950s. His parents closed all the windows, then sat down at the *mesa camilla*, a round table covered by a cloth that touched their feet and thus kept in the warmth from the brazier (*brasero*) on the floor, full of hot coals. Since most Spanish houses did not have any other form of heat, the *mesa camilla* was the warmest place in the house, the hearth and center of family life.[1] The Labradors' radio set, bought in Madrid with hard-earned savings, sat in the center of the table. In order to prevent passersby from eavesdropping, the family put a blanket over the set and their heads before tuning in Radio Pirenaica in Andorra, the ancient principality between France and Spain with the only uncensored radio in the Iberian Peninsula.

As Franco gradually nudged the Falange out of power, its influence in broadcasting and publishing waned while the Church filled the vacuum. Under the name of

Radio Popular de España, it established a network of religious stations throughout the country. Spaniards could listen to Mass on Sundays, the daily rosary in the afternoon, and the Angelus every morning, noon, and evening. The Church also had its own news agency (Logos) as well as daily newspapers.

Some private stations competed with the state and Church. The anti-capitalist tendency of the early Francoist regime made it difficult for them to survive. A government order of 1941 stipulated that radio commercials should not encourage "economic gains of a crass nature."

The fifties were the golden age of radio in Spain. It was the medium that expressed Spaniards' dreams and illusions. Lorenzo Díaz, who grew up during the period, has said that radio announcers were more important for young girls and boys than their schoolteachers. The radio set became the central piece of furniture in the house, he goes on, "the magic window in which appeared the colorful world of newscasts, serials, contests, sports shows." Soap operas had the widest audiences. The interminable melodramas of Guillermo Sautier Casaseca and other writers made half the country weep. One of the most successful, *Ama Rosa*, told the story of an upper middle-class boy who was unaware of his humble origins. Some of these serials were so popular that they were printed as books or performed on the stage. Anyone walking the streets of a Spanish town or village of the time remembers the sound of the radio coming from windows and patios, those afternoons when life seemed to come to a halt as neighbors gathered to listen to their favorite soap opera, a bullfight or the soccer *Match of the Day*.

Music was the other great star. The whole nation seemed to follow the Spanish proverb, "*Quien canta, sus males espanta*" (Singing drives our woes away). The sentimental songs popularized above all by radio—*cuplés* (see Chapter 6, "Music") and "typical" Andalusian tunes of love and loss—were part of the culture of evasion that largely ignored the real problems beleaguering the country. Radio, along with movies, was beginning to replace the oral tradition as the main transmitter of popular music. The writer Carmen Martín Gaite, in her beautiful novel *El cuarto de atrás* (The Back Room, 1978), shows that the radio songs of the 1930s and 1940s—along with the sentimental novels and films of the time—often laid bare the deep suffering and bitterness that were ignored by official discourse and offered a source of energy to resist the national conformity. Vázquez Montalbán, author of the first book to demonstrate how the radio helped form popular consciousness in the 1950s, has said, "If they took the radio from me they would take away my memory."

Songs from the New World also invaded the airwaves. Díaz says: "Latin America flooded us with uninterrupted shiploads of sambas, *corridos* [Mexican ballads], rumbas, tangos, mariachis, rancheras" (Mexican country songs). This music did more than all the diplomats to improve understanding between Spain and its former colonies.

If the 1950s was the golden time of radio, the sixties belonged to television. Some of the country's best-known radio personalities switched to TV or worked in both media. The famous announcer Matías Prats, for example, the voice of RNE and the NO-DO newsreels (Noticias y Documentales Españoles), became a popular figure on television while continuing to broadcast on the radio. In more recent years some announcers have even left television partly or completely for the radio, such as well-known talk-show hosts Iñaki Gabilondo and Concha García Campoy. The phenomenon, almost unique to Spain, suggests again the primacy of radio as the oral medium par excellence. The fact that the same government office is in charge of both media—Radio Televisión Española (RTVE)—also leads to more crossovers than in most other countries. Vázquez Montalbán has spoken of the "inevitable coexistence, cohabitation and concubinage" of the two media in Spain.

In the 1960s the government took some measures to protect radio against encroachment from television. The "radio tax" was eliminated and foreigners were allowed to invest in private stations. Pop music, especially American and British, began to compete with traditional Spanish and Latin American songs. With help from the state, a few private networks enjoyed a nearly exclusive oligopoly: Radio Intercontinental, Cadena SER (Sociedad Española de Radiodifusión) and Radio Rato. The sound of the old Spain was beginning to change.

The second golden period of Spanish radio coincided with the death of Franco and the transition to democracy. The government released its stranglehold on communications; the number of private stations multiplied by a factor of four. In 1977 Radio Exterior de España, Spanish foreign radio, began broadcasting around the world in shortwave. It now transmits in Spanish, Catalan, Galician, Basque, Sephardic, English, German, French, Arabic and Russian.

The supreme moment of Spanish radio occurred on 23 February 1981 when an attempted coup d'état nearly overturned the fledgling constitutional monarchy. That evening became known as "the night of the transistors" as Spaniards all over the country huddled around their radios to see if the rebel soldiers would surrender to the legal authorities. Juan Luis Cebrián, publisher of the prestigious newspaper *El País*, has said: "Numerous observers agree that the coup d'état failed precisely because of the King's decisive action and because of the radio. It was a new victory for the transistor." The figures speak for themselves: when Franco died in 1975, there were approximately 7.5 million listeners in Spain; by 1980 the number had risen to 13 million, and on the night of 23 February 1981 it reached a record 17 million. In the twenty years after the dictator's death, the number of radios in the country grew by one-third to more than eleven million. Nowadays almost every Spanish home has one or more sets. Although the number of radios per capita is lower than in many European countries, the audience is larger, a fact explained by the Spanish custom of listening in groups. (By way of contrast, most Americans listen alone.) According to figures from the latest General Media Survey (January–March 1996), a record 20.7 million people, or 56.5 percent of the population above the age of fourteen, tunes in every day.

The period of disenchantment in the early 1980s also affected the radio. The suspense of the attempted coup d'état ("*el 23-F*") could hardly be repeated. But as always in the past, radio managed to find new avenues of expression and survival. The movement of "free radios" began when the Catalan station Onda Lliure (Free Wave) set up a transmitter without government approval. FM stations proliferated and outnumbered AM stations by 1985; now they have nearly three times more listeners. In this time of technical innovation, networks hooked up to satellite systems for transmission.

Another important event in the 1980s was the establishment of radio and television networks in Spain's new autonomous regions—seventeen in all. First the Basques, then the Catalans and Galicians set up their own stations and channels with programs in the local language as well as Castilian. They now cover 70 percent of Spain. Some of these stations have a long and noble tradition: Rádio Associació de Catalunya (RAC) in Barcelona, for example, was created in 1929, shut down by the victorious Nationalists at the end of the Civil War in 1939, and reopened by the autonomous government, the Generalitat, in 1984. It and other vernacular stations reach 20 to 25 percent of the listening audience in the region, compared to 75 to 80 percent in Castilian. Besides competing with Spanish-language stations in their own linguistic areas, the Catalans, like the Basques, Galicians and Valencians must also contend with RNE, Antena 3, Cadena SER, Cadena 13, COPE (Cadena de Ondas Populares), Radio España, Radio Minuto, Radio Rato and all the national networks, public and private. Other autonomous regions broadcast only in Castilian: Onda Madrid, Canal Sur (Andalusia) and Onda Regional de Murcia. Spain also has several thousand local stations that belong to the Coordenadora de Emisoras Municipales. The combination of narrowcasting and broadcasting also characterizes Spanish television and seems to be the dynamic of the future.

Some networks in Spain belong to the same company, such as the powerful PRISA group (Promotora de Informaciones, S.A.), publisher of *El País*. It owns Cadena SER—the biggest private radio network in Europe, Fórmula (Top 40), Radio Minuto and Cadena Dial, which together controlled more than 40 percent of the airwaves in 1991. The government stations (RNE) had 20 percent of the audience at the same time, while the Grupo Godó (Antena 3, Radio 80) had 17 percent and COPE (Convencional, Fórmula) had 13 percent. In other words, these four giants were reaching more than 90 percent of all listeners. A fifth network, Onda Cero, owned 176 stations in 1995. In addition to these groups, powerful Spanish banks have invested heavily in both radio and television in recent years. Multinational groups have also been making inroads. This concentration of capital and influence could be one of the major threats to freedom of information in Spain, as well as in the rest of Europe, not to mention the United States.

One of the unique characteristics of Spanish radio listeners is that more than two-thirds prefer talk and news to music. Today some 15.3 million people listen to information-based shows each day, while the figure for music programs is a mere 7.6 million. Some argue that the popularity of news-talk formats is due to the fact that open political debate is still less than twenty-five years old.

In spite of its problems, radio has a promising future in the Peninsula. Spain probably has more stations per capita than any other country in Europe—about 2,000 public and 1,000 private. Radio seems to nourish the country's vibrant oral culture. Its many addicts, as Vázquez Montalbán says, will always be able to close their eyes, tune their sets and "see what we cannot see."

TELEVISION

Spanish television was born under a dictatorship and lived for its first twenty years with all the restrictions of an authoritarian regime. This has affected its nature right up to the present. As Vila San Juan says, television has always been the "den of power" in Spain.

Closed-circuit telecasts started in the late 1940s. Just as one of the first movies shot in Spain inevitably treated the national spectacle of the *corrida de toros*, the first TV transmission featured a bullfight in Madrid. The results were disastrous and the Spanish people, always ready to criticize the system, soon baptized the new medium as "*telerrisión*" ("laugh-a-vision"). The next closed-circuit telecast, this time from a bullring to the Círculo de Bellas Artes and El Pardo, Franco's palace outside of Madrid, was more successful and gave the green light for the introduction of TV in Spain.

The official inauguration took place on Sunday 28 October 1956 at 6:15 in the afternoon. Franco did not preside over the event, perhaps because he feared another technical disaster, joked some Spaniards. His private chaplain, Monsignor Boulart, offered a Mass in front of the image of St. Clara, the new patron of Spanish television. It was estimated that there were only about four hundred TV sets in Madrid.

In its early days television was an extension of radio in the Peninsula. As we have seen, announcers went from the old medium to the new, then back and forth. News and weather reports were the only programs that originated in the studio.

In 1958 the owner of a television could only watch the set between 7 P.M. and 12:18 A.M. The viewer could see one news program, one weather report and a single feature-length movie. Every Monday evening and during the entire summer there was a blackout, because the privileged classes that owned TV sets were on vacation in the mountains or at the beach.

From the beginning the Francoist state used television to consolidate its power. As a total government monopoly, TVE (Televisión Española), the television company within RTVE, was even more tightly controlled than radio, the press, publishing and cinema, which at least benefitted from private investment. For this reason television was the only medium that did not profit from the regime's various "openings." The image of Spanish life transmitted by TV showed an idyllic country in which the Caudillo, General Franco, perpetually dedicated new factories and schools while the people lived in peace and harmony. The government was not fooling anyone: this image appeared false not only when compared with foreign newspapers, but even with the Spanish press. On 20 March 1968 the Barcelona daily *La Vanguardia*, one of the most widely circulated in the country, published a comparison between the news of that day as reported on TV and in the press. The study concluded that television showed Spain as a perfect land untouched by political crises, economic problems and strikes. The news service of TVE ignored completely the reports of inflation, a strike in the city of Badajoz, student demonstrations, the conviction of various Communists by the Tribunal of Public Order in Madrid, demands by workers for open unions, and daring sermons by several priests that were all reported in the press, however summarily.

Spanish TV transmitted the same stereotyped image of the country that appeared in many films produced at the time: in a word, *españoladas. Several versions of the classic Don Juan legend were produced, as well as programs featuring flamenco music and *zarzuelas. The old Roman philosophy of "bread and circus" seemed to apply to the "imperial television" under Franco (Díaz). The regime cagily transmitted important soccer matches at crucial moments in order to distract public attention and keep Spaniards at home instead of in the streets, where they might have caused trouble.

Spanish TV was the supreme instrument of the culture of evasion. Its early development coincided with the country's economic and industrial explosion. If only 1 percent of Spanish homes had a TV set in 1960, 90 percent owned one by 1970. Television became both the symbol and the vehicle of the new society of consumerism.

One of the most characteristic initiatives of the government were the "teleclubs" (television clubs) established in underdeveloped parts of the country, such as rural areas and the poor suburbs of big cities. The idea was to make the message of TVE available to people who could not afford to buy a television of their own. The first teleclub was inaugurated in the small town of Matilla la Seca (Zamora) in 1964. Ten years later there were more than 4,000 throughout the Peninsula. Although the idea looked fine on paper, its execution left a lot to be desired. Vázquez Montalbán thought the teleclubs were "soulless." The historian Ricardo de la Cierva, who administered them in his position as director-general of Popular Culture, has said: "When I began my trips to the towns that had teleclubs, I was disconsolate. They were simple *tertulias of old people seated in front of a TV set. . . . A true revitalization of the teleclubs would require a colossal budget . . . and I had only four million pesetas to promote teleclubs in the whole country."

TVE came out with a new program to promote these locales. Called Teleclub, it was directed to the rural areas of the country where most of the clubs were established. Vázquez Montalbán, with his typical ironic style, summarized the program's ideology, which coincided exactly with that of the dictatorship: "the virtues of the country over those of the city, family ties over migration [to the city], respect for the tele-established norms of behavior, the participation of peasants in the country's growth, the necessity for maintaining the nucleus of traditional religious and cultural values." While it espoused these values, the regime was enacting an economic policy based on industrialization, tourism and speculation, which inevitably caused depression in the countryside, expansion in the cities and a breakdown of the values espoused by official propaganda.

While the government failed in its attempts, the owners of thousands of bars and cafés installed TV sets in their locales, which became the country's real teleclubs. Just as many Spaniards share the newspaper, they watch the same television set in local bars and cafés. Francisco Javier Rodríguez says: "In our bars, the TV plays while the clients, often indifferent to the multicolored message on the screen, feel themselves irresistibly attracted by the background noise it produces, which allows them to fuse the 'official' world with their own world of wines and pitted olives, paper napkins and greasy mussel shells scattered on the floor."

Spanish TV remained an impoverished medium until the time of Franco's death. Entertainment dominated the small screen—quiz shows, soap operas (many imported from Spanish America), sports, situation comedies and movies (most of them American). In comparison to the national channels of other European countries, TVE devoted far less screen time to news and education. Moreover these programs were often relegated to unpopular hours. In 1973 only 4 percent of screen time was dedicated to educational programs, compared to 22 percent on BBC-1 and 27 percent on the German ORTF-1. During the whole year only eleven hours were devoted to educational subjects, compared to 377 hours of sports.

The same year Vázquez Montalbán came out with a book that denounced the mediocrity of Spanish TV: *El libro gris de la televisión española* (The Gray Book of Spanish Television). It was a work that would have been impossible to publish before the liberalization of censorship laws during the *dictablanda*. Searching for a modern metaphor that would express the relationship between television viewers and their society, the author hit upon the French geese who are force-fed to produce foie gras: "With the membranes of their feet stuck in the soil of their cage-den-rent-controlled apartment, soups, truths, stories, concentrated news items are stuffed down the indiscriminate funnel of their throats." Vázquez Montalbán saw Spanish spectators of the Franco period as a "silenced majority" who entered "the gas chamber of the press, radio and TV. It is a poisoning that lasts a lifetime." As a total government monopoly, television was the "legitimate daughter" of the authoritarian regime, unmediated by private initiative as in the press. TVE "is power, pure power." Since it requires less effort to assimilate than either radio or newspapers, it is also the most dangerous medium and must therefore be controlled at all costs by the power apparatus. Even the best programs produced by TVE, such as the popular series *Crónica de un pueblo* (Chronicle of a Small Town, 1971–1973) inevitably revealed a false, idealized image of Spain that could have been "directed by . . . El Cid in the Middle Ages."

There were few bright spots on Spanish TV during the Franco years. In spite of Vázquez Montalbán's criticism, Antonio Mercero's *Crónica de un pueblo* represented something new in Spain. As the director said, "for the first time we dealt with the rural world and people said "Coño!" (literally "Cunt!", the most common Spanish expletive). Mercero also directed *La cabina* (The Telephone Booth, 1972), the most award-winning Spanish production in the history of TVE. It tells the story of a man who enters a phone booth to make a call in a large city but cannot get out; he will eventually die there, along with other citizens in the same plight. The work seemed to be an allegory for the isolation of people in a country where communication was inhibited by repression and censorship.

José María Pemán, a right-wing poet, playwright and novelist, wrote the script for an earlier series called *Séneca* (1968–1970). The name referred of course to the Roman philosopher from Córdoba, whose Stoic philosophy has been assimilated by certain Spanish thinkers. Pemán created the character of a modern-day Séneca who spouted obvious truths through witty maxims and proverbs. The program struck a popular chord and reminded Spaniards of the Andalusian folk dramas of the Alvarez

Quintero brothers. When Antonio Martelo, the actor who played the role of Séneca died in a car accident, many people went into mourning and Pemán decided to discontinue the show. Twenty-six years later, in March 1996, a remake premiered on Canal Sur, the Andalusian regional channel, with 140 actors and 600 extras. Among others it featured Imperio Argentina, the celebrated *folklórica* from Spanish films of the 1930s and 1940s. Old stereotypes die hard in Spain.

Some of the best and most popular programs of the Franco years were written, directed and narrated by the biologist Félix Rodríguez de la Fuente, "the animals' friend." His series *El hombre y la tierra* (Man and Earth, 1974–1977) was the most successful series in the history of TVE; both viewers and critics also admired his *Fauna* and *Planeta azul* (Blue Planet). Some of his programs were televised in as many as fifty countries. Rodríguez de la Fuente died in a car crash in 1980 while filming a documentary on dogsledding in Alaska.

The backwardness of Spanish TV was demonstrated by the death of Generalissimo Franco in 1975. Spain had to ask German technicians for help in order to cover the spectacular funeral rites. But Francoism did not die with the dictator. Censorship would continue for several years. The importance of television in Spanish life was revealed by the fact that the leading politician of the transition to democracy, Adolfo Suárez, had risen to power through his position as director-general of radio and television from 1969 to 1973. Beginning with Suárez, a new kind of leader would be spawned on all sides of the political spectrum: young, telegenic men (rarely women) who used the power of TV to reach the electorate.

The quality of programming improved slightly during the transition and the early years of democracy, especially under the leadership of the well-known film director Pilar Miró. She was an example of a different breed of Spaniard who had begun their careers in the new medium. Miró had worked her way up from the bottom of TVE to become the director of some two hundred programs, as well as six feature-length films, three theater productions, an opera, several video movies and publicity spots. "Television is the story of my life," she said. After being director-general of cinema from 1982 to 1985, she took over the position in charge of radio and television. She never lost sight of the connections between film and TV. The government gave subventions for nearly all of the best films of the period, including some adventurous works by directors like Pedro Almodóvar. Unfortunately Pilar Miró is more remembered for an alleged scandal involving the purchase of clothes with official funds and was not cleared of charges until 1992.

Antonio Mercero, one of the most talented directors under the dictatorship, continued turning out popular programs during the transition and democracy. His series *Verano azul* (1979–1980) told the story of a group of teenagers on vacation at a beach resort in southern Spain. Over the course of the summer they undergo various rites of passage related to friendship, sex, parents, nature and death. The program was a sensational success; every Sunday afternoon at four o'clock, "the country was paralyzed. . . . All Spain was in front of a TV set" (Díaz). Mercero won international prizes in Prague and Munich and his program was sold in France, Argentina, Costa Rica and other countries. With the exception of Rodríguez de la Fuente's nature series, *Verano azul* has been the most lucrative show produced by Spanish television. As we will see later, Mercero continued directing successful programs in the era of private channels.

When TVE moved to its present location in a complex capped by a kind of space needle called Torrespaña ("Spaintower"), people soon baptized the structure "El Piruli," a pointed lollipop beloved by Spanish children (see Photograph 9). The nickname reveals the amused scepticism that many Spaniards feel for the nationalized television industry. In 1997, many channels moved their studios and offices to the Ciudad de la Imagen (Image City), located in the outskirts of Madrid.

The most important change of the 1980s was the creation of television networks in Spain's new autonomous regions. The first was in the Basque Country (ETB), which began transmitting before receiving permission from the central government. It was followed by Catalonia a few months later, then by Galicia, Valencia, Murcia and Madrid itself. Like the two central public channels (TVE 1 and TVE 2), the autonomous networks are public in so far as they are controlled by government; yet they also finance themselves with commercials. By 1990 there were thirteen public channels in the country and the number was growing.

Some of the autonomous stations transmit in their own languages. In Catalonia, TV 3 and Canal 33 use only Catalan, as does Canal Nou (9) in the Valencian region. In the Basque Country, ETB 1 broadcasts in Euskara (Basque) while ETB 2 has programming in Castilian. In Galicia, TVG transmits only in Galician. The other autonomous channels, such as Telemadrid and Canal Sur in Andalusia, always use Castilian. While several other European countries have public networks that broadcast in regional languages, only the United Kingdom (Wales) and Spain have public channels that are controlled by local governments rather than the state. The Basque, Catalan and Galician regions may be nations without states, but they have their own TV networks.

Programming on the autonomous channels differs from the main government networks (TVE 1 and TVE 2). In general it reflects the ideals expressed in the Spanish Constitution and the Statutes of Autonomy: promotion of local languages and cultures and respect for political, cultural, linguistic, religious and social pluralism. There is special emphasis on local news and culture and more educational programming for children. TV 3 in Catalonia, for example, dedicates 14 percent of screen time to cultural matters, while ETB 1 in the Basque Country devotes 17 percent to children's shows; compare this to 4 percent for cultural programming and 5 percent for children on TVE 1. On the other hand, the regional channels depend on popular foreign programs to keep their ratings high. On the opening night of TV-3 in Catalonia, for example, the hit episode of *Dallas*, "Who Shot JR?", was telecast in a dubbed Catalan version.

The autonomous networks capture about 15 percent of the television audience in Spain—less than TVE 1 but usually more than TVE 2. TV 3, one of the two Catalan networks, had more than 20 percent of its region's audience in 1994 (some say 40%); Telemadrid, Canal Sur and Canal Nou (Valencia) had a share of about 18 percent each; TVG captured 16 percent of the Galician audience while ETB 2 (Castilian) reached 10 percent of viewers in the Basque Country, compared to 5 percent for ETB 1 (Euskara).

9. Torrespaña ("Spaintower") c. 1995. Headquarters of Televisión Española (Spanish National Television), Madrid, popularly known as *El Piruli* (The Lollipop). Reproduced courtesy of *Fototeca de TVE*.

The regional networks belong to an organization called FORTA (Federación de Organismos de Radio Televisión Autonómicas). It enables them to present a common front in negotiations with the national government and with European Union countries for advertising and the sale, purchase and exchange of programs. FORTA coproduces shows and films and also retransmits soccer matches of the popular Liga Española de Fútbol (Spanish Football League).

The other key change in Spanish television has been privatization. The Socialist government fought long and hard to prevent competition with national networks. In January 1988 a pirate station called Canal 10 began to telecast from London. It did not last long, but it forced Spain to yield to the inevitable process of change that was already transforming communications in the rest of Europe. In March of the same year the Law of Private Television was passed, and in 1990 the first commercial channel began to transmit. Soon afterwards Canal Plus introduced pay TV in Spain. Within four years it had 850,000 subscribers, making it the third-largest pay-for-view channel in Europe. The free private stations are Antena 3 and Tele 5. They are entertainment channels with a variety of programming for children and adults, a combination of foreign and Spanish shows, movies, contests, sports.

Privatization also opened the door to foreign investment. The state imposed a ceiling on ownership of shares at 25 percent by any person or company but did not enforce the regulation. As the Spanish proverb says, *Hecha la ley, hecha la trampa*: "A new law is broken as quickly as it is passed." The French Canal Plus has big holdings in the Spanish channel of the same name. News Corporation (Murdoch) owns shares in Antena 3, while three-quarters of Tele 5 belongs to the Italian communications mogul and politician Berlusconi (Fininvest), Kirch and the Bank of Luxembourg.

Privatization and regional television have caused radical changes. In eight years Spain went from two public stations to thirteen; from no private channels to three that are payless and about a dozen for subscribers; from 6,000 hours of programming to 65,000. One of the results of this phenomenal growth of TV is that fewer people go to the movies or rent films: the number of video outlets dropped by 35 percent in three years.

The explosion of channels in Spain has created the same results as in other countries. The major networks now control a smaller share of the audience, which is more fragmented. While the most popular program in 1989 reached 41 percent of viewers, by 1993 the share had fallen to 23 percent. The ten most popular shows had an audience of 107 million in 1989, a figure that dropped almost by half in four years. Most viewers now use remote controls and "zapping" has become a Spanish word with its variant *zapeo*.

The influence of Anglo-Saxon television is revealed by the fact that much of the vocabulary for programming and marketing has been taken lock, stock and barrel from English: "prime-time," "ranking," "share," "sitcom," "talk-show" and so on. It is curious to note that prime time in Spain is not the same as in the United States and other countries: the people's late-night habits mean that most viewers do not sit down to watch their sets until about 9 o'clock. The time with the maximum number of

viewers extends to midnight. Featured movies often begin at 10 P.M. The last newscasts on most channels are at 1 A.M. or even later. Another custom that distinguishes
Spaniards is the popularity of the "*sobremesa*" or after-lunch hour for watching TV,
since many adults and schoolchildren still return home for the big midday meal.
There is often an afternoon newscast at 3 P.M. Then television, like business and
every other activity in Spain, has to compete with the national passion for the siesta,
especially in the hot summer months. Another national passion, soccer, accounts for
the highest ratings on Spanish television. In 1994, for example, the twenty most-
watched events were all soccer matches.

Here is a table of television audience in Spain in October 1994, made available by
the website "Sí, Spain" (by thousands of viewers):

TVE 1	16,353
Antena 3 (private)	15,013
Tele 5 (private)	9,980
TVE 2	5,996
TV 3 (Catalonia)	2,692
Canal Sur (Andalusia)	2,133
Canal Plus (private)	2,000
Telemadrid	1,349
Canal Nou (Valencia)	1,170
TVG (Galicia)	736
ETB 2 (Basque Country)	695
Canal 33 (Catalonia)	555
Foreign channels	230
Municipal channels	211
ETB 1 (Basque Country)	185

(The figures refer to a total of 32,000,000 viewers over 14 years of age who live in
Spanish territory.)

The private channels have stolen some of TVE's best talent and produced popular
shows in the new era of competition. Antonio Mercero has enjoyed still another success with his latest program, *Farmacia de guardia* (All-Night Pharmacy, 1991–),
shown on Antena 3. With his sure instinct for finding situations that strike a popular chord, he has taken the institution of the all-night pharmacy—there is one in every
Spanish town—to show a microcosm of contemporary society. The adventures of the
Cano family, their assistant, friends and clients make up a lively mosaic of Spain in
the 1990s.

In spite of some good programs, privatization has also produced an abundance of
what Spaniards call "*telebasura*" (teletrash). "Reality shows" have become the new
sensation on nearly all channels. Some of the most popular are *¿Quién sabe dónde?*
(Who Knows Where?), *La máquina de la verdad* (The Truth Machine), *Al filo de la ley*

(On the Edge of the Law), *Misterios sin resolver* (Unsolved Mysteries), *Emergencia* and so forth. On one episode of *Su media naranja* (Your Better Half), for a fee of about 50,000 pesetas ($400), one woman told several million spectators that her husband's secret desire was to sodomize her, while he complained that his wife did not enjoy taking mineral baths at a spa. American spectators would not find much new on these programs.

Disappointment with the results of privatization has led to a malaise that recalls the period of disenchantment during the long transition to democracy. The old cries of "We were better off under Franco!" are now being heard with reference to television. Narciso Ibáñez Serrador, a famous TV personality in Argentina and Spain, made a typical comment in the pages of *El País* on 4 July 1994: "We thought that everything would improve with competition, but now one can say that private TV also brought deformation and impoverishment. The level of quality was higher ten years ago."

In spite of "teletrash," Spanish spectators now enjoy a variety of television offerings that must seem astounding to those who were brought up in the years of the government monopoly. Francisco Javier Rodríguez, author of *Television and Spaniards* has said:

The private channels broaden the offerings, make new choices possible; no longer would we be able to spend our free time without them. Also, their young and dynamic presence has forced the two state channels to liven up their programs and enter the competition in the daily battle for viewers. We have all come out ahead: both those who work for TV and those who watch it. At least for now.

Here is what a viewer in Madrid could watch on a Thursday night in late March 1996, assuming that she had access to the subscription as well as the public channels: local, regional, national and international news on several channels; *Barrio Sésamo* (the Spanish version of *Sesame Street*); a karaoke show; *A toda página*, news and features hosted by Sonsoles Suárez, daughter of former Prime Minister Adolfo Suárez; a soccer match (of course); *Telecupón*, a drawing for the traditional Spanish lottery for the blind, hosted by the famous *folklórica* of the 1950s and 1960s, Carmen Sevilla; a film cycle featuring the work of the Spanish director Mario Camus; Ettore Scola's *Mario, Maria and Mario*; *Cuando los dinosaurios duermen* (When the Dinosaurs Sleep), a new program on nightlife in Madrid; King Vidor's *The Fountainhead* with Gary Cooper; a program on astrology. Earlier in the day the viewer could have seen innumerable soap operas (many of them imported from Latin America) and American reruns of programs like *The Bill Cosby Show*. On that same Thursday night, spectators with a satellite dish could watch on the Hispasat channel a program about flamenco, several documentaries and a feature-length movie; on TVE's Eutelsat channel, several "Euronews" programs, a half-hour of cooking with the prize-winning Basque chef Karlos Arguiñano, and *Lingo*, a popular word game; on French Eutelsat, nearly twenty-four hours of programs from France and Quebec; on Eurosport, every kind of sporting event from horseracing to skiing, ice skating, boxing, Formula 1 racing and soccer, from 8:30 in the morning until 1:30 the next morning; on TNT, an evening of television in English, with a featured show about the upcoming Oscar awards; on BBC World, twenty-four hours of programming from London; on Astra Cine, fourteen hours of movies and programs about the movies; on Astra Classics, the original version of mostly foreign, mostly American films like *The Adventures of Huckleberry Finn*; on Astra Documenta, fourteen hours of documentaries—on Salman Rushdie, the planet Mars, the Kennedys, Mt. Everest, Emperor Hirohito; on Minimax, children's programs from 7:45 A.M. to 9 P.M., including *The Flintstones* and *The Addams Family*; on Cartoon Network, you guessed it, but you did not guess that they were all in English. Finally, a viewer could see twenty-four hours of news programming on CNN Sky News (*TeleABC* 21–27 March 1996).

Spanish television, like Spanish life in general, continues to be plagued by politics and corruption. Several major scams have rocked the country. In 1992 the opposition newspapers had headlines like these: "Public TV Costs the State as Much Every Year as 340 Kilometers of New Roads" (*ABC*, February 16); "Scandal in TVE: 90 Million Pesetas Disappear and Some Payments Made Three Times" (*ABC*, 3 June); "Private Trips, Luxury Hotels and Unjustified Meals, among the Abuses Committed by TVE Officials" (*Diario 16*, 7 June). Abuses were committed during the Franco years, during the transition to democracy, during the Socialist sway from 1982 to 1996 and under the conservative government afterwards.

Spanish television lends itself to economic and political corruption because the state has almost complete control of patronage and programming on TVE. It names the director-general, who is always a member of the party in power. During the Franco years, Spanish TV had a plethora of religious programs; under the Socialist Party, they filled a mere 1 percent of screen time on the national stations. The government also tends to slant news coverage. In March 1991 the Partido Popular (Popular or Conservative Party) accused the Socialists of not giving fair coverage to the discussion on the state of the nation. According to its figures, news reports on the two central government channels (TVE 1 and TVE 2) that day dedicated 11.11 minutes to the prime minister, Felipe González, while conceding only 7.57 minutes to the opposition. When the conservatives took over the government in 1996, they did much the same thing.

With or without corruption, public TV is a losing business in Spain and many other countries. TVE alone cost the state about 314 million pesetas ($250,000) per day in 1995. Although it and the autonomous stations all use commercials, they end up in the red each year.

In general the quality of Spanish television is lower than in other Western European countries, and sometimes it is abysmal. We should remember that in its forty years of existence, almost twenty were spent under a dictatorship; since then TVE has been manipulated by every government in power. The deregulation of both television and radio has occurred without a tradition or concept of public service broadcasting. To an American or Northern European viewer, many Spanish programs seem to resemble TV from the Third World—unsophisticated in technique and overcharged with melodrama. Many of the soap operas are in fact imported from Mexico,

Venezuela and Brazil, where a good part of the public is illiterate or subliterate. These series are known as "*culebrones*" ("long snakes") because they seem to go on forever. In both imported and local programs, women—beautiful "*mama-chichos*"—are consistently exploited; the same occurs in commercial spots. Even when television recruits some of the country's best talent, the results are usually disappointing. The superb journalist and novelist Rosa Montero, for example, wrote the screenplay for the series *Media naranja* (Better Half, 1985, not to be confused with the later reality show *Su media naranja*). The result was embarrassingly below the level of her other writing. Authors like Antonio Gala and Terençi Moix have sometimes been more successful in maintaining the quality of their work in the medium of television.

Since even the public channels use commercials in Spain, TV is a lucrative if losing business. In Europe, only the United Kingdom and Italy abuse its spectators with as many publicity spots. The private channels are the worst: in a recent survey Tele 5 had a commercial every ten minutes, followed by Antena 3, with one every seventeen minutes. The main government channels were considerably better: every thirty-five minutes on TVE 1 and every hour and fourteen minutes on TVE 2, making it almost commercial free.

Sometimes the publicity spots are better than the programs. I remember a commercial for RENFE (Red Nacional de Ferrocarriles Españoles), the national railway, which was telecast in the Madrid area a few years ago before Holy Week, a time when Spaniards enjoy a long vacation and flee the cities for the south, like American college students at spring break. The camera cut back and forth between a traffic jam and a speeding train with a "*saeta*" on the soundtrack—an ancient form of *cante jondo* or flamenco sung in Andalusian cities on Good Friday (and also a word for "arrow" in Spanish). The message was irresistible and a few days later I was on the AVE, the high-speed train between Madrid and Sevilla. This commercial spot won first prize at the Festival of Publicity Films in Bordeaux.

Television is known in Spain as "the king of the house." Sociologists have noted that it has usurped the father's chair as the privileged spot in the typical Spanish home. Spaniards spend more time in front of the small screen than most Europeans—an average of 180 minutes a day according to a recent survey, more than the French and Germans but less than the British. (They are all far behind the Americans.)

Although the 1980s were a period of immense change in Spanish television, the 1990s have been perhaps even more revolutionary: the introduction of private channels, cable and direct-broadcast satellites, digital TV and the integration of Spain in Eurotelevision. The country has become one of the fastest-growing markets on the Continent. Twenty-four hours each day, Televisión Española Internacional now broadcasts to the Americas. Spanish investors, producers and distributors are taking the lead in direct-broadcast satellite and subscription TV in Latin America—Spain's largest potential export market. At the same time, the channels in the autonomous regions are becoming more numerous and more competitive. The future of television in Spain, like that of radio and cinema, will entail a special blend of regional and global factors.

NOTE

1. "The *mesa camilla* was the Round Table of the Spanish home. There we charged our nerve cells with radio dreams while we cleaned pebbles and bugs from our lentils and kidney beans." Lorenzo Díaz, *La televisión en España 1949–1995* (Madrid: Alianza, 1994), 28.

RESOURCES

Resources for Spanish radio are limited, especially in English. The best archives are those of the individual radio stations like Radio Nacional de España and SER (Sociedad Española de Radiodifusión), in Madrid. A site on Spanish radio on the World Wide Web is "Sí, Spain" at the Spanish Embassy in Ottawa: <http://www.docuweb.ca/SiSpain/media/radio.html/>. Several stations now have their own sites whose URLs can be accessed through "Sí, Spain." The Spanish foreign service radio, Radio Exterior de España, can be contacted for information about broadcasting schedules and frequencies: Apartado 156.202, 28080 Madrid, Spain; telephone 011-34-91-346-1081, fax 011-34-1-346-1815, e-mail <radioexterior.espana@rtve.es>.

Resources for Spanish television in general are better than those for radio, but also poor in English. The Instituto Cervantes in New York has the best collection of Spanish TV programs in the United States; they are lent to members for a small fee. (See its address under "Resources," Chapter 7, "Film.") Televisión Española (TVE) has its own archives in Madrid. The Library of Congress is the most broad-ranging source for scholars in the United States. The Annenberg School of Communications at the University of Southern California and the Graduate Library at the University of California, Los Angeles also have valuable material. A website for Spanish television is <http://www.docuweb.ca/SiSpain/media/televisi.html/>. Some television stations now have their own sites whose URLs can be reached through "Sí, Spain."

BIBLIOGRAPHY

Alisky, Marvin. "Spain's Press and Broadcasting: Conformity and Censorship." *Journalism Quarterly*, no. 391 (Winter 1962): 63–69.

Boddy, William. "The New Geopolitical Landscape of Television: Rethinking Program Flows and Cultural Sovereignty." Unpublished paper presented at the annual conference of the Society of Cinema Studies, Los Angeles, 1991. Cited in Marsha Kinder, *Blood Cinema: The Reconstruction of National Identity in Spain* (Berkeley and Los Angeles: University of California Press, 1993).

Bustamante, Enrique. "The Mass Media: A Problematic Modernization." In *Spanish Cultural Studies. An Introduction. The Struggle for Modernity*, edited by Helen Graham and Jo Labanyi, 356–361. Oxford: Oxford University Press, 1995.

Callejo Gallego, Javier. *La audiencia activa. El consumo televisivo: discursos y estrategias.* Madrid: Centro de Investigaciones Sociológicas, 1995.

Campo Vidal, Manuel. *La televisión por dentro.* Barcelona: Muchnik Editores, 1985.

Carr, Raymond, and Juan Pablo Fusi. *Spain: Dictatorship to Democracy.* 1979. Reprint. London: George Allen & Unwin, 1981.

Cebrián, Juan Luis. *¿Qué pasa en el mundo? Los medios de información de masas.* Madrid: Salvat, 1983.

Cheval, Jean Jacques. *La radio en Espagne (actualité et mutation).* Bordeaux: Presse Universitaire, 1990.

Díaz, Lorenzo. *La radio en España 1923–1993.* Madrid: Alianza, 1993.

———. *La televisión en España 1949–1995.* Madrid: Alianza, 1994.

Fuenmayor, Domingo de. *Las catacumbas de la radio.* Barcelona: Juventud, S.A., 1939.

García Jiménez, Jesús. *Radiotelevisión y política cultural en el franquismo.* Madrid: Consejo Superior de Investigaciones Científicas, 1980.

Gibson, Ian. *Queipo de Llano. Sevilla, verano de 1936.* Barcelona: Grijalbo, 1986.

Jordan, Barry. "Redefining the Public Interest: Television in Spain Today." In *Spanish Cultural Studies. An Introduction. The Struggle for Modernity,* edited by Helen Graham and Jo Labanyi, 361–369. Oxford: Oxford University Press, 1995.

Las mujeres y la publicidad. Nosotras y vosotros según nos ve la televisión. Madrid: Ministerio de Asuntos Sociales, 1995.

Linde Paniagua, Enrique, ed. *Las radiotelevisiones en el espacio europeo.* Valencia: Ente Público RTVV, 1990.

Martín Gaite, Carmen. *El cuarto de atrás.* Barcelona: Destino, 1978. Translated by Helen Lane as *The Back Room.* New York: Columbia University Press, 1983.

Maxwell, Richard. "Spatial Eruptions, Global Grids: Regionalist TV in Spain and Dialectics of Identity Politics." In *Refiguring Spain: Cinema/Media/Representation,* edited by Marsha Kinder, 260–283. Durham, NC: Duke University Press, 1997.

Miguel, Amando de. *La sociedad española, 1993–94.* Madrid: Alianza, 1994.

Muñoz Iglesias, Salvador. *500 programas religiosos en TVE.* Madrid: TVE, 1965.

Palacio, Manuel. *Una historia de la televisión en España.* Madrid: Arqueología y Modernidad, 1992.

Pares i Maicas, Manuel, Lluís Badia, and Izaskun Araiko. *Spanish Bibliography on Mass Communication with a Profile of the Main Spanish Academic and Scientific Institutions in the Field of Mass Communications.* Barcelona: UAB, 1988.

Rodríguez, Francisco Javier. *La televisión y los españoles. Análisis periodístico de un vicio nacional.* Madrid: Paraninfo, 1993.

Rubin, Richard. "It's Radi-O!" *Atlantic Monthly* 281, no. 1 (January 1998): 16, 18–19.

UNESCO. *World Communications: A 200-Country Survey of Press, Radio, Television, and Film.* 5th ed. Paris: UNESCO, 1975.

Vaca Berdayes, Ricardo. *Quién manda en el mando: comportamiento de los españoles ante la televisión.* Madrid: Visor, 1997.

Vázquez Montalbán, Manuel. *El libro gris de la televisión española.* Barcelona: Ediciones 99, 1973.

Vila San Juan, Juan Felipe. *La trastienda de TVE.* Barcelona: Plaza y Janés, 1981.

—————— *Chapter 9* ——————

The Press

Mariano José de Larra, the greatest Spanish journalist of all time, wrote these words in the first half of the nineteenth century. He meant that Spain's political life was so corrupt that any newspaperman who wrote about it would be brought to tears. When he saw that his friends the liberals, once they obtained power, were no more honest than the opposition, Larra despaired and shot himself. (Of course he had other reasons too.) Ever since he has been the saint and the bogeyman of Spanish journalists.

Almost 150 years later, at the height of the euphoria following Franco's death, Juan Luis Cebrián, editor-in-chief of the new daily *El País* (The Nation), said: "In today's Spain we have advanced considerably: there is actually no reason for a Spanish journalist to shoot himself." Now, after twenty years of corrupt democratic governments, are his words still true?

Probably. Corruption continues; yet there is a vibrant free press in Spain. The quality of reporting and writing varies but it can be very good—as good as anywhere in the world. More Spaniards read newspapers and magazines than ever before. The press, to a greater degree than in the United States, for example, is virtually a "paper parliament," a fourth power along with the three branches of government. Unlike Spanish television, it has not lagged behind its European neighbors and in some ways it has even rivalled and surpassed them.

On the other hand, Spaniards still read newspapers less than most Americans and Europeans in other countries. The same multimedia groups that monopolize radio and television are moving into the publishing industry, wiping out competition. A small number of companies controls a huge part of the media. Foreign investment is making inroads every day. If a Spanish journalist no longer has reason to shoot himself, he has plenty of reasons to weep.

Like radio, television and film, the Spanish press suffered through the long night of Franco's rule (1939–1975). It also was subject to prior censorship and official sanctions. The government controlled news agencies—Agencia EFE and Pyresa—as well as the country's largest chain of newspapers: publications with symbolic names like *Alcázar* (Fortress), *Alerta* (Alert), *Arriba* (Hurrah), *El Español* (The Spaniard), *Patria* (Fatherland), *Pueblo* (The People), *Siete Flechas* (Seven Arrows), *Voluntad* (Willpower), *Yugo* (Yoke) and so on. Together they constituted the *Cadena del Movimiento*, the official organs of the Francoist Movement. Another was the *La Hoja del Lunes* (The Monday Page), the only newspaper published on Mondays, eagerly anticipated by millions of Spaniards because it printed the results of the *quiniela* or soccer pools. The Church published several dailies of its own, like the influential *Ya* (Now), in addition to magazines like *Ecclesia* and *El Mensajero del Corazón de Jesús* (Messenger of the Sacred Heart). Some private newspapers were allowed to live in competition or concubinage with the government-controlled publications, such as the monarchist *ABC* in Madrid, run by the powerful Luca de Tena dynasty, and the venerable *La Vanguardia* in Barcelona, owned by the wealthy Godó family.

The result of the government's heavy hand was "a press of inconceivable boredom, full of flat accounts of official functions" (Carr and Fusi). Like cinema, radio and later TV, the press fomented a culture of evasion. While newspapers neglected political, economic and social realities, popular magazines like *Hola* described in detail the minutiae of the Generalissimo's family life—baptisms, first communions, engagements, weddings, hunting and fishing parties, teas, receptions.

Censorship of the press was no less harsh than in radio, television and film. Enrique Bustamante, a journalist who labored under the Franco yoke and would later become a leading scholar in the field, remembers that the slightest inducement to change "came up against the watchful eye and ultra-conservative attitudes of the vast majority of the public and private media." The censors corrected, mutilated, expunged. They confiscated whole issues on the newstands. Certain editorials had to be printed in their entirety by all newspapers in the land. In addition, the government had the ultimate weapon of control: if a periodical was recalcitrant, its supply of newsprint was simply cut off.

Two examples will demonstrate the arbitrary nature of censorship under Franco. When Spain's most important philosopher, José Ortega y Gasset, died in 1955, newspapers were not allowed to reproduce archival photographs of the living man, but only of his death mask or the funeral chapel. No more than three articles could be published in any periodical—one about his life and two commentaries on his work, neither of which could neglect to mention Ortega's errors in religious doctrine. The government's orders were not empty threats; if a newspaper failed to comply, it could be fined, sanctioned or shut down temporarily or for good. So in 1963, Manuel Fernández Areal, editor of the *Diario Regional de Valladolid* (Regional Daily of Valladolid), was found guilty of "not publishing the speech delivered by His Excellency the Chief of State . . . printing only an extract of the same . . . when it was obligatory to reproduce it in full, according to the stipulations of the authorities."

In the last ten years of Franco's rule, the government started proceedings against the media no less than 1,270 times, of which 450 resulted in sanctions—an average of almost one per week. The ill-fated evening newspaper *Madrid*, controlled by *Opus Dei, was one of the unfortunate victims. It emerged in 1966, encouraged by the more liberal *Ley de Prensa e Imprenta* (Press and Publishing Law), the long-awaited statute framed by the minister of information and tourism, Manuel Fraga Iribarne. Soon *Madrid* was sanctioned for an editorial with a dangerous title: "Protest Is Not Always Morally Wrong." For the next five years the newspaper was slapped with dozens of accusations and fines. In 1971 the government closed its doors and later dynamited the building.

Cartoonists sometimes suffered less harassment than other journalists. The famous Forges (Antonio Fraguas de Pablo), for example, managed to get away with mild political satire because his cartoons in the daily *Informaciones* were so hilarious and popular. Cebrián said of him: "The so-called *establishment*, by which I mean those who give the orders in this business, feels helpless and perplexed by his criticism that is severe and funny at the same time." In *ABC*, the cartoons of Antonio Mingote were "an oasis of freedom and ingenuity" (Cebrián). Evaristo Acevedo, Kalikatres and Serafín were also fine cartoonists in the dark years. Forges, Mingote and other cartoonists, such as Chumy Chúmez, Máximo, Perich and Peridis seem to be immune to political change: they thrived under the dictatorship, during the transition and in the democratic years.

Another space for limited satire was filled by magazines; since they were more expensive and enjoyed less circulation, the regime considered them to be less dangerous than newspapers. Carr and Fusi have discussed the "vein of black humor, a characteristic reaction in the underdeveloped Spain of the forties and fifties that can be sensed in such magazines as *La Cordorniz* (The Quail)." This periodical, with its subtitle "The Most Daring Magazine for the Most Intelligent Reader," suffered its share of censorship and shutdowns over the years but consistently offered an escape to those who could read between the lines. The novelist Carmen Martín Gaite has described beautifully what *La Cordorniz* meant to young Spaniards in the darkest years of the dictatorship:

Through the window of *La Cordorniz* blew a healthy and demystifying air that little by little cleaned out the transcendental cobwebs in the minds of young people in the period after the Civil War. Apparently innocuous and frivolous, it assaulted stiffness and affectation from the only terrain allowed by the censors: light humor, a little bit absurd. . . . [It] made us understand that everything has a flip side, in a period like that of early Francoism when they only showed us one face of the coin, the one they had polished. . . . [*La Codorniz*] was like a little red balloon that had gotten away from a child in the middle of a victory parade, and some of us watched it apprehensively as it rose in the air, thinking that it might contain dynamite.

Manuel Vázquez Montalbán, who also lived through those years, said

The little ironic spark of *La Codorniz* turned into a brushfire, and the humor magazines became a critical vanguard comparable to the one made up by Diderot, Voltaire, Rousseau or D'Alembert to blow up the Ancien Régime. Periodicals like *Barrabás* [Barabbas], *El Papús* [untranslatable], *Hermano Lobo* [Brother Wolf], *Por Favor* [Please], rather than create new opinions, destroyed the old, and thus fed our sarcastic hope for a more civil society.

Other magazines in this vein were *Ajoblanco* (Whitegarlic), *La Calle* (The Street) and *El Viejo Topo* (The Old Mole). The subtitle of one periodical cited by Vázquez Montalbán, *Hermano Lobo*, reminded its readers that censorship was always there: "Humorous Weekly within the Limits of the Possible."

A very different kind of magazine was the prestigious *Cuadernos para el Diálogo* (Notebooks for Dialogue), the closest thing to a left-wing publication in Franco's Spain. It had been founded in 1963 by the liberal Catholic Joaquín Ruiz Giménez, ex-minister of education and ambassador to Rome. Imbued with the spirit of the Second Vatican Council, the journal promoted the new Vatican ideals. Because of its founder's ties to the Church, *Cuadernos* was spared by the censors more than other periodicals; yet it too was fined and had several issues banned. Ruiz Giménez stayed in the government until 1964, trying to change it from within. One writer likened his efforts to those of "a sister of charity preaching chastity in a whorehouse." His journal was more influential than his political career. True to its name, *Cuadernos para el Diálogo* opened a national debate that was the most that could be hoped for under the circumstances. Some of the best writers in Spain wrote on pressing political and cultural topics in its pages. The journal published special issues on polemical subjects like the *Proceso de Burgos*—the trial of *ETA militants in 1970—the coup d'état in Chile in 1973 and controversial writers like the poet Antonio Machado. The editor of the evening paper *Pueblo*, Emilio Romero—one of the regime's most powerful and hated journalists—accused *Cuadernos* of being in a state of "permanent orgasm."

The rebirth of the legendary *Revista de Occidente* (Journal of the West) was another happy fruit of the new press law. It had originally been founded by Ortega y Gasset in 1923 to bring the best and latest European thought to Spain. Its new editor was José Ortega Spottorno, the philosopher's son, who would later be the founder of the most important newspaper in the transition to democracy, *El País*. Journals like *Revista de Occidente* and *Cuadernos para el Diálogo* enlivened political and cultural debate and helped pave the road for change.

Another phenomenon of the times was the weekly magazine *Cambio 16* (Change 16). Following the models of *Time* and *L'Express*, it filled a necessary gap in the Spanish press. It combined comprehensive news coverage with searching criticism of the Francoist system, expressed in a clear, direct style. *Cambio 16* was an instant success: its circulation of half a million copies per week "revealed both an astonishing awakening of political curiosity in a society that had been characterised by political apathy, and the desire for substantial political changes" (Carr and Fusi). Juan Tomás de Salas, one of the leading journalists in Spain and president of *Cambio 16*, later pronounced these words that spoke for much of the opposition press: "We were more than a publication, we were more than simple witnesses, because in our pages there was a true parliament; the free parliament that had been prohibited by Franco."

Other new publications appeared: the daring magazine *Triunfo* (Triumph), which pushed legality to the limit; periodicals of the Catholic workers' movement; critical journals at the universities; clandestine Marxist pamphlets. Romero, always ready to satirize the growing opposition, said that his colleagues in the new publications "were smoking the hashish of liberalization."

Some of these magazines, like *Cambio 16*, stayed on the newsstands in the transition after Franco's death, but most disappeared, victims of the growing democratic consensus that required a different sort of writing. The disappearance of *Triunfo* was an important loss. The further relaxation of censorship caused an explosion of soft pornography. The first female nudes appeared in the Spanish editions of *Penthouse* and *Playboy*, and in the popular *Interviú*, which also published sensationalistic reports and interviews with important public figures; it became the first periodical in the country to reach a circulation of one million readers. Harder pornography followed in other publications, a natural result of forty years of censorship and puritanical mores.

Even before Franco's death, the government newspapers had begun to lose readers. Some of their problems were caused by poor management, but mostly by the public's weariness from years of lies, distortions and silences. *Informaciones* lasted until the Portuguese revolution in 1974; *Arriba*, founded in 1931, hit the streets for the last time in June 1979; *Pueblo* hung on until May 1984. The Socialist government at last agreed to privatize these leftovers from the Franco regime; some twenty publications were sold to companies throughout the country. The largest chain of newspapers in Europe had disappeared.

On 4 May 1976, six months after Franco's death, the new daily *El País* rolled off the presses. It would turn out to be the most important event in the history of modern Spanish journalism and its greatest success story. *El País* became a vehicle for the ideology of liberal consensus that Spain needed during its transition to democracy. Indeed it would be hard to imagine this period in Spanish history without *El País*; in the same way, it would be hard to imagine *El País* coming into being at any other time.

The editor of the new paper, the omnipresent Cebrián, had somehow managed to survive as a journalist under the dictatorship. If his career as reporter and editor had been the caterpillar and pupa stages in his life, Franco's death metamorphosed him into "a winged creature bent on creating a new kind of newspaper" (Charles R. Eisendrath). Under his direction, *El País* would attempt to fulfill the same role as the prestigious *El Sol* (The Sun) in the 1920s and 1930s, a Madrid daily whose guiding spirit had been Ortega y Gasset. The new publication also followed foreign models: the format of France's *Le Monde*, the tone of the *Manchester Guardian*, the independence of the *Washington Post*, the raciness of the *Village Voice*. Three years after its debut, it had become the largest-selling daily in the country and Spain's newspaper of record. By 1978 it was rated among the top fifty dailies in the world. It continues to be one of the most influential newspapers anywhere.

El País was born after a long and difficult labor. Hampered by insufficient capital and resistance from the state, its parent company, PRISA (Promotora de Infomaciones, S.A.) took four years to publish the first issue. Although Franco was already dead, Francoism lived on in the form of government harassment. Cebrián was condemned to three months in prison for contempt of authority in an editorial titled "The Press and Democracy."

At first *El País* was funded only by small investors. Gradually PRISA consolidated its position and the paper was soon turning a healthy profit, from both newsstand sales and advertising. After the Madrid edition, others were added in various regions of Spain, like Andalusia, Catalonia and Valencia. A weekly international edition on lightweight paper was also created; it has dominated the overseas market in 150 countries as effectively as the main edition has captured the national readership. In 1982, the first *Anuario El País* (Yearbook) was published, a kind of almanac or synthesis of the previous twelve months in Spain and the world; it has appeared annually since then. *El País* is now the centerpiece of a multimedia group with holdings in television, radio and publishing.

It is hard to describe the paper's unique style to readers who have not perused its pages. It preserves the tabloid format that is traditional in Spain. Otherwise its design and look represent a departure from the past. It has a simple, clear and orderly appearance. Its pages offer three kinds of reading: the headlines, the unusually long leads that summarize important articles, and the full text.

El País was the first newspaper in Spain to turn the letters to the editor section into a true forum for its readers. During the Franco years, readers had not dared to send honest letters; editors could not print honest replies. Cebrián was proud of the fact that his paper altered the situation. In its first four years, *El País* received some 100,000 letters from its readers and published about 4,000. Cebrián said

I keep letters from political exiles, émigrés, prostitutes, terrorists, prisoners, beggars, ministers, from intellectuals, laborers, students, bullfighters, bankers, artists, priests, children, military personnel, judges, ambassadors, and gypsies. Letters that insult, eulogize, criticize, tear apart, exalt, inspire, which in every case quicken the emotions because they contain the heart, the ideas, and the feelings of someone who wants to speak and express himself.

El País has also been original in its use of photographs. Many of them would not have been approved by the old censorship. Some critics have accused the paper of exploiting morbid and erotic images. During the scandalous plague of poisoned colza (rapeseed) oil in 1982, for example, *El País* published a photo of a young girl's emaciated body in a hospital. Her family requested that the newspaper refrain from publishing more photos. The editors promptly printed another image of the girl, accompanied by a statement defending freedom of the press.

The newspaper's classified pages would also shock the old censors. *El País* publishes the most explicit sexual ads to be found in any major newspaper in the world. Under the "Services" section on 13 July 1996, for example, "Sandra" claimed that she had "the best breasts and behind in Madrid. 15,000 pesetas" ($120). Another ad from the same issue says simply "From the rear," with a telephone number. A company called "Macho's!" offers men only. There are ads for "Thai job" (bathtub sex), "Greek job" (anal), "French job" (oral) and "British job" (S & M); there are also spots for transvestites, lesbians, gays. It would be hard to imagine *Le Monde* or the *New York Times* with this kind of advertising. Yet *El País* rivals these newspapers in quality and prestige.

The paper became the vehicle for the new journalism in Spain, similar to that in the United States and other countries, but freer in expression. Some of the country's best writers contributed to *El País* from the start. Rosa Montero and Francisco Umbral, well-known novelists and essayists as well as journalists, were two exponents of the new style that often combined a subjective point of view, dialogue and narrative techniques borrowed from fiction, marginal topics and people, and a new kind of realism that tried to portray the underside of modern life. Reading *El País* can be as lively as reading good creative writing. A whole generation of talented authors cut its eyeteeth in its pages: Juan Cueto, Fernando Savater, José Miguel Ullán, Manuel Vicent and many more. Older intellectuals like Agustín García Calvo, Juan Goytisolo and Alfonso Sastre appeared along with the younger figures. Other writers from throughout the world, especially Latin America, continued sending contributions: the Nobel Prize winners Gabriel García Márquez and Octavio Paz, Mario Vargas Llosa, Carlos Fuentes, Alfredo Bryce Echenique. If women's names are lacking, it is because *El País*, in spite of recent improvements, has not been able to destroy the bastion of machismo in its pages. Only one woman, Lidia Falcón, founder and director of the Partido Feminista de España (Spanish Feminist Party), has written steadily in the opinion section.

Like its competition, *El País* is more political than most American newspapers. There is not always a strict separation between the editorial pages and the rest of the paper. Cebrián says: "I have frequently insisted that before being objective newspapers should be honest. . . . Spanish newspapers—not to mention those in France—frequently adopt the custom of commenting upon events before giving an account of them." This tendency has become even more marked in recent years: *El País* and other Spanish dailies often assume that their public has already learned about breaking news from radio and television and therefore does not want to read the same facts in a newspaper.

I have granted generous space to the *El País* phenomenon because it is unique in the history of modern Spanish journalism. As well as a daily paper, this newspaper has become a public space. At the height of its influence in the 1980s, some critics called it the "dominant reference" in the country, like the *New York Times* in the United States, the *Times* in England, *Le Monde* in France or *Il Corriere della Sera* in Italy. It was an unavoidable reference for the other media, printed or audiovisual; a privileged platform for politicians, thinkers and writers; a prime source of data for diplomats in Spain and abroad. Let us take each one of these points in order. First, other newspapers, magazines, radio and TV channels had to take *El País* into account before establishing their own opinion on a news story. Second, since it enjoyed the largest circulation in the country, it was the best vehicle for reaching a large audience in print. The late philosopher José Luis Aranguren called *El País* "the collective intelligentsia of Spain." If a thinker, writer or politician did not publish in its pages, he or she lost cachet. Finally, *El País* was the first Spanish newspaper in history to have a significant impact on readers outside the national borders.

The newspaper's power had grown so much by the 1980s that it had become a part of the national identity. Some said that it not only reported and interpreted reality, but created or destroyed it like a god. If an event or a person did not appear in the pages of *El País*, it might as well have not existed. On the other hand, the stories and people blessed by its coverage acquired a public presence and prestige. More than a mere newspaper, *El País* was a ritual, a political, social and cultural standard. At a time when the Church, the state, the university and other institutions were losing their authority, this newspaper represented an attempt to save the best in traditional humanistic culture by bringing it up to date in a free society after forty years of oppression.

What about other newspapers in Spain? *El País* continues to be the leading daily, with a circulation of more than 400,000, but it has ceased to be an undisputed giant. Its strongest rival, the monarchist *ABC*, has staged a comeback after its near eclipse in the period of transition, achieving a circulation of some 335,000. Founded in 1921, this monarchist paper has known two dictatorships, one Republic, a civil war and democracy. It began to suffer from economic problems in the 1960s and 1970s, in spite of having successfully launched the first Sunday supplement in Spain (*Blanco y Negro*, Black and White). Some of the country's and the world's leading writers and thinkers have contributed to *ABC*: Salvador de Madariaga, Claudio Sánchez Albornoz, Aldous Huxley, Bertrand Russell. A few well-known conservative authors continue to write in its pages, such as Lázaro Carreter and Julián Marías. *ABC* was an important opposition paper during the Socialist rule of 1983–1996. It has a strident, polemical tone that is foreign to most American journalism. Curiously, it beat *El País* and most of its competition to the punch on the World Wide Web: *ABCe* (Electronic *ABC*) is a primary source of news and commentary for Spanish speakers in the Peninsula and throughout the world.

La Vanguardia is another old daily that has survived in the new era. Founded in 1881, it has been the most widely read paper in Barcelona ever since. It has normally maintained a centrist political stance, but after Franco's death it adapted to the new times by favoring Catalan autonomy. In spite of competition from *El País* and Catalan-language dailies like *Avui* (Today) and *Diari de Barcelona* (Barcelona Daily), it has a circulation of over 200,000.

One newspaper that suffered from the transition to democracy was the Catholic daily *Ya*. During the late 1960s and the 1970s, it was a forum for young politicians who followed the line of Europe's Christian Democratic parties. The sudden rise of *El País* hurt its circulation so much that the Church had to intervene to save it. When Pope John Paul II visited Spain and received donations of 40 million pesetas from the Spanish people, he decided to hand them over to the languishing newspaper. Little by little, *Ya* radicalized its editorial line and alienated more readers. It finally folded in 1996, only to be reborn in 1997 with an uncertain future.

The biggest splash in the decade of the 1990s has been the newspaper *El Mundo*, called by some the *El País* of the new decade. Founded in 1989 under its full name *El Mundo del Siglo XXI* (The World in the Twenty-First Century), with both Spanish and foreign capital (Giovanni Agnelli), it soon became the third newspaper in the country, with a circulation close to that of *La Vanguardia*. Its vigorous investigative journalism and muckraking were the scourge of the Socialists during the last years of their rule. *El Mundo* recruited some of the best old and new talent in Spanish newspapers: Víctor de la Serna, Melchor Miralles, Umbral, Forges. Following the model of *El País*, the new daily published its main edition in Madrid, but also established semi-independent versions in key regions throughout the Peninsula: the Basque Country, Castile-León, Catalonia, Galicia. Each edition carries some common editorials and national and international stories but also places emphasis on its particular region, sometimes in the local language. *El Mundo* is also known for its splendid illustrators, cartoonists and designers. In 1994–1995 it won more prizes from the Society of Newspaper Design than any publication in the world and was far ahead of its competition in Spain. (See Photograph 6 in Chapter 5 of this book for an example of a prize-winning drawing.)

El Mundo is a star to watch in the constellation of the Spanish press. Its sudden prosperity is even more remarkable in a country like Spain where a reader's identity may be closely tied to the newspaper he buys at his neighborhood kiosk and carries to work on foot, in the subway, on a bus or in a taxi. One journalist told me that it is easier for a Spaniard to change his wife than his newspaper. Both he and I speak of a masculine reader because in Spain, nearly 60 percent are men.

In the same way that the autonomous regions began to broadcast and televise in their own languages after the dictatorship, newspapers started to appear in Basque, Catalan and Galician or in mixtures of these tongues and Castilian. In 1975 *Deia*, the organ of the National Basque Party appeared, along with the more radical *Egin*, mouthpiece of the Herri Batasuna coalition. The next year *Avui* was born in Catalonia. Ten years later *Diari de Barcelona* began publication. In Galicia the formerly all-Castilian *El Correo Gallego* (The Galician Post) became a bilingual paper with an addditional name, *O Correo Galego*. The non-Spanish-language press can be influential but has a small circulation, rarely more than 50,000 per edition.

Here is a list of the twenty top newspapers in 1993:

Newspaper	Average Circulation
El País	401,258
ABC	334,317
Marca	333,396
El Mundo del Siglo XXI	209,992
La Vanguardia	208,029
El Periódico de Catalunya	185,517
As	140,213
El Correo Español	134,000
El Pueblo Vasco	133,954
Diario 16	109,338
La Voz de Galicia	107,446
El Diario Vasco	93,578
Sport	88,972
El Mundo Deportivo	67,373
Diario de Navarra	63,312

Heraldo de Aragón	58,401
Las Provincias	58,354
Egin	51,366
Levante	51,240
La Nueva España	47,972
La Verdad	46,919

It is remarkable that the third-largest-selling newspaper in Spain is a sports daily—*Marca* (Record)—and that two other similar publications appear on the list—*As* (Ace) and *Sport*. This explains in part the fact that most readers of the press are men, who make up a majority of sports fans in Spain.

Circulation on Sundays is about twice as large as the rest of the week. The major newspapers include supplements which resemble the *New York Times Magazine*. *El País*'s Sunday edition topped 1,000,000 copies in 1993, while *Blanco y Negro* (ABC) surpassed 600,000, *La Revista* (The Magazine, *El Mundo*) 400,000, and *La Vanguardia* 300,000.

The relation between sales and readers can be complex in Spain. Dailies are more expensive than in any other European country. For this and other reasons, Spaniards have the custom of sharing newspapers: in local bars, casinos, offices, restaurants and shops, one often sees dog-eared copies of dailies that have been read by many people. Like listening to the radio and watching television, reading newspapers can be a collective experience in Spain.

While most newspaper readers in Spain are men (about 63%), an astonishing 70 percent of magazine readers are women. Almost half of all weekly and monthly publications belong to the category of *revistas del corazón*, "magazines of the heart" or gossip rags like *Hola* (Hello), *Semana* (Week), *Lecturas* (Readings), *Diez Minutos* (Ten Minutes) and *Garbo* (Glamour); together they sell some 2,000,000 copies. *Hola* is the Spanish publication with the highest sales in the country and abroad, especially in Latin America. Adolfo Suárez admitted that one interview in this magazine won him half a million votes in the important presidential elections of 1977. Following his victory in 1982, Felipe González granted his first interview to *Hola*. This would be similar to a newly elected American president being interviewed by *People* magazine.

Another 20 percent of Spanish periodicals have to do with sewing, embroidery and other domestic activities that also attract a feminine audience. As people have achieved more affluence and enjoy more free time, other leisure publications have flourished. Some of the leading magazines of this type in 1994 were *Ciclismo a fondo* and *Bicisport* (cycling, circulation approximately 26,000 and 23,000 respectively), *Sólo 4 por 4* (4-wheel drive vehicles, 26,000), *Comer y beber* (food and drink, 24,000), *Don Balón* (soccer, 21,000), and *PC Actual* (computers, 21,000). As basketball has become more popular in Spain, the monthly *Baloncesto* has thrived. Economic and financial periodicals have also flourished in recent years, like *Gaceta de los Negocios* (Business Gazette) and *Dinero* (Money). Some of the major newspapers are now publishing special supplements on economic matters, like *El Mundo*'s *Su Dinero* (Your Money).

Magazines are also published in the minority languages of the "historic communities" in Catalonia, Galicia and the Basque Country. Their existence is precarious. Of the four Catalan news magazines launched in the 1980s, for example, only one has survived: *El Temps* (The Times), published in Valencia. A number of specialized journals reach a small audience of intellectuals: *Serra d'Or* (Golden Sierra), *Els Marges* (The Margins), *L'Avenç* (Progress). The cultural journals *Grial* (Grail) and *Luzes de Galicia* (Lights of Galicia) cater to a similar élite in northwestern Spain. Basque journals are even more marginal. *Jakin* offers an annual list of books published in the language, with critical commentary, while other journals, written mostly in Spanish, print some poems or prose in Euskara.

Almost all magazine sales are direct; very few Spaniards have subscriptions. The most popular place to purchase both newspapers and magazines is the local kiosk or newsstand. This fact creates important swings in the market. If a magazine is displayed prominently, its sales will rise; if not, they will plummet. Weekly and monthly publications therefore suffer frequent changes in revenue. Their sales depend to a great extent on the issue's ability to seduce the reader at the moment of purchase. The result is an abundance of flashy covers with provocative titles.

I have two periodicals in front of me now, one old and one new; they may give a feeling for what can be found in the popular Spanish press. The first is the popular satirical weekly, *El Jueves* (Thursday), whose subtitle is *La Revista que Sale los Miércoles* (The Magazine That Comes Out on Wednesdays). Inside there is a special page with the title "El Viernes," an independent weekly, dependent upon Thursday. Founded in 1976, the year after Franco's death, *El Jueves* has stayed on the newsstands ever since; in July of 1996 it published its one-thousandth issue. It is an almost entirely visual publication with cartoons, jokes and a little text, always humorous and irreverent. Some of the cartoonists are the best in Spain (the omnipresent Forges, Perich, Gallego & Rey). The text and the illustrations are often very explicit. This magazine turns everything upside down and spares nobody, not even the king and queen. *El Jueves* could not be said to have a political line, but there is a page sponsored by Greenpeace. Unlike most American periodicals, it does not support itself mainly through advertising: in the 10 June 1996 number, with seventy-two pages, there were only six ads (Sony, J & B, two private schools and two spreads for *El Jueves*). This important magazine will also be discussed in Chapter 10 ("Popular Literature").

The second magazine in front of me is *La Farola* (The Street Lamp), a biweekly tabloid published since 1995. Its subtitle is "The Newspaper of the Homeless and the Unemployed." Unlike any other periodical in Spain, *La Farola* is sold exclusively by carriers on the streets, each of whom must wear an identification card with a photograph; all issues are stamped with the carrier's number. On the cover of No. 33 (June 1996) is a color photograph of an Indian from the Andean region (only the front and back pages are in color). The feature article, "Air Bridge to the Third World," has to do with Spanish organizations that donate used medicines, books and bicycles to underdeveloped countries. Other articles deal with the popular Catalan singer Lluís Llach, who sets up booths for *La Farola* and Amnesty International at his concerts; the dangers of summer—traffic, sun, forest fires, abandoned pets; volunteer lifeguards from the Spanish Red Cross; Idrobús, the Mobile Service for the Social Integration of the Drug Dependent in Madrid; human rights abuses in China and other countries. Each issue also features "News on the Vendors of *La Farola*," most of whom are people who would not have jobs if they did not work for the periodical. On the back pages is a photograph of a 200-peseta piece—the price of one issue of *La Farola*—with a breakdown of how it is distributed: 150 pesetas ($1.20) for the seller, 50 pesetas (40 cents) for the newspaper. This unusual publication won several awards in its first two years: the City of Barcelona Journalism and the Human Rights Journalism prizes in 1995 and the European Artistic Forum Prize in 1996.

These examples show that the Spanish press can be lively, original and informative. As in film, radio and TV, its main problems have to do with economic infrastructure. Five groups own more than forty newspapers that control roughly 55 percent of sales. Beyond these groups, plus *ABC* and *El Mundo*, there are seventy-five more newspapers with a total circulation of a scant one-half million. In the regional press, four groups—El Correo, Grupo 16, Prensa Ibérica and ZETA—have made a series of mergers and takeovers in recent years that have done away with competition in some areas of Spain.

Only two Spanish newspaper publishers can truly be called multimedia groups. PRISA, with its flagship *El País*, has close links with the book-publishing chain Timón. As we have seen in Chapter 8 ("Radio and Television"), it also has a majority holding in the biggest private radio network in Europe, SER; a significant investment in Antena 3 Radio and other stations; 25 percent of the subscription TV Canal Plus. In addition, through subsidiaries, it has moved into audiovisual products and advertising. PRISA is the only Spanish publishing group to have embarked upon overseas expansion: *Público* in Portugal, *The Independent* in Great Britain, *La Prensa* in Mexico, the M-40 radio network in France, among other interests.

The second multimedia group is ZETA, publisher of *El Periódico de Catalunya* (The Newspaper of Catalonia), the sixth most widely circulated newspaper in Spain. The company started out with the magazine *Interviú* and now has a large regional press chain, a broad range of general- and special-interest periodicals including comic books, pornographic magazines like *Lib*, a production and distribution company for erotic films, and the television channel Antena 3, in partnership with one of the biggest banking groups, Banesto. In fact the four wealthiest banks in Spain—Banesto, Banco Central–Hispano, Banco de Bilbao–Vizcaya and Banco de Santander—have huge investments in the communication groups that prevail in publishing, radio and television.[1]

Foreign investment is closely tied to the concentration of capital that is the major threat to the health of the Spanish press. Between 1982 and 1988, the government opened the media to foreign companies. Further integration with the European Union will only accelerate this process. Two of the five largest book publishers in Spain are already non-Spanish (Bertelsmann, Springer), between them controlling 57 percent of the market.

In conclusion, Spanish journalists still have reason to weep, if not to shoot themselves like their unofficial patron saint, Larra. Since Franco's death, the country's newspapers have spearheaded a free, critical press. They probably enjoy more prestige than their counterparts in most parts of the world. A significant custom of Spanish television channels, for example, is to show the front pages of the chief dailies on evening news programs; it is still the press, not TV, that sets the agenda for what deserves attention. In cities throughout the Peninsula, some of the world's best journalists go on practicing what Cebrián calls their "nocturnal, maligned trade."

If you walk through a Spanish town or city, you will eventually come to the local kiosk; with the possible exception of the bars on the main square, where people often go to read their favorite periodical, it will probably be the most animated spot on the streets. At the newsstand you will see an exciting display of national and international newspapers, magazines, books and posters for men and women, children, teenagers. You will see people approach the kiosk, peruse the colorful assortment of periodicals, perhaps exchange a few words with the vendor, make a purchase and walk away with a periodical or two under their arms. Then you will know that the Spanish press is thriving.

NOTE

1. Banco Central-Hispano and Banco de Santander have merged into a single corporation, Banco de Santander Central Hispano.

RESOURCES

If you have a professional interest in the Spanish media, you can request a copy of the yearly *Agenda de la Comunicación* from Asistencia a la Función Informativa, Ministerio de la Presidencia, Secretaría General del Portavoz del Gobierno, Complejo de la Moncloa, 28071 Madrid, Spain; telephone 011-34-91-3214078, Fax 011-34-91-3214030 or 3214050. If you are interested in Spanish cultural magazines, you can contact Asociación de Revistas Culturales de España, Hortaleza 75, 28004 Madrid; telephone 011-34-91-3086066, fax 011-34-91-3199267. The best website for the press and magazines is through "Sí, Spain," from the Spanish Embassy in Ottawa: <http:// www.docuweb.ca/sispain/media/press/htm/>. The following newspapers have websites that you can reach through "Sí, Spain" or the Iberian Studies Web from Brigham Young University, <http://www.lib.byu.edu/~rdh/wess/iber/index. html/>: *ABCe* (= *ABC electrónico*), *Avui* (in Catalan), *El Comercio*, *El Correo Gallego/O Correo Galego* (in Castilian and Galician), *El Diario Vasco*, *El País Digital* (= *El País* online), *El Periódico de Catalunya*, *Setmanari de l'Alt Empordà* (weekly, in Catalan), *Sport*, *La Vanguardia*, *La Voz Diario de Lanzarote*. *El Mundo* has three supplements available on the web: *El Mundo del Siglo XXI (Suplemento Campus)*, *El Mundo del Siglo XXI (La Revista)*, and the economic journal *Su Dinero*. Other economic dailies and magazines that you can also find through "Sí, Spain" are *Dinero* and *Gaceta de los Negocios* (in English, French or Spanish). You can visit one sports daily: *Sport*. *El Temps* (in Catalan) and *Melibea (Revista de Cultura Hispana)* are located at the same site. Finally, you can also visit the news agency Agencia Efe through the website "Sí, Spain."

BIBLIOGRAPHY

Ayala, Francisco. *La retórica del periodismo y otras retóricas*. Madrid: Espasa-Calpe, 1985.

Benn's Guide to Newspapers and Periodicals of the World. London: Benn Brothers, annual.

Bernárdez, Asunción. "Prensa, radio y televisión." In *España hoy*, edited by Antonio Ramos Gascón, 2: 317–349. 2 vols. Madrid: Cátedra, 1991.

Bustamante, Enrique. "The Mass Media: A Problematic Modernization." In *Spanish Cultural Studies. An Introduction. The Struggle for Modernity*, edited by Helen Graham and Jo Labanyi, 356–361. Oxford: Oxford University Press, 1995.

Carr, Raymond, and Juan Pablo Fusi. *Spain: Dictatorship to Democracy*. 1979. Reprint. London: George Allen & Unwin, 1981.

Cebrián, Juan Luis. *The Press and Main Street. "El País"—Journalism in Democratic Spain*. Translated by Brian Nienhaus. Ann Arbor: University of Michigan Press, 1989. Expanded version of *La prensa y la calle*. Madrid: Nuestra Cultura, 1980.

————. *¿Qué pasa en el mundo? Los medios de información de masas*. Barcelona: Salvat, 1983.

Communication Yearbook. New Brunswick, NJ: Transaction Books, annual.

Eisendrath, Charles R. "Foreword." In Juan Luis Cebrián, *The Press and Main Street. "El País"—Journalism in Democratic Spain*, v–x. Ann Arbor: University of Michigan Press, 1989.

España 1994. Una interpretación de su realidad social. Madrid: Centro de Estudios del Cambio Social, 1995.

Foreign Newspaper Report. Washington, DC: Library of Congress, 1973. Continued by *Foreign Newspaper and Gazette Report*.

Forges (Antonio Fraguas de Pablo). *El libro de Forges*. Madrid: Ediciones 99, 1972.

Gilmour, David. *The Transformation of Spain: From Franco to the Constitutional Monarchy*. New York: Quartet Books, 1985.

Giner, Juan A. "Journalists, Mass Media, and Public Opinion in Spain, 1938–1982." In *The Press and the Rebirth of Iberian Democracy*, edited by Kenneth Maxwell, 33–54. Westport, CT: Greenwood Press, 1983.

Imbert, Gérard, and José Vidal Beneyto, eds. *"El País" o la referencia dominante*. Barcelona: Editorial Mitre, 1986.

International and Intercultural Communication Annual. Chicago: Intercultural Press, annual.

Journalism Abstracts. Columbia, SC: Association for Education in Journalism and Mass Communication, annual.

Kurian, George T. *World Press Encyclopedia*. 2 vols. New York: Facts on File, 1982.

Martín Gaite, Carmen, *Usos amorosos de la postguerra española*. Barcelona: Anagrama, 1987.

Mass Communication Review Yearbook. Beverly Hills, CA: Sage, annual.

Maxwell, Kenneth. "Introduction: The Transition to Democracy in Spain and Portugal." In *The Press and the Rebirth of Iberian Democracy*, edited by Kenneth Maxwell, 1–30. Westport, CT: Greenwood Press, 1983.

Preston, Paul. *The Triumph of Democracy in Spain*. London: Methuen, 1986.

UNESCO. *Statistical Yearbook*. Paris: UNESCO, annual.

Vázquez, Manuel. *Informe sobre la información*. Barcelona: Fontanella, 1963.

World Press Review. An English-language digest of the international press that reprints articles from Spanish newspapers.

<hr> Chapter 10 <hr>

Popular Literature

El que mucho abarca poco aprieta (He who bites off too much will not be able to swallow it).

—Spanish proverb

If you go to the Cuesta de Moyano on a Sunday morning in Madrid, next to the Botanical Garden and just a block from the Prado Museum, you will see a long row of stalls, most of them covered by awnings, where people walk up and down looking at old and new books, popular novels, comics for children and adults, manuals of sexual hygiene, sets of bound fascicles or booklets, inexpensive prints, yellowing photonovels and news magazines. Here you will see how popular literature flourishes in the center of Spain.

I have kept the Spanish proverb "He who bites off too much will not be able to swallow it" in mind more here than anywhere else in the book. Popular literature in Spain is a vast subject that embraces the extremes of popular culture itself—everything from poetry and stories in the oral tradition to comic books, detective novels and their electronic versions. Moreover, it also permeates "high" or official culture more than in other European countries. In order to avoid biting off more than a reader can swallow, I am going to limit myself to some of the most important expressions of popular literature in the Peninsula: the oral tradition, the *novela rosa* or sentimental novel, comic books and thrillers. I will touch other forms only in passing—the western, horror, spy novels, science fiction and pornography—because they are not very different from the same genres in countries throughout the world and because they do not tell us very much about Spain.

THE ORAL TRADITION

The oral tradition is as alive in Spain as in any Western country. It could be described as a great river that was born in the Middle Ages with the languages spoken in the Iberian Peninsula, then flowed above ground or as a subterranean stream for hundreds of years, crossed the Atlantic Ocean in the sixteenth century and spread throughout Spanish America, and has kept on rolling in the Old and New World until our time. Its most important expression in Castilian is the *romance* or ballad and the *copla*, *villancico* or folk songs that include love lyrics, wedding and funeral songs (see Chapter 6, "Music"). Related forms are folktales, riddles, jokes, proverbs (see Chapter 1, "Languages") and street cries. Even today there are few Spaniards, from the Peninsula to the Balearic and Canary Islands, who do not have in their memory, however deeply buried, some remnant of this ancient, vital expression of popular culture.

One of the most dramatic examples of the surviving oral tradition is the Basque *bertsolari*, a folk poet or bard. The Basque language, Euskara, did not have a written form until modern times, so we can be sure that the improvised poetry of the *bertsolariak* has reached us through oral transmission. The Basque-American writer Robert Laxalt says: "A youth begins his career as a bard . . . when those who know best have remarked on his richness of voice and magic with words. Then he is encouraged to go on, singing at weddings and village feasts and finally in contest with other bertsolariak." There are still competitions between these poets at popular festivals and *pelota* (jai alai) matches, in theaters and on television. It is curious to note that the bards are almost invariably men, whereas women tend to be the main transmitters of oral literature in other regions of the Peninsula.

Folktales have survived in Spain more than in many other countries. They are almost the exclusive domain of women, older women at that. "*Cuentos de vieja*" or "old ladies' tales" is a partly derogatory term that reveals the fact that most oral literature is transmitted by women, who are the guardians of tradition. In order to refer to remote times in the past, Spaniards still speak of "*el tiempo de Maricastaña*," or "the days of Chestnut-Mary," an expression that has parallels in other languages.

Similar folktales can be found in all parts of the Iberian Peninsula. In general they follow Vladimir Propp's basic structure as described in his classic *Morphology of the Folktale*. This structure can be simplified in the following way:

1. an initial situation in which something is lacking,
2. a meeting or assembly (the king proclaims an edict or asks that a certain task be carried out, for example),
3. a journey by the protagonist or hero,
4. a proof of his generosity or cunning,
5. the magical object (a ring, sword, etc.),
6. combat,
7. trials (the hero is submitted to difficult tests),
8. return,
9. recognition of the hero,
10. finale (the hero marries the princess, etc.).

I speak of the hero rather than the heroine because most protagonists in Spanish folklore are male.

These stories are often variants of widely known European tales, but most have been adapted or changed. Thus *Blancanieves* (Snow White) becomes *Blancaflor* (White Flower), *Pulgarcito* (Tom Thumb) becomes *Periquillo* (Little Pete), the Cyclops becomes *Ojanco* (from *ojo*, eye) and the Unicorn is *Oricuerno* (Goldhorn). Other typical Spanish protagonists are *Mariquita* (Little Mary), *Estrellita de Oro* (Little Golden Star), *Juan el Oso* (John the Bear), *Juan sin Miedo* (Fearless John), *Pedro de Urdemala* (Peter the Schemer). Witches and sorceresses are rarely called this way, but are simply *viejas* or old women, *gitanas* or gypsies, *negras* or black women. The fairy godmother does not exist; in her place appears a *viejecita* (little old woman) or *agüelilla* (little grandma). The hero is often simply called *el muchacho* (boy) or *el joven* (young man), while the heroine is *la niña* (young girl). The dragon and other fabulous aggressors are reduced to the *fiera* or wild beast. The magic wand is usually styled *la varita mágica* or *la varita de virtudes* (the wand of power).

One of the most characteristic Spanish folktales is that of Juan el Oso (John the Bear). I will tell one of its basic versions. A young girl is taking care of a herd of cattle. Following a lost cow, she reaches a distant mountain. A bear carries her off to his cave where he keeps her prisoner; they have a son. The bear forbids them to leave the cave. The son, Juan el Oso, kills his father and flees with his mother. Juan does not adapt to life in town because of his superhuman strength. He departs and has many adventures, eventually performing a heroic deed that wins the hand of a princess, whom he finally marries. Psychoanalysts would have a field day with this Oedipal narrative.

Another Spanish folktale with a similar motif is "La niña sin manos" or "The Girl with No Hands." She amputates her arms or hands in order to be less attractive to her incestuous father. She may give birth to a pair of twins, who represent incestuous descent in many primitive cultures. The girl flees the home and eventually achieves social integration through marriage outside her family.

As can be seen from the two examples, these folktales are often as violent as other expressions of Spanish popular culture. One version of a well-known story has the heroine burn the enchanted toad before he can be transformed into a prince. In *Blancaflor* (Snow White), the evil mother (rather than the stepmother) or sorceress often receives her due punishment, which is deleted from many European versions.

Like ballads, folktales can still be heard in Spain. They too have become the almost exclusive lore of old ladies in the country, small towns and villages. Some songs and stories will die with these women; others will pass on to their daughters, granddaughters and nieces; still others will continue to be saved by scholars who transcribe and record these jewels of the Hispanic tradition.

THE NOVELA ROSA (SENTIMENTAL NOVEL)

I will not deal with this genre in detail because it would probably bore most of my readers. Moreover, it is so similar to sentimental novels in other Western countries that it does not tell us much about Spanish popular culture. Yet it is so pervasive that it cannot be ignored.

The *novela rosa* is an important part of the "kiosk literature" that is so visible on Spanish streets (see Chapter 9): comics books, detective and spy novels, horror, science fiction, westerns. The sentimental novel has always been successful because it is cheap, simply written and upholds traditional values. Most of its readers are women with little education who belong to the poorest social classes.

The modern *novela rosa* is the direct descendant of the nineteenth-century *folletín* or serialized novel. The name of the genre is hard to translate into English but means something like "pink," "rosy" or "soft." Some critics now speak of a more realistic, erotic style of popular fiction or *novela roja*, the "red" or "hard-core" novel. The original "soft" form is far more popular and will be the subject of my comments. The *novela rosa* also stands in opposition to the *novela negra*, a translation of the French *roman noir* or "black novel"—the thriller, analyzed below.

The sentimental novel shows some of the same characteristics as the popular *folletines* that flourished in the late-nineteenth and early-twentieth centuries. The stories are full of hyperbole and melodrama. The plots are usually predictable from the outset but may astonish us with sudden changes and contradictions. The point of view is almost invariably the woman's because most readers of the genre have always been female. The social, political and economic infrastructure of society is virtually absent: the characters frequently exist in a historical vacuum. They are "flat" and poorly developed, types rather than individuals. Sudden psychological shifts can occur without rhyme or reason. The language is sentimental and riddled with clichés: "From the bottom of my heart, Ricardo, thank you." The narrative and the dialogue are often interrupted by armchair philosophy: "Eating . . . is homely but necessary for life," "There are thousands of women worthy of being loved who never find love." The villains are nearly always men, brutes who have not been domesticated by romance. They are often punished, beaten and chastised for daring to break the laws of love; the critic Andrés Amorós compares them to the victim who receives all the blows in puppet theater. The characters of the fathers in these novels seem to come from a different age; they use a language that sounds more archaic than that of their counterparts in other countries: "You doubt a father's honor?" Indeed the theme of honor is one of the few survivals of Spanish tradition in these books; at times they recall situations from the Golden Age theater of Lope de Vega and Calderón de la Barca. The lovers' sense of pride and honor usually gives tension to the plot and prevents them from going to bed before the story has gotten off the ground.

During the Franco years the sentimental novel sustained the cults of virginity, marriage and family. After the transition to democracy these values have evolved much more slowly in the *novela rosa* than in the society as a whole. Love still reigns supreme in the romance; it can overcome any obstacle. The underlying assumption is that "any woman, if she is truly feminine . . . possesses the necessary weapons to make any man fall in love with her" (Amorós). Premarital sex, abortion, adultery and divorce are less common than in Anglo-Saxon romances, but they are no longer taboos. Religion is hardly mentioned; the world of the Spanish romance is a secular one in which the only ideology is love.

The most famous authors of the modern *novela rosa* in Spain are Carlos de Santander and Corín Tellado. Their production is voluminous and has appeared in the form of novels, comic books, *fotonovelas* or photonovels (picture novelettes with balloon-captioned photos), in popular women's magazines and in radio and television soap operas. Some of Corín Tellado's titles will give the reader an idea of their content: *Has jugado con fuego* (You Have Played with Fire), *Tu marido está aquí* (Your Husband Is Here), *Amargo despertar* (Bitter Awakening), *La obsesión* (The Obsession), *Me siento culpable* (I Feel Guilty), *Tú y yo* (You and I), *Convivencia peligrosa* (A Dangerous Life Together), *¿Qué le pasa a tu marido?* (What's Wrong with Your Husband?), *Una historia de amor* (A Love Story), *Bendita equivocación* (Blessed Mistake), *Sólo amor* (Only Love).

I have in my hands a mercifully short novel by Corín Tellado, published in the women's magazine *Vanidades* (October 1996), printed in Miami and distributed throughout the Spanish-speaking world. Since one of the traits of the sentimental novel is its repeatability, this book will serve as an example of hundreds of others in Spain and Latin America. In *Matrimonio indeciso* (Undecided Marriage), the narrator is Anita, a thirty-eight-year-old Spanish woman married to Celso Mínguez, with whom she has had two children. Like most protagonists of the sentimental novel, they have plenty of money. Anita can't help telling the reader that she is pretty: her attractiveness "almost borders on authentic beauty." As for Celso, he "is dark, although he has a few gray hairs; he has greenish eyes and if he is not exactly an Adonis, he is an attractive, strong and athletic man." After twenty years of life together, their passion is fading. Anita discovers that Celso has a mistress. He leaves the house and goes to live with the other woman; he and Anita are legally separated. She spills her heart to her friend Sofía, the inevitable female confidante, and begins an affair with a married man named Teo. When Celso returns to the house one day, he and Anita make love with renewed fervor and he begins to spend the weekends at the house—strangely enough, without the knowledge of the children. (Their daughter is seventeen.) She continues her secret rendezvous with Teo. One Saturday Celso invites Anita to lunch with the kids at the sailing club. It is a sunny day in spring (the first time the weather and the season of the year have been mentioned in the novel). Over a meal of "shellfish, soup and lobster" (is lobster not a shellfish?), Celso tells Anita that he has left his lover and wants to live with her and the children again. She accepts. When her former lover Teo calls one day, she tells him "I'm sorry, but I've gone back to Celso. Forget me, because I will always be a faithful wife. Now I am totally happy with my husband and my two children."

In spite of the changes in sexual mores reflected in this novel, we note that the double standard continues to hold. Celso lives openly with another woman, but Anita must see Teo clandestinely in restaurants and motels on the outskirts of town. Her friend Sofía tells her clearly the rule of the patriarchal game: if her husband discovers that she is sleeping with another man, he will never forgive her, and their marriage will be lost forever. On the other hand, he expects Anita to accept the fact that he is living with another woman. So the Mínguez's remarriage will be founded on concealment and silence.

The pages of the novel are interspersed with advertisements for psychics ("Professor Cosmos," for example), a skin ointment and plastic surgery, in addition to a crossword puzzle (*crucigrama* in Spanish), called here a "Vanigrama."

The *novela rosa* has added very little to Spanish literature. Unlike the thriller (see below), it does not demand a modicum of craft by the author. If one purpose of literature is to give us a deeper knowledge of the world, the romance not only fails to fulfill that purpose but mystifies our understanding. Speaking of a series of Corín Tellado photonovels—which could just as well be her novels—Amorós says: "I have not found . . . any psychological subtlety, nor critical awareness, nor trace of intelligence or creativity, nor sense of humor. In short, nothing that surprises me in any way, that 'opens' me to some kind of interesting vital experience. Perhaps that is precisely what pleases so many readers, what they are looking for—comfortable predictability." There are few expressions of popular Spanish culture about which this stunning denial could be made.

In recent years the *novela rosa* has been a fertile source of parody for "serious" writers like Carmen Martín Gaite, Terençi Moix and Manuel Vázquez Montalbán—names that appear in this and preceding chapters—as well as Latin American authors like Gabriel García Márquez, Manuel Puig and Mario Vargas Llosa. Their works are what Stephanie Sieburth calls "mass cultural novels," "in-between works" or hybrids of low and high culture. *Don Quixote* may have been the first mass cultural novel in its blend of popular literature with the most modern narrative techniques of the time. Contemporary authors and movie directors like Pedro Almodóvar have found the sentimental novel, with its melodrama, rhetoric and absurdity, a soft target for parody. Their characters, like thousands of real Spaniards, avidly consume *novelas rosas*—and related forms like popular music, film, radio and TV soap operas—and attempt to follow their formulas in their own lives. The result is a hilarious and sometimes sad parody, in which the characters' illusions necessarily clash with a world that was not written by Corín Tellado.

COMICS

Unlike the sentimental novel, comic books have undergone a unique development that reveals many aspects of modern Spanish life. The most dreamlike of all media, they draw on the unconscious anxieties and desires of mass audiences. After the oral tradition they are probably the most pervasive and well-studied form of popular culture in the Peninsula. They are closely related to major styles of printed popular literature discussed in this chapter—the sentimental novel and the thriller—as well as other genres like pornography, the western, spy novels, horror and science fiction, all of which appear frequently as comics. In this they are a compendium of popular literature in Spain. They are also a marvelous vehicle for irrepressible Spanish humor. As one website on the genre says, "If there's something we know how to do, it's laugh at ourselves." Should the world of Ray Bradbury's *Fahrenheit 451* come true—in which comic books are the only reading material in the world—we would be better off than if we had nothing but sentimental novels to read.

Just as Anglo-Saxon critics trace the comic to Hogarth, Spaniards often trace it to Goya. Unlike the English artist's works, his humorous sketches and prints are usually not sequential: they do not tell a single story. Yet some of them, especially the *Caprichos* (Whims, c. 1798), combine image and text in a way that anticipates the cartoon and comic. Many writers, both inside and outside the Peninsula, cite Goya as a forerunner of the genre.

The early development of the form in Spain is similar to that in other European countries. The first important comic book in the country, *TBO* (1917), became so popular that it actually gave its name to the genre. Its three letters play on the Spanish words "*Te veo*" (I see you) and indicate the visual nature of the classic strip. The Royal Spanish Academy of the Language, an institution not known for its haste, gave respectability to this pioneer magazine in 1968 by officially recognizing *tebeo* as the correct word for the genre, preferable to the foreign-sounding "comic." To my knowledge Spain is the only country in the world where the title of a comic book gave a generic name to the form.

The story of *TBO* is the story of early Spanish comics. Its circulation gradually climbed from 39,000 copies a week in 1920 to 220,000 on the eve of the Civil War (1936). Although both factions produced comics during the hostilities, circulation plummeted as the conflict dragged on. In the postwar years poverty and paper shortages made all print forms a luxury. *TBO* appeared sporadically; as paper supplies slowly grew it became monthly in 1946, weekly in 1949. Largely because of its links to prewar Spain, the magazine was read eagerly by all social classes, who followed the usual Spanish custom of sharing their reading material. Juan Antonio Ramírez, one of the best historians of the genre, estimates that each issue must have been seen by some fifteen readers in the dark years of 1945–1955. Used issues were sold at special stands for exchange and resale ("*puestos de recambio y de reventa*"). With the tourist and industrial booms in the following decade the number of readers per issue dropped to ten or twelve. Collective reading continues right up to the more prosperous present, suggesting that it is an ingrained custom as much as an economic necessity.

Spanish *tebeos* must be seen against the background of the "official" children's magazines of the postwar years—publications like *En Marcha* (On the March), edited by the Female Section of the Falangist Party; *Volad* (Take Flight), produced by Catholic Action; *¡Hossana!*, sponsored by the Eucharistic Crusaders of Spain. In this stultifying atmosphere comics must have been a blast of fresh air for many children. According to Terençi Moix they were far more influential than the didactic, religious publications fostered by the state and the Church.

During the decade after the Civil War (1936–1939), comic books expressed the nation's collective unconscious as well as any other form of popular culture. They were the refuge of a people sunk in misery and pessimism, much as they had been for Americans during the Great Depression. One of the most popular series of the time was accurately called *DDT Contra las Penas* (DDT Your Pain). The censors, never known for their intelligence, assumed that comics were less dangerous than more prestigious literary forms. Yet sometimes the genre was so clearly rebellious that even the censors were not fooled. When a strip featuring a mischievous young boy called

Satanás (Satan) appeared in the mid-1940s, the government demanded that his name be deleted. Thus the character Ginesito (Little Ginés) was born; he became so popular that he outsold foreign competitors for several years. A more powerful form of coercion was "prior censorship" through the state's control of the paper supply under the Vice-Secretariat of National Education.

When it became clear, even to the dull-witted censors, that Spanish *tebeos* were expressing subversive values, the government set up legal guidelines. In Chapter III, paragraph 9 of the "Orientation of Juvenile Publications" (1952) we read: "[One will avoid] Any deviance in humor toward ridicule of parents' authority, the wholesomeness of the family and the home, respect for those who exercise authority, love for the Fatherland and obedience of the laws." Where there was smoke there was clearly fire. In a study of fifty-four Spanish strips in the period 1947–1949, Federico Revilla counted no less than thirty-three cases of children who had fun at their parents' expense. In these publications he found "dissidence, often violent, against the established order . . . a permanent frustration, an insidious dissatisfaction . . . harsh and determined opposition to the father and other adults. . . . Ferocious, surly humor and brutality." In their portrayal of the country's malaise, Spanish *tebeos* anticipated the realistic or "social" novel and poetry of the following decades.

American comics invaded Spain in the 1940s and 1950s, a period that coincided with the genre's golden age in the United States. Moix says that Spanish kids spent their childhood "literally devouring the heroes of the classic American comic . . . Flash Gordon . . . Tarzan . . . Merlin the Magician . . . Tim Tyler . . . Rip Kirby, Captain Marvel . . . Blond Panther (Sheena), etc." American and other foreign series, with their higher-quality paper and design, forced the impoverished native industry to sharpen its craft. Moix spoke of the "eternal economic underdevelopment of our *tebeos*." The underdevelopment proved to be less than eternal, since it only lasted until the late 1970s.

There were three trends in Spanish comic-book publishing during the postwar years, all located in the Catalan-speaking areas of the Peninsula. The Bruguera school, centered around the family-run publisher of the same name in Barcelona, tended to produce the most realistic and subversive collections—*DDT Contra las Penas, Pulgarcito* (Tom Thumb), *Tío Vivo* (Sharp Guy, with a wordplay on Merry-Go-Round), *Mortadelo* (Baloney). The *TBO* school (also located in Barcelona) favored a more innocuous humor. Finally, the Valencia school tended to mix the trends of Bruguera and *TBO* in collections like *Jaimito* (Little Jimmy) and *Pumby*.

Most critics also divide the comics of the postwar period into three main categories: adventure, the *historieta* or humorous strip, female comics. Each has been well studied. Some of the more famous adventure heroes, in the order of their appearance, were El Coyote, a Zorro-like figure who starred in endless pulp novels as well, created by the prolific José Mallorquí; El Cuto, a boy who had exciting adventures all around the world and in many historical epochs, drawn by Jesús Blanco, the most famous of all Spanish cartoonists; the Guerrero del Antifaz (Masked Warrior), who pursued evil Moors in the Spain of the Catholic Kings; Capitán Trueno (Captain Thunder), a contemporary of Richard the Lion-Hearted who defended the hallowed ideals of chivalry; Jabato, a kind of Iberian Spartacus who seemed to spring out of an Italian "peplum" movie; Haxtur, a creation of Víctor de la Fuente in the early 1970s, a guerrilla fighter not unlike Che Guevara, who also pursued his exploits in the jungle and died in a final episode—one of the only mortal heroes in the history of comic books. Some of these characters lasted for decades and inspired radio and television programs, plays, movies and magazines. A few are still available in new editions or in facsimile.

Of course these adventure strips embodied many of the values of Francoist Spain. In contrast to American comics, they tended to evoke heroes of the past. It is no coincidence that some of the archaic Spanish characters embodied the virtues of faith and valor at a time when the regime was attempting to revive the glory of the Catholic Kings. Moix, who has analyzed these popular heroes brilliantly, speaks of their "mystique of masculinity." They were all male and none had a normal, healthy relationship with women, who always represented the Other, either a disturbing presence or an idealized object. She was often associated with exotic-erotic types like Moorish and Jewish princesses or members of a harem. In this sense, according to Moix, the message of the comics was the same one inculcated in middle-class Spanish boys by their parents: women represented danger and "in the end, deep down, a mortal venereal disease." The muscular heroes and their younger sidekicks—following the well-known model of Batman and Robin—underwent a series of adventures and tortures that revealed a male camaraderie, a masochistic revelling in torture and a sublimated homosexuality. By the 1950s and especially the 1960s, under the influence of television, torture became less important than violence: "a punch with a fist or a blast of the bazooka . . . replaces the slow death by fire."

The second major type of comic in the postwar period was the *historieta* or humorous strip. Some of the most enduring and representative characters were Carpanta (Hunger Pain), a picaresque character in a poverty-stricken nation; Don Berrinche (Mr. Hothead), a curmudgeon who terrorized the streets with his wooden club surmounted by a nail; La Familia Ulises (The Ulysses's), a Barcelona family in a satirical comedy of manners; Zipi y Zape (Zip and Zap or Rumpus), two mischievous brothers who became the country's Katzenjammer Kids; Mortadelo y Filemón (Baloney and Fillet), an absurd private eye and his assistant who may be Spain's most famous comic characters of all time; Cucharito, the protagonist of the world's only bullfight strip; La Familia Churumbel (The Churumbel Family), a clan of Andalusian gypsies whose story is a politically incorrect example of the *costumbrista and regionalist strip, remotely comparable to "Li'l Abner." Many of these figures are household names for Spaniards; some inspired radio and television tie-ins, movies, fanzines, toys and dolls.

These characters and stories show the underside of Spanish society from the post-Civil War to the transition and democracy. Ramírez has said:

The *historieta* . . . offered a priceless testimony of our social, economic and cultural reality, far superior, without a doubt, to the cinema and "vanguardist" plastic arts of the time. . . . When official censorship was falling hard on the traditional manifestations of "high culture," a whole tragicomic pandemonium of characters was sneaking in the back door of the *tebeo*—smugglers, hoboes, workers who hate their bosses, shabby-genteel old maids, amorous maniacs, perverts, nuts of all kinds.

Even in the most innocent strips there was a depiction of daily events and concerns that was hard to find anywhere else in Spain, except between the lines of certain humorous magazines like *La Codorniz* ("The Quail"; see Chapter 9) and in the best fiction and poetry of the age. *Tebeos* were accessible to almost everyone, first- or secondhand. I remember seeing middle-class commuters reading comics on buses, streetcars and subways in the Franco years.

The best early strips of the postwar period show us a Spain racked by hunger, misery, solitude and frustration. The recently ended Civil War was prolonged in domestic warfare between husbands and wives, brothers and sisters, children and parents, or in battle at the workplace between bosses and their employees. In his study of selected *tebeos* of the late 1940s, Revilla did not find a single example of conflict resolved by persuasion rather than force, nor of a "natural and sincere" treatment of relations between the sexes.

The sexual theme in postwar Spanish comics is a subject that could fill a whole volume. In the first two decades there was a slew of tiny, solitary male characters, mortally shy, who dreamed of finding the perfect lady of their dreams, like so many diminished, modern Don Quixotes. They had long, humorous names like Cucufato Pi and Golondrino Pérez, two of the most famous. They were hungry for love at a time when many Spaniards were still hungry for food as well. When the diminutive characters spotted a beautiful *señorita* with a short skirt—who towered over them—they would go into ecstasy. The censors realized the erotic potential of these stories and clamped down on the cartoonists, who were obliged to reduce their protagonists' excitement to a series of icons: levitation, eyes popping out of heads, fluttering hearts, the inevitable bouquet of flowers. By the late 1950s, when the country was already undergoing rapid change, these lovelorn characters began to die out. They were replaced by a new breed of affluent dandies sporting well-perfumed mustaches and a carnation in their lapel, like Pilaropo and Rigoberto Picaporte.

The story of women in the postwar period was told through comic characters like Floripondia Piripi, but mostly through the subgenre of special collections published for girls. Ramírez has written a fine study on the subject. He speaks of "that peculiar mystique of femininity, so radically indigenous to Spain, that is reflected in *tebeos* for girls. . . . The story of the feminine Spanish comic is not only the story of an artistic subgenre, but also of Spanish women and their frustrations in the postwar years."

The female *tebeo* passed through several stages. In the first decade after the Civil War they resembled "notebooks for hunger," portraying a miraculous realm of little girls and angels who rewarded them for good behavior. Boys and men belonged to a foreign world because of what Moix calls the "educational apartheid between the sexes." A menagerie of talking animals, gnomes and other creatures surrounded the feminine characters. Moix believes that the "irrationality" of the stories was directly related to the movies and comics created by Walt Disney, translated into Spanish and distributed throughout the Peninsula. Some of the local collections were *Caperucita* (Little Red Riding Hood without the Red), *Hadas* (Fairies), *Idilio* (Idyll), *Mis Chicas* (My Little Girls), *Princesita* (Little Princess).

In the next decade a second or "pedagogical" stage began with the publication of *Florita*, called by Ramírez "the first feminine *tebeo* that abandons the miserable world of isolation in order to launch a conquest, in the Spanish style, of the 'American way of life.'" The title character of the magazine was a teenage girl who embodied the repertoire of feelings, ideas and behavior considered to be ideal by the emerging middle class. Florita enjoyed the unheard-of luxuries of a private bedroom, a maid, horseback riding, elegant parties, trips abroad. The American influence on her character is shown by the fact that she had a television set in her room by 1951, a full five years before the inauguration of TV in Spain. (What programs was she supposed to be watching?) By the end of the decade Florita was in fact competing with television for an audience; the new medium created a need for a more realistic kind of publication.

A third stage began with an unequalled explosion of "sentimental" comics for women. More hit the newsstands between 1958 and 1963 than in the previous twenty years. New collections like *Belinda, Aventuras de una Secretaria* (Belinda, Adventures of a Secretary), *Mary Noticias* (Mary News, a journalist) and *Lillian, Azafata del Aire* (Lillian, Air Stewardess) incarnated the ambitions of a new generation of Spanish girls who dreamed of attaining independence through glamorous jobs. The heroines worked side by side with men; they often fell in love with their male counterparts. By the mid-1960s these comics were competing not only with the *novela rosa* but also with the illustrated women's magazines and photonovels that were flooding the market. They could not match the appeal of the newer publications and started to disappear from the newsstands. By the early 1970s only a few remained.

The May 1968 revolution in France affected comic books in Spain much more than in America. The avant-garde underground strip was born. Under the Francoist dictatorship it was easy to confuse rock and roll, drugs and sex with revolution. As usual Catalonia led the rest of the country. The talented artist Enric Sió created, in Catalan, his first independent work, "Lavinia 2.016 o la Guerra dels Poetes" (Lavinia 2016 and the War of the Poets), which appeared in the monthly magazine *Oriflama* in 1968. It portrayed life in a city of the future, easily recognizable as Barcelona, inhabited by well-known personalities from the cultural Left alongside comic-strip characters like Snoopy, mythic figures from popular culture like Bonnie and Clyde, images from advertising, cinema, theater and music. (That future turned out to be the 1980s.) Sió's first color series, "Sorang," depicted a submarine society after a nuclear catastrophe, combining elements of photography and commercial art. A third strip, "Nus y Atleta" (Nus and Athlete), started as a mystery story enriched by references to pop art, photography, film and television. It showed violent contrasts between black-and-white and color as well as montages and multiple levels of reality. It connected the avant-garde comic in Spain to one of the country's most persistent artistic trends, surrealism, opening the way for new artists in the 1970s and 1980s. Other recurrent trends would also appear in underground artists—the *picaresque, satire, *esperpento* or the grotesque.

The death of Franco had less impact on comic books than on radio, television, cinema and the press. The genre had already begun to change radically before the transition to democracy. On the one hand some of the traditional forms like the feminine and the adventure comic continued to decline, never to recover their popularity. On the other hand the underground strip went on experimenting with new visual and verbal styles. Some of the most original creations—most of them still on the newsstands—were the well-known Cairo series that fused the detective format with sadomasochistic themes; Peter Pank, an ultraviolent appropriation of Peter Pan (Pank approximates the Spanish pronunciation of "punk"), with Tinker Bell sporting a mohawk hairdo; the popular El Víbora (The Viper), a hermaphrodite (as suggested by the masculine article with the feminine noun) whose sexual adventures were unrestrained by gender. The success of these works is borne out by the fact that they are sold in bound volumes whose prices match those of canonical works of art and literature.

There are no superhero comics in Spain, perhaps because the market is saturated by American imports. Nowadays adventure simply means heroes or anti-heroes who are journalists, soldiers, cops or detectives. One strip, "El Manantial de la Noche" (The Source of the Night), by Fernando Luna and Miguelanxo Prado, borrows from the famous Belgian cartoonist Hergé, creator of the immensely successful Tintin. Our hero is a rumpled Colombo-type who materializes out of the steam from the illustrator's coffee cup. His creator sends him off in search of the "source of the night," meanwhile making him eke out a living as a detective. The series is drawn with a gloomy, watery palette that caught the fancy of the editors at *Heavy Metal*, which has published a few installments in translation.

Comic books are the best medium for Spaniards' wonderful humor. Magazines like *El Jueves* (Thursday, discussed in Chapter 9) publish some of the funniest cartoon art in the world. Its offshoot, *La Puta Mili* (The Fucking Army) specializes in satirizing the ever more questionable institution of the military draft. In a recent sketch (available online), the cartoonist imagines five forms of alternate service for the country's growing number of conscientious objectors: (1) masseur of top models ("If I only had three hands!" says a recruit about to give a massage to Claudia Schiffer), (2) applier of suntan lotion for female Swedish tourists, (3) Spanish millionaire ("So they won't think we're a bunch of stick-in-the-muds"), (4) beach Don Juan ("Anything to help tourism!") and (5) mattress tester ("It's a hard job but someone has to do it").

The Catalans and Valencians continue to be the most innovative cartoonists in Spain. Their primacy has grown partly from a long tradition of good printing and graphic design, partly from their history of antifascism and anarchy that nourishes underground art. One of the few female artists in the genre, Nùria Pompeya, has used both the cartoon and the comic strip to denounce the old-fashioned socialization of women. In her syndicated "Palmira" series and in books like *Maternasis* and *Mujercitas* (Little Women), she offers frightening yet hilarious images of female children and adolescents who are brainwashed by their fathers, brothers, uncles, boyfriends and bosses.

Another well-known artist is the Valencian Nazario, who was already a famous drag queen and underground cartoonist before Franco's death. Since 1979 he has chronicled the adventures of Anarcoma, a gay man who cross-dresses, uses lurid makeup and has real breasts. He (or she) has more of the sexual attributes of both sexes than most people have of either one; the character is well hung and stacked at the same time. Accompanied by his macho boyfriend, he has adventures in a utopian, pansexual Barcelona where disease and jealousy do not exist.

Mariscal, another famous Catalan artist, has invented the Garriris, hedonistic critters who resemble Mickey and Pluto, Krazy Kat style. They cruise the endless beaches and the discos of Barcelona and the Costa Brava, drinking, stealing cars and chasing girls while cracking jokes and speaking to each other in disjointed slang. They have been exported to other countries, including the United States, where they appeared in *RAW*. Their creator Mariscal was the designer of Cobi, the mascot of the 1992 Olympic Games, and is sometimes considered the best artist among Spanish cartoonists.

Montesol is also a Catalan who sets his stories in Barcelona. Unlike Nazario and Mariscal, his art relies on a kind of everyday realism instead of fantasy. As one critic says, "His characters gossip, read, sit through pointless classes, shake down editors for more money, take road trips, talk (endlessly) about art, complain about their jobs, fuck, shoot up, sleep, go shopping, borrow records, have existential doubts and pointless affairs" (Anne Rubenstein). Montesol records the life of the post-Franco generation, which has moved in twenty years from rebellion to disenchantment and consumerism.

A final Catalan cartoonist is Martí, whose style and subject matter could not be more different from Nazario's, Mariscal's and Montesol's. His most famous protagonist is Taxista (The Cabbie), a kind of Catholic Dick Tracy on the streets of Barcelona. Martí's work has been translated into English and published in the United States. He also has a series about Dr. Vertigo, a psychiatrist who has the power of getting inside his patients' heads.

Miguelanxo Prado is an example of the new international dimension of Spanish comics. He has a weekly strip that is syndicated throughout Europe and Latin America—"El Manantial de la Noche," described earlier. He has collaborated in many animated film and television projects, has published twelve books and illustrated a recent novel by the prize-winning Mexican writer Laura Esquivel.

The manga invasion from Japan has affected Spain as well as every other country. These comics, full of violence, monsters, sex, science fiction and huge eyes—above all, eyes—have captured a small but devoted market. There are fanzines, specialized publications, TV programs, even an association of "defenders of anime and manga." Some Spanish illustrators imitate the Japanese form. Two of the most popular examples are *RYU* and *Sueños*, an erotic manga. But there is still no cause for alarm: two million copies are sold each week in Japan, compared to a mere eight thousand in Spain, a country with almost one-third as many inhabitants.

A greater threat to Spanish comics is the international market. Foreign companies headhunt for talent in Spain, a country the size of Montana with "at least as many good cartoonists as the United States" (Rubenstein). Some Spanish artists go abroad to work and live (Enric Sió), others work under foreign license, still others abandon the profession for lucrative fields like commercial art and advertising.

Comic books are one of the most important forms of popular culture in Spain. For fifty years they have tapped into Spaniards' deepest fears and yearnings. They show the evolution of Spanish society better than any other genre of popular literature. They draw on some of the best-rooted artistic tendencies in Spain—the picaresque, *costumbrismo, esperpento* or the grotesque, surrealism. They have bridged the gap between young and adult audiences: unlike their counterparts in other countries, Spanish cartoonists do not draw mainly for 13-year-old boys. Underground strips are published regularly and paradoxically have come to be a part of the mainstream. The best newspapers in the country review the *álbumes* or bound albums of comics alongside the latest novels and essays.

In 1997 the Biblioteca Nacional (National Library) in Madrid celebrated an exhibition entitled "Comics: The First 100 Years"—one year late, Spanish style. The organizer, Antonio Lara, called *tebeos* "the absolute and faithful mirror of Spanish reality." In addition to this one-time event, an annual "Semana de la Historieta" (Comic Strip Week) is held in the capital, while Barcelona has its yearly "Salón del Comic y la Ilustración" (Comic and Illustration Show). Both events involve "massive advance publicity, expositions, numerous social events, formal inaugurations and lectures, authors autographing their volumes and drawing cartoons, video and cartoon showings, daily bulletins, radio and television coverage and critics' ratings of the expositions" (Janet Pérez and Genaro Pérez). To top it off, the Spanish government actually supports these activities—something that would be unimaginable in the United States. For all these reasons the comic appears to have a long and dynamic future in Spain.

THRILLERS

The story of thrillers is one of the most fascinating in popular Spanish literature. They and the political novel are probably the two most important new fictional forms in post-Franco Spain. For different reasons, neither genre existed during the old regime; since the Generalissimo's death they have grown and reached maturity in a single generation.

Following the usage of other critics, I will employ the term "thriller" to refer to the hard-boiled detective novel—the Spanish *novela negra*, from the French *roman noir*, which of course is well-known in its cinematic form as film noir. In this sense the thriller is a subgenre of the mystery, the whodunit or detective novel. What separates it from these other subgenres is its emphasis on action, violence and sexuality, and its "dark" view of human nature and society.

During the nineteenth century in Spain, under the influence of Romanticism and *costumbrismo*, ballads, colportage or string literature and serialized novels (*folletines*) told stories of famous bandits and criminals. Spanish society was still too rural and preindustrial for a native crime fiction to take root. The first translations of detective novels in the early years of the twentieth century stimulated the interest of a few Spanish writers. The novelist Emilia Pardo Bazán, a Galician countess who had been an early champion of French naturalism in Spain, wrote reviews of Sir Arthur Conan Doyle and short stories that were clear imitations of foreign models. During the 1920s popular collections of crime novels copied American pulps. It was not until after the Civil War, in the 1940s, that certain Spanish authors could make a precarious living from writing mysteries. Since the genre was associated in the popular mind with Anglo-Saxon novelists, these writers used English-sounding pseudonyms: Alexis Barclay (A. Viader Vives), Clark Carrados (L. García Lecha), Lou Carrigan (A. Vera Ramírez), Donald Curtis and Curtis Garland (J. Gallardo Muñoz), Mark Halloran (J. Gubern Ribalta), Silver Kane (F. González Ledesma), Fel Marty (Félix Martínez Orejón), Charles Mitchell (Carlos Miguel Martínez), Joe Mogar (José Moreno García). Their novels were usually set in the United States with American protagonists. The tireless José Mallorquí, who worked in nearly every genre of popular literature, translated American mystery novels and invented popular characters of his own like La Sombra, an evident imitation of The Shadow. These writers published in cheap collections like Bruguera's *Serie Policíaca* (Police Series), Cliper's *Colección Misterio* (Mystery Collection) and Molino's *Hombres Audaces* (Men of Daring). In the 1950s, Bruguera initiated new series like *F.B.I.*, *Servicios Secretos* (Secret Service) and *Punto Rojo* (Red Spot), which emphasized the spy novel and reflected the atmosphere of the cold war; in fact they did not disappear until the collapse of the Soviet Union.

The pulp fiction of the Franco period tended to imitate the classic detective or mystery novel more than the thriller or the *roman noir*. Censorship would not have allowed the realism, the critical point of view, the loose sexual morals or the cynicism of the hard-boiled novel. When the publisher Mateu had Raymond Chandler's *The Lady in the Lake* translated in 1962 under the flashy title of *La 'dolce vita' en América* (exploiting the sensation of Federico Fellini's recent movie), the censors deleted several passages. It was not until the thaw of the *dictablanda in the early 1970s that foreign thrillers could be translated freely, circulate and influence Spanish writers.

There were other reasons for the late development of the hard-boiled novel in Spain. For years the *novela negra* had suffered from a kind of racial segregation in the elitist Spanish literary establishment. As Román Gubern has said, "it is a black man and literature is a fancy neighborhood where he doesn't have the right to live." Until the 1970s critics tended to classify detective novels along with the *folletín* or newspaper serial, the sentimental novel and science fiction as "subliterature." By the time of the transition from dictatorship to democracy, the line between "high" and "low" culture had begun to dissolve, making it possible for Spanish mystery novels to be accepted in the literary mainstream.

Historians of the detective novel have also argued that Francoist society did not have the structures necessary to make this kind of fiction plausible. The legal system contained obsolete laws and an archaic penal code that the regime in any case often ignored. The economy was controlled largely by the government, which prevented the kind of social mobility required by the thriller. Gubern believes this kind of fiction can only flourish in modern industrial countries with their "philosophy of insecurity" and "philosophy of anguish." (His words almost seem to define Spain's democratic transition, a time of sustained crisis at all levels of society.) He defines the detective novel as "a consequence of economic greed and the institution of private property; in other words, [it is] the scandal sheet and the anti-epic of capitalism."

In Spain the bourgeois revolution, industrialization and economic liberalism did not develop fully until the final years of Francoism and the transition to democracy. (Catalonia and the Basque country were notable exceptions.) Of course these are the same forces invoked to explain the rise of the modern novel in the nineteenth century. In Spain there was a cultural lag of almost a hundred years. With the modernization of national life in the 1970s, new realities emerged: massive emigration to the cities, urban violence, crime, terrorism, drugs. After Franco's death the fledgling democracy gave writers a freer approach to these new social problems, not to mention older ones like corruption, bribery, extortion and army or police brutality. At about the same time quality magazines devoted to mysteries appeared, specialized literary prizes for the genre began to abound and several authors won awards for detective novels.

Is it a mere coincidence that the thriller began to prosper precisely at the time of political transformation? Rob Rix has said with a fine sense of humor:

Whether the connection is merely coincidental, or whether the boom in thriller writing reflects a deep-seated cultural response to the mysterious plot of the Transition, constitutes an enigma which the critic as detective may attempt to solve, or which the investigator of cultural form and substance may choose to overlook. . . . Genre fiction, in a post-modernist world, is as deadly serious as any other construction of reality which lurks, in the guise of literature, to entrap and implicate that quintessential victim, the reader.

Spanish writers in fact took their work in a deadly serious way. The ubiquitous Manuel Vázquez Montalbán—poet, essayist, journalist, novelist and political commentator—who published the first Spanish thriller exactly one year before Franco's death, made his anti-hero an ex-Marxist and based the plots of several novels around political events. Since that time he has published many more works in the same series, claiming that he does not write detective fiction but realistic novels in the manner of Honoré de Balzac, Charles Dickens, and Benito Pérez Galdós—the great chronicler of nineteenth-century Spanish life. He has even affirmed that the detective novel as such does not exist in Spain, since it lacks a long-standing tradition and because good writing of any kind should not be classified as genre literature. This comment could be seen as an act of professional suicide, since Vázquez Montalbán is the author of the most popular thrillers in the Spanish-speaking world.

The spectacular emergence of detective fiction should also be seen against the wider background of other literature in democratic Spain. By the mid-1970s the experimentation and social realism that marked the post–Civil War novel—as seen in writers like Camilo José Cela (Nobel Prize 1989) and Juan Goytisolo—had run their course. Other literary genres like poetry had already renovated themselves and created a new language for different times. In this situation detective fiction, especially the American hard-boiled variety with its penchant for social criticism, appealed to Spanish writers as a new vehicle for exploring their quickly changing world. Vázquez Montalbán said "the best contribution of the *novela negra* to the Spanish novel in general has been an injection of realist poetics that surpasses all the other tired and worn-out realisms." At the same time masters like Hammett and Chandler were published in new and better translations while a flux of noir films (foreign and Spanish), television programs and comic books also appeared on the scene. Spanish writers, while realizing that it would be impossible to maintain a kind of virginal purity in the postmodern world of electronics and the global village, nevertheless adapted the conventions of the thriller to local realities, or actually subverted those conventions in order to avoid still more neocolonization by American culture. They created Spanish characters in Spanish settings, dealt with Spanish problems and no longer had to hide behind the mask of Anglo-Saxon pseudonyms.

It would be hard to speak of a single school of detective fiction in contemporary Spain. What most writers in the genre have in common is a desire to write unmistakably Spanish novels, frequently recurring to national traditions like the picaresque, *costumbrismo*, surrealism, *esperpento* or the grotesque. I will discuss here a few of the most well-known writers of detective fiction in Spain.

Francisco García Pavón (1919–1989) is the only writer to adopt the cozy English detective story to a Spanish setting. Born in the town of Tomelloso (Ciudad Real) in La Mancha, he spent most of his life in Madrid as a drama critic and professor at the Royal School of Dramatic Art. He won several important literary awards for his mystery stories, including the Critics' Prize (Premio de la Crítica) in 1968, the Nadal in 1969 and the Piggy Bank (Hucha de Oro) for short stories in 1975. His career shows the increasing respectability and acceptance of detective fiction by the Spanish literary establishment and readers.

García Pavón wrote a series of short stories and novels with his Holmes-Watson or Poirot-Hastings protagonists, Manuel González (alias Plinio) and Don Lotario. Plinio is a small-town man with a wife and daughter, not terribly educated but with plenty of common sense and intuition (his "*pálpitos*" or hunches). He works as chief of the police force in Tomelloso and has a reputation for being the best criminal investigator in Spain. His helper, the retired veterinarian Don Lotario, often helps him and also serves as narrator, like Dr. Watson. García Pavón's plots are not nearly as well constructed as those of classic English or American mysteries. He often neglects to give the reader sufficient clues and the crime sometimes seems to be a mere pretext for descriptions of the life and characters in a small Spanish village: Plinio's wife and daughter, the Secretary of City Hall Don Tomaíto, the police corporal Malez, Braulio "the philosopher," Rocío the baker of *buñuelos* or fritters, the practical joker "Faraón" (Pharaoh), the waiter Manolo. More than mysteries, these stories and novels are *costumbrista* writing in the frame of detective fiction. When Plinio solves a crime, which he does as infallibly as Sherlock Holmes or Hercule Poirot, life returns to its normal routine in a society that is basically honest and just.

García Pavón's stories are collected in *Historias de Plinio* (Stories of Plinio, 1968), *Nuevas historias de Plinio* (New Stories of Plinio, 1970), *El último sábado* (The Last Saturday, 1974) and *Cuentos de amor . . . vagamente* (Stories of Love . . . Vaguely, 1985). Two of his best-known novels are *Las hermanas coloradas* (The Red-Headed Sisters, 1970) and *El hospital de los dormidos* (The Hospital of the Sleepers, 1981).

García Pavón soon developed a cult following and was the first serious Spanish author to concentrate on the detective novel. He gave the genre a new dignity that would open the way for younger writers. Most of them would be drawn to the urban private-eye novel rather than the English-style rural mystery.

The protean Manuel Vázquez Montalbán was the first practitioner of the hard-boiled detective novel in Spain; he is still the most successful. In addition to writing more than a dozen volumes of short stories and novels in the genre, he has been its main spokesman ever since he founded and edited the magazine *Gimlet* in 1981–1982. (It was named after the bitter gin-and-lime cocktail drunk by Philip Marlowe in *The Long Goodbye*.) Speaking of his early career as a mystery writer he said "as a handful of crime novelists . . . we were almost treated like criminals." Since the publication of *Tatuaje* (Tatoo, 1974), he has been treated like a celebrity. In that novel we find fully developed the unusual character of Pepe Carvalho, a *charnego* or son of immigrants to Barcelona (like the author himself), an ex-Communist, ex-agent of the CIA, now a world-weary private detective who believes in the underdog, good food and sex. ("Sex and food are the most serious things in the world.") He is an educated private eye who despises high culture; one of his hobbies is burning books from his highly selective library. Carvalho is a good cook who also likes to drink wine and ice-cold *orujo* or Galician firewater (revealing his peasant background from northwestern Spain). He is almost as cynical and violent as some of the criminals he pursues. His presence imbues the novels with a sense of irony and moral ambiguity. Like Chandler's Marlowe he appears to be cynical and tough-skinned; yet inside he is a sentimental loner with his own sense of what is right. Carvalho's true enemies are not petty wrongdoers but a corrupt capitalist society that encourages competition rather than solidarity and in which the big fish usually eat the small. The protagonist knows that he cannot change the system. All he can do is perform his job and right a few wrongs in a fallen world that will always be ruled by power and greed. "I tell you that this society is rotten. It doesn't believe in anything," he tells his sidekick Biscúter, a reformed delinquent. His other confidants are Bromuro, a bootblack, and Charo, a call girl with whom he maintains an on-and-off relationship.

If García Pavón used the frame of the mystery to write *costumbrista* fiction, Vázquez Montalbán used the frame of the noir to record the life of contemporary Spain. His style has a unique blend of realism, satire, lyricism and humor. If a rural Spanish village was the normal setting for García Pavón's work, the metropolis of Barcelona is the usual backdrop for the younger writer's books. Vázquez Montalbán shows the Catalan city with all of its vitality and shame: the Ramblas, Vallvidrera, the port, the Barrio Chino or red-light district, the sordid proletarian neighborhoods. It is a postindustrial, postmodern world with abundant allusions to the media, mass communication and popular culture—street slang, radio, television, film, the press, advertising. The author mixes the collage technique with lyrical insights, bespeaking his longtime career as a poet. Here are a few phrases from *Tatuaje*: "And one of the young woman's hands slipped like a cold dove inside of Carvalho's shirt," "The surf of the bed sheets," "The soul of the wooden stairway," "His eyes nipped green horizons."

Vázquez Montalbán's work constitutes an original mosaic of contemporary Spain. Some of the novels contain lucid commentaries on current issues: the *desencanto or disillusionment of the transition to democracy in *Los mares del Sur* (The Southern Seas, 1979), the internal crisis of the Spanish Communist Party in *Asesinato en el Comité Central* (Murder in the Central Committee, 1981), the preparations for the 1992 Olympic Games in *El delantero centro fue asesinado al atardecer* (The Center-Forward Was Murdered at Dusk, 1988). This novel establishes the first stage in Pepe Carvalho's inevitable decline with the death of Bromuro, his principal informant about the Barcelona underworld. The aging investigator suffers from fractious health and becomes increasingly obsessed with retirement, or rather with the likelihood of ending his days in penury and solitude. In *El laberinto griego* (The Greek Labyrinth, 1991), Carvalho's lover Charo abandons Barcelona, where she can no longer make a living as a menopausal hooker. The characters' lives progress in the real time of contemporary history in contrast to the frozen time of most detective fiction and genre novels in general. In this way Vázquez Montalbán's thrillers have not turned into a stylized and monotonous serial. He has decided to write a few more novels and to end in 1999 with a final work, appropriately called *Millennium*. No doubt many readers, including this one, will miss their old friend Pepe Carvalho.

Vázquez Montalbán has won numerous awards for his detective novels: the Planeta (1979) and the International Prize for Detective Fiction (1981) for *Los mares del Sur*; the National Prize of Literature, the Europa and the International Crime Fiction Writers' Guild Prize (1992) for *Galíndez* (1990). The author has also been recognized by popular acclaim. The "Serie Carvalho" is the first collection to be devoted to a single native detective in the history of Spanish publishing; it has been adapted to television, the movies and even mystery puzzles. In *Las recetas de Carvalho* (Carvalho's Recipes, 1989), the author gathered together some of the best food passages from the series, adding ingredients and instructions for preparing them. Vázquez Montalbán is also the first author to export the Spanish thriller: his novels have been translated into many languages. They are probably too loosely constructed to win favor among Anglo-Saxon mystery buffs: he could use a few basic lessons about constructing plots. This is a clue to the way that Vázquez Montalbán and other Spanish writers see the thriller: they tend to ignore the rigid structure of the classic detective story while embracing the milieu of the hard-boiled American thriller. Like Raymond Chandler they are often careless about such minor matters as consistency or even clarity in the plot.

Eduardo Mendoza is another pioneer of detective fiction in Spain. Like Vázquez Montalbán he is a native of Barcelona, the city that has given rise to the genre in the Peninsula. He studied law and worked as an interpreter for the United Nations. His first published novel, *La verdad sobre el caso Savolta* (The Truth About the Savolta Case, 1975) was an instant success, winning the Critics' Prize and going through many editions. It was an original but fairly standard mystery, which would be followed by a pair of off-beat parodies that are two of the most outlandish thrillers ever written in Spanish—*El misterio de la cripta embrujada* (The Mystery of the Enchanted Crypt, 1979) and *El laberinto de las aceitunas* (The Labyrinth of Olives, 1982). Their unnamed narrator-protagonist is an inmate at an asylum for criminal lunatics during the transition to democracy; he is freed by the cops to help them solve shady crimes in which there is a suggestion of silent complicity. He is a sort of contemporary rogue in the Spanish tradition of the picaresque novel, a schizophrenic petty thief who drinks Pepsi-Cola. After solving the crimes in each novel, he is promptly recommitted to the asylum "so that the bold gendarmes can get on with their peaceful lives without interference from lunatics who, if left to their own devices, might catch all the criminals in Barcelona" (Leo Hickey).

Mendoza's two novels are a wild parody of both the classic mystery and the hardboiled thriller—with possible influence of Donald Westlake—as well as the metaphysical detective story in the style of the Argentine master, Jorge Luis Borges. He also draws on diverse traditions of classic Spanish literature, especially Miguel de Cervantes: the picaresque, the sane madman in a crazy world (Don Quixote), the labyrinthine plot of the Byzantine novel, the interpolated story, historical fiction, melodrama, the *esperpento* or grotesque. Combining all of these elements with the techniques of experimental fiction, Mendoza has created a brilliant pastiche which is hard to compare to the work of any other writer. The critic Ian Michaels, himself a practitioner of the mystery novel, calls Mendoza an honorable exception to the rule of sloppy construction in Spanish thrillers. Unlike Vázquez Montalbán, however, the author apparently does not plan to write a series of detective novels and has moved onto other genres in his later work: biography, travel-adventure and science fiction. The extent to which the thriller has been accepted in the literary canon is proven by the fact that both Eduardo Mendoza and Vázquez Montalbán are required reading in the national curriculum of Spanish high schools, side by side with heavy hitters like Federico García Lorca and Camilo José Cela.

A third author of thrillers from Barcelona, the capital of crime fiction in the Peninsula, is Andreu Martín. He is very different from Mendoza and Vázquez Montalbán in the sense that he has no qualms about being considered a professional mystery writer. He has created a highly personal style in the psychological thriller or what he prefers to call the novel of urban terror. Like Hammett's work, Martín's reveals the connections between crime and the violence of the social structure itself. He is also the most prolific author of thrillers in the country, with more than twenty novels and collections of short stories to his credit since the late 1970s. Unlike most writers in the genre, he has not based his works around a single private eye: sometimes his protagonist is the criminal, other times a cop, a detective or an amateur crime solver.

Andreu Martín studied psychology in college and has worked in various fields as a journalist and writer—comics (*Sam Balluga*, an American sleuth), theater, film, science fiction. He has been president of the Spanish Association of Crime Writers and a member of the International Association. To my knowledge his thrillers have not been translated to other languages, probably because they are so rooted in their Spanish context; yet they are tightly plotted and have the kind of simple, direct language preferred in the American noir. Martín surpasses all his models in violence: some passages in his books are so crude and bloody that they are hard to stomach even for the most hard-boiled reader. He has said: "The violence in my novels is usually the kick in the shins that we would all like to give once and for all when we find ourselves oppressed by the more subtle kind of violence that is exercised against us." Martín's best-known novel is probably *Prótesis* (1980), which was turned into the movie *Fanny Pelopaja* (1984), directed by Vicente Aranda. His novel *Barcelona Connection* (1988) was based on the screenplay for a film of the same title. It is not by chance that Martín's work has been compared to that of Luis Buñuel, the master of cinematic cruelty, violence and satire of bourgeois morality.

Juan Madrid is the only major Spanish detective novelist whose work is not set primarily in Barcelona. Born in the Andalusian city of Málaga, he studied literature and history in college. Since 1959 he has lived in Madrid and has made it the scene for most of his seventeen novels, three novellas, many stories and screenplays for the popular TV series *Brigada Central*. In them he evokes the capital of Spain with all its contrasts—the old Plaza Mayor, the modern suburbs, the Gran Vía, Plaza de España, Calle Princesa, the elegant Salamanca quarter, the seedy Calle Carretas and Lavapiés; the bars and clubs of the nocturnal city—Casa Domingo, Bar Durán, La Luna de Medianoche, Club Melodías, Cervecería de Hamburgo. This world is inhabited by a motley crowd of petty criminals, drug dealers and addicts, pickpockets, barmaids, strippers, prostitutes, gypsies, police confidants and corrupt cops. In his work as an investigative criminal reporter for the magazine *Cambio 16*, Madrid became acquainted with the milieu of his novels in person. It has been said that he "resembles a character taken out of a vintage *roman noir*" (José F. Colmeiro).

Juan Madrid is probably the closest thing to a Spanish reworking of Raymond Chandler. His portrayal of Madrid recalls the American writer's Los Angeles of the 1930s and 1940s, but with a rawer edge and echoes of Spanish traditions like *costumbrismo*, the picaresque and *tremendismo*, an exaggerated form of social realism popularized by Cela and other writers in the 1950s. Vázquez Montalbán calls Madrid a combination of the purest *roman noir* plus Pío Baroja, the Spanish neonaturalist admired by Hemingway. Many of his novels, short stories and scripts feature Toni Romano, a private investigator in the line of Chandler's Philip Marlowe. Toni is the son of an alcoholic bootblack, an ex-policeman and ex-boxer, who works as an unlicensed detective. He sells his services to whoever needs them, rescuing people in distress or settling accounts on his own. He is often obliged to imitate his beloved Rocky Marciano in the line of duty, but is he a sensitive man inside, with his own sense of justice. Toni is also the narrator; he tells his stories in a terse and rapid prose full of street talk and criminal slang. Two of the novels that include Romano's adventures—the first and a more recent one—are *Un beso de amigo* (A Friend's Kiss, 1980) and *Oídos sordos* (Deaf Ears, 1990).

More than any other Spanish detective writer, Juan Madrid captures what Chandler called the "smell of fear." In fact he believes that fear is the atavic impulse behind the thriller, one that used to be confined to the underworld but now permeates all levels of society. "Fear is no longer a unique characteristic of the bourgeoisie" he has said. "Now, everyone is afraid of everyone else." Martín believes the true *roman noir* died in America with Ross MacDonald, but it crossed the Atlantic and arrived in Spain where it gave rise to the Spanish thriller. This is only fitting, since Humphrey Bogart/Philip Marlowe, the archetypal hero of the American noir film, was also the protagonist of the movie *Casablanca*: the tough-skinned but soft-hearted Rick, the ex–international brigader who had fought for the Spanish Republic before moving to northern Africa during World War II. The connection between literature and cinema in the American and Spanish thriller comes full circle.

Other novelists who would be treated in a longer study include Jorge Martínez Reverte, Carlos Pérez Merinero and Julián Ibáñez. I have not discussed the writers who have made occasional incursions into the genre: Rosa Montero in *Te trataré como a una reina* (I'll Treat You Like a Queen, 1983) with a new feminist approach to the form; Fernando Savater in *Caronte aguarda* (Charon Is Waiting, 1984); Antonio Muñoz Molina in his novels *Invierno en Lisboa* (Winter in Lisbon, 1987) and *Beltenebros* (1989); Arturo Pérez Reverte in *La tabla de Flandes* (The Flanders Panel, 1990). I have not dealt with the crime novelists who write in the Catalan and Galician languages like Jaume Fuster, Maria Antònia Oliver, Manuel de Pedrolo and Carlos G. Reigosa. Clearly the future of the Spanish thriller looks far from black.

RESOURCES

The International Museum of Cartoon Art in Boca Raton, Florida, has the world's largest collection of cartoons, including many examples from Spain: a total of some 160,000 works by more than 1,000 artists spanning 200 years and all genres of the form—comic books, comic strips, editorial cartoons, caricatures, illustrations and animation. The address is 201 Plaza Real, Boca Raton, Florida, tel. (407) 391–2200. There is also a Cartoon Art Museum of California in San Francisco. Spain has nothing like these or the French comic museum in Angouleme.

For Spanish comics online, see the special issue of *El Mundo. Campus* (<el mundo.campus@offcampus.es/>). Two World Wide Web cites for Spanish comics are: <www.readysoft.es/home.tebeo/bruguera.html/> and <http:/magina.ugr.es/gente/ jbernier/COMIC/comic.es.html/>. Through these websites you can locate some Spanish comics, such as the famous "Mortadelo and Filemón".

The Ultimate Mystery/Detective Web Guide is at <www.magicdragon.com/Ultimate Mystery/Mystery-Index.html/>. Spain has no equivalent to the Bibliothèque des Littératures Policièrs in Paris.

You can reach The Asociación Española de Ciencia Ficción (Spanish Society of Science Fiction) online at <www.geocities.com/Athens/7037/guiahi.html#arch/>. The Asociación Española de Fantasía y Ciencia Ficción (Spanish Association of Fantasy and Science Fiction) has a site at <http://www.ualm.es/~egallego/aefcf.htm/>. You can find The Ultimate Science Fiction Web Guide at <www.magicdragon.com/ Ultimate SF/SF-Index.html/>.

BIBLIOGRAPHY

Allard, Albert, and Robert Laxalt. *A Time We Knew: Images of Yesterday in the Basque Homeland.* Reno: University of Nevada Press, 1990.

Alvar, Manuel. *El romancero en la tradición oral moderna.* Madrid: Gredos, 1972.

Amorós, Andrés. *Sociología de una novela rosa.* Madrid: Taurus, 1968.

———. *Subliteraturas.* Barcelona: Ariel, 1974.

Aulestia, Gorka. *Bertsolarismo.* Bilbao: Bizkaiko Foro Aldundia, 1990.

Barceló, Miquel. *Ciencia ficción: Guía de lectura.* Barcelona: Ediciones B, 1990.

Barrier, Michael, Bill Blackbeard, Javier Coma, and others. *Historia de los Comics.* 4 vols. Barcelona: Toutain Editor, 1982.

Caro Baroja, Julio. *Ensayos sobre la cultura popular española.* Madrid: Editorial Dosbe, 1979.

Clute, John, and Peter Nichols, eds. *The Encyclopedia of Science Fiction.* New York: St. Martin's Press, 1993.

Colmeiro, José F. *La novela policiaca española. Teoría e historia crítica.* Barcelona: Anthropos, 1994.

———. "The Spanish Connection: Detective Fiction after Franco." *Journal of Popular Culture* 28 (1994): 151-161. The best general treatment of the subject in English and one that I have used extensively in this chapter.

Coma, Javier. *Del gato Félix al gato Fritz: Historia de los cómics.* Barcelona: Gustavo Gili, 1979.

———. *De Mickey à Marlowe: La edad de oro.* Barcelona: Península, 1987.

———. *El ocaso de los héroes en los cómics de autor.* Barcelona: Península, 1984.

———. *Los cómics: Un arte del siglo XX.* Barcelona: Labor, [1978].

Cottam, John. "Understanding the Creation of Pepe Carvalho." In *Leeds Papers on Thrillers in the Transition. "Novela negra" and Political Change in Spain,* edited by Rob Rix, 123-135. Leeds: Trinity and All Saints College, 1992.

Diez Borque, J. M. *Literatura y cultura de masas.* Madrid: Al-Borak, 1972.

Dorfman, Ariel, and Armand Mattelart. *How to Read Donald Duck: Imperialist Ideology in the Disney Comic.* Translated with introduction by David Kunzle. New York: International General, 1975.

Espinosa, Aurelio M. *Cuentos populares de Castilla y León.* Madrid: Consejo Superior de Investigaciones Científicas, 1987-1988.

———. *Cuentos populares españoles, recogidos de la tradición oral de España.* 3 vols. Palo Alto, CA: Stanford University Press, 1923-1926. Spanish edition, 3 vols. Madrid: Consejo Superior de Investigaciones Científicas, 1946-1947.

Fernández, Juan José, and Luis Vigil, eds. *El cómix marginal español.* Barcelona: Producciones Editoriales, 1976.

García Pavón, Francisco. *Cuentos de amor . . . vagamente.* Barcelona: Destino, 1985.

———. *El hospital de los dormidos.* Madrid: Cátedra, 1981.

———. *El último sábado.* Barcelona: Destino, 1974.

———. *Historias de Plinio.* Barcelona: Plaza y Janés, 1971.

———. *Las hermanas coloradas.* Barcelona: Destino, 1972.

———. *Nuevas historias de Plinio.* Barcelona: Destino, 1973.

García Tortosa, Francisco, ed. *Literatura popular y proletaria.* Sevilla: Universidad de Sevilla, 1986.

Gasca, Luis. *Los cómics en España.* Barcelona: Lumen, 1969.

———. *Tebeo y cultura de masas.* Madrid: Editorial Prensa Española, 1966.

Giardinelli, Mempo. *El género negro.* 2 vols. Mexico City: Universidad Autónoma Metropolitana, 1984.

Gubern, Román. *El lenguaje de los cómics.* Barcelona: Ediciones Península, 1972.

———. *La literatura de la imagen.* Barcelona: Salvat, 1974.

———, and others. *La novela criminal.* Barcelona: Tusquets, 1982.

Guelbenzu, José María. *Cuentos populares españoles.* 2 vols. Madrid: Siruela, 1997.

Hart, Patricia. *The Spanish Sleuth: The Detective in Spanish Fiction.* Rutherford, NJ: Fairleigh Dickinson University Press, 1985.

Hickey, Leo. "The Incongruence Factor in Eduardo Mendoza's 'Ceferino' Novels." In *Leeds Papers on Thrillers in the Transition. "Novela negra" and Political Change in Spain*, edited by Rob Rix, 75-104. Leeds: Trinity and All Saints College, 1992.

Horn, Maurice, ed. *Women in the Comics*. New York: Chelsea House, 1981.

————, ed. *The World Encyclopedia of Comics*. New York: Chelsea House, 1976.

La nova historieta: 30 dibuixants. Barcelona: Generalitat de Catalunya, 1989.

Laxalt, Robert, and Albert Allard. *A Time We Knew: Images of Yesterday in the Basque Homeland*. Reno: University of Nevada Press, 1990.

Lent, John A., ed. *Comic Art of Europe. An International, Comprehensive Bibliography*. Westport, CT: Greenwood Press, 1994.

Luna, Fernando, and Miguelanxo Prado. *El manantial de la noche*. Barcelona: Norma Editorial, 1989.

Madrid, Juan. *Oídos sordos*. Madrid: Cuadernos del Asfalto, 1990.

————. *Un beso de amigo*. Madrid: Sedmay, 1980.

Mariscal. *Historias de Garriris*. Barcelona: Editorial Complot, 1987.

Martí. *The Cabbie*. New York: Catalan Communications, 1987.

Martín, Andreu. *Barcelona Connection*. Barcelona: Ediciones B, 1988.

————. *Prótesis*. Madrid: Sedmay, 1980.

Martín, Antonio. *Historia del cómic español: 1875-1939*. Barcelona: Gustavo Gili, 1978.

Martín Martínez, Antonio. "El ayer próximo," "Breve reseña histórica de publicaciones seleccionadas." In *Prensa infantil y juvenil: pasado y presente*, 15-36, 72-107. Madrid: Comisión de Información y Publicaciones Infantiles y Juveniles, 1967.

Mendoza, Eduardo. *El laberinto de las aceitunas*. Barcelona: Seix Barral, 1982.

————. *El misterio de la cripta embrujada*. Barcelona: Seix Barral, 1979.

————. *La verdad sobre el caso Savolta*. 1975. Reprint. Barcelona: Seix Barral, 1992. English translation *The Truth About the Savolta Case*. New York: Pantheon, 1975.

Michael, Ian (David Serafin). "From Scarlet Study to Novela Negra." In *Leeds Papers on Thrillers in the Transition. "Novela negra" and Political Change in Spain*, edited by Rob Rix, 17-47. Leeds: Trinity and All Saints College, 1992.

Minc, Rose S., ed. *Literature and Popular Culture in the Hispanic World: A Symposium*. Gaithersburg, MD: Hispamérica and Montclair State College, 1981.

Moix, Ramón-Terençi. *Los "cómics": Arte para consumo y formas "pop."* Barcelona: Llibres de Sinera, 1968.

Moliterni, Claude, ed. *Histoire Mondiale de la Bande Dessinée*. Paris: Pierre Horay Editeur, 1989. Has a section on Spain with reproductions of comics from the early twentieth century through the 1980s, with text by Luis Gasca and Edouard François.

Montero, Rosa. *Te trataré como a una reina*. Barcelona: Seix Barral, 1983.

Montesol. *Vidas ejemplares: Las guerras domésticas*. Barcelona: Editorial Complot, 1989.

Montesol, and Ramón de España. *La noche de siempre*. Barcelona: Especial Star, 1982.

Muñoz Molina, Antonio. *Beltenebros*. Barcelona: Seix Barral, 1989.

————. *El invierno en Lisboa*. Barcelona: Seix Barral, 1987.

Paredes Núñez, Juan. *La novela policiaca española*. Granada: Universidad de Granada, 1989. Contains Vázquez Montalbán's controversial essay, "Sobre la inexistencia de la novela policíaca en España" (pp. 49-62) and other essays by mystery writers like Juan Madrid, Andreu Martín, Jorge Martínez Reverte, and Julián Ibáñez.

Pérez, Janet W., and Genaro J. Pérez, eds. "Hispanic Marginal Literatures: The Erotic, the Comics, *novela rosa*." Special issue of *Monographic Review/Revista Monográfica* 7 (1991).

Pérez Reverte, Arturo. *La tabla de Flandes*. Madrid: Alfaguara, 1990. English translation *The Flanders Panel*. New York: Bantam Books, 1996.

Pompeya, Nùria. *Maternasis*. Barcelona: Kairós, 1977.

———. *Mujercitas*. Barcelona: Kairós, 1977.

Propp, Vladimir. *Morphology of the Folktale*. Austin: University of Texas Press, 1968.

Ramírez, Juan Antonio. *El "cómic" femenino en España: Arte sub y anulación*. Madrid: Cuadernos para el Diálogo, 1975.

———. *La historieta cómic de postguerra*. Madrid: Cuadernos para el Diálogo, 1975.

Ramos, Rosa Alicia. *El cuento folklórico: una aproximación a su estudio*. Madrid: Pliegos, 1988.

Revilla, Federico. *Los tebeos de la posguerra*. Barcelona: Centro de Estudios Postuniversitarios, 1990.

———. "Psicosociología del 'tebeo' español de la posguerra." *Arbor* (March 1982): 107–116.

Rix, Rob. "Loners, Losers and Centre-Forwards: Vázquez Montalbán's Poetics of Memory." In *Leeds Papers on Thrillers in the Transition. "Novela negra" and Political Change in Spain*, edited by Rob Rix, 137–161. Leeds: Trinity and All Saints College, 1992.

———, ed. *Leeds Papers on Thrillers in the Transition. "Novela negra" and Political Change in Spain*. Leeds: Trinity and All Saints College, 1992.

Rodríguez Almodóvar, Antonio. *Cuentos al amor de la lumbre*. 2 vols. Madrid: Anaya, 1983–84.

———. *Los cuentos maravillosos españoles*. Barcelona: Grijalbo, 1982.

———. *Los cuentos populares o la tentativa de un texto infinito*. Murcia: Universidad de Murcia, 1989.

Rubenstein, Anne. "La Ciudad de Toons: Spanish Comics Get Serious." *The Village Voice*, Literary Supplement, February 1990, 21.

Sainz Cidoncha, Carlos. *Historia de la Ciencia Ficción en España*. Madrid: Sala Editorial, 1976.

Santonja, Gonzalo. *La República de los libros: el nuevo libro popular de la II República*. Barcelona: Anthropos, 1989.

Savater, Fernando. *Caronte aguarda*. Madrid: Cátedra, 1981.

Sempere, Pedro. *Semiología del infortunio: lenguaje e ideología de la fotonovela*. Madrid: Felmar, 1976.

Sieburth, Stephanie. *Literature, Mass Culture, and Uneven Modernity in Spain*. Durham, NC: Duke University Press, 1994.

Tellado, Corín. "Matrimonio indeciso." *Vanidades* 36, no. 21 (8 October 1996): 105–108, 110–119.

Thompson, Stith. *Motif-Index of Folk-Literature*. 6 vols. Bloomington: Indiana University Press, 1955.

Valles Calatrava, José R. *La novela criminal española*. Granada: Universidad de Granada, 1991. Contains articles by Andreu Martín and other writers in the crime genre.

Vázquez de Parga, Salvador. *De la novela policíaca a la novela negra (Los mitos de la novela criminal)*. Barcelona: Plaza y Janés, 1986.

———. *Los cómics del franquismo*. Barcelona: Planeta, 1980.

Vázquez Montalbán, Manuel. *Asesinato en el Comité Central*. Barcelona: Planeta, 1981. English translation *Murder in the Central Committee*. London: Pluto, 1984.

———. *El delantero centro fue asesinado al atardecer*. Barcelona: Planeta, 1988.

———. *El laberinto griego*. Barcelona: Seix Barral, 1991. English translation *An Olympic Death*. London: Serpent's Tail, 1992.

———. *Galíndez*. Barcelona: Seix Barral, 1990. English translation *Galíndez*. New York: Atheneum, 1992.

————. *Las recetas de Carvalho*. Barcelona: Planeta, 1989.

————. *Los mares del Sur*. Barcelona: Planeta, 1979. English translation *The Southern Seas*. London: Pluto, 1990.

————. *Tatuaje*. Barcelona: Planeta, 1974.

————, and others. *Novela negra/novela política*. Zaragoza: Ibercaja, 1993.

El Wendigo. Spanish magazine, good source of information on comics.

Glossary

Black Legend. *See* Leyenda negra.

Costumbrismo (costumbrista). Fostered by the Romantic cult of local color, this movement in Spanish literature and art of the nineteenth century portrayed the unique customs (*costumbres*) and figures of the country's regional life. *Costumbrismo* was often a vehicle for a shallow, sentimental vision of rural Spain, its various regions (especially Andalusia) and the picturesque. Related to *españolada* (see below).

Desencanto. The mood of political disappointment in the late years of the transition to democracy (1979–1982), anticipated by the film *El desencanto* by Jaime Chávarri (1976).

Dictablanda. Name for the period of "soft" dictatorship during the last years of Franco's rule in the early 1970s, a pun on the Spanish word *dictadura*, or "hard" dictatorship.

Españolada. Any action or work that exploits the typical stereotypes of Spain and Spaniards. The *españolada* usually presents the image of Spain as an exotic, "different" country full of local color, superstition and picturesque characters like gypsies and bullfighters. Books, films, plays and *zarzuelas* based on the *españolada* are usually set in Andalusia; they exploit the flamenco culture of this region, which is mistakenly seen as the most "typical" of Spain.

Esperpento. Defined in dictionaries as a scarecrow, nonsense, macabre story or tale, the word was used by the great Spanish writer Ramón del Valle-Inclán (1866–1936) for a series of fictional works characterized by exaggeration, satire, caricature and the grotesque; life "reflected in a concave mirror." The term is often used to refer to a current in peninsular art that can be traced through the picaresque novel, the Golden Age author Francisco de Quevedo, Goya, surrealism and Dalí to the present. In short, Spanish black comedy.

ETA (Euzkadi Ta Askatasuna, Homeland and Freedom). Clandestine terrorist organization formed in 1959 to support Basque independence; still in existence but greatly weakened and opposed by the majority of Basques and other peoples in Spain.

Leyenda negra **(Black Legend).** "The persistent idea that Spaniards are backward, cruel, humorless, and violent, the Spain of the Inquisition, of poverty and ignorance, a 'legend' begun, some authors have it . . . by Protestants in northern Europe to counteract the religious, military, and political power of Spain during the Catholic Monarchs and Philip II in the sixteenth century." Peter Besas, *Behind the Spanish Lens: Spanish Cinema under Fascism and Democracy* (Denver, CO: Arden Press, 1985), 9.

Movida. Loosely translatable as "the movement" or "the scene," sometimes called *movida madrileña* because of its center in Madrid. A complex artistic movement that characterized youth culture in the early period of Spanish democracy from the late 1970s through the mid-1980s. It influenced art forms such as cinema, photography, painting, literature, popular music, fashion and interior design. It could be seen as the Spanish version of punk. The film critic Fernando Rodríguez Lafuente has described the exponents of the *movida* as "a heterogeneous group of musicians, painters, photographers and filmmakers who were searching for a total transformation of taste and cultural values. . . . To that end, any act of transgression was acceptable, as long as it was destructive, absurd, blasphemous and ironic" ("Cine español: 1939–1990," in *España hoy: Cultura*, ed. Antonio Ramos Gascón, 2 vols. [Madrid: Cátedra, 1991], 1: 265). The director Pedro Almodóvar has been the most successful member of the group both in Spain and abroad. The term has also been applied to later expressions of youth culture, like the *movida galega* (Galician *movida*).

Opus Dei. Founded by José María Escrivá de Balaguer in 1928, a lay Catholic organization with an ultraconservative, ultramontane philosophy. Some 40 percent of its 70,000 members are in Spain. Unlike the Dominicans and Jesuits, the other most important religious organizations founded by Spaniards, the Opus Dei (Work of God) includes men and women, single and married people, religious and secular. It has penetrated educational, business and governmental institutions around the world and achieved its greatest prominence during the Franco regime. The Opus controls influential schools, a university and publishing houses in Spain.

Pasotismo. The flight into the private world of drugs and alcohol by the once highly political youth of Spain, especially in the period of transition and early democracy (late 1970s and early 1980s). The *pasotas* have been described as burnt-out people who have "been there, done that."

Picaresque. A tradition beginning with the anonymous novel *Lazarillo de Tormes* (ca. 1550), depicting a down-and-out protagonist who is usually a sort of anti-hero. He moves about from place to place seeking a livelihood, passing through a cross-section of a corrupt society ruled by false pride, selfishness, hypocrisy and greed. The picaresque has been a constant in many Spanish art forms, from literature (Quevedo) to painting (Goya) and film (Buñuel).

Tertulia. A social gathering in a public place, often on a regular basis, of a group of friends or people with a common interest. Writers, journalists, musicians, artists, lawyers, doctors, bullfight and soccer fans are examples of social groups who gather at *tertulias* in cafés and bars of Spanish towns and cities. Some of these gatherings have endured for decades and have played an important role in the intellectual history of modern Spain, such as the literary *tertulia* at the famous Café Gijón in Madrid.

Zarzuela. Spanish comic opera of courtly origin that became increasingly popularized in the later eighteenth century. "It takes its name from the Palace of La Zarzuela (a royal country seat near Madrid, comparable to Versailles) where festive representations, called 'Fiestas de Zarzuela,' were given, the earliest on record being Lope de Vega's eclogue, *La selva sin amor* (The Forest without Love), of 1629" (*Harvard Dictionary of Music* [Cambridge, MA: Harvard University Press, 1967], 821). The *zarzuela* appears in various expressions of popular culture like song, drama, film, radio and television and is often related to the *españolada* (see above).

Index

About the Author

EDWARD F. STANTON is Professor of Spanish and was named in 1998 the first Bingham Professor in the Humanities at the University of Kentucky. He is the author of numerous books and articles on various aspects of Hispanic life and culture.